The Dome and the Rock

"The gold dome of things is the perfected spirit."

THE DOME AND

STRUCTURE IN THE POETRY

by James Baird

Wallace Stevens: From the "Adagia"

THE ROCK

OF WALLACE STEVENS

The Johns Hopkins Press: Baltimore

Library of Congress Catalog Card Number 68–19701

Permission to quote from previously unpublished writings of Wallace Stevens, which appear for the first time in this book, must be obtained from Holly Stevens, c/o Alfred A. Knopf, Inc., 501 Madison Avenue, New York, N.Y.

The following permissions from holders of copyrights are gratefully acknowledged:

Alfred A. Knopf, Inc.

For "Tattoo," Copyright 1923 by Wallace Stevens. Renewed, 1951. Reprinted by permission of Alfred A. Knopf, Inc., from *Collected Poems of Wallace Stevens.* For "A Mythology Reflects Its Region," Copyright 1957 by Elsie Stevens and Holly Stevens. Reprinted by permission of Alfred A. Knopf, Inc., from *Opus Posthumous* by Wallace Stevens.

The scattered passages and quotations from the published writings of Stevens in this book are reprinted by permission of the publisher Alfred A. Knopf, Inc., from the following copyrighted editions: *The Necessary Angel* by Wallace Stevens (1951), *The Collected Poems of Wallace Stevens* (1954), *Opus Posthumous* (1957), and *The Letters of Wallace Stevens* (1966).

New Directions Publishing Corporation

For permission to reprint lines from *Paterson* by William Carlos Williams, Copyright 1948, 1958 by William Carlos Williams; from *Selected Essays* by William Carlos Williams, Copyright 1931 by William Carlos Williams; from *In the American Grain* by William Carlos Williams, Copyright 1925 by James Laughlin, 1933 by William Carlos Williams.

Giulio Einaudi Editore, Turin, Italy

For permission to quote from the translator's notes appended to *Mattino Domenicale* by Wallace Stevens, translated by Renato Poggioli (Turin, 1954).

In tribute to
Rosemary Park Anastos
George Boas
Dorothy Bethurum Loomis

Homer, *Iliad*, VI

Glaukos to Diomedes:

"High-hearted son of Tydeus, why ask of my generation?
As is the generation of leaves, so is that of humanity.
The wind scatters the leaves on the ground, but the live timber
Burgeons with leaves again in the season of spring returning.
So one generation of men will grow while another dies."

The author wishes to express his indebtedness to Miss Holly Stevens for her generous permission to reproduce passages from the letters of Wallace Stevens hitherto unpublished.

Contents

Introduction: The Grand Poem

TWO DISTINGUISHED RECENT STUDIES OF WALLACE
Stevens have extended a mode of scrutiny frequently applied to this
poet during the last decade. It is a mode founded primarily in philosophical assumptions. One can be grateful for it. The fortunes of
Stevens with the critics, when one traces these across a span of some
thirty years, are impressively erratic. There is an early raffishness in
answer to the supposed *dandyisme* of *Harmonium*; there is a subsequent academic insistence, *faute de mieux,* upon eccentricities, in
which the poet would seem to appear as some master cryptographer;
there is the mounting legend, from the late thirties, of a poet indifferent to the so-called social burden. On the other hand, one finds
much to admire in a critical labor, however intermittent, devoted to
problems in form and rhetoric and to independent mastery of selected poems, as in the task of the anthologist. This honest work
has been supported and extended, since mid-century, by a fully responsible attention to the last poems of Stevens. The present emphasis upon philosophical readings may be said to derive its strength
from the metaphysical concerns of this attention. High seriousness
is its mark; a hard-core criticism is its objective. Philosophical intent

has done much to establish the eminence of Stevens. It has its own claim to authority. But one must question its exclusiveness, despite the sophistication and the ardor with which its adherents proceed. Are there limited advantages here? And if there are limitations, have we now reached an impasse?

J. Hillis Miller, the first of the two critics, quotes the following from "An Ordinary Evening in New Haven": ". . . Of this, / A few words, an and yet, and yet, and yet—" (*CP*, 465).[1] Mr. Miller observes: "Apparently this is the whole story about Stevens. From one end of his work to the other he reiterates a single idea, and all his work is an attempt to explore the endlessly variable perspectives from which reality can be viewed by the imagination. He is resolutely carrying out Nietzsche's injunction that man the survivor of God should experiment tirelessly with new truths, new representations, new life forms."[2] Later one finds this reflection on the separateness of Stevens. "There is no rich echo of nuance and meaning from the poetic tradition, as in Eliot or Yeats. God is dead, and with him died the heaven of consecrated symbols coming down through the Christian or Platonic ages. Stevens' earth is flat and bare, and a bowl of flowers is just a bowl of flowers."[3] This strain of observation concludes with the following judgment. "His poetry is not dialectical, if that means a series of stages which build on one another, each transcending the last and moving on to a higher one in some version of the Hegelian sequence of thesis, antithesis, synthesis. It is impossible to organize the stages of Stevens' thought in this way. A new stage merely contradicts the first, and the first remains just as valid in its own way. In fact there is no first stage. They are all equally prior and equally final. There is no progress, only an alternation between contradictory possibilities."[4] The philosophical reading here may well be impeccable. Mr. Miller's way of cognition reaches, I take it, an admission to an "anti-philosophy" which he finds in the poet. Stevens' untiring concern with problems of reality admits him to the company of other modern writers examined in Mr. Miller's study, Yeats and Eliot among them. But the

---

[1] I use here the method of citation of passages from Stevens followed by recent commentators: *CP* for *Collected Poems* (New York, 1954); *OP* for *Opus Posthumous*, ed. S. F. Morse (New York, 1957); *NA* for *The Necessary Angel* (New York, 1951). Arabic numerals following the letters indicate page numbers. The abbreviated title *Letters* represents *Letters of Wallace Stevens*, ed. Holly Stevens (New York, 1966).

[2] *Poets of Reality* (Cambridge, Mass. 1965), p. 225.

[3] *Ibid.*, p. 230.

[4] *Ibid.*, p. 259.

conclusion would seem to be that Stevens stands in paradox: the reality sought remains unreality without the exertion of a dialectical method. On other grounds, e.g., Stevens' desertion of the tradition, Mr. Miller's criteria are, of course, respectably his own. They rest in his persuasions concerning the nature of poetry.

The second critic at hand is Joseph N. Riddel, whose study is of chief value in its adroit readings of the major long poems. Less committed to the philosophical method than is Mr. Miller, this commentator nonetheless notes: ". . . Stevens' view of the poem as an 'act of the mind' makes him available to the kind of phenomenological scrutiny of romantic and symbolist literature exercised so effectively by continental critics like Gaston Bachelard, J-P Richard, René Girard, and Georges Poulet, among others. For example, Poulet's phenomenological reading of Bergson, in his *Studies in Human Time,* offers a salient approach to Stevens and helps to define the quality which makes the later poetry so appropriately and revealingly modern."[5] Mr. Riddel appears as a liberal when he later contends: ". . . one need not make an exclusive choice with Stevens."[6] His catholicity is welcome. The supposition seems to be that Stevens is susceptible to a number of approaches that will together demonstrate the idiom of an American poet unsurpassed in difficulty throughout the history of literature in English. Apparently Mr. Riddel expects further philosophical evaluations. Phenomenology, being much in the critical mode of present literary studies, would seem to be the next phase. To a degree Mr. Miller has already applied it. So has Richard A. Macksey, in a searching essay of recent date. His study provides some impressive affinities between Stevens and Husserl.[7]

I have suggested that there may be limits to the value of philosophical approach. Impressive as its achievements have been thus far, it seems to me more an imposition of the critic's will than an exposition of the poet at hand. Certainly there is the critic's frame of reference; he would not be a very good critic without it. Nonetheless, the commanding design is, or should be, the poet's. Mr. Miller has spoken of the impossibility of organizing the stages of Stevens' thought according to the principles of an established ontology. Then, shall we say that these stages cannot be organized on

[5] *The Clairvoyant Eye* (Baton Rouge, 1965), pp. 271–72.
[6] *Ibid.,* p. 278.
[7] "The Climates of Wallace Stevens," in *The Act of the Mind: Essays on the Poetry of Wallace Stevens,* ed. R. H. Pearce and J. Hillis Miller (Baltimore, 1965), pp. 185–224.

other principles? I think not. Stevens himself has left us the means of organization. His signs are clearly visible if the critic limits himself to exposition and organization. Ideally, the critic of Stevens should seek to become a transparency. I so determine, knowing as I do that my ineptitudes will sometimes fail the design which I wish to study. I shall recognize Stevens' long association with formal philosophy as the progenitor of one theme—and only one—in his work. I wish to oppose a wide application of philosophy *qua* philosophy, however adroit and stimulating this has been, and to turn to the variety and the energy of the total poet. When Mr. Miller urges a line from "An Ordinary Evening in New Haven" as a description of the total poetic range, I must answer negatively. The line does not reveal "the whole story about Stevens." It is merely a small part of it.

A number of years ago Newton P. Stallknecht spoke of Wordsworth's poetry as embodying "a good deal of philosophical energy."[8] The phrase is exact. Philosophy as a formal discipline is not the issue. The thrust of the mind encounters questions appropriately expressing the nature of philosophy. In this sense Stevens displays a philosophical energy of comparable intensity. But the differences between the two poets are enormous. Wordsworth's inevitable progression, as in *The Prelude,* ranges through the levels of consciousness to the thresholds of infinity. The exploration of Stevens is deliberately self-contained. It explores the metamorphoses of consciousness, repeatedly imposing questions on the data of the senses and strictly maintaining an absoluteness of temporality. Wordsworth's energy flows toward a Kantian *noumenon.* That of Stevens remains within the sense of the physical world. The poet's subject, he said, is *his* [Stevens'] *sense of the world (NA,* 121). I propose that he regarded any systematic philosophy that he knew— and he read widely in several such systems—as a description of the philosopher's *sense of the world.* For instance, he wrote in 1948 to Delmore Schwartz, then editor of *The Partisan Review*: "It seems that poetic order is potentially as significant as philosophic order. . . . [A theory of poetry] does what poetry itself does, that is to say, it leads to a fresh conception of the world."[9]

It must be understood that Stevens did not here think of poetry as *within* philosophy, nor did he, to my knowledge, anywhere else. He thought of it as a companion art. It was the lyrical rather than the didactic element of philosophy, the immediate and the singular

---

[8] *Strange Seas of Thought* (Durham, 1945), p. 23.
[9] In a letter dated at Hartford, April 26, 1948, in *Letters*, p. 590.

rather than the traditional, which appealed to Stevens. I very much doubt that he saw any system—Platonic, Cartesian, Berkeleyan, Hegelian, or existentialist—as having any power of sovereignty over his own sense of the world. On the other hand, I feel quite certain that every system which aroused his curiosity appeared to him as an intriguing structure expressed in another man's metaphor of the world. A Platonism, however second-hand (as some of us believe Wordsworth's to have been, from Coleridge), may generate a surging philosophical energy, as it apparently did in *The Prelude* of 1805. But when it comes to Stevens, what is he speaking of, other than an energy self-committed, as he writes in "Esthétique du Mal" of "attributes / With which we vested, once, the golden forms / . . . Before we were wholly human and knew ourselves" (*CP*, 317)? These *attributes* are energies. Once they flowed to a transcendent Platonic absolute. In an age in search of a new humanism they flow within the temporality of men. One need not question the poet's play within the old range of the golden forms. It is simply the metaphor that fascinates him, another man's description of his sense of the world as *he* went about making a "philosophic order." Plato must descend from the myth of Plato and take his place in an equation with other "wholly human" men. By analogy, even the remote God himself must descend and enter the equation, moving silently "as Plato's ghost / Or Aristotle's skeleton . . ." ("Less and Less Human, O Savage Spirit," *CP*, 327).

Somewhere in this concern for Stevens and philosophy there must be an encounter with the mode of poetic wisdom. The "wise passiveness" of Wordsworth will accord nowhere with the inclinations of Stevens. This point need not be urged. But in the contemporary sense this matter of wisdom is serious enough to notice. Wystan Hugh Auden, lecturing at Oxford in recent years, extended his elaborate analogy between Shakespeare's Prospero and the quest for wisdom in lyric poetry. Robert Frost was his subject. He had found, he said, "some signs of a rivalry between Ariel and Prospero . . . one might say, [in] every poem. . . ."[10] Mr. Auden concluded that Frost is a "Prospero-dominated poet."[11] "And, when it comes to wisdom, is not having a lover's quarrel with life more worthy of Prospero than not caring and looking coldly?"[12] This bifurcation leaves Ariel as the unwise. He is the careless spirit, darting in the sun, working magic

10 *The Dyer's Hand* (New York, 1962), pp. 337–38.
11 *Ibid.*, p. 341.
12 *Ibid.*, p. 353.

and metamorphosis, essentially indifferent to humanity. Ralph J. Mills has chosen to extend the analogy to Stevens. "The latter category, in which he [Auden] placed Frost, is representative of the search for wisdom; the former, including Rimbaud and Mallarmé, seeks the earthly paradise. There is little doubt . . . that Stevens moves with Ariel. Poets in his path hunger after that transformation which will bring a lost history full circle and restore to man the image and nature from which he once defected."[13] Both Mr. Auden and Mr. Mills apparently agree on the nature of wisdom as advanced here. Neither defines it. As we read, we should suppose that the Prospero-dominated poet, whoever he is, aspires to universal statement, as in Prospero's reflection: it is the *we*, not the *I*, of humanity that must flourish in the stuff of dreams.

In an essay of 1951, "A Collect of Philosophy," Stevens proposed that "a poem in which the poet has chosen for his subject a philosophical theme should result in the poem of poems" (*OP*, 187). If philosophy seeks wisdom, then Stevens did not write this Prospero poem. The texture of his largest expression of philosophical energy, "Notes Toward a Supreme Fiction," of course shows substantial strands of philosophical inquiry. But it is not a performance on a purely philosophical theme. It is a poem, or a sequence of poems, about poetry. In my opinion, no poem of Stevens' deals with wisdom unless it returns to the frequent view of the *we* in a universal human poverty; and, correspondingly, no poem deals primarily with philosophy. Yet assigning him to the category of Ariel does not serve any definition. It may, however, emphasize the differences between Frost and Stevens.

For this distance between the two is informative to criticism. Robert Lowell has recorded the following anecdote, which he heard from Frost. It is about a Florida train trip that brought Frost and Stevens together. "The two poets were nervous with each other. Stevens however was more in the vacationer's mood. He made witty remarks, and finally said, 'The trouble with your poetry, Frost, is that it has subjects.' " Mr. Lowell observes that "Frost had an unfashionable hold on subjects." He finds a "whimsical rightness" in the taunt of Stevens'.[14] But it would be nonsense to assume that

[13] "Wallace Stevens: The Image of the Rock," *Accent*, XVIII, No. 2 (Spring, 1958), 89.
[14] In a memorial note on Robert Frost, *New York Review of Books* (Special Issue, n.d. [May or June], 1963), p. 47. The first meeting of Frost and Stevens apparently took place at Key West in the late winter of 1935. In a letter to Harriet Monroe on March 13 of that year Stevens speaks of having recently returned to

this is Ariel as nay-sayer to Prospero. Stevens had his subjects. His encompassing subject—the poet's sense of the world—has been noted. I shall later identify the major subjects that persevere within the sense and shape it. The introductory point which I wish to make here is that the sense of the world is the particular subject of Stevens only when it is seen as *process*. In the whole of Stevens' work there is no poem in the slightest degree comparable *in resolution* to, for instance, "The Axe-Helve" of Frost. Certainly this master lyric shows process. The poem itself moves in a sense of crafting, from the violation of design by an indifference of machine-turning to the hickory lines of the good helve "native to the grain before the knife / Expressed them. . . ." A poet's sense of the world is projected. As the poem moves, it appears in correspondence to the fashioning of the helve, a speeech "native to the grain," a speech of poetry discoursing upon the poetry of a native sense. Thus far the poetic condition is fully admissible to the sense of Stevens. But then the crafting ends. The helve stands erect in its waving lines. The final metaphor comes. Now it is the erect serpent in the Garden. It becomes a sign of the Fortunate Fall. The human condition at the bone is the sharing of human flesh and human fate, no matter what the degree of individual isolation. The process has led to the subject. Privacy of vision is relinquished for wisdom. The mode of *I* in which the poem begins becomes the mode of *we*.

To say that Stevens nowhere used poetry to this end is to name the major obstacle for his critics. Vision in Stevens is strictly contained within the I. Except in those moments of urgency, when he turns to the use of symbols of the imaginative faculty common to humankind, he is unyielding. Presuppositions of ends to be sought by the critic are useless, and, more often than not, they leave him in the position of an assailant storming an enclosure and writing of the

---

Hartford from Florida. He writes of entertaining Frost at Key West and notes that he and Frost were classmates at Harvard, "although we did not know each other at Cambridge" (*Letters*, p. 278). The two poets again met at Key West in February, 1940 (*Letters*, plate facing p. 342, and n. 2, p. 355). In October, 1942, Stevens sent to Frost a copy of the Cummington edition of *Notes Toward a Supreme Fiction* (*Letters*, p. 422); a day later he mentioned lunching with Frost in Hartford (*Letters*, p. 423). The correspondence provides no evidence, however, that the friendship was at any time close. After 1940 the published letters present only four brief references to Frost, the last of which, dated in March, 1954, suggests a measure of indifference. Stevens had declined an invitation to the celebration of Frost's eightieth birthday at Amherst College. Writing to Mrs. Henry Church, he suggested more than was said. "Frost is greatly admired by many people. I do not know his work well enough to be either impressed or unimpressed." (See *Letters*, p. 825).

outside walls. A means of entrance must be found; once found, it must involve the assailant in the total process. He must expect, as long as he lives in the domain of Wallace Stevens, to accept isolation as fact. There is no wisdom looming beyond it. Isolation is not a subject. It is the condition of intellectual being, as the vital bodily processes are the conditions of physical being. Process and privacy are the subjects as Stevens writes of "A text of intelligent men / At the centre of the unintelligible, / As in a hermitage, for us to think, / Writing and reading the rigid inscription" ("Things of August," *CP*, 495). At the end of the process there must be an enclosing, "The roundness that pulls tight the final ring . . ." ("A Primitive Like An Orb," *CP*, 442). In order to understand this final act of pulling tight, the critic will have had to know the full poem-as-process. Stevens must be taken at his word: "One poem proves another and the whole . . . The essential poem begets the others . . ." ("A Primitive Like An Orb," *CP*, 441). The begetting must be fully traced. From poem to poem, an intricacy of relationships must be mastered. One meets in the language of the poetry the structure that memorializes the total process. It must be seen as a whole, if one intends to grasp the poet's intent.

The question of relationships in this poetry, as in certain other totalities of literary expression, must in any case be answered. A number of years ago I contended in another study that a major obligation of criticism is the arrangement of cognate texts that will illuminate one another through an ordered adjacency. At that time I was concerned with symbols and images occurring in the literature of modern primitivism.[15] My principle may be stated simply: literature has within it the power of commentary upon itself; the critic may free this power by his acts of arrangement and by collation. Something of the same principle will govern the present study. The process of a total poetry is to be examined. The total poem-as-process is to be defined through a study of relationships, deliberately established by the poet, among the separate exertions of the process. Each poem within the whole is, to use Stevens' words just quoted, *one poem proving another and the whole.* For the moment I wish to specify possibilities by citing a metaphor of *dryness* of the imagination which occurs at three points in the full range of Stevens: in "dry guitars," "dry catarrhs" of "The Ordinary Women," the ninth poem of *Harmonium* in the chronological order provided in the collected edition

15 *Ishmael* (Baltimore, 1956) and *Ishmael: The Art of Melville in the Contexts of International Primitivism* (New York, 1960).

of 1954; in the "dry men blown / Brown as the bread," from "Dry Loaf," standing near the opening of *Parts of a World*, a sequence that memorializes the destitution of the imagination in the years of the Depression; in the "dryness" of Professor Eucalyptus in "An Ordinary Evening in New Haven," written six years before the poet's death (*CP*, 12, 199, 475). In order to indicate what is meant by process, let it be said that the desiccation of the imagination as a modern ill is the subject. In the first instance the dryness is of poets; in the second it is of man in the American social context at one point in national history; in the third it is of men of "wisdom" in the academies. But the subject will not illuminate the process. It is the play of the imagination upon the theme, its boldness of encounter with words, its command to metamorphosis, and its endurance in movement which together make the poetry of the total structure. Wisdom is not the end. It is the ground of beginning. Like isolation in the hermitage, it is a fact at the inception of process, not an end to be sought. Such wisdom is of the rock of being. It becomes the stuff of poetry only as the imagination plays upon it. Since this imagination is singular, precisely like no other man's, its movement is contained within the enclosure. The vision is obdurate in privacy. Herein, then, rests the difficulty. The assailant from the outside will not fully see the mind of the poet. Nothing less than a committed entrance upon the vision will suffice. The poems are not written in Coptic. They stand in English, even when they astound us with an English employed with frequent indifference to tradition. As the critic reads, he must assume the imagination of Stevens as though it were his own.

The subject of the total poem is poetry, a poetic process. As one confronts it, he will remember that Stevens insisted upon it as a process of rejoicing. No reader will have overlooked his emphasis upon the *gaudiness* of poetry. Here his fondness for an utter radicalism in diction appears. The word springs anew from the Latin *gaudere*. The poet in an ideal nakedness, a full freedom from the authority of tradition inherited from other men, washes his world clean of secondhand metaphor. He becomes the hero of his own imaginings. He is the "plus gaudiest vir," ("Montrachet-Le-Jardin," *CP*, 262); he knows "a passion merely to be / For the gaudium of being . . ." ("Owl's Clover," *OP*, 71). *Gaudeamus te* is lifted from liturgy. It becomes "I praise thee, O free imagination." Moving upon the mind's frame of ideas, the imagination is free to flourish. Again and again, relentlessly moving, it makes its "floraisons of imagery" ("The Sail of Ulysses," *OP*, 102). Process becomes the beauty of poetic experience, the satisfaction of rejoicing in a poet's life. The poet has made a new metaphor of the world. It is his own. He has answered the demands of his subject: his unique sense of existence.

The epigraph prefacing "Evening Without Angels," a lyric from the collection *Ideas of Order,* is derived from Mario Rossi:[16] ". . . *the great interests of man: air and light, the joy of having a body, the voluptuousness of looking*" (*CP*, 136). The value of the source, a philosopher-critic of meager abilities, is inconsequential. It is merely strange that the poet in this particular choice reveals an attitude of so little interest to established criticism. The late Randall Jarrell, in a second appraisal (almost totally reversing his earlier dismissal of Stevens) wrote in a review of the *Collected Poems* in 1955: "Setting out on Stevens for the first time would be like setting out to be an explorer of Earth."[17] Precisely. The judgment seems to speak almost alone of an Earth to be seen anew through the refreshing vision of Stevens. The eye and language meet in the poet's art of seeing. "A poem is a meteor. . . . The tongue is an eye," wrote Stevens in the notes of the "Adagia" (*CP*, 158, 167). The poem of the earth must engage him, the earth in a present vision of one man, neither past vision of a past man, nor the possibilities of future men, neither a horror of Hell, nor a dream of Heaven. We are physical beings in a physical world. "The adventurer / In humanity has not conceived of a race / Completely physical in a physical world" ("Esthétique du Mal," *CP*, 325). There is a voluptuousness of looking. It urges praise. Save Whitman, there is no poet in American literature who fully anticipates Stevens in this sense.

Thus I come finally to the prospect of the Grand Poem of Stevens. Mr. Riddel notes: "The reception of *Harmonium* [1923] reveals the wisdom of Stevens' editors in refusing his title of 'Grand Poem.' For even in the most generous reviews, and there were several, it was considered a miscellany, a book of poems all too insular."[18] I can

---

[16] Co-author with Joseph M. Hone of *Bishop Berkeley* (New York, 1931, introduction by W. B. Yeats), and *Swift* (New York, 1934). According to Holly Stevens, Elizabeth Yeats sent to Stevens in February, 1934, a copy of Rossi's *Pilgrimage to the West* (Dublin, 1933). (See *Letters*, p. 347, n. 2.) Stevens in a letter to Hi Simons dated at Hartford, January 9, 1940, confesses that he is unable to recall the source of the quotation in Rossi's published work. It may have come, he concludes, "from something in the LONDON MERCURY" (*Letters*, p. 347). In turn, I have been unable to identify the source.

[17] "The Collected Poems of Wallace Stevens," *Yale Review*, XLIV (1955), 341.

[18] *The Clairvoyant Eye*, pp. 8–9. On March 12, 1923, Stevens suggested to his publisher, Alfred A. Knopf, his preferred title for the volume: "THE GRAND POEM: PRELIMINARY MINUTIAE." On May 18, evidently after further correspondence with his editors, he sent a telegram to Knopf reading "Use HARMONIUM" (*Letters*, pp. 237–38).

only suppose that the editors might be praised had they reserved the title for the collected poems to follow some thirty years later. Yet Stevens did not acquiesce entirely. *Harmonium* as a title is doubly endowed. It names with fine wit the old American parlor organ, squeakily accompanying the family hymn-singing.[19] It confirms the Americanness of the poet's imagination. But it also suggests a harmony of relationships. The collection is not a miscellany. It is a whole within itself. Nor is it insular. It is prototypic for the Grand Poem. As a small design within the whole, it prefigures the designs to come. The first poem, "Earthy Anecdote" (*CP*, 3), introduces a figure of the imagination about to pounce upon the endless movement of life. It is a firecat, cousin to every clawed and winged creature-symbol of Stevens' full array, even to the faint birdcall heard in one of the last poems of his life ("Not Ideas About the Thing But the Thing Itself," *CP*, 534). The last poem of *Harmonium*, "To the Roaring Wind" (*CP*, 113), points to the final vistas near the poet's end. "Vocalissimus," it seeks the syllable (poetic utterance) of the future, the syllable to succeed the voice of Wallace Stevens. As the point of beginning, *Harmonium* is a description of genesis in a total process intent upon the Grand Design.

Mr. Riddel admits to the Grand Poem, "however imperfect."[20] But he declines commitment to it.[21] On the other hand, Louis L. Martz, in a retrospective essay shortly after the poet's death, seems closer to acceptance of the whole but less aware than Mr. Riddel of implications in the *grandness* of the poem. Mr. Martz recognizes process. But he does not see it as continuous, Stevens in mid-career having set out to evolve "another kind of poetic self."[22] In the opinion of this critic the "hedonism" of the first poetry is the source of elements developed in the late poetry. It is an early poetry giving place to the poetry of meditation.[23] Since Stevens spoke nowhere in his own critical appraisals and confessions of hedonism, I exclude the term. In place of it I use his own concept of a *gaudium* of being. The *gaudium* of the first volume perseveres to and through the last, waning at the end only with the diminution of physical energy and imaginative vigor. As for meditation, its presence is inescapable in the opening lyrics of *Harmonium*, in, for instance, the frequently anthol-

[19] See Lloyd Frankenberg, *Pleasure Dome: On Reading Modern Poetry* (Boston, 1949), p. 198.
[20] *The Clairvoyant Eye*, p. 50.
[21] *Ibid.*, p. 278.
[22] "Wallace Stevens: The World as Meditation," in *Literature and Belief*, English Institute Essays, 1957 (New York, 1958), p. 157.
[23] *Ibid.*, p. 143.

ogized "Domination of Black" (*CP*, 8). Process, both meditative and joyful, begins in absolute sureness. The poet knows himself. He knows the courses of vigor, from its first assertions, through the full strength of the zenith, and into the meditation of age. He will not stop to rebuild. Imagination is the bird of majestic wing and gripping claw. It has left the egg.[24] It will not return.

Nothing less than the grand reading will bring comprehension of the scope. But it is agreed that Stevens will probably never be a popular poet. He did not expect to be; nor did he expect to be long remembered. His contempt for poetry used as a means to fame was genuine. Some critics have thought of his use of his art as "innocent." Be that as it may, in Stevens' view of history the facts are severe: the winds and the weather of men change; artists, politicians, what-not, are forgotten. The past has very little relevance to the present; it exacts nothing of us in the human (as opposed to the scientific) sense. Stevens contended, "Poetry is the scholar's art" (*NA*, 61). If history is "a cemetery of aristocracies" (as he borrows from Vilfredo Pareto, *NA,* 35), then scholars alone will work there. He was not, I think, speaking of academic scholars. He was approximate to Emerson's concept of *man thinking.* A poetry achieved in the ardor of thought will be answered only by a reading of comparable ardor. Apologetics or objections directed to this view seem to me to be irrelevant. Whitman wished to be carried in the pockets of his countrymen. Who, exactly, reads Whitman today apart from Emersonian scholars? Who will read Ezra Pound tomorrow? With the exception of poetry in the unaltered tradition of the epic or the ballad, or the pretensions of the poet *manqué,* what poetry is there which does not require the labor of thought?

The labor for Stevens will, of course, be the more intense because he cannot be read with any techniques of earlier habitude. Randall Jarrell's exceptional essay of 1955, for instance, is unique in its use of a metaphor from music as he arrives at certain problems of the late poems. He is reminded "of the slow movements of some of Beethoven's late quartets and sonatas. . . ." Again, the earlier orchestration of the poetry "has been replaced, most of the time, by plain chords from a few instruments. . . ."[25] One can rejoice in this critical bold-

[24] See "Things of August," Sec. 2, *CP*, 490, for an exposition of the symbol of the egg.
[25] "The Collected Poems of Wallace Stevens," pp. 343, 345.

ness. Yet it is less boldness than care when one recognizes that the art of Stevens is distinguished by a vocabulary from music: variations, scales, fugues, modes of the tonic and the dominant, keys, instruments of the major orchestral choirs, modulations, and effects which should be named as arpeggios and glissandos. Furthermore, the play of the imagination in the poetry of Stevens, its brilliance and its swift passage especially in the early and middle periods, suggests Stevens as the musician's poet. If Randall Jarrell thought of the late Beethoven quartets as analogies for the late poetry of Stevens, so there are close affinities between the earlier performances and the *Carnaval* of Schumann or Hindemith's *Symphonic Metamorphosis of Themes by Carl Maria von Weber*.

Or there is the relationship of Stevens to painting, an area which has only recently begun to receive critical notice, thanks to the initial work of Michel Benamou.[26] Stevens' methods of coloration and design are now seen as genuinely significant in their affinities to the theory and practice particularly of the impressionists. Yet criticism has remained reluctant, even with the spur of Stevens' essay "The Relations between Poetry and Painting," read at the Museum of Modern Art in New York in 1951. Again, there is his interest in architecture, which has shaped the course of the study to follow.

Happily for scholars, in the sense of Stevens, the reading of his poetry must comprehend the fine arts that interested him, at least in some part of his knowledge and enthusiasm. Note, for instance, the range of metaphor in the following, from "A Primitive Like an Orb": "The essential poem at the centre of things / The arias that spiritual fiddlings make, / Have gorged the cast-iron of our lives with good / And the cast-iron of our works" (*CP*, 440). The arias make the iron of banal fact endurable. Or consider the shifting ocean-blooms in "Sea Surface Full of Clouds." The mode of vision is that of impressionist painting, of Monet, if one prefers. Of what relevance is any bristling against privacy of vision? Who berates poetry about poetry? Will the same one object to Johann Sebastian Bach in *The Art of the Fugue* or *The Well-Tempered Klavier*? Is not this music about music? Or will he disdain Paul Cézanne for having painted about painting in his sequence of Mont Sainte-Victoire? Are not Bach and Cézanne celebrated for a sovereign privacy of the imagination in these works?

[26] See, for instance, his "Wallace Stevens: Some Relations between Poetry and Painting," *Comparative Literature*, XI (1959), 47–60.

If one takes a long look at any art which has flourished in privacy, he will find it entitled to a free standing from typicalness. As an aesthete Stevens is an internationalist. Perhaps he is a Royalist in his view of art. And, if he is, presumably he deserts the Republic. One may suppose that the eighteenth-century *décor* of *Harmonium,* and its metamorphoses in the manner of a court masque deriving from Ovid, appeared to some readers as the insignia of a Royalist. In the end, however he has been judged, he was writing of poetry. Whether popular or not, the symphonies of Charles Ives or John Marin's sequence of pictures of the Maine coast do not raise objections. Yet a poet who stands close to them in his metamorphoses on American themes may be held suspect.

But poetry, it will be answered, is different. Just how? Perception through a sense of the world and the struggle toward design are common to all three arts. Must the poet, then, be a moralist, a purveyor of wisdom to his society? In "The Noble Rider and the Sound of Words" Stevens contends: "I do not think that a poet owes any more as a social obligation than he owes as moral obligation, and if there is anything concerning poetry about which people agree it is that the role of the poet is not to be found in morals" (*NA,* 27–28). The trouble is that they do not so agree. Stevens was complimenting his Princeton audience. His true freedom is claimed in a later essay as he quotes from Henri Focillon's *The Life of Forms in Art*: *"The chief characteristic of the mind is to be constantly describing itself."* He continues: "This activity is indirect egotism. The mind of the poet describes itself as constantly in his poems as the mind of the sculptor describes itself in his forms, or as the mind of Cézanne described itself in his 'psychological landscapes' " (*NA,* 46).

The American public approach to poetry will be given some attention in the concluding chapter of this study. For the moment, let it be said that public sentiment in the Republic seemed to Stevens to be constant: one man's poetry ought to be every man's truth. Poetry describes the ordinariness of every day or it is useless. Stevens' ruminations on the constancy of the democratic ideal may be found in "Owl's Clover," in particular in the section which he entitled "A Duck for Dinner" (*OP,* 60–66). The maker of art for the scholar, unhappily, cannot compete with the duck. The hunger to be assuaged by the duck is large; the hunger for the artist is small. Stevens is in agreement with Cézanne, who measured the audience in a letter to his friend Émile Bernard. "Taste is the best judge. It is rare. Art only addresses itself to an excessively small number of individuals."[27] But in this agreement Stevens should be clearly regarded as an artist accepting a reality of his time. Contrary to all judgments of his aloofness, the fact is that he did not value poetry, or any art, as an exclusive *mystique.* The small audience was not a desirable proof of American limitations related to a oneness of humanity. He wished for his country a poetry of singular creators, each shaping his art in faithfulness to himself, offering nothing for the sake of popular acclaim and yet everything for the sake of example to other men. For him a singular art was a proof of the possible, and in this sense a gift of encouragement, revealing the faculty of the imagination as a redeeming power for every life. That he found little public receptivity in his time to this encouragement from poetry may be for some readers evidence of an aloofness. I regard it only as honest appraisal.

Of Stevens' attitude toward the cult of modernism, however, there may be little question. He knew his own unorthodoxy in poetry quite thoroughly. Yet he detested all assumptions of a "modern" right on the part of cultists to create an incomprehensible art, closed to public understanding. His distaste for *avant-gardisme* should be read as a firm rejection of a corrupt aesthetic: "art" created for the sake of obscurity. In the twentieth century his desire was fixed upon an American freedom of the self, a desire as simply American as the desire of Thoreau. Posterity should fully recognize this ardor as it reads the Grand Poem that he left. The poem was, of course, modern while it was being written. But the time of its composition is no longer modern, in the sense of the immediate present; and now, seen in its fullness and at a distance, it towers, like nothing else in the literature of poetry in its time, and like very little from any literature of the past. If it endures, as many of us believe it will, it then will stand as a memorial to every art of private vision, in itself a vision of a new "explorer of Earth." Randall Jarrell understood the perennial possibility of this new sight.

My purpose is to trace the process of the Grand Poem and the total structure that it accomplished in language. I shall not aspire to more than the firm lines of this structure and some of the poet's ventures along them. The full art of Stevens is organized with an architectural precision. The shape of the mind becomes a building, the

---

27 *Letters,* ed. John Rewald, trans. Marguerite Kay (Oxford, 1941), p. 235. The letter is dated at Aix, May 12, 1904.

framework of which is founded in a willed symmetry of design. In the chapters that follow I wish to expose the native capacity of the poet for this design and to reveal the craftsmanship of his acts as builder. My course with this shaping of a mind will proceed from a theory of possibilities to concern with the elements of the poet's crafting, with the accomplished structure, and with a consideration of its significance in this century. "The gold dome of things is the perfected spirit," Stevens noted in the "Adagia" (*OP*, 168). The Grand Poem is a dome upon the rock of being.

The letters of the poet, recently selected for publication and edited by his daughter, Holly Stevens, have been fully considered throughout this study. The generous representation provided by Miss Stevens, her unobtrusive notes, and her attention to significant phases of the chronology establish the image which she promises in her introduction: "Wallace Stevens as an 'all-round man.' "[28] Readers of the poetry become indebted to her in a deepening knowledge of the mind, how it is that the young writer of the journal at Harvard and in New York prefigures the maker of an art, and how it came to be that the maker sought out in correspondence men and women of companionable imaginations and sympathies. The man in the world has been disclosed. We learn his poet's dimensions of confidence, his delicacy of respect for people of selfless good will toward the arts, his regard for his family and for the memorials of his Pennsylvania boyhood. We discover a particular delight, as well, in his letters revealing his pleasure in imagined lands made of reports to him from afar, for instance, those addressed to his correspondent in Ceylon, Leonard C. van Geyzel, whom he never met; or those affirming his warm interest in the aspirations of youth, as he carefully respects a young Korean friend, Peter H. Lee; or those hearty statements from his widest American observation sent to his Cuban friend, José Rodríguez Feo. We recognize, subsequently, a man who chose to keep his life of the business day apart from his letters. The fullness of the image does not derive from the realities of a business office. Why, after all, should he have spoken of them, any more than he should have written to a friend of the activities of the Works Progress Administration in the state of Connecticut? His poet's aesthetic governs his taste in correspondence, even to his delight in describing a few pieces of perfect fruit purchased in New York and carried home on

[28] *Letters*, p. xiii.

the train to Hartford. The "all-roundness" of the man is the fullness of a poet's prose of the world he perceived.

Yet with those reviewers of the *Letters* who have contended that the correspondence is assiduously explicative of the poetry I must strongly disagree. There are, of course, the careful notes of Stevens addressed to Hi Simons, an early scholar-admirer, and to Renato Poggioli of Harvard, as this eminent translator prepared the text for an Italian edition of selected poems. But these notes are not fully explicative, even with their breadth of disclosure. When the total body of the letters is considered, it is apparent that explication is not the customary act of Stevens. Furthermore, contradictions in the persuasions of the poet himself must be added to ellipsis in explication. Stevens has not disclosed the elements of structure in his great design. He did not enjoy talking of his poetic process, save in the wider range of his affirmations of the art of poetry as an art of living. In relation to the full body of his achievement the number of poems and parts of poems which he chose to explicate in any way is remarkably small.

As for the contradictions, one should say only that these are of the prerogatives of any creator who is not as a letter-writer to be held to consistency. As they stand in the correspondence, these contradictions are engaging in their ways, and yet irrelevant to the poetry itself. A single letter of 1935, for instance, proposes what I must call a prevailing taste for the contradictory. Stevens contends that he knows very little of Paul Valéry, though he has "a number of his books." The poetry itself, as I shall attempt to show, either refutes this contention or reveals an affinity that is nearly incredible as a chance occurrence. In the same letter Stevens writes: "Yes. I think I have been influenced by Chinese and Japanese lyrics." Yet fifteen years later, as his editor notes, he disclaims any influence whatsoever. He writes that at one time he was interested in Japanese prints; but his having a "half dozen volumes of Chinese and Japanese poetry somewhere in the house . . . is purely casual."[29] Any careful reader of the letters will discover other examples of contradiction as he proceeds. I find it unthinkable that Stevens in his last year would have turned to the writing of a preface for an English translation of Valéry without a warm and profound admiration springing from this earlier time when he professed scarcely any knowledge of the French

[29] Wallace Stevens to Ronald Lane Latimer, dated at Hartford, November 5, 1935. The comment of 1950 is contained in a letter responding to an inquiry by Earl Miner of November 30; *Letters*, pp. 290, and 291. n. 9.

poet. I must note, too, that he makes no mention of Jules Laforgue, whom he certainly studied in his earlier years. As for the influence of the Japanese *haiku* on the maker of "Thirteen Ways of Looking at a Blackbird," who can know?

Any study of Stevens which is intent upon influences and analogies as primary approaches to a measurement of his art will not, in any case, answer his requirement. It is a requirement which one finds stated at several points in the correspondence. I choose three of these statements. In 1940 he wrote: ". . . I think that the critic is under obligation to base his remarks on what he has before him. It is not a question of what an author meant to say but of what he has said."[30] In the following year the assertion became even more firm: "What I intended is nothing. . . . A poet, or any writer, must be held to what he puts down on the page. . . . The basis of criticism is the work, not the hidden intention of the writer."[31] Two years before his death Stevens pared his requirement to the bone. "I believe in pure explication de texte. This may in fact be my principal form of piety."[32] In summary, the critic is to read what is before him.

The requirement is, of course, salubrious. One thinks of the old days of the academic critic, the days of searching for influences with the philologists. In our readings of Stevens they had better be gone forever. As I preface this study, I wish to say that where I have fallen into error the fault was one of ineptness rather than of intention. I have placed my confidence in the rightness of Stevens' dicta on the critic of poetry. "There seem to be very few people who read poetry at the finger tips. . . . Most people read it [poetry] listening for the echoes because the echoes are familiar to them. They wade through it the way a boy wades through water, feeling with his toes for the bottom: the echoes are the bottom."[33] I have intended a finger-tip reading of Stevens, whatever the errors. For it is clear that he was thinking of an instrumentalist, the right reader, the man at the keyboard who plays the master score before him. As far as Stevens is concerned—and here one is again grateful for the evidence of the letters—this is the way all poetry should be read, a playing of the score of a composer who was uniquely himself and no other, with as much faithfulness as one can bring to what is set down in black notes on white paper. To recognize the presence of Italian operatic

[30] Wallace Stevens to Hi Simons, from Hartford, January 9, 1940; *Letters*, p. 346.
[31] Wallace Stevens to John Pauker, from Hartford, June 3, 1941; *Letters*, p. 390.
[32] Wallace Stevens to Bernard Heringman, from Hartford, July 21, 1953; *Letters*, p. 793.
[33] Wallace Stevens to José Rodríguez Feo, from Hartford, January 22, 1948; *Letters*, p. 575.

style in the youthful scores of Beethoven, to acknowledge an imagination initially placed in the tutelage of a foreign model, does no injustice to the composer, certainly; such a recognition in the scholarship of the performer of early Beethoven scores will inevitably deepen his reading. But to assume that the expression of the mature shaper of music is a complex of reflected influences and affinities is to deny the vision of the creator. The "leaves" of Stevens, separate poems which clothe the great ribs of the dome, are to this extent separate scores which require our faithfulness as "finger-tip" readers. The frequent metaphor of Stevens for himself as composer is insistent: he inscribes his notation at the keyboard. We endeavor to perform his music, to read it as he conceived it and as he wrote it. The originality of the artist is supreme.

Value judgments may possibly be inevitable in all readings of works of art. If, in the sense of Stevens, a reading of a poet's structure is proposed as analogous to an instrumental performance, then it may be answered that the "player's" emphases themselves imply judgments of comparative worth among "scores." Nevertheless, I have intended a demonstrative rather than an evaluative study of Stevens. I believe that the work of this poet requires demonstration similar to that applied in studies of master structures in related arts. The chosen analogy of Stevens refers primarily to music. But he thinks as well of total idiomatic structures in the history of painting, as in the work of Claude Lorrain, or in the evidence of dominant styles in architecture, as in the neo-Gothic designs of Viollet-le-Duc. The scholar intent upon a master idiom and its sequential forms in the achievement of a composer, a painter, or an architect seems to enjoy a particular freedom from obligation to judge the artist's personality. There are difficulties inherent in claiming the same freedom for explicators of lyric poetry. A long habitude of regarding the character of poetic art seems endlessly to require presuppositions: that, although we may grant the autonomy of a poet's work, we nonetheless insist upon biography among our implementations for reading, or, if we have not very much of that, clues within the poetry which point to the poet's deficiency or his excellence, his indifference or his sympathy, as a man among men. An evaluative criticism of Stevens will measure, as it wills, his humanity, or his poet's acts of truth or falsity relative to what he believed of human worth, or did not believe but tried to believe. The full portrait of a poet as a man among men and the demonstration of the artistic design of that man are, as I take them, sharply differing eventualities from one's reading. I have chosen to seek the second of these ends since I consider it to have been the one which Stevens himself respected. In this objective I have had two purposes: to examine the method and the inclusive shape of Stevens' design, and to relate these to the character of a creative mind in solitude. It is my hope that this demonstration may appear justified in relation to methods in the study of arts other than poetry, studies in which obligation to a measurement of personality is not presupposed.[34]

Of the method which I have followed I wish finally to offer a brief word of defense. Every student of lyric poetry justly regards the separate poem as an entity, containing organic relationships of images and themes which determine the degree of its vitality. Cutting through these entities in a poet's work, as one traces thematic elements of a total life structure in poetry, may seem to some readers intolerable. However, it was Stevens, not his readers, who designed the Grand Poem. To recall his stated principle in "A Primitive Like an Orb" (*CP*, 441), "One poem proves another and the whole. . . ." The principle in the Grand Poem is realized through a recapitulation of themes and of images as well. The separate poems of Stevens are all parts of the total poem, "proofs" of one another and of the whole. In a demonstration of the principle, a cutting through entities, as we regard them separately, is inevitable. I propose that a tracing of interrelationships among the parts does no violence to any one full text, singly read. "Sunday Morning" remains free-standing. But a knowledge of its relatedness to the total poem should enrich its significance and deepen the responses of which we are capable. This master lyric is momentary in the speech of the whole; and in the context of the whole the meditation which it preserves is enlarged. Thus I have intended, with respect to the separate poems, to contribute toward a deeper reading of Stevens at any chosen point in what he was pleased to call "the amassing harmony" (*CP*, 403). The musicologist may choose to read the full range of a composer as a harmony of relatedness among separate works; and when he does he will demonstrate affinities that make the peculiarity of a total accomplishment. His reference must cross from part to part as he defines the whole. Because the poetry of Stevens is uniquely what it is, his concepts of his

---

[34] Of biographical readings I wish finally to note that I am aware of possibilities, e.g., those presumably to be recognized in "Le Monocle de Mon Oncle" (*CP*, 13–18) and "Red Loves Kit" (*OP*, 30–32), of intimate disclosures concerning Stevens' marriage. Holding these to be inadmissible to a study of Stevens as an artist, I decline them.

art are alone essential for his readers. Because he chose to write the Grand Poem and to hold himself to a strict discipline for its realization, we should assume his theory throughout our study of his work. As his reputation advances and his readers increase in number, it may be better, in the end, to regard him as an artist among artists rather than a poet among poets.

The Shaper

I

Architecture

1

THE ADVENTURE IN THE TOTAL STRUCTURE AND THE ritual of its making—in the view of Wallace Stevens these are the acts of the poet. As the supreme motions of the mind in its encounter with a world in motion, they justify the will of the artist. In a comment on the critic Paul Rosenfeld, Stevens wrote: ". . . [he] was a shaper, that is to say, a *Schöpfer*, who lived for the sake of *Schöpfung*. . . . This constant shaping, as distinguished from constancy of shape, is characteristic of the poet."[1] *Schöpfung*. The English equivalent will not serve. Stevens returns to his European heritage. He must be satisfied in his naming of creative restlessness. His urgency here matches his insistence upon the *gaudium* of being. A leeched-out English will not match the force of the Latin; nor will it match the satisfying fullness of the German. The subsequent observation on the character of the poet celebrates process as the end in itself. A poem is made; its shape is a constancy. But the poet leaves this momentary achievement for the making of another. It is his restlessness, rather than the endurance of the poem, that characterizes him. Unlike the Lord

[1] See, for instance, Rosenfeld's *Men Seen* (New York, 1925). Stevens' note (1948) appears in *Opus Posthumous*, pp. 262–64, under the title "The Shaper."

of Creation, he will not rest on the Seventh Day. An American poet, he is ploughing North America on Sunday, as the feathers of the imagination "flare / And bluster in the wind" ("Ploughing on Sunday," in *Harmonium, CP,* 20). The ploughing is of his *Schöpfung.* It goes on every day, as the wind of constant change blows upon the poet and the land. Yet a good ploughing goes on a line. It has its own geometric precision. In this very early lyric, meditating on a poetic act of turning the surface of American reality, Stevens discloses his love of the precise. His *Schöpfung* will be masterly in his command of design. It will be a creation shaped without compromise. The line on the soil will hold him fast.

The ground, he knew, was *blue.* I shall not purpose to review Stevens' symbolism of color. Every reader knows it well. Blue, of course, is the sign of a potentiality of or for the imagination. A little farther on in *Harmonium* the poet observes in "Anecdote of the Prince of Peacocks": "I knew from this / That the blue ground / Was full of blocks / And blocking steel" (*CP,* 58). Two personae figure in the poem: Berserk, who is the presence of the endless imaginative faculty in man, his power to make poetry, and the beginning poet, who is challenged in the dialogue. The potential is at his feet, the earth of the ploughman. It is full of materials for a structure, *materia poetica,* as Stevens was later to call them (e.g., "The Noble Rider and the Sound of Words," *NA,* 33). There is "blocking steel" here, as well. It is a material to carry the weight of an art. The ploughman's furrow will become the determinant of a certain element in a steel framing. It will become a major theme taken from the circumstance of the poet's reality. Those constancies of crafted poems which are left in the structure as the imagination ceaselessly moves will be supported at this chosen point. The steel element will become an arc. It will become a part of what Stevens in retrospection near the close of the process calls ". . . that which in an altitude would soar, / A vis, a principle or, it may be, / The meditation of a principle. . ." ("A Primitive Like an Orb," *CP,* 442).

The nature of architecture is the nature of the process celebrated as *Schöpfung.* This study cannot be concerned with a formal philosophy of art. But I wish to note that the concept behind architecture as an art of shaping was mandatory for Stevens. There is a passion for shaping within the dynamics of any primary work of art. We seem to call upon architecture to name the passion as we speak of the architectonics of Milton in *Paradise Lost,* or the lineaments of design in the last quartets of Beethoven, or architectural precision in the mythological canvases of Poussin. It is the organic evidence of architecture which captures us. Beneath the crafted object is the living and moving idea of the object. The Platonic metaphor of the golden form is merely another name for the fact of organicism. In art, by whatever name, it was always there. At the risk of offense to professional theorists in aesthetics, one may assert that it is the architectural element which is the force of movement captured in the work as it stands completed. The ribs of the Gothic vault *spring*; the exterior buttresses *thrust*. Or the lateral motion of glass tiers in a new building on Park Avenue *repeats* a process without a finial, as though to suggest an infinite series rising into space. Architectural evidence appears to be an endless demonstration of original movement in the mind and hand of the shaper. He has finished his work, but the building continues to express movement.

Aesthetic theory may be, in the rigidness of doctrine, what one chooses. But for Stevens the dynamics of architecture were commanding in the sense just described. The power of the concept was obsessive. Almost literally, his first and last choices as a craftsman were posited upon architecture. If we assume that his fully serious reflection upon his own potentiality for poetry began in about 1912–14, scarcely four years had passed before he began to identify his poetic future with the shaper in architecture. In 1918 he published in *The Little Review* a poem given the name of the art. If on the authority of Samuel French Morse,[2] his posthumous editor, we take as his last significant work his prefaces for the newly translated *Dialogues* of Paul Valéry,[3] then Stevens' reflections upon the shaper in fact close his life. He completed the prefaces in March of 1955.[4] His death occurred in the following August. Yet these reflections had been deepening since 1952, particularly in his poem addressed to Santayana, "To An Old Philosopher in Rome," and in his witty survey of his own poet's architecture in "St. Armorer's Church from the Outside" (*ca.* 1954). The span from the announcement of an intention upon architecture to the last long look at the completed building encompasses, then, the forty

[2] See *Opus Posthumous,* the introduction, p. xxxvi.

[3] Bollingen Series, XLV, No. 4 (New York, 1956), Stevens' prefaces are directed to "Dance and the Soul" and "Eupalinos, or The Architect." A subsequent volume (1958) in this series presents an English translation of Valéry's *The Art of Poetry,* translated by Denise Folliot, with a preface by T. S. Eliot.

[4] On April 20, after he had finished his prefaces, Stevens wrote to Jackson Mathews at the University of Washington: "This man's [William McCausland Stewart's] translation of the *Eupalinos* is a beautiful thing: severe and with a kind of old-fashioned idiom." (Stevens' carbon copy of the letter in the possession of his daughter, Holly Stevens.) By permission of Miss Stevens.

years of Stevens the poet. The full satisfaction of the shaper is not a final matter at issue. The design was completed. There was reason to rejoice in the late retrospective lyric, "The Planet on the Table," deliberately placed by Stevens at the close of his last arrangement in the *Collected Poems*: "Ariel was glad he had written his poems. / . . . It was not important that they survive. / What mattered was that they should bear / Some lineament or character, / Some affluence, if only half-perceived, / In the poverty of their words, / Of the planet of which they were part" (*CP*, 532–33).

The poem "Architecture,"[5] of 1918, was excluded by Stevens from the collected edition. Reclaimed by Mr. Morse and now restored to the canon, it is indispensable at the threshold of examining the act of design. "Let us build the building of light, / Push up the towers / To the cock-tops. / These are the pointings of our edifice, / Which, like a gorgeous palm, / Shall tuft the commonplace . . ." (*OP*, 17). There will be portals, east and west. This building of light will rise, "Our chiefest dome a demoiselle of gold." "Pierce the interior with pouring shafts, / In diverse chambers. / Pierce, too, with buttresses of coral air / And purple timbers, / Various argentines, / Embossings of the sky" (*OP*, 18). The poem stands as an exploratory sketch. Its prefigurings are numerous; and the early poet's awareness of the shape to come is startling when one surveys the later achievement. The poem is a paradigm. One begins a listing here with *light* as the phenomenon to be celebrated by the poet's building. The *cock-tops* introduce the persistent metaphor to come: the imagination symbolized by birds and clawed creatures—parakeet, dove, eagle, or that greedy lion favored by Stevens. The palm with its symmetrical crown anticipates the symmetry of the dome. It is the symbol of a total design, the design that is to figure in a poem of Stevens' last year, "Of Mere Being" (*OP*, 117–18). This lyric has been regarded by recent interpreters as cryptic. In relation to "Architecture" it springs to openness and to an arresting beauty. The palm stands at the end of thought. The imaginative process is about to cease as the poet feels the approach of his own end. The structure alone endures. It is the palm "on the edge of space," now foreign to its maker, whose process ends; yet it is an achieved structure. But in the poet's beginning the palm spreading over the ground of reality suggests the majesty of the dome to be built. The points of the compass will dictate its orientation. The *demoiselle* capping the dome will be of gold, the

5 "Architecture" was included in the first edition of *Harmonium* and omitted in the second edition; see *Letters*, p. 259.

gold of the sun. She foretells the presence of the eternal feminine throughout Stevens' art. She will become, as she assumes various guises and passes through scores of metamorphoses, the attendant genius of poetry. Since poetry is of that essential freedom of air, an air of Ariel, the buttresses of this structure will be fashioned of it; and the timbers will be purple, in the poet's persistent color-symbol for ceremony and rite.

Light, bird, palm, woman of gold, air and freedom, a poet's ritual —all these announcements as the poet begins to anticipate certainties in the process of the structure to come—are to be reasserted in the major poetry, each time with wider significance as the mind grows and the process intensifies. Furthermore, one must notice the four-squareness of the building. Stevens thinks of his own poet's life as moving from South to North. Youth is in the South. Thus he takes his leave of the Florida of the imagination (*Harmonium*) as his second volume, *Ideas of Order*, opens. At the far North, toward which he moves after Florida, lies the end of mind described in *The Auroras of Autumn* and "The Rock." Throughout the Grand Poem, Nature moves in a counter direction from East to West, as in the course of the sun and the duration of a day's light. In "Architecture" the poet projects a building to celebrate natural process in the East-West portals. For the present he will exclude the inevitable certainty: the life of the mind moves from South to North. The sketch foretells the future with a certain awesomeness, as though the "sybil of the self" had spoken (as in "The Sail of Ulysses," *OP*, 104).[6]

The projected building is to stand as a memorial to the shaping of a self, a mind. For Stevens, of course, the self and the mind were to be realized in poetry. But the need for individual shape was to remain omnipresent in his thought. The promise of *life* as a self-established meaning in defiance of meaninglessness was here in this need, and in the answer to be exerted by the will intent upon structure. The imagination, then, is subject to the discipline of the will. To exert it under discipline is to shape. Poetry need not be the end any more than is the architecture of the real building of steel, stone, and glass or, for that matter, the accomplishment of any man distinguished as a shaper.

One should note the concept of shape as a poetic subject. I intend three instances at this point. The first appears in "The Good Man Has

[6] The poem was written for New York Delta of Phi Beta Kappa and was read at Columbia University on May 31, 1954, in honor of the Columbia Bicentennial Celebration.

No Shape," from *Transport to Summer* (1947). The poem turns upon the irony of man freed to himself. "Through centuries he lived in poverty. / God only was his only elegance." Then generation by generation he grew a little stronger. He saw the promise of the good life. The good life came. But "Lazarus betrayed him to the rest, / Who killed him, sticking feathers in his flesh / To mock him." Entombed, he was left with sour wine and an empty book to read. "And over it [his grave] they set a jagged sign, / Epitaphium to his death, which read, / The Good Man Has No Shape, as if they knew" (*CP*, 364). *They*, the rest, are the shapeless, compelling the perseverance of shapelessness. The mockery of the feathers in the flesh is a tragic summation. The feathers are the signs of the bird of the imagination, of the power of self-shaping. They adorn the good man in death, just as the thorns of the Crucifixion were a mocking adornment. A second instance follows almost immediately in the chronology, in "A Lot of People Bathing in a Stream" (*CP*, 371). We are in the stream of time, with our children splashing about us. We are old. They are young. We see them near us, "angular anonymids / Gulping for shape among the reeds." We are creatures of natural process in this desire for shape; and our final compulsion to relinquish it is the proof of the desire. Thus the poet stands at last beneath the *aurora borealis* of autumn. Now, "This is form gulping after formlessness . . ." ("The Auroras of Autumn," *CP*, 411). We begin in a desire for form. We gulp among the reeds. Society defies the shape of the individual. It will dispossess, if it can, the strength of the individual imagination. But the supreme irony lies at the end. Children of the physical world, we reach a time in age when we feel compulsions to relinquish form. As the strength of the imagination wanes, we seek a return to the anonymous. Shape is thus unsubstantial, save in the substance of the total building governed by the shape. For shape is itself organic. It is process. There is no stasis of individual being. The architecture of the self flourishes through the duration of vitality. In the Introduction I have contended that Stevens did not write poetry in the mode of wisdom. Process remains all. It is a matter of what the individual does with the power to shape himself. His success or his failure in shaping the self, his experience with process, are simply facts of the human condition. Wisdom, if it is here at all, is in the earnestness of confronting the facts.

It may be that Stevens had known the *Eupalinos* of Valéry (originally published in Paris in 1923) for some years prior to his undertaking of the preface of 1955. One would suppose a long acquaintance.[7] Phaedrus addresses Socrates in the Dialogue: "By dint of constructing . . . I truly believe that I have constructed myself." Socrates replies, "To construct oneself, to know oneself—are these two distinct acts or not?"[8] Stevens commented on this exchange in his preface: "This elevation of aesthetics is typical of Valéry's thought. It is itself an act of construction. . . . His partiality for architecture was instinctive and declared itself in his youthful *Introduction to the Method of Leonardo da Vinci.*"[9] Whether or not Stevens had looked upon Valéry's architecture of the self when he most needed this correspondence of vision (during the 1920's), he was, I think, quite aware of this French "elevation of aesthetics" at an early date in his career. In the next chapter I intend to demonstrate some affinities between Valéry and Stevens. The title chosen by Stevens for his preface of 1955 is "Gloire du long Désir, Idées." The elevation of ideas projected by Valéry in the *Eupalinos* complements the glory of Stevens' desire, certainly. As he asserts in his preface, the total need for a craft, the true understanding and the exact practice of it are "immeasurably the most important things in the world, through which the world itself comes to the place of the divine."[10] This craft will be of the shaping of the self, as in the observation of Eupalinos: ". . . true beauty is precisely as rare as is, among men, the man capable of making an effort against himself, that is to say, of choosing a certain self and of imposing it upon himself."[11] One feels that the Socrates of the Dialogue is near the poet who sees the children of the stream, the beginners, the "anonymids." So said Socrates: "I told you that I was born *several* and that I died *one.* The child when it appears is a countless crowd, which life reduces soon enough to a single individual, the one who manifests himself and who dies."[12] One feels, too, that Stevens rejoiced in this vision of the self as he read Valéry's proposal through Eupalinos: the artist of the self is the inconstant; the sculptor's model is impressed in the sand; the molten bronze is

[7] Stevens, with characteristic disinclination to speak of influences upon his work, wrote to Ronald Lane Latimer from Hartford on November 5, 1935: "I have read very little of Valéry, although I have a number of his books and, for that matter, several books about him. If there are any literary relations between my things and those of other writers, they are unconscious. . . . Of course, a man like Valéry emerges from his books without a close reading" (*Letters*, p. 290).

[8] Bollingen edition, trans. Stewart, p. 81. Eupalinos, by Valéry's confession, is the name of an engineer of Megara taken from the article "Architecture" in the *Encyclopédie Berthelot.* (See Stevens' preface, pp. x and xi.)

[9] *Ibid.,* p. xvi.

[10] *Ibid.,* p. xviii.

[11] *Ibid.,* p. 86.

[12] *Ibid.,* pp. 109–10.

poured; the wax from the shaping hand disappears; the Corinthian metal endures as a constant memorial to an inconstant being.[13] Or, finally, what more fitting agreement could Stevens have discovered than that contained in the words of Socrates? "[N]o geometry without the word. Without it, figures are accidents. . . . [W]e are able . . . without paying any more heed to sight or movement, to recognize the properties of the combinations we have made; and as it were, to construct or enrich space, by means of well-linked sentences."[14] Thus, at the end of a life in poetry, Stevens turned to that architecture of the self long ago projected, and now realized. The geometry of the word had been ruler of the craft; space had been enriched through "well-linked sentences." The structure of the self had become, in this sense, the structure of the world perceived through the sovereign eye.

The poet's address to George Santayana in 1952 has been read correctly as an elegy of the first magnitude. As a commemorative poem it is unsurpassed in the range of literature in English; and it has as much to tell us of a singular poetic being, of questions of fame and the endurance of art, as has "Lycidas." The subject is the death of a man loved, yet distantly known. The setting is of a city which the poet had never seen. Stevens did not enter Santayana's course in the philosophy of art at Harvard during his student days there (1897–1900). But it is clear from Stevens' early journal and from his letters that Santayana took a more than passing interest in the young poet-president of the *Harvard Advocate*.[15] The admiration, at any rate, was of long standing. It deepened with the years, as the poet read the philosopher; and it led Stevens to assess Santayana's life as one in which the life of the imagination had "a function similar to its function in any deliberate work of art or letters" (*NA*, 147–48). Stevens' commemoration is of Santayana the shaper; it is also, in the wider sense, a lyrical address to the human power of shaping. Who can read this poem without sensing the majesty of the Roman back-

[13] *Ibid.*, pp. 88–89.
[14] *Ibid.*, p. 105.
[15] On January 4, 1945, Stevens wrote from Hartford to his friend José Rodríguez Feo: "While I did not take any of his [Santayana's] courses and never heard him lecture, he invited me to come to see him a number of times and, in that way, I came to know him a little. I read several poems to him and he expressed his own view of the subject of them in a sonnet which he sent me, and which is in one of his books." Santayana's sonnet is "Cathedrals by the Sea," replying to Stevens' student effort, "Cathedrals are not built along the sea." See the note by Holly Stevens relating to the above quotation from the letter, in *Letters*, pp. 481–82. See also a reference to the friendship with Santayana in Stevens' journal of the early New York years, in *Letters*, p. 96.

ground, a Rome crowded with structures, a Rome exalted through the centuries by its sovereign art, architecture? Who can escape the majesty of this death of a shaper amid the shapes? The old man lies in the poverty of human ends. Yet he lies in triumph, his own achievement complete in a succession of shapes. "The bed, the books, the chair, the moving nuns, / The candle as it evades the sight, these are / The sources of happiness in the shape of Rome, / A shape within the ancient circles of shapes, / And these beneath the shadow of a shape . . . " (*CP*, 508–9). *The domes* of the city are the *architecture* of the bed (*CP*, 510). "Total grandeur of a total edifice, / Chosen by an inquisitor of structures / For himself. He stops upon this threshold, / As if the design of all his words takes form / And *frame* from thinking and is realized" (*CP*, 511).[16] A shaper dies, himself an inquisitor of structures. "The life of the city never lets you go, nor do you / Ever want it to" (*CP*, 510). The testament of Rome is the testament of the shaping power. It is comfort; it is triumph.

The design was chosen. At the end of the act of building, the thinker pauses, *as if* the design were a *frame* in its total realization. The long retrospective pause of Wallace Stevens begins with "The Auroras of Autumn." As in Valéry's metaphor from *Eupalinos*, the flames burning away the presence of the creating self, so the poet reaches the autumnal, the northern blaze in this sinister flaring of night skies. "He opens the door of his house / On flames. The scholar of one candle sees / An arctic effulgence flaring on the frame / Of everything he is" (*CP*, 417). The imagination's "shape and mournful making move to find / What must unmake it . . ." (*CP*, 418). An inquisitor of a structure—his own—stands in prospect of both the house to be abandoned and the shape of himself, which, remaining as process until he dies, now moves inexorably to its own "unmaking." It is, nonetheless, the realization of the structure, the *frame*, that preserves meaning in the meaningless.

The paradox is nowhere more firmly stated by the late Stevens than in his last look at the building, "St. Armorer's Church from the Outside":

> *Its chapel rises from Terre Ensevelie,*
> *An ember yes among its cindery noes,*
> *His own: a chapel of breath, an appearance made*
> *For a sign of meaning in the meaningless,*

16 Italics mine.

No radiance of dead blaze, but something seen
In a mystic eye, no sign of life but life,
Itself, the presence of the intelligible
In that which is created as its symbol.

It is like a new account of everything old,
Matisse at Vence and a great deal more than
*   that....*   [*CP*, 529]

From Terre Ensevelie it rises as a symbol; it is one man's knowledge of existence. It expresses his sense of the world. Another sense of the world, another knowing of existence, was expressed by Henri Matisse, the maker of the chapel at Vence. The making of structures is old. It is part of that life of imagining mankind, "which is always beginning, over and over" (*CP*, 530). No "radiance of dead blaze" is left on the poet's building. Yet what is left will survive for a little time as he perishes, an ember among the cinders of entombment. This image of the ember is of the highest significance in any examination of Stevens' poetics. It urges the vitality of poetry lived by its creator, the process of poetry. Poetry is immediate; it is a flourishing in private vision, "his own." Abandoned at death by the individual imagination that shaped it, the achievement yet knows an endurance. But it is to be endurance among the cinders, the past to which every present moves, cinders of that landscape projected by the poet in "A Postcard from the Volcano" (*Ideas of Order, CP*, 158).

Stevens' imagery and symbols of achieved structure throughout his poetry are dominated by the *dome*. In the poem to Santayana the domes of the ancient city are the architecture of the philosopher's bed (*CP*, 510): they are the shapes antecedent to the shape that lingers there. The brilliance of this dome imagery comes from a poetic mastery of long habitude. The dome is first seen in the poem "Architecture." It reappears in "The Comedian as the Letter C," as the American "cabin" of Crispin's New-World imagination becomes a dome and halidom, a sanctuary for his four daughters (*CP*, 43). Images of pillars and arches related to the dome structure assume prominence in related expressions of the theme, as in "Botanist on Alp (No. 1)" and "A Fading of the Sun" (*CP*, 135, 139). But it is in "Owl's Clover" (1936), suppressed[17] by Stevens in the *Collected Poems*, that one en-

---

[17] Suppressed, one supposes, because of the poet's dissatisfaction with the socio-political content. In long-standing critical agreement, this sequence is flawed by its ineptitudes of expression in treating as subject the American cultural hiatus during the years of the Depression.

counters the fullest description of the sovereign dome of the self. The passage that follows occurs in the section of the poem entitled "The Greenest Continent" (*OP*, 53–54). Full quotation is required here. The concept of dome and halidom is projected in its entirety. The poet speaks of an earthly paradise of domes, each man the possessor of his middle dome among the structures of other men.

> *There was a heaven once,*
> *But not that Salzburg of the skies. It was*
> *The spirit's episcopate, hallowed and high*
> *To which the spirit ascended, to increase*
> *Itself, beyond the utmost increase come*
> *From youngest day or oldest night and far*
> *Beyond thought's regulation. There each man,*
> *Through long cloud-cloister-porches, walked alone,*
> *Noble within perfecting solitude*
> *Like a solitude of the sun, in which the mind*
> *Acquired transparence and beheld itself*
> *And beheld the source from which transparence*
> *   came;*
> *And there he heard the voices that were once*
> *The confusion of men's voices, intricate*
> *Made extricate by meanings, meanings made*
> *Into a music never touched to sound.*
> *There, too, he saw, since he must see, the domes*
> *Of azure round an upper dome, brightest*
> *Because it rose above them all, stippled*
> *By waverings of stars, the joy of day*
> *And its immaculate fire, the middle dome,*
> *The temple of the altar where each man*
> *Beheld the truth and knew it to be true.*

These domes of solitary builders crowd a lost paradise. The middle dome is the possessed structure of each man. In the metamorphoses of the poetry of Stevens it becomes the dome of Santayana's bed; it becomes the poet's own St. Armorer's Church.

Between this "greenest continent" of "Owl's Clover" and the last look at the Church, some two decades of Stevens' poetry intervene. The imagery of the structure is unceasing. Here and elsewhere in this study, in citing examples from the poetry, I shall wish to avoid exhaustive chronologies. The fullness of the vision, as I have contended in the Introduction, can be mastered only by a close reading of the Grand Poem. But metamorphosis in language must be illustrated at this point. The dome, as it is seen in the long passage just quoted, is present in each of the following examples. In "The Man with the Blue Guitar" (1937) the crowd of the "shapeless," those who determine that "the good man has no shape," announce: "Do not speak to us of the greatness of poetry . . . Of the structure of vaults upon a point of light" (*CP*, 167). In "The Sail of Ulysses" (1954) the language changes to "The living man in the present place . . . the difficult inch, / On which the vast arches of space / Repose . . ." (*OP*, 103). Human duration in each instance is a point, an inch in space. Upon this difficult limitation space is enriched, as in those "well-linked sentences" named by Valéry's Socrates. This act of the poet-builder, as I shall later consider it, is Stevens' qualification for the hero.

But there is an unheroic youth, who begins as a would-be shaper intimidated by the structures of other men. He is the youth addressed in "Notes Toward a Supreme Fiction," the one who begins in tentativeness and weakness. He looks from his attic window. "You look / Across the roofs [of structures of other men] as sigil and as ward / And in your centre mark them and are cowed . . ." (*CP*, 384). This imagery of structures within the vision of the youth has opened with the poet's observation that "it is the celestial ennui of apartments / That sends us back to the first idea, the quick / Of this invention . . ." (*CP*, 381). The building of life must be a place of the sovereign self. We return to the first idea, of shaping, to escape the tenant's boredom. We behold the academies "like structures in a mist" (*CP*, 386). We long for a "castle-fortress-home." Viollet-le-Duc[18] may help us build it; and we may set a man, MacCullough, to live there, as though we installed, let us say, some American industrial baron in one of those neo-Gothic palaces of old upper Fifth Avenue. But the MacCullough of crass imagination, if of any imagination at all, is a tenant, of course. The apartments, however new, are old. "It does not follow that major man [the man in all of us who needs the *first idea*, the quick of imaginative invention] is man" (*CP*, 386).[19]

As he surveyed New Haven on an "ordinary evening" toward the close of his life, reading quietly from a long poem to the Connecticut Academy of Arts and Sciences,[20] Stevens observed of "Alpha" beginners and "hierophant Omega" men, the young men and the old, that ". . . both alike appoint themselves the choice / Custodians of the glory of the scene, / The immaculate interpreters of life." The lines

[18] French architect (1814–1879), exponent of the Gothic revival.
[19] Italics mine.
[20] The Sesquicentennial Celebration, November 4, 1949.

immediately following he did not read on that evening. "In the presence of such chapels and such schools, / The impoverished architects appear to be / Much richer, more fecund, sportive and alive" (*CP*, 469).[21] "Conceptions of new mornings of new worlds" have been lost (*CP*, 470). The vision of "The Greenest Continent" from "Owl's Clover," with its many domes of many men, is aspiration to the "ordinary" reality of this view, with its impoverished architects as custodians of the scene. The heroism of great imaginers, great builders of domes, is now exchanged for tenancy. Academies and chapels rise in the evening air of New Haven. Are these MacCulloughs who live there, these custodians of tradition? The trouble is that the MacCulloughs refuse to be major men. One wonders just how much of Stevens' meditation, even with the omission of the impoverished architects, was understood by this august academy gathered in the Yale Art Gallery! The sybil of the self speaks, of course, in her own language.

Socrates in the *Eupalinos* of Valéry discloses that he was born *several* and died *one*. What has become of the *others* of that several? asks Phaedrus. Socrates replies: "Ideas. They have remained in the condition of ideas. They came, asking to be, and they were refused." So the two converse, in the realm of the dead on the banks of the Ilissus, the river of Time.[22] Socrates speaks of the idea of the self chosen to become the self. The others were possibilities, ideas not chosen. The suggestion is of an apriorism, innate possibilities in the beginning shaper of the self, which Stevens would reject, certainly, unless innateness were limited to the imagination alone. In Stevens' view the difference between the traditional philosopher and the traditionless poet may lie just here. In "An Ordinary Evening in New Haven" he says of the search for reality: "It is the philosopher's search for an interior made exterior / And the poet's search for the same exterior made / Interior . . ." (*CP*, 481). The distinction is fully expressive. The philosopher begins with his imposition of an *idea* upon the world; the poet begins with the phenomena of the world and

[21] The total poem contains thirty-one sections, each consisting of six unrhymed triplets, a favorite stanzaic form in the late poetry. Of these sections Stevens read to the Academy only eleven, chosen from various sequences of the poem. The full text was published in *The Auroras of Autumn* (New York, 1950). The abbreviated version may be found in *Transactions of the Connecticut Academy of Arts and Sciences*, Sesquicentennial Celebration, Proceedings, Pt. I, Vol. 38 (December, 1949), pp. 162–72.

[22] The Stewart translation (see above, n. 3), pp. 109–10.

reaches the *idea*. The philosopher's interior seeks proof of its authority in the exterior; the poet's encounter with the physicality of the
exterior determines the reality of the interior. In other words, the
philosopher builds upon the unreal of his own dream, very much as
though he wills the formulas of a world before turning to the world
itself. The poet first receives the world through his senses; his
reality, his *sense of the world* eventuates from the play of the mind
upon the data of the senses. Yet more simply, with the philosopher—
Professor Eucalyptus of "An Ordinary Evening" in this case—*idea*
proceeds to *object*; with the poet Stevens, *object* proceeds to *idea*.

The contention here intensifies Stevens' view of physicality as
the condition of being. Without the world of the concrete, the real, or,
if one wishes, the world of measurable phenomena, we would have
no ideas. Being would become nonbeing, existence without feeling
and without any power of response. In "Esthétique du Mal" Stevens
submits that pain "is a part of the sublime / From which we shrink.
And yet, except for us, / The total past felt nothing when destroyed"
(*CP*, 314). The point is that pain is not human pain without the
power of response of a mind structured in ideas. It is a part of the
sublime because the power of ideas and idea-making is contained in
it. It is this concept of pain which directs the poet's prospect of his
own end, "The Auroras of Autumn." "Farewell to an idea . . . A cabin
stands, / Deserted, on a beach." Again, "Farewell to an idea . . . The
mother's face, / The purpose of the poem . . ." (*CP*, 412–13). The
cabin is the house of a poet in poverty; the mother's face is the face
of Earth. Yet it is not the leave-taking addressed to the poet's craft
or the farewell to this physical Earth that inflicts pain. It is the loss
of the idea of each that torments: ideas in the structure of the mind.
The imagination wanes. Now existence becomes a duration of "mere
being," to recall the title of a late poem already discussed, or the state
of minor living presented in the last poem of the collected edition,
"Not Ideas About the Thing But the Thing Itself." The thing
sensed is now merely the thing. No ideas spring from it in the mind.

My final remarks on the poet's architecture must then have to
do with ideas as materials intricate in the act of the shaper. The best
of contemporary theory from professional architecture illustrates the
presence of inner shaping, of object becoming idea, of idea imposing
form upon material. The work of the Saarinens, father and son, discloses in each American building shaped by their hands the authority of inner reality. There are differences between the two with respect to a theory of source. The elder, Eliel, contended for the origin

of architectural form in the object in nature.[23] The younger, Eero, rejected natural form for "the total of man's man-made physical surroundings . . . man-made nature."[24] Thus his Trans World Airlines Terminal at Kennedy Airport in New York was conceived of as a building "in which the architecture itself would express . . . the drama of travel."[25] But these distinctions within the source of ideas are not of our concern here. Whether a natural form, e.g., the trunk of a tree, or a social form, e.g., the movement of travelers at an airport, serves as the progenitor of an idea, the object is nonetheless the point of beginning. The process is not that of the "superficially decorative form" discussed by Eliel Saarinen: ". . . Our rooms, homes, buildings, towns and cities have become the innocent victims of miscellaneous styles, accumulated from the abundant remnants of earlier epochs."[26] It is clear that both father and son, like every other contemporary architect of eminent vision, intended to free an art from a metaphor of cluttered accretions. Every architecture of past or present which issues from an idea prototypic in the mind alone, without any *raison d'être*, save the imposition of form unrelated to a primary object, is the opposite of this modern purpose. The same difference is apparent when one considers Stevens' ideal dome of ideas formed in an inner reality, and the banal roof-top of the timid youth addressed in "Notes Toward a Supreme Fiction." This youth has been discussed in his relationship to a tenancy of old (and artificial) forms. The poet is specific. "But you, ephebe, look from your attic window, / Your mansard with a rented piano" (*CP*, 384). That persistent mansard roof, to some of us appearing as an infallible mark of the late Victorian style, is a dubious French gift, no matter what the original excellence of Pierre Lescot and François Mansart. What has it to do with a first idea for us, the quick of imaginative invention?

In a study of Stevens, then, it must come to this: no ideas without a requisite antecedence in the physical world; and no ideas worth the keeping which do not preserve the quick of invention. To

---

[23] See his *Search for Form: A Fundamental Approach to Art* (New York, 1948), pp. 11–48.
[24] See *Eero Saarinen on His Work,* ed. Aline B. Saarinen (New Haven, 1962), p. 5. Yet, even with this contention, Eero Saarinen's description of theoretical approaches to the design of the Auditorium, Massachusetts Institute of Technology, runs: " . . . [T]his one-room building is spanned with a dome at three points. . . . The auditorium floor . . . is essentially a reverse dome shape. The building was thus two shell shapes, like a clam" (p. 34).
[25] *Ibid.,* p. 60.
[26] *Search for Form,* p. 12.

speak in this way is to argue for an old premise from the philosophers. Mr. Miller is exact when he notes that "Stevens uses the word 'idea' in its original meaning of 'direct sense image.' "[27] But we should remember that the process is not wholly direct. The imagination will alter the image according to its own individual requirement. The possible sources in philosophy for Stevens are numerous. Santayana's *The Sense of Beauty,* published in 1896, may have challenged him in the assertion: "Visible objects are . . . nothing but possibilities of sensation."[28] More particularly, one supposes that the following tribute to the imagination from Santayana had an appeal that was never forgotten in the poet's mature craft.

[T]he feeling of significance signifies little. All we have . . . is a potentiality of imagination; and only when this potentiality begins to be realized in definite ideas, does a real meaning, or any object which that meaning can mean, arise in the mind. . . . To learn to see in nature and to enshrine in the arts the typical forms of things; to study and recognize their variations; to domesticate the imagination in the world, so that everywhere beauty can be seen, and a hint for artistic creation—that is the goal of contemplation. Progress lies in the direction of discrimination and precision, not in that of formless emotion and reverie.[29]

No doubt Stevens found in this power of domesticating the imagination in the world the center of Santayana's act as a maker of a total edifice. But the poetry of Stevens does not show a concern for preserving the typicalness of form in nature; neither is beauty its persistent end. "Art," he wrote in the "Adagia," "includes vastly more than the sense of beauty" (*OP*, 159). It seems to me, as I have contended in the Introduction, useless to attempt to fit him to the frame of any philosopher. The points of contiguity are important, these and nothing else. His tastes in philosophy were highly eclectic. Any insistence upon this potentiality of imagination operating upon the thing, making of it an idea, appealed to him, whether he was reading in idealism, materialism, phenomenology, or what not.

The range of possibilities within this eclecticism is interesting, even though I wish to exclude questions of wide indebtedness. George Berkeley's principle *Esse est percipi* is exactly appropriate for Stevens. So are its refinements in the "Essay on Vision": ". . . [I]f we take a close and accurate view of things, it must be acknowledged

[27] *Poets of Reality*, p. 248.
[28] I use the New York edition of that year, p. 69.
[29] *Ibid.*, pp. 151–52.

that we never see and feel one and the same object. That which is seen is one thing, and that which is felt is another."[30] Or one may turn to the essay "Concerning Motion": "No light can be thrown on Nature by adducing anything that is neither accessible to the senses nor intelligible to reason."[31] He continues: ". . . For nothing can be formed in imagination that cannot by its nature be perceived by sense, since imagination is simply the power of representing sensible things actual or possible."[32] Yet Stevens cannot be related in any act of coercion to Berkeley the theologian, who reserves for the intellect, as apart from the "extending" imagination, the power of treating "spiritual and unextended things."[33] The only *things* are the things sensed, things made ideas, and things produced by the imagination in its play upon the ideas. For Stevens no faculty is absolute except the imagination. Frank Doggett, one of the best of recent critics of Stevens, finds his subject very closely related to Francis Herbert Bradley in the premises of *Appearance and Reality* (1893): "the skeleton of primary qualities," "a strictly physical explanation of the Universe."[34] But though there is reason to suppose that Stevens read Bradley, one cannot overlook the unsuitableness to the poet's view of Bradley's progression. The physical world, in his system, is reduced to essences. Instead of remaining essences of the object serviceable alone to the imagination, they become signs of a perfect and changeless reality. Bradley was an absolute idealist. One is left again with an uncommitted Stevens; and I cannot suppose here, any more than in those instances from Santayana and Berkeley, that the poet was interested in more than method and metaphor. A "domestication of the imagination," *Esse est percipi*, "the skeleton of primary qualities"—in this realm of object and idea these are points of agreement for Stevens.

The affinities just noted precede the twentieth century as an aggregate of theory useful to the poet. There is also a critical gain in prospect through recognition of contemporary theory. The work to be done for Stevens in this area is both attractive and demanding. Much of it must await the appearance of a critical biography and a full exposition of Stevens' reading. Yet the purposes of my study are dependent only on the internal evidence of the poet's published work. I wish merely to note certain possibilities of development in a knowl-

[30] *Philosophical Writings*, ed. T. E. Jessop (London, 1952), p. 9.
[31] *Ibid.*, p. 205.
[32] *Ibid.*, p. 211.
[33] *Ibid.*
[34] "Abstraction and Wallace Stevens," *Criticism*, II (1960), 35.

edge of this background of the contemporary. For the most part, it is a background compounded of aesthetic assumptions rather than of total systems. In "The Pure Good of Theory," a poem in four parts from *Transport to Summer*, Stevens asserts quite simply, "It is never the thing but the version of the thing . . ." (*CP*, 332). His relation to the nonrepresentational in the art of this century need no longer be urged. I am concerned only with his insistence upon theory as a pure good. The philosopher-critic Ramon Fernandez, certainly read by Stevens,[35] spoke in the mid-twenties (in his essay "Of Philosophical Criticism") of *psychic equivalents* set up in the mind encountering the object. In the mode of this century the transformation of object into idea is met head-on with analysis. "Through the concentration of impressionism reality is translated into human tendencies and these in turn have to be translated by analysis. The thing to be understood is displaced and situated between common-sense reality and intelligence: that is . . . the astral body of the object."[36] This astral position of the object seems to appear in a poem of Stevens, "So-and-So Reclining on Her Couch." Executed under its title as though an *odalisque* were in process, the figure "floats in the contention, the flux / Between the thing as idea and / The idea as thing. She is half who made her" (*CP*, 295). The poem seems deliberately intended to suggest the painter's craft. But its real concern is rather with the area between object and idea open to the imagination. I propose that two levels of perception are apparent here. First, there was a psychic equivalent, to use the term of Fernandez—that equivalent which became idea after the first sense impression; second, there was an imposition of the idea upon the thing now encountered a second time. But the second encounter takes place inside, not apart from, the mind. It is the meeting of the retained idea and the flourishing imagination.

In the poet's architecture this genesis and this later encounter are of supreme importance. The poet Howard Nemerov has noted that ". . . this may now be said about the figurative center of Stevens' poetry: that every object, in the poet's mind, becomes the idea of itself, and thereby produces the final illumination which in the platonic philosophy would have been produced by the view of the arche-

---

[35] The name of a persona in the much celebrated "'The Idea of Order at Key West." Stevens disclaimed any knowledge of Ramon Fernandez. See his note written for the reprinting of the poem in the anthology *Modern Poetry*, ed. K. Friar and J. M. Brinnin (New York, 1951), p. 538: "I used two everyday names. As I might have expected, they turned out to be an actual name."
[36] *Messages*, trans. Montgomery Belgion (New York, 1927), p. 43.

types themselves. . . ."[37] Mr. Nemerov is right about the finality of illumination through idea. Nothing exists beyond this private illumination. With that admission Stevens is set apart from much of the philosophical antecedence of his century. He enters the company of European theorists of contemporary reality. He becomes closely related to Juan Gris, the cubist who insisted that there is a kinship between poetry and painting, since both, through graphic signs, are *writing*.[38] As a theorist Gris contended that ". . . the mental image which has formed in the creative imagination of the artist exists for him alone." By taking shape through this graphic "writing," it will exist for others.[39] Or Stevens knows the object as it becomes idea in the sense of the poet Tristan Tzara: "Under each stone, there is a nest of words, and it is out of their rapid whirling that the substance of the world is formed."[40] Again, to transfer this privacy of idea leading nowhere beyond itself, one may turn to Jean-Paul Sartre in his description of object-consciousness: "The object as image is never anything more than the consciousness one has of it. This is the phenomenon of quasi-observation."[41] An object, as in Tzara's potential nest of words, is "an infinity of aspects."[42] Quasi-observation we may take to be the mode of Stevens' thought as he writes in "So-and-So Reclining on Her Couch" of "the flux / Between the thing as idea and / The idea as thing." The idea alone cannot govern; neither can the object alone. In the modern sense, one must inquire into the nature of the artist's thought as it precedes structure.

"A thought," Odilon Redon observed, "cannot become a work of art . . . except in literature."[43] The literature of thought recognized by this painter will not include Stevens. The flux between thing and idea will not permit a poetry of thought alone. An interaction between the two is for Stevens essential, unquestionable. To recall the Sunday ploughman over his furrow, the very possibility of a controlled architecture, a shaping sense of the physical world, lies here. Nothing in the vision of Stevens the poet will so sharply set him apart from a contemporary poetry of thought alone as this interaction. One thinks

[37] "The Poetry of Wallace Stevens," *The Sewanee Review*, LXV (Winter, 1957), 8.
[38] Daniel-Henry Kahnweiler, *Juan Gris: His Life and Work*, trans. Douglas Cooper (New York, 1947), pp. 40, 45.
[39] *Ibid.*, p. 40.
[40] Quoted by Marcel Raymond, *From Baudelaire to Surrealism* (New York, 1950), p. 316. The translator appears by initials only, "G. M."
[41] *The Psychology of the Imagination*, translator unnamed (New York, 1948), p. 20.
[42] *Ibid.*, p. 9.
[43] Quoted by Etienne Gilson, *Painting and Reality* (New York, 1959), p. 157, continued in note 33a, p. 361, after *À soi-même* of Redon.

of the *Duino Elegies* of Rilke or the *Four Quartets* of Eliot. They are built upon thought; and to such a theorist as Redon their kind may be admissible. So may they have been admissible to Stevens. But they bear no kinship whatsoever to Stevens' poetry. With Stevens reality requires the act of constructing from objects of earth made into ideas, and that alone.

The feathers of the imagination fly from its encounter with the object-made-idea. In"Ploughing on Sunday" the feathers of the white cock's tail "flare / And bluster in the wind" (*CP*, 20), as the furrow cuts into the earth. Twenty-five years later, in the poem "The Bouquet" (published in *The Auroras of Autumn*), Stevens is still intent upon the original theme of this encounter, but now with a dazzling mastery of lyric statement. "Through the door one sees on the lake that the white duck swims / Away—and tells and tells the water tells / Of the image spreading behind it in idea." "Here the eye fastens intently to these lines / And crawls on them, as if feathers of the duck / Fell openly from the air to reappear / In other shapes . . ." (*CP*, 449–50). The other shapes assure the possibility of structure. The feathers contribute to the certainty of an architecture of the Grand Poem, and of the self. This certainty points to an ontology, one quite independent of the ontologies of philosophy. A great building, as I have suggested, is made of the sequence of thing-idea-thing. Phenomenology is wholly inappropriate to a reading of Stevens, as much as it is essential for a reading of William Carlos Williams. Poetry, if one wills as Dr. Williams did, may be compelled to *Das Ding an sich*. Whether this be poetry or not will depend, of course, upon one's private assumptions and requirements. Stevens thought of the poetry of Williams as "rubbings of reality."[44] This reality is, of course, the hard fact of earthly reality *unaltered by the imagination* since no idea whatsoever was made of the fact. One takes a rubbing of a gravestone or a stele, or Sunday in the park, or a concupiscent pair in a hidden nook of the park, to particularize from the work of Williams. But the rightness of Williams is neither here nor there. He had his own temperament, and his own persuasions. For us, what can more fully demonstrate the distance between Stevens and Williams than this sauntering way of a poet along the Passaic River, the contents of the mind, the contents of the object, and nothing

---

44 See the essay on Williams under this title in *Opus Posthumous*, pp. 257–59.

else? In Book II of *Paterson* the poet writes of a cloud of grasshoppers whirring from the red basalt shelf of the river bank: "They fly away, churring! until / their strength spent they plunge / to the coarse cover again and disappear / —but leave, livening the mind, a flashing / of wings and a churring song." The passage ends: "AND a grasshopper of red basalt, boot-long, / tumbles from the core of his mind, / a rubble-bank disintegrating beneath a tropic downpour. . . ."[45] This concluding image is absolutely precise for the poetry of Williams. One is compelled to set the rubble-bank mind in sharp opposition to the crafted dome intended by Stevens. The perceiver-poet encounters red basalt and grasshopper. A simple association occurs. A red basalt grasshopper falls from the mind. There is no progression to the idea of grasshopper. There is no reappearance in other shapes. This is phenomenological poetry. It is not a poetry of the shaper. The mind wishes to represent itself as a series of dictations from the phenomenal world. There will not be a seeking of an architecture of the self. Life is observation, certainly; but it is seeing only for the sake of seeing, at happenstance.

Stevens chose to inscribe in a notebook, "Sur Plusieurs Beaux Sujets, I," the following quotation from Graham Bell, writing in *The New Statesman and Nation* (1937): "But these . . . qualities (of 'varied and inimitable' colour and his [Cézanne's] handling) . . . do not account for the look of hard and unrelenting authenticity that distinguishes his work from that of lesser men. It is Cézanne's peculiar determination to pin down his sensation, and the exactness and intensity of notation resulting from this, that made Cézanne pre-eminent. . . . With Cézanne integrity was the thing . . ." (*OP*, xxxix). The poet added: "I note the above both for itself and because it adds to subject and manner the thing that is incessantly overlooked: the artist, the presence of the determining personality. Without that reality no amount of other things matters much." The inference to be made is clear. It is Cézanne the shaper who is revered. The presence of the determining personality is the governor of structure. His work is *Schöpfung*. It is a "pinning down of his sensation," his sense of the world, and an exactness of notation. It is, we may add, an architecture.

---

[45] "Sunday in the Park," in the New Directions edition (New York, 1963), p. 62.

Adjacent Structures: English and French Antecedents

2

A little while of Terra Paradise
I dreamed, of autumn rivers, silvas green,
Of sanctimonious mountains high in snow,

But in that dream a heavy difference
Kept waking and a mournful sense sought out,
In vain, life's season or death's element.

Bastard chateaux and smoky demoiselles,
No more. I can build towers of my own,
There to behold, there to proclaim, the grace

And free requiting of responsive fact,
To project the naked man in a state of fact,
As acutest virtue and ascetic trove.

THIS MEDITATION OF STEVENS' STANDS NEAR THE close of "Montrachet-le-Jardin" (*CP*, 263). Published in *Parts of a World* (1942), the poem bears in its title the name of a rare French wine. Both the rarity and the memory of a French pleasure are significant. The resolve "no more" seems to suggest a poet's rejection of an earlier quest. In 1942 Stevens was sixty-three. The "mournful sense" seeking out "life's season" or "death's element" is crucial. The time has not arrived for last assertions. But it approaches. William Butler Yeats, at seventy-four in the year of his death, 1939, had published "The Black Tower."[1] Did Stevens think of the vision of the first lines: the men of the old black tower, who feed as goatherds, their wine gone sour, their final lot the obduracy of soldiers? Stevens' resolve upon "acutest virtue," radically emphasized from the Latin *virtus*, may propose a relationship between the two poems. But there is no real similarity. In each the delights of the wine are over. "The Black Tower," with its vision of winds from the shore blowing against the dark mountain, shaking the bones, is a surrender to natural process. Furthermore, it is a surrender executed in the plural. But in the poem of Stevens, although "life's season" and "death's element" assert the reality of natural process, the inevitable end is confined to the singular; and, more impressively, the resolve upon architectural purpose to the utmost limits is intensified.

Yet the dream of the earthly paradise appears to be negated by the "mournful sense." William York Tindall finds that the poem "seems to have nothing to do with this great wine. . . . [It] has to do with its opposite." "The bottle is empty. Good-by, says Stevens, to the 'bastard chateaux and smoky demoiselles' in which he once delighted."[2] The question isolated by Mr. Tindall is, of course, at the center of the poem. But the *chateaux* and *demoiselles* appearing here cannot be understood without reference to Stevens' intention in his use of them elsewhere. The castle-fortress-home of MacCullough and the gold *demoiselle* atop the dome in the early design named "Architecture," as these have been discussed in the preceding chapter, must be related to the disclosure of "Montrachet-le-Jardin." It is not the *chateau* and the *demoiselle* of the poet that one finds rejected. His act of building will continue to completion, to that "ascetic trove" of "naked man" at the end. If the banquet is over, he will nonetheless persevere. It is the *unusableness* of structures other than his own, *bastard* and *smoky* to his purpose, the work of other men now disqualified for the poet's attention, that is at issue, as though one posed the question: After trying one's hand at the

[1] The date of the poem is January, 1939; see *Collected Poems* (New York, 1959), p. 340.
[2] *Wallace Stevens*, No. 11 in *Pamphlets on American Writers* (Minneapolis, 1961), p. 22.

architecture of an earthly paradise, does not one leave his own and enter another structure, for his final comfort? The refusal of Stevens in the "heavy difference" is unquestionable. The tower for the last look at the facts—facts of things only, without ideas beyond, without acts of the imagination upon ideas—will be his and no other's. He will keep to the singular. Nothing of his earlier dream is rejected. It is simply that the banquet must now give place to other concerns for the extending craft. The process of the shaper will be maintained. "And yet what good were yesterday's devotions?" the poet asks (*CP*, 264). The doubt is human. Knowing Stevens as the maker of a complete structure, we will answer: of no absolute good; the act of devotion was process; it will remain so. It is the assertion of the living self.

This wholly human doubt of the value of the structure had disturbed Stevens as he wrote the closing lines of the early "The Comedian as the Letter C": ". . . [W]hat can all this matter since / The relation [of each man] comes, benignly, to its end? / So may the relation of each man be clipped" (*CP*, 46). To be clipped is to be shorn of the power of imagination, that which makes the relation, the telling of the process. The doubt disturbed him again, this time heavily, in "The Bed of Old John Zeller." This meditation (in the volume *Transport to Summer*, 1947) stands as a major statement among the confessional poems of Stevens. It is human, he reflects, to wish for the structures of other men. Between the Comedian and Old John there is overwhelming evidence of that utter solitariness which urges the doubt: the solemn midnight of "The Reader" (*CP*, 146) or the awesome wakefulness of "The Men that Are Falling,"[3] with its premonition of finality (*CP*, 187–88). The bed and the pillow, as the only witnesses to a midnight speech, have become looming presences in a solitary room. They will reappear in the Roman bed of Santayana.

Old John Zeller was the poet's grandfather. Santayana was a builder-philosopher. Santayana's bed is a "difficult inch" of life (to recall the imagery of "The Sail of Ulysses") upon which a structure rises, completed. But then there is the doubt of John Zeller in bed, that "habit of wishing as if one's grandfather lay / In one's heart and wished as he had always wished, unable / To sleep in that bed for its disorder. . . ." "It is more difficult to evade / That habit of wishing

---

[3] Of this poem Stevens wrote to Bernard Heringman from Hartford on September 1, 1953: ". . . I did have the Spanish Republicans in mind when I wrote *The Men that are Falling*" (*Letters*, p. 798).

and to accept the structure / Of things as the structure of ideas" (*CP*, 327). The promise of the poet's end is his thought of the *structure of things*, his things made intricate among themselves, in "the old peak of night" (*CP*, 327). This imagistic darkness anticipates one of the most perplexing passages in the full range of Stevens' poetry, the second section of the Canon Aspirin sequence in "Notes Toward a Supreme Fiction" (*CP*, 403.) The Canon is major man, *naked* man, the perseverance of the wholly human in an imagining humankind. By the act of the poet he is contemporized and embodied. The Canon flew "With huge pathetic force / Straight to the utmost crown of night." At this zenith of the dark—ultimate, as though it were an apex of the *aurora borealis*—"The nothingness was a nakedness." There he had to choose. But the choice lay not between the nothingness and a structure. It was the choice of a structure. "He chose to include the things / That in each other are included, the whole, / The complicate, the amassing harmony." The examples that I cite here are widely distant from other expressions of the earlier poetry. The doubt of the significance of shaping from things-made-ideas and finally from things alone was endless.

The wish for the structures of other men as possible houses for one's tenancy was always there, "as if one's grandfather lay / In one's heart. . . ." "Montrachet-le-Jardin" does not speak of bastard structures in which the poet once delighted. It is a statement of a strengthened resolve against other structures, as the wine bottle lies empty and solitariness increases. The Canon Aspirin's resolve is of the same mold. Only the metaphor has changed. The banquet which he leaves is that of youth, an imagining of a world in richness as of a bottle of Meursault, of "lobster Bombay with mango chutney" (*CP*, 401). The adjacent structure which he shuns is that of his "sister." Stevens does not name her. Probably she is Ecclesia. She has daughters as Crispin had daughters. They are her progeny of the imagination. She dresses them "The way a painter of pauvred color paints. . . . appropriate to / Their poverty . . ." (*CP*, 402). She is a widow, sister-with-pale-children to the poet-as-his-own-priest, the maker of his own chapel. The Aspirin is the touch of the old poet-comedian who went in youth to the banquet: the priest in need of a later sobriety. There comes a time, as Mr. Tindall might agree, when the dream of terra paradise must be exchanged for the sober view of finalities. At this point an iron will must govern the process to the end. The movement of the poetry must be inexorable. The Canon will not take refuge with his sister. At the peak of night he will choose the final harmony. His architecture will remain his own.[4]

With this preface I have intended to suggest the relation of adjacent structures to the architecture of Stevens. This adjacency, I must strongly assert, does not impose questions of imitation. To recall the builders of domes in "Owl's Clover,"[5] each man is the architect of his middle dome, "The temple of the altar where each man / Beheld the truth and knew it to be true" (OP, 54). Other buildings in proximity display possibilities of a full shaping, of a life lived for the sake of a total structure. I wish now to discuss these possibilities as Stevens probably saw them. I refer primarily to poets as builders of the self, reserving for Santayana the one place among philosophers singled out by Stevens for praise. My test of the poet's interest in these adjacencies will be a strict one. I wish to inquire into possibilities of total design as Stevens may have observed these in his acquaintance with the work of certain English and French poets, and with a few models of oriental origin. In applying this test, I shall have to minimize and sometimes exclude interesting questions of a passing enthusiasm—that, for instance, which rests briefly on the elegance of Verlaine and Mallarmé.[6] The reading of Stevens has not been fully traced; nor will it be until a definitive biography has appeared. But one may assume that this reading, when it is known, will propose two possibilities: an impression of total design projected or achieved by poets known to Stevens; or a particular attribute in symbolism or in imagery which captures the attention of the poet's imagination. Although I shall note briefly certain matters of interest within the second of these possibilities, I am primarily interested in the first. To every serious student of Stevens it will already be apparent that the

---

[4] Stevens in comment on the Canon Aspirin is scarcely clear. His remarks to Hi Simons in a letter dated at Hartford, March 29, 1943, seem designed to convey ambiguity rather than to elucidate. He speaks of return to the side of the children's bed "with every sense of human dependence. . . . [But] if he is to elude human pathos, and fact, he must go straight to the utmost crown of night: find his way through the imagination or perhaps to the imagination" (Letters, p. 445). I take this comment, veiled at best, to mean that the poet in the persona of the Canon returns after the banquet of youth to the possibility of that human dependence represented in the church. But he chooses "to elude human pathos," to take the independent way of his singular imagination, no matter what the "utmost crown" of a dark solitude.

[5] See above, p. 11.

[6] For a discussion of Stevens and Verlaine of the Fêtes galantes, see Tindall, Wallace Stevens, pp. 16–17.

major attention is directed to French achievement. A French wine is precisely chosen as it passes into a poetic title. The following discussion, then, is directed toward Stevens' relation to foreign literatures. His relation to the American lineage I shall reserve for limited comment in the next chapter.

One can scarcely imagine a life more decorous and conforming than that of Stevens as an executive of an insurance company. But of that life of the artist apart one has only to say that it was wholly unconcerned with contracting itself to any acts other than its own. As I have said, it is useless to attempt to coerce Stevens the artist into any structure of other hands. He will inevitably burst the doors and disappear. Furthermore, the critic, whoever he is, will use the word *influence* with respect to Stevens at his own peril. I take Stevens at his word; and I shall heed the warning. Two letters of his, addressed to the poet Richard Eberhart in 1954, some eighteen months before his (Stevens') death, are uncompromising. The first asserts: ". . . [I]n my own case, I am not conscious of having been influenced by anybody and have purposely held off from reading highly mannered people like Eliot and Pound so that I should not absorb anything, even unconsciously. But there is a kind of critic who spends his time dissecting what he reads for echoes, imitations, influences, as if no one was ever simply himself but is always compounded of a lot of other people."[7] The second letter expands upon the first:

It seems to me that the true answer is that with a true poet his poetry is the same thing as his vital self. It is not possible for anyone else to touch it. For my own part, let me say now . . . that I had never for a moment thought that I had any influence on you nor, for that matter, on anyone else. Every now and then I notice that somebody is supposed to have influenced me but, personally, I have never been able to recognize the influence. And, of course, I am no more interested in influencing people than you are. My interest is to write my own poetry just as yours is to write your own poetry.[8]

This much is quite clear: the poet's view of himself will not be respected by any study that attempts to drag the poetry through the old combing process used by a critical regimen intent upon influences. We note, parenthetically, that the dangers of this error are now minimal, the dominance of traditional philology having given place in our time to the healthier study of literature. We understand that an influence is a *flowing into*: it represents penetration and assimila-

---

[7] The letter is dated at Hartford, January 15; *Letters*, p. 813.
[8] The second letter to Eberhart, dated at Hartford a few days later, January 20; *Letters*, p. 815.

tion. Stevens did not permit this for himself. He permitted only suggestions of possibilities. If the critic is to honor Stevens, he will regard any adjacencies that interested the poet as exterior objects for the architectural process: they are seen and studied; passing into the mind, they become ideas for the poet's own unique acts. His imagination alone dictates his poetry. The central self, the naked man, will be answered in no other way.

Crispin, the old European imagination traveling to a new shore, a green wilderness of possibilities, failed to establish in America the grandeur that he might have had. He "built a cabin who once planned / Loquacious columns by the ructive sea" ("The Comedian as the Letter C," *CP*, 41). Humble cabin or no, it was his, in a country where a poverty of the imagination seemed to Stevens to have persisted. The poet himself was willing to equate the structured dome of his own art with this national poverty, as he wrote of the deserted cabin on a beach in "The Auroras of Autumn" (*CP*, 412). But the vision of the loquacious columns was tenacious. Casting his eye over the poetry of past and present which appealed to him, Stevens was persuaded of grandeur in the visions of other men. It is clear that what made the difference between the grandeur of loquacious columns and the American cabin style was *milieu*—intellectual, imaginative, artistic. A richness of milieu urges the temple as a structure. It is a milieu of abundant myth and bold men.

There is a passage in "The Auroras of Autumn" (Sec. 9, *CP*, 419) which is beautifully explicated by a quotation from Coleridge in Stevens' essay "The Figure of the Youth as Virile Poet." The poem goes: "We were as Danes in Denmark all day long / And knew each other well, hale-hearted landsmen. . . ." In that time once "[we] of each other thought— in the idiom / Of the work, in the idiom of an innocent earth, / Not of the enigma of the guilty dream." In the essay[9] the poet turns to Coleridge's account of his voyage to Germany. Aboard ship, Coleridge falls into the company of some high-spirited Danes. Because of his black garb his new friends dub him *un philosophe*. Chagrined at this title, the unhappy man becomes impatient. But he is soon comforted when a Dane assures him that "all in the present party [are] Philosophers likewise. . . ." Then they drink and talk, sing and dance (*NA*, 41). Stevens thinks of the *milieu* celebrated in the "Auroras" as a good. Once we were as Danes in Denmark, in another age. Each man was his own philosopher. Each was supreme for himself in imagination. The use of life was, in this

[9] Read as a lecture at Mount Holyoke College in 1943.

sense, heroic and affirmative. The happy condition of the Danes is, of course, metaphoric in Stevens' poem. A certain "idiom of innocent earth" is not named. But we know that Stevens thought often and intently of Periclean Athens.

One has only to exchange this concept of milieu for Stevens' familiar symbol of *weather*. Every age knows a weather. For some ages the weather was harsh and evil; for others it was benign and enfolding, to such a degree that men lived in it with primary force. Good weather, whenever it comes, is a rightness of a time of man; and in Stevens' historical view it was above all else a rightness made rich with ideas. This is to say: no columns beside the ructive sea without a wealth of being asserted near a wealth of other beings. I have contended in the Introduction that Stevens regarded the past, in its humanistic aspect, as having no authority in the present. A man may regret the time-placed point of his life. But a past weather cannot be invoked. It was; it is now dissipated. All that remains to us *in memoriam* is the prospect of structures reared within it. Great Ozymandias is entertained as a subject by both Shelley and Stevens. But the similarity between the two poets ends there. Shelley's vision in his sonnet is romantically directed to the sweep of time passing in the drifting sands. Stevens' concern in the Ozymandias section of "Notes Toward a Supreme Fiction" (Pt. II, Sec. 8, *CP*, 395–96) is with naked, central man weaving a "fictive covering" for the woman-genius of poetry, the *demoiselle* ancient and ever new. Yet this Ozymandias memorialized by Diodorus and by Shelley was a man of another weather.

Stevens made several long reaches into the past. Each time he explored a freshness of vision in a time of ideas springing from the acts of the native element, the *central* man. Ulysses and Penelope become symbols of this perennial possibility of freshness in the late poems, "The World as Meditation" (*CP*, 520–21) and "The Sail of Ulysses" (*OP*, 99–105). But Stevens' meditation on Greek structures in his proposal "From the Packet of Anacharsis" (*Transport to Summer*, 1947) suggests his attention to an architecture wrought by the imagination, as he writes of a Hellenic precision of sight:[10] " 'The farm was white. / The buildings were of marble and stood in marble

[10] The image of this clarity of Greece seems to have taken form very early in Stevens' mind. In 1907 he wrote from New York to Elsie Moll [Kachel] his description of its brilliance. "The impression of Greece is one of the purest things in the world. It is not a thing, however, that you get from any one book, but from fragments of poetry that have been preserved, and from statues and ruins, and a thousand things, all building up in the mind a noble conception of a pagan world of passion and love of beauty and life. It is a white world under a blue sky, still standing erect in remote sunshine" (*Letters*, p. 101).

light. / It was his clarity that made the vista bright" (*CP*, 366). The farm is near Athens; the clarity is that of Anacharsis. Clarity of vision must then be equated with clarity of perception. It is new vision in the sense that the art of seeing the world springs from the sovereignty of central man. Immediately, the poet turns to the murals of Puvis de Chavannes. What would he have done with this farm of white buildings seen by Anacharsis? It would be "gray-rose with violet rocks," second-hand vision rendered in pastel. The vibrant light upon Pentelic marble would have been lost. One cannot inherit or re-create the weather of another age. This principle of Stevens' cannot be overstressed. The "primitive line" (*CP*, 366) of another man cannot be repeated by means other than fakery.

Thus it may be supposed that Stevens, who knew his Virgil, had examined the prospect of the grand structure in the *Georgics*.[11] The image of the poet-builder of the temple in Book III is a precise example in answer to Stevens' requirement. The shape is of Virgil's Mantua, freshly conceived in a poet's clarity:

> *If life allow, my epic verse will show*
> *The Muses have left Helicon for Rome;*
> *I shall be the first to bring to you,*
> *O Mantua, the palms of victory;*
> *And, beside the noble Mincio's sinuous stream*
> *That takes its wandering course past reed-lined*
>   *banks,*
> *Build a marble shrine on the verdant plain.*
> *Within my temple Caesar will hold sway.*
> *And I, set off by purple robes as victor,*
> *Will lead, to honor him, processional ranks*
> *Of a hundred four-horse chariots past the shore.*[12]

The weather, the milieu, of Virgil was what it was. In the poet's temple, in a firm and predictable cosmos, Caesar will be celebrated. Virgil was a builder. But what shall the poet build two thousand years later? His cosmos is incipient;[13] there is no myth that sub-

---

[11] See his reference to Virgil in "The Effects of Analogy" (*NA*, 116), read at Yale University in 1948. The translation used is that of C. Day Lewis.

[12] In the translation by Smith P. Bovie (Chicago, 1956), pp. 57–58.

[13] Cf. "July Mountain":

> We live in a constellation
> Of patches and of pitches . . .
> Thinkers without final thoughts
> In an always incipient cosmos,
> The way, when we climb a mountain,
> Vermont throws itself together.   [*OP*, 114–15]

sumes him. The purpose of the shaper in architecture must become subjective. The act of building becomes the reason for his structure. The poet's process must create a myth of the self as its proceeds. Every element of design must be newly conceived.

Stevens is generally taken to have been unusually well read in the major English literature from the Elizabethans to the mid-twentieth century. No doubt he was. But I do not wish to urge affinities between Stevens and the primary poets before romanticism. The conditions of preromantic expression in England, as on the Continent, are of course fully marked by tradition. The inheritance of ideas in a complex distinguishing every major writer from the High Renaissance through the rationalism of the eighteenth century may be commanding for us. One doubts that this complex was of primary interest to Stevens. At the same time, he was immediately willing to grant the perseverance of masterworks, whatever the degree of traditionalism. It is simply that he could not find useful to his own purposes literature in that tradition which offers structure as metaphor for a state of being beyond the work itself. This exclusion of the tradition which Stevens was impelled to make is entirely clear in a brief examination of Bunyan at the opening of his essay "Effects of Analogy": With respect to the allegory of *Pilgrim's Progress,* "we are less engaged by the symbols than we are by what is symbolized. . . . [I]t is the other meaning that is the solid matter . . ." (*NA,* 109). In praise of La Fontaine at the same point of his argument he notes: ". . . the solid matter is the story" (*NA,* 109–10). The fable is fable and nothing else. The maker of a fiction, whether poet or prose narrator, in the sense of Stevens, is either the maker of the work referring to a state of being beyond itself, serving in this way as plural rather than singular metaphor, or the maker of the work self-contained. One must pose Bunyan the allegorist against La Fontaine the fabulist; and the question of solid matter, imperious in being solely for itself, is demanding. Let it be said that the story-telling of Bunyan is an act of passage to abstraction, and that the narration of La Fontaine is nothing other than story for the sake of story. Stevens adds in his essay: "The difference may be a national difference" (*NA,* 110). Perhaps. We reserve judgment, however, pending an examination of the poet's French affinities.

An analogy from the recent history of painting will be useful in getting at Stevens' preference, in fact, his requirement. If one considers his taste for impressionism, the reference of an impressionist picture is at issue. In the first place the subject, whatever it is, proceeds into design as fresh vision. Claude Monet's studies of London, for instance, present the traffic of the Thames with traditionless attention. The moment of vision is captured and recorded in the medium. The picture framed by its outer limits refers solely to that momentary vision. In the second place, then, the picture does not exist to support a tradition or to represent abstraction. It does not refer beyond itself, save to the infinite possibilities of seeing London. So to speak is to invoke Stevens' insistent image of central, of *naked*, man. To illustrate a sharply opposed act of the artist, let us take the painter's pageant of François Boucher. In a poem of mid-career, "Asides on the Oboe" (*CP*, 250), Stevens reflects on "the gods that Boucher killed; / And the metal heroes that time granulates. . . ." Immediately thereafter he sets the figure of central man in opposition. The gods killed by Boucher are the tradition worn threadbare; the metal heroes are figures of the past copied and now "granulated" with the accretions of time. They are "metal" abstractions.

This rebellion against servitude to abstractions is the act of Stevens the modernist, if one dares use a term that he detested. It accounts for his strenuous opposition to centuries of literary history read as categories, as he surveys this reading in "Lytton Strachey, Also, Enters into Heaven" (*OP*, 38–39). The stamp of an age belongs to Mademoiselle de Lespinasse or Horace Walpole or Mrs. Thrale. Lytton Strachey was bewitched by the "Dixhuitième and Georgian and serene." Racial memory would seem to have no quarter here, that "serene" of recollection sweeping over the past, making bloodless abstractions at each turning. There can be no mistaking Stevens, either, when he turns to Samuel Johnson as a maker of abstractions. In "Owl's Clover" the objection seems denunciatory: "The civil fiction, the calico idea, / The Johnsonian composition, abstract man, / All are evasions like a repeated phrase, / Which, by its repetition, comes to bear / A meaning without a meaning" (*OP*, 65). What is Stevens thinking of: *Rasselas, Prince of Abyssinia*, or *The Vanity of Human Wishes*? One may advance Pope of the *Essay on Man* as a comparable maker of the abstraction. Stevens will not accept it. Man is ideally man only as he flourishes individually and contemporaneously. Art, at any rate, will not be fully art if it confines itself to abstractions of the human circumstance. I have already suggested the nature of this exclusion on the part of Stevens as I discussed his distance from the poetic mode of wisdom. By "a meaning without a meaning," Stevens,

the lover of paradox, implies abstraction without respect to the particular. His question would be: How can abstraction or an abstracted
tradition allow for the act of naked man expressing himself and no
other?

These exclusions of tradition make a heavy barrier against attempts to relate Stevens to traditional English structures of the mind
in art. His observation from the "Adagia" should be heeded: "Nothing
could be more inappropriate to American literature than its English
source since the Americans are not British in sensibility" (*OP*, 176).
We may be unable to attack this problem of Stevens' reading of
British sensibility with absolute accuracy. But this much appears
certain: he was disinclined to celebrate any poetry dominated by allegory, however atypical, or by abstraction having to do with supposed
universal states of human existence. I suspect that what he most objected to in this British sensibility was its inherent passion for poetic
empiricism. Eschatology, theism, morals, wherever one finds them—
these habitudes of English poetry tend always, in the view of Stevens,
to invalidate the solid matter of the creating artist. The comparison
between Bunyan and La Fontaine holds.

Thus one turns in vain to such attractive possibilities as the
architecture of Spenser in *The Faerie Queene* for an examination of
adjacent structures.[14] Each structure, whatever one pleases—the
House of Holiness or Castle Joyous or another—is founded in a

---

[14] Stevens in "Effects of Analogy" (*NA*, 111–12) takes note of *The Faerie Queene*
in an equation with Bunyan. Allegory, in a long work, induces a state of sensibility
which, because of sustained involvement, produces "an emotional effect" on the
reader. But this effect is, we infer from Stevens' analysis at this point, ephemeral.
For the time of involvement, the images (analogies) of the long work *seem* to be
expressive of *singular* emotion on the part of the artist; hence the imagination
revealed in the work seems to be of the particular rather than the general.
Stevens goes on in the same essay to speak of two theories of imagination which
confront the poet: (1) ". . . his imagination is not wholly his own but . . . may be
part of a much larger, much more potent imagination, which it is his affair to try
to get at . . ."; (2) ". . . the imagination . . . [is] a power within him to have such
insights into reality as will make it possible for him to be sufficient as a poet in the
very center of consciousness." He continues: "This results, or should result, in a
central poetry" (*NA*, 115; italics mine). It appears that the poet who regards his
art as a part of a larger imagination is an allegorist. The poet sufficient at the
center is the poet self-contained. Stevens concludes these reflections with the following remarks on the claim made by poetry upon time. "The proponents of the
first theory believe that it will be a part of their achievement to have created the
poetry of the future. It may be that the poetry of the future will be to the poetry
of the present what the poetry of the present is to the ballad. The proponents of
the second theory believe that to create the poetry of the present is an incalculable
difficulty, which is rarely achieved, fully and robustly, by anyone. They think that
. . . in any art, the central problem is always the problem of reality" (*NA*,
115–16). Obviously Stevens is allying himself here with the present poetry of incalculable difficulty, the poetry from the *center* of present consciousness.

consummate draftsmanship. But these structures of the imagination are abstractions of moral codes. When one has recognized fully the excellence of Spenser's craftsmanship, one still knows them to be symbols of values outside the poem. Like the bastions of the old *Castle of Perseverance,* these well-laid walls and turrets point to ethical absolutes. On similar grounds one must accept the eschatology of Donne and Milton as the element overreaching the grandeur of architecture, however majestic (to us) the precision of Donne's compass points or the dynamic symmetry of Milton. Before the inception of the nineteenth century in England there are houses of the poetic mind in plenty for the regard of Stevens. But the final requirement would seem to be that which he exacted of himself: the poet's house as his total process, the discipline of the mind freed to itself alone, answering to no traditional authority and strictly exemplifying the self that determined it. The abstraction is of the self, and only that.

Nothing, we may suppose, separates Stevens from Eliot so much as this requirement. The distance between the two becomes scarcely measurable. For Stevens, tradition, especially that which would make of art the point of intersection of all human diversities, an abstraction of, let us say, "life" as it is to "Johnsonian man," is the perennial enemy of poetry; for Eliot it is the essential continuum, no matter how great the newness in the contemporary expression that delivers it. Eliot began with T. E. Hulme's denunciation of romanticism; Stevens began with the contention that the romantic is the end of all true poetry. Late in life he concluded: "The whole effort of the imagination is toward the production of the romantic" (*OP*, 215).[15] Nor is there the slightest doubt that he lived as a poet by the principle recorded in the "Adagia." I must insist quite literally upon his exclusion of poetry that abstracts beyond the self, and his regard for the *pure* poetic act. "To give a sense of the freshness or vividness of life is a valid purpose for poetry. A didactic purpose justifies itself in the mind of the teacher; a philosophical purpose justifies itself in the mind of the philosopher. It is not that one purpose is as justifiable as another but that some purposes are pure, others impure. Seek those purposes that are purely the purposes of the pure poet" (*OP*, 157).

Since poetic structures are ordered by purpose, one must then look at this matter of adjacencies for Stevens with attention to his in-

[15] In "Two or Three Ideas," read before The New England College English Association in 1951.

sistence upon the pure. Within the English heritage this purity is by his requirement romantic and is descriptive of fresh perception, self-posited vision. Tradition must cease to be the ontological end of poetry. The only ontology is to be found in the realization of a pure structure. The full estate of English romanticism would seem to be the first realm of the possible and the satisfying for Stevens. I shall attempt, then, with some swiftness to indicate why it is not *purely* sufficient and why Stevens turned in strong preference to the memorials of late French romanticism. Early criticism of Stevens has considered, with good reason, the problem of his affinities with English romantic theories of the imagination. But it appears that his insistence upon freshness and purity, exactly as he defined these in his notebook, was then unsuspected.

Wordsworth, as everyone knows, intended in the original version of *The Prelude* in 1805 to trace the growth of a poet's mind. In that it records a singular process demonstrating constantly a theory of associated emotional states and of a private reality achieved through memory, it is a wholly original English poem. Stevens' requirement of a poetry of the center would seem to be answered: it stands free of poetic tradition; it explores the shaping self; it proposes a wholly personal vision; it realizes a biography of a mind like no other mind. The fourteen books of this structure present a true architecture. Furthermore, the poem is a massive statement about the nature of poetry; and in its perception of the poetic art of object-into-idea there is a full freshness of sight. This new vision, this way of looking at the world, becomes sovereign. The dynamics of a mind are described; a full design emerges. Beyond it the grand design is anticipated, as Wordsworth sketched this in the prefatory note to *The Excursion* in 1814. An entire life-architecture is projected. *The Prelude* is autobiographical and "preparatory." It is to be regarded as the "Ante-chapel" of a Gothic church. This church, *The Recluse,* is to represent Man, Nature, and Society. *The Excursion* as Part II of *The Recluse* is finished. If nave, transept, and chancel are the intended major projections, then only the second of these reaches completion. The "minor pieces" of his poetry, Wordsworth directs, "when they shall be properly arranged, will be found by the attentive reader to have such connection with the main work as may give them claim to be likened to the little cells, oratories, and sepulchral recesses, ordinarily included in these edifices."[16] The cruciform structure, with its

[16] *The Poetical Works of William Wordsworth,* ed. T. Hutchinson (London, 1928), p. 754.

cluster of small units bound to it, seems at first glance an ideal prototype for Stevens. Here in a poetic adjacency is an architecture of an original mode. A poet's life will be lived there.

The Prelude, taken singly, may have been demonstrative for Stevens. To record in poetry the structure of a mind is a supreme act. Yet the method of *The Prelude,* the *building up* (the Wordsworthian "growth of mind") in a Platonic progression, of reality transcending earlier reality, of absolute spiritual identity finally dismissing the synthesis of sense impression, is foreign to every objective of Stevens'. When one turns to *The Excursion,* the morality informing the poem becomes wholly unacceptable. The initial "paganism" of Wordsworth has given place to a Christian sensibility. Stevens himself seems to provide his own answer in an early portrait, "A High-Toned Old Christian Woman" (*CP,* 59). He opposes a Christian design with a Greek design. "Take the moral law and make a nave of it / And from the nave build haunted heaven." "But take / The opposing law and make a peristyle, / And from the peristyle project a masque / Beyond the planets." This antimoral masque projected from the peristyle makes all the difference. The architecture of the poet is inadmissible as a nave; it is rejected as a moral structure. It must be of the self and its exclusive vision of the world. An abstraction of man is inappropriate to the poet. One is inclined to pause on the threshold of Wordsworth's unfinished cathedral, regarding intently those small recesses bound to the "main work." Stevens' principle of *the poem of the whole* seems to be anticipated. But the barricade is Wordsworth's interdicting purpose: the Gothic cathedral is to exist as a moral structure; man abstracted to universal man is to be the master of its vaults. As for the "Ante-chapel," *The Prelude,* its "pagan" architecture of 1805 is "Christianized" in the revisions of 1850, the privacy of its first discoveries now coerced to a theological end. The poem has been rebuilt to conform with an adjacent structure, that of Christian faith. Certainly the revision exemplifies fully Wordsworth's rejection of the central poem for a final tenancy in another structure. It is as though he had known the restless bed, particularized by Stevens in those nocturnal tossings of Old John Zeller.

There is no need to review once more Stevens' possible derivations from Coleridge as a theorist. Important similarities frequently have been urged by criticism. Certainly the imagination known to Stevens establishes correspondences; it fuses the data of the senses; it compels the similar from the dissimilar; through synthesis it achieves a poetic reality. In the terminology of Stevens, this synthesis is the process of imagination at work upon things made ideas. It seems to me ill-advised to cite these attributes of imagination as proof of Stevens' dependence upon, let us say, the *Biographia Literaria*. The influence of this work alone upon romantic poetry in English is much exaggerated. If one must consider influences at all, would not the aesthetics of Hegel have served Stevens equally well? An advancement of the imagination as the agent of synthesis is one of the marks of romanticism, wherever it occurs. We may suppose immediate affinities when we consider the Coleridge of the ode "Dejection": that lamented suspension of ". . . what nature gave me at my birth, / My shaping spirit of Imagination" (Sec. 6). In the succeeding section the mountain wind is a "mad Lutanist"; the imagination confers form upon a primal force of nature. One then turns to Stevens at work with the symbol of the lutanist in "The Man with the Blue Guitar" (Sec. 19, *CP*, 175). In this poet's vision there is a lion, "the lion in the lute / Before the lion locked in stone." The stone is this reality of great nature; a fierceness of the lion couches within it, a "monster" to be "reduced." The poet would be "Two things, the two together as one, / And play of the monster and of myself. . . ." The old Aeolian harp image, originally of German romanticism, natural force sweeping the strings of the dynamic imagination, is battered and unstrung by this insistence of Stevens'.

Coleridge, it is true, has confessed in "Dejection" that ". . . in our life alone does Nature live" (Sec. 55). Joy (through imagination) is "the spirit and the power, / Which wedding Nature to us gives in dower / A new Earth and a new Heaven . . ." (Sec. 5). One need not quibble about this joy. It is an affirmation of the shaping power; and so it is as well for Stevens. But the passiveness of the lutelike imagination receiving the strains of the lute in nature, like the "wise passiveness" of Wordsworth, bespeaks the difference. Man, as the receiver, evinces a divine plan. Coleridge's poem spreads outward, into abstraction. Stevens, the lion lutanist, confronts the lion locked in stone. He will unlock it, flay it, make it roar. Wind will not be a compelling force from a divine purpose, as it is with Coleridge. The music will proceed from the poet's will, and that alone. There is no forthcoming "dowry" from nature. So to contend would be to argue for a homocentric cosmos. The orthodoxy of Wordsworth and Coleridge need not be reviewed. Plainly asserted, these apriorisms of English romanticism do not agree in any way with Stevens' view of the essential "impoverishment" of humanity in the twentieth century. The individual wrests whatever is to be his from the pure obstinacy of the stone upon which he must live.

The one architectural form in the poetry of Coleridge that may have engaged Stevens' attention is, of course, the pleasure-dome of "Kubla Khan." But as a fanciful structure it is dream alone, wholly unrelated to things of a "stone" reality-made-ideas. The dome of Stevens rests upon the rigid, indifferent base; it preserves a total poetic process, steel above stone. Coleridge's dome of Xanadu is scarcely attributable to the hand of an adjacent architect, any more than the peculiar power of Alph, the sacred river, is measurable, as it flows through caverns to a sunless sea. The pleasure-dome has "caves of ice"; its shadow floats "midway on the waves." Remarkable as this poem is in hallucinatory power, it is a water-borne mirage. The imagination dictates images in a state of riot unchallenged by poetic will. Such antecedence is of no value in a study of Stevens. One may as well attempt to urge a prefiguring eminence for the white radiance beyond Shelley's "dome of many-coloured glass" in "Adonais" (Sec. 52). These domes are imposed, rather than integral, structures.[17]

A brief note on Keats and Shelley remains. Of the two, Shelley appears the more central, in the sense of Stevens. Keats, in the diffuse proposals of "Sleep and Poetry," seems to begin in a search for the center. Impressions from the senses crowd the mind, flooding the early vision with possibilities of imagistic experience. The poem is a celebration of the imaginative faculty. The shapes of a day become "a poet's house, who keeps the keys / Of pleasure's temple" (ll. 354–56). There is every reason to suppose that the perseverance of the poet-as-priest in the major poetry that follows accords with Stevens' elevation of the priestly acts of imagination. Furthermore, the enshrinement of Psyche, the installation of Melancholy among her trophies, and the fashioning of magic casements at the close of the "Nightingale" are acts clearly related to the power of the architect. One may also cite the brilliance of "The Eve of St. Agnes" as a display of architectural obsession. But these inclinations of Keats are overruled by the search for tradition, the return to the Elizabethans and

---

[17] The aptitude of Shelley for visualizing architectural forms in natural phenomena, particularly in the Italian imagery of the late poetry, receives a brilliant discussion by Milton Wilson in *Shelley's Later Poetry* (New York, 1957), pp. 115ff. Of especial interest here is his attention to Shelley's "dome" imagery in "Ode to the West Wind" and "Lines Written among the Euganean Hills." Mr. Wilson submits that Shelley reflects in this imagery the strength of impression from prospects of domical architecture in Venice and Rome, particularly. Whether or not Stevens was aware of Shelley's tendency "to give the processes of nature an architectural and geometric stiffening" in his Italian poetry I cannot say.

to the dream of mythological Greece. The possibilities of "Sleep and Poetry" are directed into the mainstream of the neomythic. The weather of other ages in the human span, as Stevens would see it, is the objective. Yet this much is pervasive in Keats, as one proposes the question of the central poem: there is in him an enduring presence of the woman-genius of poetry. All the female figures of the odes, of *Endymion,* and of "La Belle Dame" reveal her in metamorphosis. In a later discussion of Stevens' mythological canon I shall wish to show that this presence in metamorphosis is one of the certain marks of the romantic in his poetry.

For it is this presence alone which invites a close comparison of Stevens with Shelley, even though in a limited sense. The poem of chief concern is "Epipsychidion." Whatever its disaccord with the poetry of Stevens, particularly in its passive character as reverie, it proposes an image of *naked,* untraditional man, the central poet, to recall Stevens' Ozymandias, weaving "a fictive covering" for this woman-genius, the demoiselle ancient and ever new. Emilia Viviani of Pisa, to whom the poem is addressed, is not the woman clothed. The "radiant form" is that of the eternal genius of imagination. The young Emily is transmuted. She becomes the Being whom the spirit of the poet meets "on its visioned wanderings. . . . In the clear golden prime of . . . youth's dawn" (ll. 191–92); she is the moon "waxing and waning o'er Endymion . . ." (l. 294); she is "soft as an Incarnation of the Sun . . ." (ll. 333–35); she presides over the poet's image of the "azure heaven" (l. 373). The Aegean island advanced as a haven of union with this presence wears "The light clear element . . . heavy with the scent of lemon-flowers" (ll. 446–47).[18] It is an island of

18 Cf. Stevens, in "An Ordinary Evening in New Haven," Sec. 21. The island of death, represented in name by Baudelaire's Cythère, is adjacent to another island, a place of the senses:

> . . . an isolation
> At the centre, the object of the will, this place,
> The things around—the alternate romanza

> Out of the surfaces, the windows, the walls,
> The bricks grown brittle in time's poverty,
> The clear. A celestial mode is paramount

> If only in the branches sweeping in the rain:
> The two romanzas, the distant and the near,
> Are a single voice in the boo-ha of the wind. [*CP,* 480–81]

The black isle of death is the "will of necessity." The "celestial mode" of the isle of the senses is the beauty of the physical world. The two become "a single voice" in the wind of change. Shelley's island is a symbol of fresh sensuousness, e.g., "the light clear element."

It is perhaps worth noting that Stevens describes a land of lemon trees in Sec. 29 of "An Ordinary Evening in New Haven" (*CP,* 486–87).

the senses, where a total freedom of the imagination is to be known. The Greek compound in the title of the poem names a state of being beyond intellect. In this island realm of the poem, sense and imagination alone will govern. To the student of Shelley's Platonism it may appear as the ideal-beyond-the-ideal this "soul out of soul" (l. 238), this sphere of being, distinguished from the sphere of universal being (l. 361). The imagery of the last section of the poem (ll. 513–91) is dominated by architectural vision. "This isle and house are mine, and I have vowed / Thee to be lady of the solitude . . . our home in life . . . Under the roof of blue Ionian weather."[19]

If freedom from tradition, freshness of vision, expression from the center of the poet in his time, are answers to the requirements posed by Stevens, then "Epipsychidion" stands in adjacency. At the same time, the differences that separate the poem from the art of Stevens are wide. In the first place, the architecture in which the poem closes is not structural in poetic method. It is imposed and incidental. In the second place, the poem is, or is intended to be, autobiographical. In the third, it advances an absolute state of love as universal law. In these respects it is distinctly unlike any poem of Stevens'. Yet one cannot dismiss its possible significance to Stevens as a reader of English romanticism. In its radical departure from tradition, its assertiveness toward an ideal primacy of the poet singular in his imagination, it stands with *The Prelude* as romantic English poetry without antecedence. It abstracts nothing save the self.

One thinks of later works of the nineteenth century devoted to a poetry exerted in prospect of older forms: Rossetti in an "Italian" service to the sonnet in *The House of Life*; Morris in tribute to the archaic saga; or Tennyson in his masterly evocation of an epic past. These were makers of structures, the greatest among them being the architectural achievement of Tennyson in the *Idylls*. Of other Victorian masters, Browning seems to anticipate certain aspects of a central poetry on the "primitive line"; and one supposes that his early admiration of Shelley came of his search for an essential freshness of perception. But my concern remains limited to possibilities within English romanticism. As far as Stevens bears any discernible relationship to the mainstream of English poetry, the

[19] The poem was composed at Pisa in January and February, 1821, the year preceding Shelley's death. One of Shelley's three early drafts of the preface sets forth an account of a young Englishman who had recently purchased one of the islands of the Sporades. He died on his passage from Leghorn to the Levant. See *The Complete Poetical Works of Percy Bysshe Shelley,* ed. T. Hutchinson (London, 1929), p. 420. Shelley's legend in which he masquerades as the young voyager is fictive.

important affinities will be found in romantic expression. Among the English antecedents in poetry, works of abstraction apart from the primacy of the central poet are irrelevant to his purpose. Ezra Pound's latest, and perhaps last, reflection on T. S. Eliot poses the eminence of Eliot's abstraction: "His was the true Dantescan voice. . . ."[20] This judgment is declaration. Pound reminds us of Eliot's vision of *man*. He proclaims Dante as the ultimate prototype. In a judgment of Stevens, it must be admitted that he has no commanding prototype. But the major antecedence of his art may be said to lie in French poetry of the late-nineteenth and the twentieth centuries.

"Most . . . [reviewers] seem to think that one writes poetry in order to imitate Mallarmé, or in order to be a member of this or that school. It is quite possible to have a feeling about the world which creates a need that nothing satisfies except poetry and this has nothing to do with other poets or with anything else."[21] So Stevens wrote in a letter of 1953. In a consideration of his French affinities, I shall again follow the injunction of the poet. Yet, when the question of imitation is put aside, there remains this matter of "feeling." The sensibility that governs in the French poetry of immediate interest to Stevens is related to his compulsion toward fresh perception and a speech of central man. In the "Adagia" he observes that "French and English constitute a single language" (*OP*, 178). That is, they do for Stevens. Nothing in his idiom is more strongly related to his search for the center than his preference for radicalism in diction. This aptitude is closely associated with his technique. A full examination of the compulsion toward a central diction must await another study. I am concerned only with the "feeling" preserved in radical imagistic usage. Adverse critical opinion has occasionally condemned Stevens' fondness for the obsolete in English. To read him, it has been said, requires a frequent dependence upon the New English Dictionary. This judgment tells us little of the poet's search for a language that would suggest the primacy of the central poem. If French and English constitute a single language, then clearly Stevens is mindful of that central English made in the admixture of French loanwords after the Battle of Hastings. It is not that he summons this distant language

[20] "For T. S. E.," *The Sewanee Review*, LXXIV, No. 1 (Winter, 1966), 109.
[21] Quoted by S. F. Morse, ed., in *Wallace Stevens: Poems* (New York, 1959), pp. v–vi. The letter is addressed to Thomas McGreevy, to whom Stevens dedicated the poem "Our Stars Come from Ireland" (*CP*, 454).

to his own use, but rather that he displays in his search for archaic speech an attention to semantic interplay, as though French and English might be captured in a process of fusion. The feeling is intent upon compounding a language of French and English used interchangeably. The only American poet who approximates him in this attention to French diction descriptive of the "primitive line" is Whitman. But Whitman had no formal French. He had only an ear receptive to the sounds of a few French words. Probably Stevens would not have claimed an unusual competence in French. Nonetheless it was a competence of very wide range, idiomatic and meticulous. His reading in French literature was wholly intent upon poetic purity as he understood that state of the center.

My observation concerning interchangeableness no doubt implies a wider incidence of French in the poetry of Stevens than is actually the case. Yet one has to recognize his fondness for French titles throughout his poetry. The signs of Stevens' early identification of his imagination with French expression lie very deep in his diction. The French refrain dominating each section of "Sea Surface Full of Clouds" is an obvious mark. I add two examples of considerable obscurity. At very widely separated points in the poetry they indicate the French disposition of the poet. In the early poem "Depression Before Spring," published in *Harmonium* (*CP*, 63) two symbols are set in opposition. As the scene opens, "The cock crows / But no queen rises." The imagination is awake, but the woman-genius of poetry does not appear. Hence a depression is confessed: "Ki-ki-ri-ki / Brings no rou-cou. . . ." The onomatopoeic sign of the cock's cry is posed against the cry of the dove, fashioned here from the French *roucouler*. It is the "French" aspect of the imagination which is absent. The poem is of the young imagination. There can be no question of French reference when this dove cry is traced through the later poetry. It is the cry at daybreak heard in the lyric "The Beginning" from *The Auroras of Autumn*. The dress woven for the woman of poetry lies cast-off, and ". . . the first tutoyers of tragedy / Speak softly, to begin with, in the eaves" (*CP*, 428). The *tutoyer*, the speaker in the second person of a wholly intimate address, supports the poem at a point where no English word will serve. It is the imagination, a bird of dawn in the eaves, speaking of the tragedy of finality, as though in a French perception. In the last sequence, "The Rock," the sun and the day have become "ordinary" in "Song of the Fixed Accord" (*CP*, 519–20): "Rou-cou spoke the dove, / Like the sooth lord of sorrow. . . ." The French cry is the same, but now diminished, as the imagination wanes and the long process reaches its end. These impositions of French are more than deliberate; they are integral in process, as the imagination traces its life through the signs of words. In the late poetry such a French endowment of diction is again striking in "An Ordinary Evening in New Haven": In the city, men walk ". . . in need / Of majesty, of an invincible clou, / A minimum of making in the mind, / A verity of the most veracious men . . ." (*CP*, 473). This *clou* is the center of the passage. It is the nail of the joiner, recalling "Peter Quince at the Clavier" from the earliest display of Stevens' technique. Peter Quince, the joiner of Shakespeare's *A Midsummer Night's Dream*, is the symbol of the poet-craftsman. The French *clou* refers to him in the initial French imagination of the poet. At this late hour Peter is the sign of the poet-builder to come, the next in succession, not that of the aging poet-speaker. The new skill is to be that of a new craftsman. Stevens' poetry invites comprehensive analyses of this French usage in diction. But the end of this future study is already apparent when one recognizes the French word as metaphor for the central act of imagination.

It should be noted in passing that modern French (with very few exceptions) serves in this metaphor. Conversely, in his use of English Stevens is inclined at those points requiring a description of the center to compel obsolete forms to conform to his purpose, or to dare a newness of his own in derivatives, as though an original freshness lay beneath the surface of the word. Hence, in the early poem "Banal Sojourn" (*Harmonium*), human temporality represented by *sojourn* is modified by the poet's own willful act. The word is not used in the sense of *commonplace*; it is made of *bane*, occurring midway in the poem. The meaning of *banal* is that of *ruinous*. Death lies beyond the green of summer and all seasonal progressions. Overhead there is a "bliss of stars, that princox of evening heaven" (*CP*, 63). It is very nearly safe to say that *princox* has been obsolete since its Elizabethan usage, and even that was infrequent. It denotes "a precocious one" or "an upstart boy." The blazing star of the summer evening is *princox* to this human eye, looking upon a transient seasonal green, seeing an earth-bound human destiny as a poet feels his urge toward the impossible, the temporal endurance of a star. The precocious star mocks, as an upstart. "One feels a malady." The feeling projected here is one of purity. It is of archaic central man living in the poet. The original poetic act in the use of *banal* and the consciously sought archaism of *princox* together reveal the poet's objective, one of the oldest in the history of poetry: to speak of human bondage to time.[22] The poem by Stevens seeks the center and finds it as surely as does Andrew Marvell's "To His Coy Mistress." But the speech, I submit, is wholly his own, traditionless, like nothing before seen. These archaisms of Stevens', then, are not mere affectations. They are valid and necessary poetic objectives, just as the choice of French bespeaks the struggle toward the center, major man in the singularity of the poet intent upon a new speech.

Thus the identification that Stevens chose to establish for his acts of imagination must, in its primary character, be traced through his reading in French. Again I intend only to suggest possibilities; and again adjacencies of poetic structures, as Stevens saw these early in his career, must be primarily regarded. At some point in the late twenties Stevens wrote to René Taupin, who then was preparing his study of French influences on American poetry, in answer to questions concerning his taste for French authors: "The lightness, the grace, the sound and the color of French have had an undeniable and precious influence on me."[23] One might suppose that this admission disagrees with Stevens' frequent refusal to confess to influences. I do not think it does, since he is speaking here only of qualities of the language which appealed to his imagination. Taupin concludes his brief discussion of Stevens: "His tradition is French."[24] I must resist this judgment. Stevens has no tradition, in the critical sense proposed by Taupin. His reading in French was very wide, stretching from La Rochefoucauld and Buffon to Malraux, Claudel, and Bernanos late in his life.[25] It appears to have been a constant activity, as though proximity to the best of French *style* (in the renowned sense of Buffon) might possess an inestimable suggestiveness for

[22] An interesting comparison may be made between Stevens' treatment of this theme and that of Wordsworth in the sonnet "I watch and long have watched with calm regret / Yon slowly sinking star. . . ." Wordsworth's traditionalism in form, the development of the theme, and the diction should be noted.

[23] See Taupin's *L'Influence du Symbolisme Français sur la Poésie Américaine* (Paris, 1929), p. 276, n. 2. Here and elsewhere throughout this study I have chosen to offer English versions of French texts quoted. I have prepared all translations.

[24] *Ibid.*, p. 277.

[25] The published letters of Stevens, especially those written to his Paris book dealer and agent, Miss Paule Vidal, provide a spectrum of his interests in French literature. Orders placed with Miss Vidal range through poets, art historians, essayists, and philosophers. A second source of information exists in the records of the library of Trinity College, Hartford, Connecticut, where an exhibition of certain French books of Stevens' was arranged, by permission of his daughter, in May, 1963. Maeterlinck, Apollinaire, Stuart Merrill, Henri de Régnier, Huysmans, and Verlaine appear in the list of the exhibition.

his poetry. Warren Ramsey, in one of the most perceptive studies yet written on Stevens and France, recognizes this suggestiveness. "The most obvious common ground between Stevens and French poets . . . is not with any particular one of them." He continues: ". . . The compounding of so much French with more muscular native vocables contributes largely to making his diction the wonderfully fresh thing it is."[26] One notes with interest that the objectives of Stevens are opposite to those of Eliot. As Malcolm Cowley has observed, Eliot's pursuit of objectives one at a time in the French canon was rigorous and methodical. Thus "The Love Song of J. Alfred Prufrock" is "the great example of the Laforguean poem in English"; the scene of Prufrock on the beach, presumably Laforguean, is "one of the great moments in twentieth-century English poetry . . . not equaled by anything in *The Waste Land.*" From Laforgue, Eliot "went on" to Tristan Corbière.[27] The method of Eliot was scholarly. His interest lay in tempering his craft with a discipline of study in foreign models. The breadth of Stevens' interest is not demonstrated in particulars. Direct influence from a carefully studied model was not his experience. His objective was a deep immersion in French feeling. It was a matter of admixture, as in the instance of French loanwords in English. What he sought most rigorously, as the following examples will seek to show, was the central poem, the French experience of *naked* man, who must build his own reality.

Stevens was fully acquainted with the French debate in the academies on the question of pure poetry. The doctrine of Henri Brémond in the late twenties had challenged every modern theorist. "There are poets who know how to make verse because they are poets; and there are poets who are poets because they know how to make verse."[28] *La poésie pure*, since it cannot be reduced to words, is that which lies back of the poem. It is a search for God impelled by religious emotion.[29] Lamartine and Hugo belong to the first class of poets; Racine and Valéry to the second.[30] But Stevens does not agree with these judgments of Brémond's. The innateness of a reality beyond the poem is rejected. In a preface to a public reading of his

[26] "Wallace Stevens and Some French Poets," *The Trinity Review*, VIII, No. 3 (May, 1954), 36–37. Mr. Ramsey demonstrates in Stevens' early poetry the interesting appearances of Mallarmé, Verlaine, Laforgue, Toulet, Baudelaire, in that order.

[27] "Laforgue in America," *The Sewanee Review*, LXXI, No. 1 (Winter, 1963), 72–73.

[28] Henri Brémond, *La Poésie Pure, avec Un Debat sur la Poésie par Robert de Souza* (Paris, 1926), p. 69.

[29] *Ibid.*, p. 71.

[30] *Ibid.*, p. 69.

poetry Stevens wrote: "In spite of M. Brémond, pure poetry is a term that has grown to be descriptive of poetry in which not the true subject but the poetry of the subject is paramount" (*OP*, 222).[31] This judgment is faithful to Stevens' contentions elsewhere: pure poetry can be only that purity of the self encountering the subject; it will not exist for the sake of the subject, a reality outside the "pure" poem. Hence one concludes that Stevens sought in his French reading the second group rejected by Brémond: poets who are poets because they know how to make verse. Process is all.

Henry James, considering *Les Fleurs du Mal*, wrote of Baudelaire, "an altogether inferior genius to Gautier" in his estimation: ". . . One is constantly tempted to suppose he cares more for his process . . . than for the things themselves. . . ."[32] James makes the exact distinction for Stevens. It is, indeed, process in Baudelaire. In the opinion of Mr. Benamou the beautiful analysis that Stevens made of the opening lines of the "La Vie Antérieure" is perhaps the most rewarding published document of his way of reading French poetry."[33] It would seem unquestionably to be so. This tribute to Baudelaire appears in the essay "Two or Three Ideas" (*OP*, 203–4).[34] Stevens begins with the opening line: "*J'ai longtemps habité sous de vastes portiques*" or "A long time I lived beneath tremendous porches." He continues in his translation: "Which the salt-sea suns tinged with a thousand fires / And which great columns, up-

31 The piece is entitled "The Irrational Element in Poetry." Samuel F. Morse fixes the date at about 1937 (*OP*, 301).

32 *French Poets and Novelists,* ed. Leon Edel (New York, 1964), p. 59, first published in England in 1878.

33 "The Symbolist Imagination," in *The Act of the Mind: Essays on the Poetry of Wallace Stevens,* p. 96.

34 "Two or Three Ideas" was read before the New England section of the College English Association and was first published in the *Chapbook* of the Association in October, 1951. (See Morse, *OP*, xxxvi and 301.) It is difficult to reconcile the devoted attention to Baudelaire in the essay with the disclosures made by Stevens to his friend in Ireland, Thomas McGreevy, with respect to the Baudelaire of the same poem. He wrote to McGreevy from Hartford in March, 1949, that he found Baudelaire "beginning to date." The reflection continues with observations on "the demand for reality in poetry." Stevens was at the time in search of "a poetry that is not poetical," "a poetry divested of poetry." "The bare idea makes everything else seem false and verbose and even ugly. It is from that point of view that J'ai habité longtemps etc. becomes repulsive" (*Letters*, p. 631). I have called attention in the Introduction to inconsistencies and paradoxes in the correspondence. The letter seems to me a direct refutation of the argument of the lecture-essay yet to follow. One or the other must be chosen here. I choose the public statement, noting as I do that for the moment of his writing to McGreevy, Stevens was for some immediate reason weary of "poetical" poetry, which in his view was insufficiently based in reality. But then the lesson of Baudelaire, which is my subject here, came, of course, much earlier in his life. This lesson, as the comment of the essay shows, was of poetry as a habitation. This endured.

right and majestic, / At evening, made resemble basalt grottoes."
"The poem," he says, "concerns the life among the images, sounds
and colors of those calm, sensual presences." He concludes in prospect of this architecture: "We stand looking at a remembered habitation. All old dwelling-places are subject to these transmogrifica-
tions and the experience of all of us includes a succession of old
dwelling-places: abodes of the imagination, ancestral or memories
of places that never existed." The kinship of Stevens with this vision
of Baudelaire strikes us with a stunning force. For all that has been
said of architecture and process in Stevens seems to be supported
here, as we follow his way into a French master. Poetry is a habitation. It is a structure made by a ceaselessly moving principle, life
among the images, sounds, and colors that only the self knows. Yet
this structure, as real as it is in the shape given it by words, is a
habitation only of transience. The poet's faith that this colonnade by
the sea could be a habitation of endurance is *innocence* as Stevens
regards it in "The Auroras of Autumn": ". . . we partake thereof, /
Lie down like children in this holiness . . ." (*CP*, 418).

The lesson of Baudelaire for Stevens seems immeasurable in
consequence. Some paraphrases of Dore Ashton, who considers the
significance of Baudelaire for modern painting, are useful here. They
are equally appropriate for Stevens. "The connoisseur [the artist]
. . . must never become entangled in a system. It is a kind of damna-
tion that leads only to painful recantations. The 'infinite spiral of
life' will always defeat the inventor of a system. . . . [H]e must cast
out the notion of progress, 'avoid it like the very devil.' Proofs are
abundant in the history of art that 'every efflorescence is spontaneous, individual' at its core."[35] What we have been saying of Stevens'
theory of the center is exactly equal to this spontaneity of efflorescence at the core. As Baudelaire wrote in the treatise "L'art roman-
tique," "The entire visible universe is only a storehouse of images
and of signs to which the imagination will assign a place and a relative value. . . . All the faculties of the human spirit must be sub-
ordinated to the imagination. . . ."[36] The center is the domain of
imagination. Baudelaire shapes it into a woman's form. She is the
Queen of the Faculties;[37] and one reflects on the evocations of this
majesty, over and over named a Queen, in the poetry of Stevens. She

[35] *The Unknown Shore: A View of Contemporary Art* (Boston, 1962), p. viii.
[36] *Oeuvres Complètes* (Paris, Calmann Lévy, n.d.), III, 10.
[37] Charles Baudelaire, *The Mirror of Art*, trans. and ed. Jonathan Mayne (New
York, 1955), p. 232.

exerts absolute sovereignty. Baudelaire extends his metaphor: ". . . Those men who are not quickened thereby are easily recognizable by some strange curse which withers their productions like the fig-tree in the Gospel."[38] The metaphor belongs to the master image of Baudelaire's theory: Art is the mirror, the glass in which we see reflected the freshness of the artist in the "infinite spiral," unencumbered by systems. It captures the spontaneity at the core. One finds in Stevens' "Notes Toward a Supreme Fiction" a lyric transcription of this aesthetic. "The freshness of transformation is / The freshness of a world. It is our own, / It is ourselves, the freshness of ourselves, / And that necessity and that presentation / Are rubbings of a glass in which we peer" (Pt. II, Sec. 10, *CP*, 397–98). The passage appears to be a summation of Baudelaire.

Studies of the relationship of Stevens to Mallarmé and Laforgue have already demonstrated important instances of similarity.[39] A comparative estimate by the late Hi Simons identifies some fourteen reflections of Mallarmé in the early poetry. Half of these suggest strong correspondences in imagery; the others propose affinities in theories of diction. Evidently Stevens had in mind Mallarmé's "Don du poème" as he fashioned the imagery of death in "The Emperor of Ice Cream."[40] But if this is a clear derivation, it is an example only of retention from the poet's reading. It can scarcely be more important than the fact that Stevens became interested in Mallarmé in about 1916, during the time of his closest association with Walter Arensberg in New York.[41] Very probably Mallarmé's theory of the "poetical radiation" of words,[42] considered apart from their denotative and connotative functions, words free-standing and distinguished by a singular and unrelated power, entered Stevens' regard for the *gaudiness* of poetry. But Mallarmé's indifference to the reality of natural phenomena (e.g., in the renowned "L'Après-midi d'un faune") and his persistent symbol of *azur*—ultimate reality—have no significance in the work of Stevens. *Azur* cannot be equated with

---

[38] *Ibid.*

[39] See Hi Simons, "Wallace Stevens and Mallarmé," *Modern Philology*, XLIII (No. 4), 235–59; H. R. Hays, "Laforgue and Wallace Stevens," *The Romanic Review*, XXV (No. 3), 242–48; Michel Benamou, "Jules Laforgue and Wallace Stevens," *The Romanic Review*, L (No. 2), 107–17.

[40] Simons, p. 238. In a letter of 1949 to Bernard Heringman Stevens disclaimed much of the influence of Mallarmé which Simons had sought to define; see *Letters*, pp. 635–36.

[41] Arensberg published in that year a translation of "L'Après-midi d'un faune" in his volume of verse *Idols* (Houghton, Mifflin); see Simons, p. 257.

[42] See Georges Lemaître, *From Cubism to Surrealism in French Literature* (Cambridge, Mass., 1941), p. 86.

blue, Stevens' sign of the imagination-in-process. It represents "a higher truth."[43] One encounters here the same disqualifying ontology that, for Stevens, renders unacceptable much of English romantic poetry.

Laforgue in prospect suggests other and more striking associations with French expression. One critic has found in Laforgue a model for Stevens of Ezra Pound's *logopoeia*, "the dance of the intellect among words."[44] The experimental early poems, as represented in the dance movements of "The Plot Against the Giant" or the acrobatic tumblings of the first and the last sequences of "The Comedian as the Letter C" (*CP*, 6, 7, 27, 46), emphasize this creation within the movement of speech alone. This mode belongs to Stevens' masquelike interludes, when the poetry takes on the costume and the motion of the *commedia dell'arte*. The "Pierrot" poems of Laforgue (in *L'imitation de Notre Dame la lune*) seem to have been fully suggestive to Stevens. A theatrical structure is inherent in these French antecedents. I am speaking of Laforgue's controlled design in his intermittent return to the Pierrot theme. But this *logopoeia* seems to me less important than a meeting of *logos* and *nous*. Here the poetry appears as the act of speech and the governing mind, rather than of speech and the improvisations of an "intellectual" dance.

For Stevens the lesson of Laforgue has the more significant consequence of imaginative play upon the idea made of the object from an implacable reality. The "Dimanche" poems of Laforgue's *Des Fleurs de Bonne Volonté*—a title exactly compelling for Stevens, flowers, flourishings from a will (imposed upon the commonplace)— seem to me to be of real consequence in a later American expression. "Dimanche" is the symbol of the banal, the quotidian. The eleventh poem of the *Fleurs* opens with "O forbidden Sundays of the infinite . . ." and continues, "Sunday citizens, entirely quotidian. . . ."[45] Sunday becomes the symbol of the banality of bourgeois commonplaceness, the quotidian of the "old cancan" (the *only* bourgeois dance), of sordidness, of rain, of "damp tobacco" in an endless succession.[46] Sunday-made-idea is rendered again and again by the imagination. Each time it reappears, it is cast in a different mode. The subject remains the same. This method of imaginative play upon mediocrity, the quality of the quotidian—in other words, the flat and

[43] See Christopher Gray, *Cubist Aesthetic Theories* (Baltimore, 1953), pp. 13–14.
[44] Hays, "Laforgue and Wallace Stevens," pp. 246–47.
[45] Jules Laforgue, *Oeuvres Complètes* (Paris, 1922), II, 28.
[46] *Ibid.*, p. 28 and p. 41 (in poem 18 of the series, again using "dimanches" as a title).

senseless endurance of a commonplace reality untransformed by imagination—is the method of Stevens. The symbol of Sunday perseveres in him: it is first exploited in "Ploughing on Sunday"; it is asserted again in "Sunday Morning"; it is recast in the fourth section of "Owl's Clover"; it reappears in a distant poem of the last meditations, "The Old Lutheran Bells at Home." It has its own architectural significance in the continuity of the poetry. When one adds to this evidence Stevens' speculation upon the quotidian in "The Comedian as the Letter C," this sapping power, this insidious weight that gives nothing in return save an "unkeyed" music (*CP*, 42–43), it seems clear that Laforgue had been regarded intently and closely remembered.

Yet, as Michel Benamou notes, Stevens loved the sun; Laforgue hated it.[47] It was "the artist in Laforgue, and not the Pierrot, who attracted Stevens most."[48] Pierrot, we add, may defy the quotidian; but to each poet his own way. Subsequent studies will no doubt reveal as many points of divergence between Stevens and Laforgue as similarities. The regularity of Sunday, a flat festival measuring out life as a Prufrock-life (after Eliot) is measured out in coffee spoons, is common to both. One stops there. Beyond this realm of the possible at war with the quotidian there is the artist at the center, naked man in Stevens' sense of the traditionless. Or, if one prefers, he is Baudelaire's spontaneous individual at the core. I shall not consider here Stevens' reading in Rimbaud and Apollinaire. As architects of the self in poetry, they offer impressive possibilities for study. Stevens read them, but I suspect that he did so very much later than he read Laforgue. In any case, both must certainly have appeared to him as spontaneous poets of the center, wholly independent of tradition. It is in this appearance and this testament that these poets must have been received through Stevens' earlier reading of Baudelaire and Laforgue. In French expression he had found what he was looking for: naked poets flourishing in the weather of an age, and no other.

Thus Stevens came to Valéry across a solid foreground. This third poet of adjacency seems to me the most important of Stevens' French experience. I have suggested as much in the foregoing discussion of Stevens and Valéry's *Eupalinos*. Marcel Raymond notes bluntly of Valéry's poetics: "To construct a poem is to construct

---

[47] "Jules Laforgue and Wallace Stevens," p. 111.
[48] *Ibid.*, p. 107.

oneself."[49] I shall not repeat Valéry's claim for poetry as an act of the architect. My earlier comment must suffice. The question of Valéry's adjacency *as a poet* now becomes the matter for regard. Two poems, *La Jeune Parque*[50] and "Ébauche d'un Serpent," should be considered as primary antecedents for Stevens. The first was published in Paris in 1917, the second in 1921. In the great monologue of the youngest of the Fates, Valéry establishes his symbol of the central self and the imagery of the serpent that embodies it. The young Fate is a mistress of human destiny. She is menaced by a serpent who comes to murder her.[51] It is the human *moi* that denies her authority, that self exalting the day, the light, senses, joy, love and spurning her whose rule is darkness and the threat of death. The sixth section of the poem requires quotation. The young Fate laments:

> *And I living, sternly*
> *Wait, secretly armed with my nothingness,*
> *But, as a cheek inflamed by love,*
> *And the nostril made one with the scent of the*
> *orange tree,*
> *I yield no more to the day than a strange gaze . . .*
> *Oh! how can this mysterious part grow in the*
> *strange night*
> *Of my separated heart,*
> *And from dark trials my art become deeper! . . .*
> *Far from my pure environs I am captive*
> *And, defeated by the evanescence of aromas,*
> *I feel my image tremble beneath the beams*
> *Of freaks of gold, its marble pervaded. . . .*

Her stern gaze, the threshold of infernal regions, is dissipated. Her reverie of doom is challenged "by the mirror of a winging bird, / That a hundred times under the sun plays with nothingness."[52] In the resolution of the poem it is the serpent-self that subsumes and transforms this Fate. The destiny of the human is the self. So in the later "Ébauche"—the sketch of the tempter of Eve, a serpent—a self

---

[49] *From Baudelaire to Surrealism*, p. 155.
[50] The poem was addressed to André Gide with this note: "For a great many years, I have neglected the art of verse: trying to commit myself to it again, I have made this exercise, which I dedicate to you." I use here the Pléiade edition of Valéry, ed. Jean Hytier (Paris, 1957), I.
[51] *Ibid.*, p. 97.
[52] *Ibid.*, pp. 100–1.

imposes the *moi* of Being, the same serpent *moi* that conquers the young Fate. It is the sun that prevents men's hearts "from knowing / That the universe is but a flaw / In the purity of Non-being."[53] For this was Eve tempted by the Tree: the temporality of the self is all, and in it wakes the certainty of earthly beauty, the day, the sun that beguiles, the immediacy of existence.

This triumph of the serpent over Fate, and the celebration of the Fortunate Fall, in the sense of Valéry, bear no relationship to traditional systems. They speak only of the majesty of the central self. So fully informed is Stevens' poetry with this concept of Being exerted in the prospect of Non-being, the nothingness masked by sun-radiance, that it seems pointless to illustrate. The images of Valéry made their enduring impression. The darkness of a Fate who would impose death upon life is countermanded by this winging bird "that a hundred times under the sun plays with nothingness." It is but a step to Stevens' metamorphic bird of the imagination, appearing again and again in the symbolism of the poetry. Under the sun it plays constantly with image-making in defiance of nothingness. It is the expressive agent of the serpent-self. Far down the long vista there stands the late poem "A Golden Woman in a Silver Mirror": ". . . In the woods, belle Belle alone / Rattles with fear in unre-flecting leaves. / Abba, dark death is the breaking of a glass" (*CP*, 460). The beautiful presence, the woman-genius of a poet, is now one with the serpent of the self. It is late. She knows fear. The leaves of the tree reflect no light. "*Abba*," the poet writes, using, presumably, the term for *father* in the rite of the Syrian and Coptic churches, death will break the mirror. The poet addresses himself as father of his images. Yet the images, he continues, "disembodied, are not broken. / They have, or they may have, their glittering crown, / Sound-soothing pearl and omni-diamond, / Of the most beautiful, the most beautiful maid / And mother . . ." (*CP*, 460–61). Even here, far from an early French vision, the poet remembers. For the diamond-image of the enduring crown recalls the Fate of *La Jeune Parque* on the threshold of her metamorphosis to the *human*: she reaches a "half immortal state," "dreaming that the future itself be-comes only a diamond closing the diadem,"[54] this jewel displacing the night of a mere endurance of destiny (a death, so to speak, in life).

[53] *Ibid.*, pp. 138–39.
[54] *Ibid.*, p. 101.

The image of the serpent-self is present at the opening of Stevens' second volume, *Ideas of Order*, as he takes leave of the South and youth. Now the self begins its metamorphoses. "The snake has left its skin upon the floor" ("Farewell to Florida," *CP*, 117). It is present again, far distant, at the opening of "The Auroras of Autumn": "This is where the serpent lives, the bodiless" (*CP*, 411). At the end, the self loses shape. In mid-course, Stevens reflected on the serpent in "Owl's Clover." Will the statue (art) rise next in Africa? he asks. But there was never a heaven in Africa, a heaven of life in life. Africa is death-ridden. Its life is death in life. It is the "black sublime." "Death, only, sits upon the serpent throne" (*OP*, 54–55). Lest it be supposed that Stevens anywhere displays the marks of primitivism, this judgment is absolute negation. The concept of the self belongs to civilized man alone.

A reference to another French poet among the aphoristic stanzas of "Like Decorations in a Nigger Cemetery" is not, I think, of major significance. "Serve the rouged fruits in early snow. / They resemble a page of Toulet / Read in the ruins of a new society, / Furtively, by candle and out of need" (*CP*, 153). This is not the place for comment on the ingenuity of this title, save to say that the several short sections are in metaphoric relationship to brilliant decorations in a black ("nigger," and thereby American) cemetery: therefore, the *gaudiness* of poetry, in a time of national disaster. The poem comes from the deepest point of the Depression. Perhaps Stevens had in mind Paul-Jean Toulet at work on his *Contrerimes* during the horrors of Verdun and the anguish of France.[55] The snow has fallen. It is not a time for fruits. Yet poetry will be read in the ruins of a new society; and the act of writing it is then a defiance of snow. Toulet belongs to the wider reading of Stevens. I do not find that the poetry is touched in any way by Toulet's technical brilliance in the *contrerime* as a form. Some of his landscapes may have attracted Stevens. But I prefer to think of a reading of Toulet as it signifies the artist's will to endure: the persistence of an American poet in a time of despair.

For future studies of Stevens and France there will be need of caution. Mr. Benamou has proposed that "it is not to Baudelaire, Mallarmé, or even Valéry that Stevens should be compared, but rather to Saint-John Perse, the only modern French poet to have rehabili-

---

[55] See Pierre O. Walzer, *P.-J. Toulet, Poètes d'Aujourd'hui*, No. 42 (Paris, n.d.), p. 10.

tated the myth of the fertile woman."[56] I find this judgment remarkably exclusive. It may be that Perse's woman-genius of poetry is considerably more fertile and earthy than the wraith-figure gracing the visions of other poets of modern France. But there is no reason to suppose that Stevens needed a French model in order to make his own woman fully vigorous. The *Élogues* of Perse appeared in 1911, the *Anabase* in 1924. The remaining poetry, published after the beginning of Perse's exile in the United States,[57] came too late to be of significant bearing on the work of Stevens. But even those volumes available for early reading seem inappropriate to Stevens' interests. Both establish settings intent upon evocations of the total civilized past, not the present. Architectural images of this past do, indeed, occur. But it is difficult to see how the conclusion of the *Anabase* could have recommended to Stevens any of the "excavations" of Perse. "Ploughland of dream! *Who talks of building?*—I have seen the earth parcelled out in vast spaces and my thought is not heedless of the navigator."[58] This ploughing will not accord with the act of Stevens. Nor will a return to a past architecture accord with Stevens' insistence upon the poet's need of his present, his own structure established in his own weather.

A concluding note remains. Stevens wrote to his Paris bookseller in 1953, with reference to his acquisition of paintings: "I hate Orientalism."[59] He refers here to the oriental pose in Western painting. But this late admission invites caution as one examines the poetry. It was inevitable, of course, that Stevens as a beginning poet in the second decade of the twentieth century would be aware of orientalism in the scene. He was looking upon the aegis of imagism; and he must have recognized the exotic strain in Amy Lowell and John Gould Fletcher, among others. Thus his early work reflects a temporary interest in oriental sources. Beginning with the poems from "Lettres d'un Soldat,"[60] published by Harriet Monroe

---

[56] "Beyond emerald or amethyst," *Dartmouth College Library Bulletin* (December, 1961), IV (n.s.), No. 3, p. 66.
[57] Following the collapse of the Vichy Government, Perse (Leger) published the following: *Exil* (1942), *Vents* (1947), *Amers* (1953).
[58] *Anabasis*, trans. T. S. Eliot (New York, 1938), p. 71.
[59] *Letters*, p. 796. The letter to Miss Paule Vidal is dated at Hartford, August 19, 1953. Stevens had been temporarily interested in acquiring a painting by Bezombes, a Parisian artist.
[60] The epigram, in French (*OP*, 10), is derived from a preface by André Chevrillon (1864–1957), French orientalist, written for Eugène Emmanuel Lemercier's *Lettres d'un soldat (août 1914–avril 1915)* (Paris, 1916). (The work was published in an English translation by a Chicago press in 1917.) See *Letters*, p. 202.

in *Poetry* (1918), Stevens' "oriental" canon includes "Thirteen Ways of Looking at a Blackbird," "Six Significant Landscapes," and the striking third stanza of "Le Monocle de Mon Oncle" (*CP*, 14). All these examples fall within the earliest chronology, as presented in *Harmonium*. Undeniably, the method of "Thirteen Ways" and the "Landscapes" reflects the Japanese *haiku*.[61] But the imagery of Chinese and Japanese reference in "Le Monocle" poses a different matter. The beards of the Chinese poet-sages and the braids of Uta-maro's beauties belong, in this symbolism of hair, to a central metaphor of Stevens': the style of the imaginative act in art. A careful reading of the stanza in question clearly indicates that the poet does not intend "to play the flat historic scale." His music must be his own. It would be a pleasant task to demonstrate that Stevens was attracted to the four-square precision of the classic Chinese mind, expressed in the formal balance of the Temple of Heaven in Peking, or to the strict order of Japanese Buddhist art, as in the Noh, with its particular appeal to Yeats and Pound. But, on the basis of present evidence, such proposals as these seem hazardous. Of the play that Stevens suppressed, "Three Travelers Watch a Sunrise" (*OP*, 127–43), with its Chinese characters, this may be said: These Chinese do not invoke the Orient; they represent a principle that was to be demonstrated throughout the poetry—the multiplicity of human vision governed by independent acts of the imagination. "Sunrise is

---

[61] Robert Buttel in his skillful recent study, *Wallace Stevens: The Making of Harmonium* (Princeton, 1967) presents, very probably, all that can be known of Stevens' early reflection of American orientalism. In a chapter bearing the exact title "Abodes of the Imagination" (approximate, as I regard it, to my concept of adjacent structures) he points to Stevens' association, in his Harvard days, with Arthur Davison Ficke and Witter Bynner, fellow students who were experimenting with poetic themes inspired by oriental art (pp. 64–65). Mr. Buttel, whose study traces important relationships between Stevens' efforts in poetry between 1900 and 1915 and the mature art of *Harmonium*, demonstrates the oriental reference of the period primarily in terms of color. (See, in particular, pp. 64–74). One may grant this early fascination of Stevens' most easily and still return to his later disavowal of orientalism. The fact is that he discarded the "Oriental pose" as unsuitable for the full aesthetic of *Harmonium*. Thereafter the early "abode" has little significance. Stevens' initial interest in Japanese prints and *haiku* is discussed by Mr. Buttel as a mark of his preference for "fresh, unsentimental, non-rococo values" (p. 67, n. 12). We conclude that his youthful brush with orientalism had its own importance in the emerging character of his taste.

My estimate of Stevens' later attention to the Orient has already been suggested in the Introduction. The *Letters* reveal his occasional delight in "imagined lands," for example, that delight to be found in his correspondence with Harriet Monroe about Peking, or with Leonard C. van Geyzel in Ceylon, or, late in his life, with his young Korean friend Peter H. Lee. Whether he would have chosen to travel in the Orient, had he been able to do so, is another matter. I take the view that Stevens as an American poet chose to keep strictly to his American locus, a choice that was essential to his discipline as an artist.

multiplied. . . . By the eyes that open on it . . ." (*OP,* 143). Stevens, in my opinion, was temperamentally opposed to all forms of exoticism in poetry. He held professional orientalism suspect, quite as he spurned allegiance to any traditional mode of regarding the world. Yet I do not wish to deny the interesting presence of oriental reference traced by Henry W. Wells in a distinguished recent study,[62] or the possible appearance of Chinese landscape painting as suggested by Albert W. Levi.[63] A full record of the poet's reading may provide wider possibilities of judgment in this area.

Finally, it must be of commanding significance that the house of the poet remained an English-French structure. I opened this chapter with the image of a "French" architecture as one discovers it in "Montrachet-le-Jardin." But an earlier poem, "Gallant Chateau" (*Ideas of Order*), tells us much of the poet's resolve. There is a bed in the "chateau." One day, as we know from our reading of the Grand Poem, it will be the final bed, a bed either for Old John Zeller in his restless tossings, or for Santayana in repose, or for Wallace Stevens. As yet, this bed of the poet is "empty." The wind of change does not blow; the curtains at the windows of the room are "stiff and prim and still." Here in this chateau are the poet's "few words tuned / And tuned and tuned and tuned" (*CP,* 161). He has studied adjacent structures; he has chosen his design. The *central* man in him will make a choice of continuing *gallantry.* He will seek the harmony of final tunings. The *things,* to recall the choice of the Canon Aspirin, are to be his alone.

Lest Stevens' faithfulness to *major man* appear to propose an abstraction, it should be clearly understood that this enduring presence in an ever-new *nakedness* is the certain human continuum. The eternal being at the core is none other than the freedom of each man to imagine of the world what he will. *Major man* is not the presence of an age, abstracted, or of a fate, a morality, a belief, or whatever one prefers to name, making all men one. He is the one human treasure ("ascetic trove," *CP,* 263). For a poet, poetry expresses him anew.

[62] *Introduction to Wallace Stevens* (Bloomington, Ind., 1964).
[63] "A Note on Wallace Stevens and the Poem of Perspective," *Perspective,* VII, No. 3 (Autumn, 1954), 137–46.

Stevens in the American Grain

3

IN SEARCH OF THE AMERICAN PAST, WILLIAM CARLOS
Williams determined to reclaim Poe from a misdirected reputation.
He was not, he wrote, "a find for French eyes." "It is the New
World, or to leave that for the better term, it is a *new locality* that
is in Poe assertive; it is America, the first great burst through to
expression of a re-awakened genius of *place*."[1] Stevens would not,
I think, have agreed. His work does not show any antecedence
whatsoever in Poe. One need not search for reasons beyond
his disinclination toward an aesthetic such as Poe advanced: poetry,
for instance, as "the rhythmical creation of beauty." I must refer
again to Stevens' rigid qualification, already cited: "Art involves
vastly more than the sense of beauty" (*OP*, 159); or to a second
principle, equally unyielding, "Poetry and materia poetica are interchangeable terms" (*OP*, 159). Poe accords with neither. But to this
contention of Dr. Williams' for an American genius of *place* Stevens
would have fully assented. The newness of the American locus, or
what should be regarded as new and unique, lay at the center of his

[1] *In the American Grain* (New York, 1956), p. 216, in the reprint series of New
Directions, No. 53. The work was first published in 1925.

poetic consciousness. His way with French literature was his own. Yet this chosen way would never have been followed without his strict adherence to his own principle: for *materia poetica*, one's own soil and no other. Stevens was initially disposed toward a French tutelage for his imagination. But it was tutelage, and nothing else. Except for an early venture to the Canadian Rockies, two brief acquaintances with Cuba, and a trip through the Canal to Tijuana and the California coast, his traveling was largely confined to the southern and the eastern United States;[2] and as the years passed there was less even of that. Let it be said for him that an American intelligence is inappropriate to French place, or any other foreign place, if one is speaking of a life in an American art. His principle has nothing to do with chauvinism. A man of Stevens' persuasion will hold to his own native reality, American or what not.

I turn, then, to Stevens' comprehension of the American grain with a limited inquiry into his sense of an American poetic genius of place. The question addressed to this sense must have to do with elements of American poetic experience as these are shared by Stevens. Affinities pertain; imitation and restatement do not. The American grain imposes problems of the self in an exclusive relation to native experience. The grain that Dr. Williams thought of is the intricacy of markings in the American hand, "whorls of meaning." The metaphor is exactly suited to his practice as a poet: unique tracings of life lines, heart lines, scorings, wrinkles. The grain for Stevens is not of this hand. It is *nakedness* in the sense of that French expression which has just been considered. With a strong fondness for Pennsylvania Dutch aphorism and riddle, Stevens published in *Ideas of Order* two lines entitled "Nudity at The Capital": "But nakedness, woolen massa, concerns an innermost atom. / If that remains concealed, what does the bottom matter?" (*CP*, 145). The capital is the self. The figure addressed is uniquely American. As a symbol, it is related to the title, "Like Decorations in

2 The evidence of the published correspondence with respect to Stevens' traveling is presumably final. The journey to British Columbia was made in August, 1903, in the company of W. G. Peckham, a New York attorney, in whose law office Stevens was employed as a clerk. See Holly Stevens' note, and Stevens' entries in his journal, in *Letters*, pp. 57, 64–65. See also Stevens' letter to José Rodríguez Feo from Hartford, January 26, 1945, on his traveling in Cuba, and another to Bernard Heringman from Hartford, September 1, 1953, in a summary statement on his foreign experience, in *Letters*, pp. 483–84, 798. The correspondence presents an ample record of Stevens' travel through the southern and the middlewestern states on business trips shortly after his marriage, and of his intimate knowledge of Florida through frequent vacation trips, especially those to Key West. His traveling in New England is less fully recorded.

a Nigger Cemetery": the Negro is a native genius of American place. Nakedness is the "innermost" of the American self. If this naked-ness is concealed, the *bottom* is insignificant. Three lines from a later poem, "Yellow Afternoon" (*CP*, 236), explicate this concluding image in a typical American testament of Stevens': "It was in the earth only / That he was at the bottom of things / And of himself." These texts in juxtaposition describe the American principle: the poet seeks "the bottom" of American things unadorned by tradition; his nakedness is the central self; American earth is his home. This was the place of central man for Stevens, as it was for certain other American artists. It may be noted that it is this requirement of an American quintessence which eludes many European critics of our poetry. An intimacy with American place, as of Hart Crane at Brook-lyn Bridge, or of Stevens at Key West or Pemaquid, is frequently prerequisite to understanding.

The struggle of the American poet *from the bottom* has been described in Theodore Roethke's metaphor of a native process; and thereby the American intent of Stevens is considerably illuminated. In an introduction to a group of his poems chosen for an anthol-ogy, Roethke spoke of an American necessity. "To begin from the depths and come out—that is difficult; for few know where the depths are or can recognize them; or, if they do, are afraid. Some of these pieces . . . begin in the mire; as if man is no more than a shape writhing from the old rock. This may be due, in part, to the Michigan from which I come. Sometimes one gets the feeling that not even the animals have been there before; but the marsh, the mire, the Void, is always there, immediate and terrifying. It is a splendid place for schooling the spirit. It is America."[3] Roethke's poem, "A Rouse for Stevens" (1955) has been read exclusively as a tribute to the "Imagination's Prince."[4] But it may be very much more, in a second sense: Stevens as a discoverer of nakedness at the "innermost atom." The greenhouse poems of Roethke, if one con-sidered no others, bear full witness to the struggle. The mire from which the self springs is there. It is immediate, and American. It is like the "dirt" of the native element that Stevens thinks of in "The Comedian as the Letter C": the American Crispin, the would-be maker of "the fables that he scrawled / With his own quill,

[3] *On the Poet and His Craft*, ed. Ralph J. Mills, Jr. (Seattle, 1965), p. 40.
[4] The poem appeared in *7 Arts*, No. 3 (The Falcon's Wing Press, Indian Hills, Colo., 1955), p. 117. The last line, particularly, "Brother, he's our father!" is to be noted.

in its indigenous dew, / Of an aesthetic tough, diverse, untamed, / Incredible to prudes, the mint of dirt, / Green barbarism turning paradigm" (*CP*, 31). Stevens' reference is to the paradigm of the American self. Certainly Roethke was an inheritor of the master design. What else than an austere American nakedness orders his vision of Michigan greenhouses in a storm, the old rose-house of his childhood riding out the wind and rain, "Carrying her full cargo of roses"?[5] This poetry is written in indigenous dew. Its ferocity and tenderness are characteristic of an American poet and no other. Its flowering is that of the American self, in "a splendid place for schooling the spirit."

If my objectives were intended to demonstrate an American continuity of poetry, there would be little reason to pursue this discussion. Roy Harvey Pearce's massive study of this continuity is definitive, and it offers a summary that is well-nigh irrefutable. Mr. Pearce concludes with the fact of an "insistent opposition" in the total American poetic record: "the egocentric as against the theocentric, man without history as against history without man, the antinomian as against the orthodox, personality as against culture, the Adamic as against the mythic." A brief reduction follows. "These are the theoretical limits. In practice the opposition is perhaps a simpler affair: man against himself."[6] Undeniably, this opposition belongs to the history of American culture. It represents again and again defiance of tradition, and a mandate for singularity. I wish to examine the province of Wallace Stevens, as though, for the time being, this were the total of the possible in a native American experience. To regard the world with Adamic vision is for Stevens simply to *shape* the world as one wills. When one has considered the vision of recent French poetry studied by Stevens, it appears that an Adamic stance abroad is no less singular than the American. Certainly French egocentrism is quite as unique as the exalted self in American poetry. It is therefore clear that the American distinction is precocious rather than unequaled. For it happened that American transcendentalism became the first expression in Western civilization of what we wish to call a modernism of the self. I am speaking of the American insistence upon *nakedness*, in the sense of Stevens, and not of degrees of literary excellence. Man, to use Mr. Pearce's phrase, was against himself, or man the artist was against

---

[5] "Big Wind" (*The Lost Son and Other Poems*, 1948) in *Words for the Wind* (London, 1957), pp. 44–45.
[6] *The Continuity of American Poetry* (Princeton, 1961), p. 423.

man in the abstract, in this country before man was so disposed in England and in Europe. Thus I take the American paradigm of a "green barbarism" as an inheritance of Stevens which must be recognized.

My purpose is not to review American poetry of the twentieth century which approximates Stevens—that of Roethke or any other—but rather to call attention to major evidence from certain of his predecessors in whom the paradigm may be studied. There can be no doubt of an American nakedness in the poetry of Hart Crane, or in that of Frost or Jarrell or Lowell. In this naming rests the bedrock conviction of Stevens: ". . . his soil is man's intelligence" ("The Comedian as the Letter C," *CP*, 36). It seems now quite certain that the American answer to the requirements of this intelligence is the condition of the fact: in variety, integrity, lyric range, and technique American poetry in the second quarter of the twentieth century is unequaled by any other like expression of the modern English-speaking world. This abundance came of an American liberation of poetry to a native nakedness deliberately sought by the first draftsmen of the paradigm. The precocious modernism of American poetry is to be identified in them. Stevens, echoing Baudelaire[7] in the French address of the following, seems to dismiss the past with an Emersonian sweep: "And you, my semblables, in gaffer-green, / Know that the past is not part of the present" ("Dutch Graves in Bucks County," *CP*, 291). Each generation brings with it its own nakedness. It is clear again that the Emersonian *constant present* is within the American paradigm as Stevens writes of the self in a late essay. "There was always in every man the increasingly human self, which instead of remaining the observer, the non-participant, the delinquent, became constantly more and more all there was or so it seemed; and whether it was so or merely seemed so still left it for him to resolve life and the world in his own terms" ("Two or Three Ideas," *OP*, 207).

The American opportunity, stripped to its bareness, was none other than a naked self confronted with a "green barbarism" of possibilities. This is the major idea of "The Comedian as the Letter C," as though the self, coming to these shores, stood free of its European garments, and, like John and William Bartram in the savannahs and swamps of Florida and Georgia, marveled at so much

---

[7] Preface to *Fleurs du Mal*; see Eliot's use of the same in *The Waste Land*, Pt. I, l. 76. Eliot employs this image of human "likenesses" in an abstraction of continuity; Stevens employs it in the sense only of "likenesses" in human form.

green and untried newness. The opportunity of this nakedness is dominant in one of Stevens' last long poems: ". . . The self as sibyl, whose diamond, . . . whose jewel found / At the exactest central of the earth / Is need." The sibyl's shape is "A child asleep in its own life" ("The Sail of Ulysses," *OP*, 104).[8] This child is the everlasting present: its life is its own in nakedness. The sibyl of the self is the American opportunity. In this land there should have been the self alone, "the chrysalis of all men" ("An Ordinary Evening in New Haven," *CP*, 468).

But the American opportunity was never fully realized. "O buckskin, O crosser of snowy divides, / For whom men were to be ends in themselves. . . . For you, / Day came upon the spirit as life comes / And deep winds flooded you; for these, day comes, / A penny sun in a tinsel sky. . . ." So Stevens reflects in "Owl's Clover" (*OP*, 61). The contrast here between the image of original vastness and the insignificant sun of an urban America is characteristic of Stevens in every year of his writing. To recall the image of adjacent structures discussed in the last chapter, the evidence of heroic imaginings, even those structures of heroic individuality known in our European origins, is a lost proof of the possible. "The scholar's outline that you had, the print / Of London, the paper of Paris magnified / By poets, the Italian lives preserved / For poverty are gaudy bosh to these" (*OP*, 61). Dr. Williams was prepared to accept the phenomenal of the modern. He remained undisturbed. Yet is is interesting to find him at one point agreeing with Stevens' evocation of the American past in this "crosser of snowy divides." Writing of Daniel Boone and the Kentucky wilderness, he begins: "There was, thank God, a great voluptuary born to the American settlements against the niggardliness of the damning puritanical tradition. . . ."[9] One discovers that this antipuritanical "voluptuousness" is wholly sufficient to Dr. Williams. It is not, for Stevens. In the affecting portrait of "Extraordinary References," Stevens presents a mother who plaits her daughter's hair with ribbons. She addresses the child: *"My Jacomyntje! Your great-grandfather was an Indian fighter"* (*CP*, 369). Hair and braids appear again as signs of a style, a way of the imagination. The poet observes: ". . . the extraordinary references / Of ordinary people, places, things, / Compose us in a kind of eulogy." A child, we may reflect with him, re-

---

[8] Cf. the imagery of the diamond in Valéry's "La Jeune Parque," p. 53 above, and Stevens' late lyric "A Child Asleep in Its Own Life" (1955, *OP*, 106).
[9] *In the American Grain*, p. 130.

quires its own being, a child asleep in its own life. Indian fighter, buckskin hero, or Daniel Boone, these are of the past. The American opportunity should have remained the same, as nakedness in one's own present. This alone is faithful to the hero. Ordinary people make extraordinary bondage to the past; the present becomes a eulogy.

Thus the American paradigm is an ideal freedom of imagination. The "buckskin crosser" was its first embodiment. Against the image of a major American frontiersman, Stevens poses that of Cotton Mather with rejoicing such as one finds in Dr. Williams' thunder against puritanism. Superbly ironical, Stevens writes in a mock declaration of pseudo-autobiography: "Cotton Mather died when I was a boy." The books Mather read "had got him nowhere." A doubt makes him preach the louder. There is an "eminent thunder" from a mouse in the wall, "the grinding in the arches of the church, / The plaster dropping. . . ." "Over wooden Boston, the sparkling Byzantine / Was everything that Cotton Mather was / And more." The Byzantine-sun, lord of time and lord of light, is the master of change. "Look down now, Cotton Mather, from the blank. / Was heaven where you thought? It must be there. / It must be where you think it is, in the light/ On bed-clothes, in an apple on a plate" (*CP*, 217). The title of the poem is utterly exact: "Blue Buildings in the Summer Air." Sun and light are constant; they make an earthly paradise; every blue building of the imagination one day falls. With irreverent amusement Stevens could have been thinking of Mather's renowned introduction to the *Magnalia Christi Americana*: "I WRITE the *Wonders* of the CHRISTIAN RELIGION, flying from the Deprivations of *Europe,* to the *American Strand* . . . His Divine Providence hath *Irradiated* an *Indian Wilderness.*"[10] To every reader of Stevens this purpose of Cotton Mather should be a treasure. The drama of this transatlantic passage is precisely opposite that of Stevens' voyager in "The Comedian as the Letter C." Crispin comes to these shores from the inanition of old Europe. He will *irradiate* the wilderness, but with a human providence. The devil of a "green barbarism" will become the angel of his imaginings.

Contemplating the American past with Stevens, one may hear with him enough of other mice nibbling in the walls, of grindings in the arches. Mice are at work everywhere. That faithful Byzantine-

[10] *Selections from Cotton Mather,* ed. Kenneth B. Murdock (New York, 1926), p. 1.

sun may seem to be the only constant. But there is one American prerogative of American man which challenges this dominion. It is the supreme heresy to a Cotton Mather: the eminent right to *shape* the self, the world appearing to that self, the art to describe the shaping. In Stevens' conviction, the exertion of this right makes the shaper a sun-child. With us, the signs of the American future of this self seem now unpropitious. Perhaps the mice are at work in its vitals. One surveys the counteraction and negation of Dr. Williams, with his "rubbings of reality," as Stevens called them, and wonders. For, as Mr. Miller[11] and other observers have noted, the act of shaping in both America and Europe becomes less and less frequent in our immediate present. Perhaps, then, I may be speaking of a self-shaping that rapidly loses authority as I consider Stevens in the company of Emerson, Thoreau, Whitman, and Emily Dickinson. In the decade since Stevens' death, we have heard other and different grindings in the arches. It is as though new arches were in collapse before the "blue buildings" of our present were even inhabited. But I have cautioned in the Introduction that Stevens is no longer modern. If the paradigm of the shaper that he exalted now fails, then he once knew it in a company of supremely exuberant American poets.

A mountain eminence in New Hampshire casts a shadow. It is Chocorua "In an immenser heaven, aloft, / Alone, lord of the land and lord / Of the men that live in the land, high lord. / One's self and the mountains of one's land . . ." ("The Man with the Blue Guitar," *CP*, 176). There is the eminence of Mt. Penn, near the Reading of the poet's boyhood ("Credences of Summer," *CP*, 374). There are his "thought-like Monadnocks" of a late reflection ("This Solitude of Cataracts," *CP*, 424). Every mountain in the poetry of Stevens is a symbol of the American land. It is the rock of American being, the place of flourishing of a sovereign American self. In this American place one discovers a means of entrance into questions of correspondence between Stevens and Emerson. It is also a point informative of differences. The Emersonian principle, every natural fact as a symbol of spiritual fact, blazes with poetic intensity in "The Sphinx": "She spired into a yellow flame; / She flowered in

---

11 *Poets of Reality*, p. 310. This discussion of Williams seems to me easily the best of Mr. Miller's concerns with his poets; there are six: Conrad, Yeats, Eliot, Thomas, Stevens, and Williams.

blossoms red; / She flowed into a foaming wave; / She stood Monad-noc's head." This is characteristic Emersonian metamorphosis. The world is a moving manifestation of the transcendent, encountered by the constant reception of the restless eye. Monadnock, solitary in New Hampshire, is approached in Emerson's poem through the movement of verbal sequence: apotheosis is reached in the last line; the mountain eminence becomes monumental. A metamorphic dance takes place before us; and this poetic swiftness, with a dynamic text of Stevens in proximity, rests upon mountain vastness. Yet the distance between the two poets is striking. With Emerson, nature moves as an outward display of inner reality; with Stevens it moves in a pattern willed by the observer's self alone, and it displays noth-ing save the reality made by the imagination. Emerson should be regarded as on the American way to Stevens.

But one notes immediately that the province of central man is the paradigm common to both poets. Within this native America area, the self is wholly the tyrant of the field of vision. Emerson is the first theorist, the archdisputant. His terminology, of course, differs from that of Stevens. In "Self Reliance" he frames the resounding American question: "What is the aboriginal Self, on which a univer-sal reliance may be grounded?" It is "that source, at once the essence of genius, of virtue, and of life, which we call Spontaneity or In-stinct."[12] In Stevens this "instinct" is the continuum, generation to generation, of the human power to imagine. Nonetheless, he dis-plays with Emerson a process of exfoliation from the center. It is Emerson's contention in "The American Scholar" that the whole of society in any present is *man divided,* made multifarious. "[T]he gods, in the beginning, divided Man into men, that he might be more helpful to himself. . . . [You] must take the whole society to find the whole man. . . . Man is priest, and scholar, and statesman, and producer, and soldier."[13] We grant the limitation which Stevens makes—that supreme acts of the imagination are con-fined to the arts. The shapers of poetry, painting, music, architec-ture, are of first interest to him. Yet the correspondence with Emerson is close, when the total evidence from Stevens is considered: an age of superior *weather* distinguishes itself with multifarious artisans springing from central man.

Beyond this concept of exfoliation is the impressive agreement

[12] *The Complete Essays and Other Writings of Ralph Waldo Emerson,* ed. Brooks Atkinson (New York, 1940), p. 155.
[13] *Ibid.,* pp. 45–46.

to be seen in the phenomenon of the representative man of an age. There is Emerson's initial proposal: ". . . [I]f Napoleon is France, if Napoleon is Europe, it is because the people whom he sways are little Napoleons."[14] It is but a step to Stevens' observation that each age imagines its heroes. "The major men— / That is different. They are characters beyond / Reality, composed thereof. They are / The fictive man created out of men. / They are men but artificial men . . ." ("Paisant Chronicle," *CP*, 335). Or again, in "An Ordinary Evening in New Haven," Stevens reflects upon "A century in which everything was part / Of that century and of its aspect, a personage, / A man who was the axis of his time . . ." (*CP*, 479). The dangers surrounding this axis-man, Napoleon or another, seem to have left Emerson undisturbed. In the violence of twentieth-century reality Stevens found the dangers urgent. It is these that he thinks of in "Sketch of the Ultimate Politician," that "final builder of the total building . . ." (*CP*, 335). In the political circumstance a century beyond Emerson, any national presence of major man is portentous. If the imaginings of a society are made unanimous in the axis-politician, it is then apparent that a single building is entire and unrivaled. The axis-ruler may become the dictator of life and its ends. Yet it is the master presence in both Emerson and Stevens that we recognize. In his benign aspect, major man is the author of multifariousness; and he is the maker of the poetry of life.

Emerson is again a threshold for Stevens in his American decree of the poet as "the namer." We understand this master author to be the poet-self, the originator of the essential name. "He stands among partial men for the complete man. . . ."[15] "He is sovereign, and stands on the centre."[16] In the poem "Certain Phenomena of Sound" Stevens poses two figures: Eulalia, the light, and Semiramide, the dark. The first is of the sun; she is the illumination of the world. The second is the namer in the poet, "dark-syllabled." "I write Semiramide and in the script / I am . . ." (*CP*, 286). But Emerson would have it that the poet names the spiritual fact of total being. In prospect of the domineering poet satirized in "Bantams in Pine Woods," Stevens protests: "I am the personal. / Your world is you. I am my world." (*CP*, 75). His emphasis upon privacy of speech, his words of Semiramide, may be described in this recent observation of Mircea Eliade. It is a view of poetry for the twentieth century.

[14] *Ibid.*, p. 501: "Napoleon; or, The Man of the World."
[15] *Ibid.*, p. 320.
[16] *Ibid.*, p. 321.

"All poetry is an effort to re-create the language; in other words, to abolish current language, that of every day, and to invent a new, private and personal speech, in the last analysis *secret*."[17] Stevens advances the poet-self in this "secrecy" as he writes in "Examination of the Hero in a Time of War": "The highest man with nothing higher / Than himself . . . / Makes poems on the syllable *fa* . . ." (*CP*, 280). His speech on the scale will not be at *do-re-mi*. Certainly the poet remains Emerson's namer. But it is clear that he names only that world of his own making. Emerson's poet-self is Homeric; Stevens' poet-self is the inscriber of his text "At the centre of the unintelligible" (*CP*, 495). For the poet, there is a quick at the center of his own life; there is an enigma at the center of the reality that he lives. Major man will speak through the poet of the center. The language will be secret. The poet in his time will be singular as man. With Stevens we see major man in the great continuum of the central presence, as Mt. Chocorua looks down upon this persevering giant of humanity. ". . . of human realizings, rugged roy [king] . . ." ("Chocorua to Its Neighbor," *CP*, 302).

"Travelling," wrote Emerson, "is a fool's paradise."[18] The American self will not be confirmed abroad. The poetry of Stevens is a later recasting of Emerson's injunction. The poet ". . . has not / To go to the Louvre to behold himself. . . . [to] monarchies beyond / The *S. S. Normandie* . . ." ("Prelude to Objects," *CP*, 194–95). He continues in Emerson's strict Americanism: "Poet, patting more nonsense foamed / From the sea, conceive for the courts / Of these academies, the diviner health / Disclosed in common forms. . . . Take the place / Of parents, lewdest of ancestors. / We are conceived in your conceits" (*CP*, 195). This place of parents is the place of the central American man. American health is to be disclosed in common American forms.

The proof of Stevens' contemplation of Emerson is found in a late poem, "Looking Across the Fields and Watching the Birds Fly." Mr. Homburg of the scene had an "irritating minor idea," "during his visits home to Concord." Not to transform the grass, the trees, the clouds, into other things "Is only what the sun does everyday . . ." (*CP*, 517). "The spirit comes from the body of the world, / Or so Mr. Homburg thought . . ." (*CP*, 519). But Stevens answers: ". . . there may be / A pensive nature, a mechanical / And slightly

---

[17] *Myths, Dreams and Mysteries: The Encounter between Contemporary Faiths and Archaic Realities*, trans. Philip Mairet (New York, 1960), pp. 35–36.
[18] "Self Reliance," *Complete Essays*, ed. Atkinson, p. 165.

detestable *operandum* . . ." (*CP*, 517). No doubt human beings live beyond themselves, beyond nature, "in air." It is "a transparency through which the swallow weaves, / Without any form or any sense of form . . ." (*CP*, 518). Mr. Homburg of Concord was wrong: spirit does not come from the body of the world (nature); the body of the world comes from the spirit. Natural facts, then, are not symbols of spiritual facts; and one does not, in answer to the self, think away grass and trees and clouds, as the indifferent sun does every day. One imagines the world through that weaving of the swallow; the will of the poet demands shape of this weaving; it transforms the "slightly detestable *operandum*." Things are not concealments with golden ideas behind them. There are no ideas until the human mind forms them. One has, then, to acknowledge anew the proximity of Emerson and Stevens in the dominion of the American self. The question of this self remains: how will it meet and use the phenomena of its world? The two differ. The mind of Emerson reaches toward Plato; the mind of Stevens flourishes upon the phenomenal reality of his century, described again and again in the dogmas of modern art: an *operandum* of nature so grave in monotony that only the play of imagination and the act of artistic making can make it endurable. But the Monadnocks of Emerson and Stevens have remained unchanged. Bastions of American place, they tower above transition. They are rock eminences in the country of the self.

It is obvious, I think, that Thoreau's experience in the domain of the self differs in degree from Emerson's. It is private. One senses the absence here of Emersonian declamation. The speech of Thoreau is less doctrinaire. If one regards *Walden* as a singular inscription, in the sense of Stevens, its lyricism is bounded by the limits of one unique vision. Certainly it is an exploration of self. In the American grain its legacy is primary. It is the record of a deliberate act at the center. For its time, it is a realization of *nakedness* nearest to Stevens' requirement of the "innermost atom." The "backing of life into a corner" at Walden is a stripping of consciousness to the bedrock of the self.

But it is with Thoreau in prospect of possibilities for the poet that we are most concerned. In 1854 he recorded in his journal a conviction of the poet's power of shaping the world. "Every important worker will report what life there is in him. It makes no odds into what seeming deserts the poet is born. Though all his neighbors pronounce it a Sahara, it will be a paradise to him; for the desert which we see is the result of the barrenness of our experience."[19] The rhetoric is of Thoreau's time. But the thought will not be found to differ very much from that of Stevens in "The Man with the Blue Guitar." In this passage Stevens begins with the individual. In him there lives the central man, named here as an *animal*, in a radical use of the world, a *sentient, living organism*, and hence the presence of the vigorously human. "The person has a mould. But not / Its animal. The angelic ones / Speak of the soul, the mind. It is / An animal. The blue guitar— / On that its claws propound, its fangs / Articulate its desert days" (*CP*, 174). Thoreau's worker makes his own paradise of the desert; this central act anticipates Stevens' modern articulation of desert days. We are inclined to forget the vehemence of Thoreau. If the poet's claws and fangs in Stevens represent a rapacious invasion of life, are they not well-matched by Thoreau's metaphor in a deceptively quiet passage of *A Week on the Concord and Merrimack Rivers*? "The talent of composition is very dangerous—the striking out the heart of life at a blow, as the Indian takes off a scalp."[20] This poet's hatchet falls with the force of the ax at Walden Pond!

An American myth of the self is the true subject of Thoreau's *Week*. When this remarkable work is considered as a poetic act, executed with a precision of purpose in its own way as measured as the Canonical Hours, its advancement of an aboriginal self becomes far more impressive than Emerson's. Day by day it is a record of interplay: the naked self turning outward upon the phenomena of an American region, and turning again inward upon an imaginative freedom, which the self knows. It is a declaration of independence from the inheritances and the tyrannies of all other myths. The image of the poet is the master of these water courses. He emerges with a steady consistency from the preface on the Concord River, where we find rude and sturdy men of country and forest, "greater men than Homer, or Chaucer, or Shakespeare, only they never got time to say so; they never took to the way of writing."[21] These are men of the center, we may say, without a verbal record. Thoreau's

---

[19] *The Writings of Henry David Thoreau*, ed. Bradford Torrey (Boston, 1906), XII (Journal, VI), 237. The entry is of May 6, 1854. The passage is anticipated by the following contentions: "There is no such thing as pure *objective* observation. Your observation, to be interesting, i.e. to be significant, must be *subjective*."
[20] From "Thursday," in Vol. 1 of *The Writings of Henry David Thoreau* (Cambridge, Mass., 1894), p. 434. *A Week* was first published in 1849.
[21] *Ibid.*, p. 7.

meditation of "Sunday" then falls upon the "mythus" of "the Christian fable,"[22] and upon the equivalence of all religious fables in the mythology of mankind. Every myth fades. The legacy of Judaism, in Thoreau's response, is vaporous. "As for me, Abraham, Isaac, and Jacob are now only the subtilest imaginable essences, which would not stain the morning sky. Your scheme must be the framework of the universe; all other schemes will soon be in ruins."[23] This transience of all mythological schemes is re-examined in the speculation of "Monday." "Every sacred book, successively, has been accepted in the faith that it was to be the final resting-place of the sojourning soul; but after all, it was but a caravansary which sup-plied refreshment to the traveler. . . . Thank God, no Hindoo tyranny prevailed at the framing of the world, but we are freemen of the universe, and not sentenced to any caste."[24] In the hours of "Friday," the image of central man has become the poet-self. Beyond the Emersonian figure of the namer, the poet now becomes the builder of his own unique form. We may venture Thoreau's image as the first of its kind in American literature. Furthermore, it is an American paradigm wholly predictive of the commitment of Ste-vens. "The true poem is not that which the public read. There is always a poem not printed on paper, coincident with the production of this, stereotyped in the poet's life. It is *what he has become through his work*."[25] This is precocious poetic humanism. Before the close of "Friday," the final reflection comes as a kind of coda. "Yet the universe is a sphere whose centre is wherever there is intelligence. The sun is not so central as a man."[26]

In the last contention alone Thoreau seems to leave this re-markable correspondence with Stevens. As I shall wish to show later, the sun is the center of the "other" world, phenomenal reality upon which the imaginative act of the poet is exerted. With Stevens, intelligence will govern the shaping of a universe imagined. But it is not an ontological center, in any case. Thoreau, despite his disci-pline, proposes a wealth of humankind in a homocentric cosmos. There is no gainsaying here the authority of his religious inheri-tance, any more than one may overlook the same in Emerson. Ste-vens, with a comparable ardor of discipline of his own kind, asserts the poverty of humanity in a universe of total "apartness," a cosmic *operandum*, to recall his answer to Emerson as Mr. Homburg, remote

22 *Ibid.,* p. 84.
23 *Ibid.,* p. 88.
24 *Ibid.,* p. 193.
25 *Ibid.,* p. 452.
26 *Ibid.,* p. 461.

from any human power save that of the transforming imagination. Yet Stevens, as one considers the central span of Thoreau's *Week,* is fully anticipated in this transcendental vision of the self. We read the aboriginal self and the later image of central, major man interchangeably.

Whitman in the American lineage is the expansion of the poet-self celebrated by Emerson and Thoreau. We have long known this inheritance. "Song of Myself" is the master redaction of the theory. In a new consideration, *Leaves of Grass* may seem, at first glance, to be a prefiguration of Stevens' Grand Poem. Whitman's *leaves* are "uttered" in praise of a major theme, the subsuming self of all humankind. In the closer sense they are acts of the poet as a shaper of himself. Stevens obviously knew his Whitman. At certain points he writes like Whitman. In the following passage from "The Man with the Blue Guitar" (Sec. 23, *CP,* 177) I have changed the lengths of lines and abolished divisions between pairs:

> *A few final solutions, like a duet with the*
> *   undertaker:*
> *A voice in the clouds, another on earth, the*
> *   one a voice*
> *Of ether, the other smelling of drink,*
> *The voice of ether prevailing, the swell of*
> *   the undertaker's song in the snow*
> *Apostrophizing wreaths, the voice in the clouds*
> *   serene and final,*
> *Next the grunted breath serene and final, the*
> *   imagined and the real,*
> *Thought and the truth, Dichtung und Wahrheit,*
> *All confusion solved, as in a refrain one keeps*
> *   on playing year by year,*
> *Concerning the nature of things as they are.*

Of especial interest here are participial suspension and the absence of periodic statement. The single long line is left open, in the manner of Whitman, without resolution in the predicate. The "open end" of the line in Whitman is deliberately intended to represent encounter with an infinite series. The same stylistic objective is apparent in this passage from Stevens. The mode of vision and expression is thus established at an assumed center of observation: the poet, in Emerson's sense, "stands among partial men for the complete man." From his position at the center, he sees into continuity rather than intermittence. Whitman's turgid late essay, "Have We a National Literature?" calls for "mighty authors" apart from "that vast abnormal ward or hysterical sick-chamber which in many respects Europe . . . would seem to be." It follows that Whitman thinks of the American voice as alone capable of "typifying the era." Yet this voice is inadequate: "Modern verse generally lacks quite altogether the modern. . . ."[27] It is clear that Whitman urges an assertion of the American poet-self. If modern verse for Whitman's age is lacking in "the modern," then it is not Whitman's poetry that is insufficient. Our estimate remains unchanged in the twentieth century: Whitman is one of the great innovators in American expression.

In this mark of innovation Whitman has his equal in Stevens. Throughout the range of American poetry there are no others more daring in the making of poetic language wholly of the American imagination. Whitman's spontaneity (as in "Savantism," "Spontaneous Me") or any of those affected-French key terms, such as "cantatrice," "imperturbe," "feuillage," can be seen and heard only as signs of a poetic immediacy, as though the poet-self were, like Stevens' sibyl, speaking from the center. Stevens matches Whitman again and again, but in an astounding array of totally original diction. Every reader knows his aptitude. There is a *spick*-ness of the sea, an evening star that *prinks*, a *dibbling* in waves of porpoises, a *skreaking* and *skrittering* of American grackles, a *dithering* of grass.[28] The language is of the American self.

But, again, Stevens will not accept a transcendental reality. It is not his purpose to restore man to nature through the act of the poet. In "Passage to India" Whitman announces: "Nature and Man shall be disjoin'd and diffused no more, / The true son of God shall absolutely fuse them" (Sec. 5). One suspects that it is this fusion which Stevens distrusted in Whitman. The poet is not in Stevens' conviction a wonder-working son of God. In answer to a letter of Joseph Bennett requesting a contribution to an issue of *The Hudson Review* commemorating the centenary of *Leaves of Grass*, Stevens wrote of the "disintegration" of Whitman. "Crossing Brooklyn Ferry" seemed to him a mark of this process. In the same

[27] The essay as printed in the *North American Review*, Vol. 152 (March, 1891), p. 337.
[28] In this order (*CP*): "The Paltry Nude Starts on a Spring Voyage" (p. 6); "Homunculus et La Belle Étoile" (p. 25); "The Comedian as the Letter C" (p. 27); "Autumn Refrain" (p. 160); "Variations on a Summer Day" (p. 234).

judgment he praised "Song of the Broad-Axe" and "Song of the Exposition." But his admiration was qualified. "He seems often to have driven himself to write like himself. The good things, the superbly beautiful and moving things, are those that he wrote naturally, with an extemporaneous and irrepressible vehemence of emotion."[29] I relate this view of Whitman's "vehemence" to Stevens in prospect of the poet-self. The poetry of the center is natural and extemporaneous. The poet driving himself to write like himself is the poet by his own election the maker of national epic. At no point that I know of was Stevens tolerant of the poet who decorates himself with the mantle of the poet-priest for the nation. Every true poet is a sun-child. But the sun remains the great and indifferent lord. No poet-priest is equal to him. Thus Stevens meets Whitman formally with the irony of "Like Decorations in a Nigger Cemetery." "In the far South the sun of autumn is passing / Like Walt Whitman walking along a ruddy shore. / He is singing and chanting the things that are part of him, / The worlds that were and will be, death and day. / Nothing is final, he chants. No man shall see the end. / His beard is of fire and his staff is a leaping flame" (Sec. 1, *CP*, 150). We note well: the sun is chanting of endurance, and his truth is beyond Whitman. He *passes*, like Walt Whitman on a ruddy shore. No man shall see his end. He will come again. But Whitman's was a human fate. Stevens regarded his disintegration.

"To expunge all people and be a pupil / Of the gorgeous wheel. . . ." Stevens speaks of the wheel of the seasons, the wheel measured by human time ("Sailing After Lunch," *CP*, 121). I am aware that an application of this purpose to Emily Dickinson will appear to some critics inadmissible. But it seems to me a purpose mandatory for both poets. There can be no question of Miss Dickinson's faithfulness to the poet-self. Her act of penetration to the center can be no less revealing than that of Thoreau confronting essential being at Walden Pond. Furthermore, the making of the sovereign self of this center is the supreme achievement of her poetry. Mr. Pearce has noted as much. "Writing poems, she writes herself. She claims to do nothing more and dares to do nothing less."[30] If this judgment is certain, as I take it to be, then conversely it will serve for Stevens. The matter for emphasis is that Miss Dickinson had no

[29] The letter is dated at Hartford, February 8, 1955; see *Letters*, pp. 870–71.
[30] *The Continuity of American Poetry*, p. 179.

more concern for epic pretensions than had Stevens; and the two
here seem to me to agree more closely with Thoreau than with
Emerson and Whitman. Furthermore, whatever the differences between the two in the mainstream of ideas—Miss Dickinson in the
endless attention that she gave to the nuances of the emotional life
and Stevens in his persistent exploration of poetry-as-process—the
variety of reaction to physical phenomena remains the dominant and
common concern. Miss Dickinson's oriole poem, "One of the ones
that Midas touched," is a brilliant testimony to this reaction. The
"golden fleece" in this New England orchard, drenched with sunlight,
filled with the "badinage divine" of the oriole, is a thing of celebration beneath the gorgeous wheel. No people are about. One may
think of the early Stevens in "Nomad Exquisite," "Beholding all
these green sides / And gold sides of green sides, / And blessed
mornings / . . . And lightning colors / So, in me, come flinging /
Forms, flames, and the flakes of flames" (*CP*, 95). Again, there are
no people; and the gorgeous wheel turns.

Miss Louise Bogan finds Emily Dickinson related to Blake,
Wordsworth, Coleridge, Shelley, and Keats in the belief that "the
imagination was nothing less than God as he operates in the human
soul."[31] This may be. Stevens began an entry in his notebook: "God
and the imagination are one" ("Adagia," *OP*, 178). But I do not
think that theocentrism, as opposed to egocentrism, is authoritative
in these poets. Stevens seems to me to regard being in ways quite
unlike those prevailing among the English poets of romanticism. On
the same ground I find Miss Dickinson unrelated. In the final analysis, the difference is one existing between a poetry that moves toward a theistic resolution and one that struggles toward the unique
self shaped from the aboriginal source in man. The latter is the
predominant American course. To recall the confession of Theodore
Roethke, it is the struggle of the shape "writhing from the old
rock." A genius of the shore presides. It is the genius of American
place, of a new locality of Western man. To this immediacy of American being, this freedom upon the rock, Stevens dedicated his poet's
life. With the evidence of the possible from structures adjacent to

[31] In *Emily Dickinson: Three Views*, with Archibald MacLeish and Richard Wil-
bur (Amherst, Mass., 1960), p. 29. On the equivalence of God and the imagination in Romantic doctrine, see C. M. Bowra, *The Romantic Imagination* (New
York, 1961), p. 34. See also Blake's annotations to Berkeley's "Siris" in *Poetry
and Prose of William Blake*, ed. Geoffrey Keynes (New York, 1932), p. 638:
"Man is All Imagination. God is Man and exists in us and we in him. . . . Imagination is the Divine Body in Every Man."

his own and with his awareness of the American grain, one has finally to consider his aptitude for design. His urge toward his own architecture is finally a matter of his own temperament and no other. As he noted in "Effects of Analogy," "a man's sense of the world comes of his personality and his temperament." This sense is not a literary problem. "It is the problem of his mind and nerves" (*NA*, 122). The remaining part of the foreground for attention in this study is the aptitude native to Stevens: mind, nerves, or whatever at the source, it is the unique compulsion of the draftsman.

The Passion for Design

4

IT IS ASSUMED HERE THAT ANY FIRST-RATE POETRY
displays the artist's will to impose an order upon the phenomena of
existence.[1] A late assertion from Stevens speaks for this poetic
objective:

> *This is the true creator, the waver*
> *Waving purple wands, the thinker*
> *Thinking gold thoughts in a golden mind,*
> *Loftily jingled, radiant,*
> *The joy of meaning in design*
> *Wrenched out of chaos. . . .*
>
> ["The Sail of Ulysses," *OP,* 100]

One reflects upon Yeats, the builder of "a sorrowful loveliness"
from "the battles of old times,"[2] another thinker of "gold thoughts,"
a master of design. But the difference marking the poetry of Stevens

---

[1] For a contention against art as imposition of order see Morse Peckham, *Man's Rage for Chaos: Biology, Behavior, and the Arts* (Philadelphia, 1965).
[2] "He Gives His Beloved Certain Rhymes," in *The Collected Poems of W. B. Yeats* (New York, 1959), p. 61.

springs from the nature rather than the degree of his intensity. The soaring cry at the close of "The Idea of Order at Key West" rings with the full authority of a master singer. "Oh! Blessed rage for order. . . ." The process of design leads to this celebration of a poet's rage:

> . . . tell why the glassy lights,
> The lights in the fishing boats at anchor there,
> As the night descended, tilting in the air,
> Mastered the night and portioned out the sea,
> Fixing emblazoned zones and fiery poles,
> Arranging, deepening, enchanting night.
>
> [CP, 130]

There is no better example in Stevens of poetry as process. One thinks again of the tongue as an eye (OP, 167). As we read, the data of the senses are organized by an act of seeing and an act of words. The scene rushes to composition. These emblazoned zones and fiery poles are established by the imagination as points of reference. We are spectators before an act of poetic will. But it is the movement directed by this will which distinguishes Stevens as the poet. If a similar experience were possible in a painting, it would run in this fashion: We regard the finished composition; but at the very moment of this regard we are admitted to the process of the painter as he once fixed dominant points of light against the dark and by these established the arrangement of other elements in his composition. With Stevens this talk of zones and poles is a clear sign of the architect in poetry. The scene at Key West, as the final resolution, is literally built upon spatial relationships. The passion mastering the night reveals the nature of the poet's intensity. I have not said that Stevens in the act of imposing order is superior to Yeats or any other poet. I have said that the nature of his rage is distinctively his; it is a matter of native aptitude.

An examination of Stevens as architect must encompass this feeling of structure as process. To see the act of the artist in terms of geometric forms and relationships is to recognize the compulsion of the draftsman. We note in the passage just quoted a *tilting* of the night, a sea *portioned out* as though divided into sectors, each vast area related to *zones* and *poles*. These strong thrusts of movement are controlled by the will exerted in the dominant points. We discover in this minimum evidence a strict geometry of the spirit.

The only other notice of this aptitude which I have encountered comes from Robert Pack's study of Stevens. Of "Anecdote of the Jar" he writes: "[Jar and hill] . . . become circles within the larger circle of the 'slovenly wilderness,' exerting a pressure that shapes things into a geometric figuration."[3] Yet this now-famous jar placed on the hill in Tennessee (*CP*, 76) is, in fact, minor in its disclosure of the geometry.

One of the widest of all geometric metaphors to be found in Stevens occurs in a poem standing very close to the jar, "Stars at Tallapoosa."[4] "The lines are straight and swift between the stars." In this moonless night these lines are of the imagination in a severe aspect. "The mind herein attains simplicity." "Let these be your delight, secretive hunter, / Wading the sea-lines, moist and ever-mingling, / Mounting the earth-lines, long and lax, lethargic. / These lines are swift and fall without diverging." In the self there is an imagined likeness to these: "A sheaf of brilliant arrows flying straight, / Flying and falling straightway for their pleasure . . ." (*CP*, 71–72). These arrows, "nimblest" motions, are of a "young nakedness." At this point we have come to understand the poet's requirement of nakedness. This beauty at Tallapoosa is austere. The composition contains nothing save the self and imagined star-lines, sea-lines, earth-lines. It is as though an enormous grid ordered in the mind were imposed upon the universe. Spacious sky and land and sea are plotted with a master print. But now the metaphor turns inward. These lines are traced from a sheaf of arrows, sent from the imagination, flying on soaring and descending arcs. The nakedness of the poet is that of Stevens—the self, these imposed lines upon nature, these arrowy flights of imaginings. This austere vision is of the utterly solitary poet writing in *Harmonium*. The same night sky will soar above him in "The Auroras of Autumn," as the northern lights sweep in "gusts of great enkindlings" and the stars "put on their glittering belts" (*CP*, 413, 419). Then the arrows will be falling. The draftsman will be near his end. In *Harmonium*, again starkly prefiguring, it is the Creator of the universe who struggles "toward his harmonious whole." For the sake of this struggle

[3] *Wallace Stevens: An Approach to His Poetry and Thought* (New Brunswick, 1958), pp. 57–58.
[4] An entry in Stevens' youthful New York journal, November 10, 1900, is prophetic of his later fascination with these gusts of the Florida night. "The moon has not been bad of late. The stars are clear and golden and geometrical and whatever else they try to be, I rather like that idea of geometrical—it's so confoundedly new!" See *Letters*, p. 48.

"we endure brief lives, / The evanescent symmetries / From that meticulous potter's thumb" ("Negation," *CP*, 97–98). If life is brief and evanescent, then it may at least achieve symmetry. Herein the defiance of the poet rests. Star-lines, sea-lines, earth-lines propose the irony of evanescence. The arrows of the draftsman-like imagination are sure.

Certainly a geometry of the spirit is the subject of the piece entitled "Someone Puts a Pineapple Together."[5] The symmetry of this fruit, in its checkered rind and barbed tuft of green, appealed to Stevens. Like the mango, frequently employed in his metaphor, it evoked a remarkably strong sense impression. The anonymous one in the poem is Stevens himself; and the lines proceed as revelation in metaphor of the draftsman's act in poetic composition. As is poetry itself, the pineapple is made of the earth from which it springs. But it is a design transcending its physical elements.

> *It is more than the odor of this core of earth*
> *And water. It is that which is distilled*
> *In the prolific ellipses that we know,*
>
> *In the planes that tilt hard revelations on*
> *The eye, a geometric glitter, tiltings*
> *As of sections collecting toward the greenest*
> *   cone.*

> [*NA*, 87]

Ellipses, planes tilting, geometric glitter, and these sections "collecting toward" the cone reveal in a microcosmic sketch the process of Stevens' total architecture. One need not look very long to discover the movement contained here. Once again, it is the architectural sense of process memorialized in the finished object which impresses us. This pineapple is related to the poet's order imposed upon night at Key West and at Tallapoosa.

In another sense the pineapple suggests in its ellipses and planes the range of Stevens' concern with universal forms. To the painter it will recall Cézanne in his injunction to Émile Bernard: ". . . Treat nature by the cylinder, the sphere, the cone, everything in proper perspective so that each side of an object or a plane is directed towards a central point."[6] The appeal to Stevens of the architectural sense in Cézanne has already been noted. It is this sense

---

[5] In the series "Three Academic Pieces," read at Harvard in 1946.
[6] *Letters*, ed. Rewald, p. 234. The letter is dated at Aix, April 15, 1904.

alone from Cézanne which survived in the cubists. Although I shall later advance certain reasons for Stevens' dislike of cubist painting, it is worth noting here that cubist mathematics developed contemporaneously with Stevens' first major achievement in *Harmonium*. Georges Lemaître speaks of cubist mysticism as "blended with a thoroughly mathematical conception of the world." He finds this "a remnant of the age-old reverence for the power of human reasoning."[7] Certainly a mathematical conception is apparent in Stevens. But it proceeds from an aptitude for structure; reverence for reasoning has little to do with it. Looking at the surface of the contemporary in "The Common Life," he found a two-dimensional flatness: the town stands in a morbid light, "Like an electric lamp / On a page of Euclid" (*CP*, 221). There are no "shadows." Stevens may then be related to Cézanne in a master analogy. The pineapple is to be regarded first as a natural object under study. The vision of the object *qua* object recalls the method of Cézanne, not that, certainly, of the cubists. There is movement here, as opposed to a cubist stasis. The object, in the second sense, becomes a metaphor of a total poetic structure. Here the poet is like no other artist. The sections of his work *collect toward* the cone. As a structure it is unique.

The movement and the depth of Cézanne and the metamorphic qualities of his color were lost, as we know, in the mathematics of cubist painting. In the mind of Stevens it was this dynamic range of the Cézanne-like imagination that had, at all costs, to be preserved. He must certainly have known well, and feared, his closeness to a pure mathematics. We may take this to be a threat of bondage to the oppressive *operandum* of nature which he names in his lines on Emerson ("Looking Across the Fields and Watching the Birds Fly," *CP*, 517). It is the tyranny of mechanisms which must be avoided. Thus the poem "Contrary Theses (II)" (*CP*, 270) is a confession of the resolve. "One chemical afternoon in mid-autumn, / When the grand mechanics of earth and sky were near . . .," a man walked "toward an abstract." His year-old boy is on his shoulder. The dog barks. The sun, the boy, and the dog are "contours" of an abstract. Cold is in the air; winter threatens. There is a chemistry of autumn earth and autumn sky, an inexorable mechanics. But motion and color fend off the "bombastic intimations" of winter. Negroes play football in the park; flies and bees seek the chrysanthemums' odor, the autumn fragrance that comes in another poem ". . . to disguise

[7] *From Cubism to Surrealism in French Literature*, p. 80.

the clanking mechanism / Of machine within machine" ("Like Decorations in a Nigger Cemetery" *CP,* 157). The contrary theses are
clear: there is a mechanism of earth; there is a saving abstract, "The
premiss from which all things were conclusions . . ." (*CP,* 270).
We know this to be the one abstraction of Stevens, major man,
the imagination. We understand that any art devoted to a thoroughly
mathematical conception of the world was for him insupportable.
The imposition of free movement by an imagination playing upon
physical nature is there denied. Surrender to the "clanking mechanism" amounts to an endless winter of the artist.

I have wished to demonstrate closely the limits that Stevens determined for mathematical vision. With him it is strictly reserved
for the technique of design. The architectural sense is never permitted to pass into the abstract—hence the difference between the
aesthetic of Stevens and that, let us say, of Piet Mondrian. No matter
what the degree of his delight in geometric order, Stevens holds to
the plane or, like Cézanne, to the cone and the sphere as elements of
structure beneath the artist's play of light and shadow, color and
movement, over the face of nature. The imagination remains sovereign in its will. With these distinctions fully stated, we may enjoy
greater freedom in considering certain examples of Stevens' poetry
revealing a mathematical sense. These are illuminating in an approach to the system of projections upon which the Grand Poem
is constructed; they reveal the power of the draftsman.

It was Cézanne's insistence upon the structure of physical reality,
the authority of natural form beneath imaginative rendering, which
finally marked his separation from pure impressionism. The same
insistence is obvious in Stevens, even when one considers his judgment of impressionism as "the only really great thing in modern
art."[8] It is certainly of some significance that Cézanne is mentioned
far more frequently in the critical prose of Stevens than is any other
modern painter. This preoccupation would seem to come of an awareness of Cézanne's postimpressionist advance into problems of structure. Ramon Fernandez, in the essay "Of Philosophic Criticism,"
which Stevens no doubt knew, provides the following analysis of
impressionistic prowess. "The sketching out of an intuitive nature,

[8] "Notes on Jean Labasque," *OP,* 293. This estimate, dated 1940–41 (?), speaks
of preoccupation with "civic" painting, a "moral axis" in painting, hostility to
the egocentric as evident in Labasque's *Preface à une Peinture.*

intermediate between reality and idea, and essential principle of the latter, has been the work of what is called *grosso modo* impressionism. . . . This greater intimacy with things is an illusion. What one should say is a greater intimacy with self. . . ."[9] Stevens will be found in agreement with these distinctions; but to them must be added his obsession with structure. Thus *intuitive nature* is extended by acts of imagination encompassing the structure of phenomena.

One of Stevens' most frequently cited poems on the imagination, "Connoisseur of Chaos," opens with an image of mathematical precision. Two "propositions"[10] are fixed: "*A*. A violent order is disorder; and / *B*. A great disorder is an order. These two things are one" (*CP*, 215). Section 2 of the poem proceeds with an illustration of *A*.: In a violently imposed (an old or inherited) order there is a disorder apparent in a unity achieved through "a law of inherent opposites." In Section 3, proposition *B*. (apparently the new and the modern) argues a disorder exhibiting order which is imaginative process, as the "squirming facts exceed the squamous mind." Thus order in the second proposition is the inevitability of proliferation from disorder. In Section 4 proposition *A*. returns to an old order as offering a truth, but in so doing it expands the disorder of truths. Proposition *B*. takes up again the process of Section 3. The winds of change in a new spring season are blowing. Ergo, all truths of old orders together make a disorder; all disorders of the new make together an order in the endless succession of change. Thus man's life is chaos; and here it must be understood that Stevens uses the term in his own way. The sense is radically Greek: the primordial *abyss*. It lies potential to the creator (here the *connoisseur*, the poet-knower). There can be no doubt of this intent as one comes to the final image of Section 5: "The pensive man . . . / He sees that eagle float / For which the intricate Alps are a single nest" (*CP*, 216). The eagle-imagination makes a nest of the abyss. To note as much is perhaps to repeat the conclusions of other readers. But it is, first, the logical precision of the poem which I wish to stress, and, second, the phenomena intricate in the mountain rocks beneath the eagle. These will be known and measured in their structures before they are made into poems. Chaos will be made art

---

[9] *Messages*, p. 38–39.
[10] This fondness for propositions and lettered points of perspective may be seen again in "So-and-So Reclining on Her Couch," Projections *A, B,* and *C* (*OP*, 295); in "An Ordinary Evening in New Haven," Sec. 6 (*OP*, 469), "Naked Alpha . . . hierophant Omega . . . infant A . . . polymathic Z"; and in "The Rock," Sec. 3 (*OP*, 528). ". . . Point A / In a perspective that begins again / At B. . . ."

by the shaper. Cézanne's renderings of Mont Sainte-Victorie, the structure of reality first mastered, and then altered as imagination dictates, do not differ theoretically from Stevens' acts upon chaos. Certainly there was "a greater intimacy with self," to repeat Fernandez; but "the greater intimacy with things" was not an illusion.

The logic just noted further reveals the mathematical bent of the poet's mind. As in the lights of Florida fishing boats and of Florida stars, he shows again his obsession with points of measurement. Thus the reflection of "The Motive for Metaphor" presents the poet in autumn: then, "You like it under the trees . . . / Because everything is half dead." Or, in spring, he was happy "With the half colors of quarter-things, / The slightly brighter sky, the melting clouds, / The single bird . . ." Things then "would never be quite expressed, / Where you yourself were never quite yourself / And did not want nor have to be. . . ." In these seasons there was a motive for metaphor. There was a "shrinking from / The weight of primary noon— / The ABC of being." The searching light, the fullness of this noon is a "ruddy temper, the hammer / Of red and blue, the hard sound— / Steel against intimation—the sharp flash, / The vital, arrogant, fatal dominant X" (CP, 288). Thus noon is summer, *primary* noon, ABC; it is the zenith at X. The mathematics of music enters the imagery of this poem. It appears first in the "quarter-things," *quarter-tones*, of "half colors" in spring. It reappears in the *dominant* qualifying X, the perfect fifth above the *tonic*. The base of these images from music is found in the "half colors" and in the *tonic*, referring as well to the general effect of color or of light and shade from the theory of painting. Thus the mathematically precise X, "Of red and blue, the hard sound," is rendered in images compounded from the theoretical language of two arts adjacent to poetry. The brilliance of summer is apotheosis. Its effect in color is red and blue against the half-colors of spring. Its effect in music is the dominant against the earlier quarter-tones. These four figures are central points of reference. The *motive for metaphor* is found in the incompleteness of autumn and spring, when the imagination freely moves in its own dominance. The hammer of summer, "steel against intimation," primary noon, is arrogance. This primacy of being places an ultimate burden upon the poet. "Summer, jangling the savagest diamonds and / Dressed in its azure-doubled crimsons," bears "its heroic fortunes / For the large, the solitary figure" ("Examination of the Hero in a Time of War," CP, 281). It is interesting to find this burst of imagery closing the volume named *Parts of a World*. In the chronology it precedes the next collection, under the title *Transport to Summer*, in which "The Motive for Metaphor" appears as the third poem.

Toward the close of "Notes Toward a Supreme Fiction" and very near the end of *Transport to Summer* the poet addresses the whistling wren and the "practicing" robin. Summer appears as a containment in a circle. In this season of arrogance and jangle, there is a repetition of both bird song and poet song: ". . . the going round / And round and round, the merely going round, / Until merely going round is a final good . . ." (*CP*, 405). "Steel against intimation," the poet has said of summer in "The Motive for Metaphor." Spring and autumn, in their incompleteness, are seasons of intimations; they are transitions, toward the authority of summer, toward the blank of winter. Summer is imagined as an endurance in a ring of steel. It is this geometric image which governs the late lyric "Celle Qui Fût Héaulmiette."[11] Intimations of the poet's winter, his own end, determine the tone of the poem. The woman-genius of his poetry reappears. Here, in the ring, she finds "a helping from the cold . . . / Like a shelter not in an arc / But in a circle, not in the arc / Of winter, in the unbroken circle / Of summer. . . ." Yet she is "at the windy edge, / Sharp in the ice shadow of the sky . . ." (*CP*, 438). The ice shadow in the summer blue is the poet's intimation of a winter finality of his own. Thus in summer she is helmeted against the threat of cold. These imagistic tracings of summer circles have their own significance in the seasonal progressions of the Grand Poem. For the moment they should be seen in

---

[11] In this preference for an earlier French of the Renaissance, compare the archaic title of the early poem from *Harmonium*: "Cy Est Pourtraicte, Madame Ste Ursule, et Les Unze Mille Vierges." "Héaulmiette" is the diminutive chosen by Stevens as he makes use of Villon's lyric "Les Regrets de la Belle Heaumière déjà parvenue à vieillesse." The second line provides the title of Stevens':

Advis m'est que j'oy regretter
La belle qui fut heaulmière. . . .

I use the Villon text printed by André Gide, *Anthologie de la Poésie Française* (Paris, 1949), p. 21. For assistance in this identification I am indebted to Professor Konrad F. Bieber. I am also grateful to Mr. Bieber for his reading of my translations of texts of French poets, particularly those chosen from Valéry, which appear in this study.

Stevens' title, however, is not wholly dependent upon Villon's lyric. According to a disclosure in a letter to Bernard Heringman dated at Hartford, July 21, 1953, his tribute to the helmet-maker's wife was suggested by Rodin's sculpture on the same subject. This figure, in the Metropolitan Museum of Art, New York, is popularly known as "The Old Courtesan." The original title from Rodin derives from the second line of Villon's poem used by Stevens. The disclosure to Mr. Heringman appears in the full text of the letter, Stevens Collection, Baker Library, Dartmouth College. It is used here with the permission of Miss Holly Stevens.

relation to every other geometric figuration presented here. A mathematical precision is at the base of design. I shall return to this helmet image as being of major significance in the poet's structure with subsequent comment on the crafting of the dome.

A final evidence from Stevens, and one considerably more open to analysis, is his preference for a metaphor of compass points. I have already noted his symbolism of individual human duration and of the dynamic continuum of nature. The poet moves in his vision from South to North. The continuum of nature moves endlessly from East to West. It should first be noted that these are of the four-squareness which engages the imagination of Stevens in his attention to seasonal progression or to an absolute precision of direction. A good example of the second appears in the composition of "Vacancy in the Park." In this last collection, "The Rock," the aging poet examines his house of the mind. The scene is shaped in the quadrangular balance of a Renaissance painting. "It is like a guitar left on a table / By a woman, who has forgotten it. . . . / The four winds blow through the rustic arbor, / Under its mattresses of vines" (CP, 511).

One begins with the early Stevens in "desire for day / Accomplished in the immensely flashing East," and, in the same poem, with a prophecy of "Desire for rest, in that descending sea / Of dark. . ." ("Evening without Angels," CP, 137). Freshness is of the East. But he knows that it is more "than the east wind blowing round one. / There is no such thing as innocence in autumn . . ." ("Like Decorations in a Nigger Cemetery," CP, 157). Again, in a picture of the young poet as a priest lingering on a pilgrimage at a hospice, Stevens writes these prophetic lines in "Certain Phenomena of Sound." "Eulalia, I lounged on the hospital porch, / On the east, sister and nun, and opened wide / A parasol, which I had found, against / The sun. The interior of a parasol, / It is a kind of blank in which ones sees" (CP, 287). I shall not anticipate here my later discussion of Stevens' crafting of the dome of the Grand Poem save to say that its design is sketched in the East. The early poem "Architecture," already discussed, demonstrates this beginning. The parasol, like the pineapple, is a microcosmic sketch. It is a roof, a shelter, a small dome. The seeing beneath it is the poet's unique seeing. It is related to other roofs and domes, as I have noted them earlier, and to the "collective being," major man, who "knew / There were others like him safely under roof . . ." ("Chocorua to Its Neighbor," *CP*, 299). East is the point of beginning of a life symmetry, each builder the possessor of his sovereign structure. East is the morning of all poet-builders, "Ulysses that approaches from the east, / The interminable adventurer . . ." ("The World as Meditation," *CP*, 520). Or, in our language, Ulysses is major man endlessly sending up a new poet with the dawn.

Every future rises in the East. Every present moves from East to West. There is an antic play with the theme in the poem of mid-career, "Of Hartford in a Purple Light." "A long time you have been making the trip / From Havre to Hartford, Master Soleil, / Bringing the lights of Norway and all that" (*CP*, 226). When the poet returns to the same theme late in life, the sun has gone. Now only the stars reign. The title announces the inexorable progression: "Our Stars Come from Ireland." The second section is named *The Westwardness of Everything:*

> *These are the ashes of fiery weather,*
> *Of nights full of the green stars from Ireland,*
> *Wet out of the sea, and luminously wet,*
> *Like beautiful and abandoned refugees.*
>
> *The whole habit of the mind is changed by them,*
> *These Gaeled and fitful-fangled darknesses*
> *Made suddenly luminous, themselves a change,*
> *An east in their compelling westwardness. . . .*
>
> [*CP*, 455]

This solemn music is of the late Stevens. The metaphor recalls another presentation of the same westwardness: an invalid refugee from old Europe, lying in bed in a Brazilian hotel, on the *west wall of the sea* ("The Pure Good of Theory," Pt. II, *CP*, 331). The final bed of every man is in the West. A poet moves from South to North in the life of the mind. The natural process to which he is bound moves from East to West. So in the late confessional "One of the Inhabitants of the West," Stevens himself becomes "A reader of the text, / A reader without a body . . ." (*CP*, 503). The serpent has shed his shape. The West disclosed is the poet's own.

A passion for design commands, as we reflect with Stevens, "The ultimate elegance: the imagined land" ("Mrs. Alfred Uruguay,"

CP, 248). Yet he cautions against hope for the perfect elegance. Life, even with the passion for perfection, cannot be reduced to an absolute purity. Once he paints for us, with a perfect delicacy, his pink and white carnations in a brilliant bowl of clear water ("The Poems of Our Climate"). All is light here, and snowy scents. But the I is "evilly compounded." "The imperfect is our paradise. / Note that, in this bitterness, delight, / Since the imperfect is so hot in us, / Lies in flawed words and stubborn sounds" (*CP*, 193–94). Imperfect in ourselves, we struggle toward purity. Delight lies in the encounter with the endless stubbornness of language. In the wider sense applicable to Stevens, the shaper, we know that delight lay for him in the passion for design. To exert the will to formalize the stubborn, to seek to "wrench" meaning from chaos, is only to aspire to the pure. But the imperfect remains in us.

In 1942 Stevens offered in *Parts of a World*, as the last world war increased its slaughter, the third section of "Asides on the Oboe":

> *One year, death and war prevented the jasmine*
> *   scent*
> *And the jasmine islands were bloody martyrdoms.*
> *How was it then with the central man? Did we*
> *Find peace? We found the sum of men. We found,*
> *If we found the central evil, the central good.*
> *We buried the fallen without jasmine crowns.*
> *There was nothing he did not suffer, no; nor we.*

> [*CP*, 251]

On this, and the world that followed it, poets of that central man were to raise their several structures. Stevens proceeded in answer to his power of shaping. A geometric precision remained the prize above the imperfect. He continued to order the points of his reference. The arrows described their arcs. They fell at the points that he plotted. It is perhaps not generally recognized that the arrangement of the last four lyrics in the *Collected Poems* is the final evidence of precision. I take these strictly in the order presented: "St. Armorer's Church from the Outside," the survey of the design completed, however imperfect to the poet, however rare to us; "The Planet on the Table," the farewell to the imagination; "The River of Rivers in Connecticut," the farewell to American earth and American being; "Not Ideas about the Thing but the Thing Itself," the salutation to the new poet to follow, the next voice in the endless succession of central man.

Poetic Geometry: The Arc

5

A THEORY OF STRUCTURE PROCEEDS FROM THE aptitude for design. In "An Ordinary Evening in New Haven" Stevens represents himself as a "scholar" who left a note, his "Segementa," as follows: " 'The Ruler of Reality, / If more unreal than New Haven, is not / A real ruler, but rules what is unreal. / . . . He is the consort of the Queen of Fact.' "

> *"Sunrise is his garment's hem, sunset is hers.*
> *He is the theorist of life, not death,*
> *The total excellence of its total book."*

[CP, 485]

The going down in the West is the inevitable Fact. The dawn springing in the East edges the poet's garment of light. Life, in particular the life of his imagination, is his Fact. His total book is his sovereign theory applied to the Fact; its total excellence is his singular vision. He is the maker of an unreal above the real, the ordinary as New Haven on any evening is ordinary, and commonplace. The total book is the Grand Poem in the Fact of Wallace Stevens.

A final question in a definition of the shaper, then, is one of determining the means employed to express the theory in a poetic totality. What principle is used to achieve the symmetry of the "total book"? The principle will at once be assumed to spring from the native power of the draftsman. It will be a constant rule of establishing relationships, of intermeshing parts, of maintaining control of the future point of vision, as the mind pauses for description of the present moment. Wassily Kandinsky thought in 1912 of the dynamics of vision in his painter's life as a moving triangle, advancing and ascending. The triangle is divided horizontally "into unequal parts, with the narrowest segment uppermost. The lower the segment, the greater it is in breadth, depth and area . . . Where the apex was today, the second segment will be tomorrow; what today can be understood only by the apex, is tomorrow the thought and feeling of the second segment."[1] This endless motion of mind and feeling is commensurate with every modern aesthetic which has had to do with the dynamics of the creating self. Perception is the constant variable. Stevens states of himself quite simply in "This Solitude of Cataracts": "He never felt twice the same about the flecked river, / Which kept flowing and never the same way twice, flowing. . . . " How would it feel, he asks, to be a bronze man "Breathing his bronzen breath at the azury center of time"? (*CP*, 425). Enough has already been said of poetry as process to indicate the acceptance that Stevens made of constant motion in the self as well as in the phenomena encompassed by vision. He will not differ appreciably from Paul Klee, who contended in his period of teaching at the Bauhaus: "Ingres is said to have created an artistic order out of rest; I should like to create an order from feeling and, going still further, from motion."[2] With respect to Kandinsky, it is this *visualization of a principle of theory* in the metaphor of the triangle which is appropriate to a study of Stevens. To the initial question, What *principle* is used to achieve the symmetry of the whole? another inquiry must be added: *What is seen in the mind's eye as the shape of the principle?* Kandinsky saw a moving triangle. Stevens saw an arc.

The principles of Cézanne must apply again as I consider

---

[1] *Über das Geistige in der Kunst,* trans. as *Concerning the Spiritual in Art* by M. Sadleir, with revisions by F. Golfing, M. Harrison, and F. Ostertag, Documents of Modern Art (New York, 1947), p. 27.
[2] *The Thinking Eye: The Notebooks of Paul Klee,* trans. R. Manheim, ed. Jürg Spiller (New York, 1961), p. 5. This principle, used by Klee in his lectures at the Bauhaus, appears in the notebooks as of September, 1914.

Stevens' visualization of theory. "In art above all, everything is theory developed and applied on contact with nature," wrote Cézanne. Of the shifts of perception, he noted: "The appearance of objects depends upon the total visual field in which they are found, and upon definite attitudes and experiences, in short, upon the total organization of the observer."[3] We take this to be the totality of organization at the time of contact. Certainly it is this momentary organization of the observer in the poetry of Stevens which determines the nature of metaphor. As he observes of the poet in "Things of August": "He does not change the sea from crumpled tinfoil / To chromatic crawler. But it is changed" (*CP*, 492). Here motion is the subject: a motion in the phenomenal world, a motion in individual perception. The sight and the metaphor of the poet shift as motion encounters motion. It is well that poetry "increases the aspects of experience," as he frames the nature of its achievement at another point ("Reply to Papini," *CP*, 446). But we know that for Stevens this increase, however plenteous, is not enough. There must be a governing control toward an ordered totality. It is our present purpose to examine the arc, as both a control of increase and a master line of the poet's architecture.

The arc is inevitable in the preference of Stevens. One adds to his feeling for mathematical precision his attention to spheres and ovoid shapes. If we follow Cézanne—that art is theory applied on contact with nature—then an aspect of the *shape* of Stevens' theory is to be seen in each of these examples, chosen at random from the poetry: the orb, in "A Primitive Like an Orb" (*CP*, 441), "As if the central poem became the world, / And the world the central poem, each one the mate / Of the other . . ."; the planet, in "The Planet on the Table" (*CP*, 532–33); the hive, in "Esthétique du Mal" (*CP*, 315), "His firm stanzas hang like hives in hell . . ."; the egg, in "Things of August" (*CP*, 490), ". . . the egg of the earth lies deep within an egg. / Spread outward. Crack the round dome." I shall later demonstrate the evolution and the completion of the dome shape in the total range of Stevens. For the present, the arc as related to spherical curvature is the matter for emphasis. This image of curvature is not new in the poetry as one reaches the staunch resolve upon the full structure. But the resolve itself should be clearly marked. It occurs in the second poem of the

---

[3] Charles E. Gauss, *The Aesthetic Theories of French Artists: 1855 to the Present* (Baltimore, 1949), pp. 44, 48.

second volume of the chronology, *Ideas of Order*, following immediately upon the turning from South toward North ("Farewell to Florida"). In "Ghosts as Cocoons," encased "spirits" prophetic of the shape of things to come, Stevens urges upon the poet-self the charge ". . . the house is not built, not even begun." There is to be "This mangled, smutted semi-world hacked out / Of dirt . . .," a "ghost of fragrance falling / On dung . . .," "While the domes resound with chant involving chant" (*CP*, 119). This *rounding* of ideas into cocoons announces the resolve upon a design of curvature.

The fifth poem of *Harmonium* displays the first image of the arc. In "The Plot Against the Giant" the looming titan is major man. We know that his successive manifestations in imagining individuals may be of various expression: violence or serenity, beauty or ugliness. But he is the source of all imagining. In this masquelike poem the speaker enters three personae. The first girl will "check" the giant with flower-scents; the second will "abash" him with colors; the third will "undo" him with "Heavenly labials in a world of gutturals" (*CP*, 6–7). It is in the second voice that the prefiguration of the arc appears: "I shall run before him, / Arching cloths besprinkled with colors / As small as fish-eggs. / The threads / Will abash him." The colored stuff will be *arched*; the *threads* as units of structure in the cloth will control the giant. Beneath the delicate metaphor of the poem lies the first sketch of the draftsman. The first voice proposes an organization of sensuousness; the second, a visualization of structure; the third, an authority of structure realized in the poet's language of "labials" as opposed to the "gutturals" of commonplace speech. As in many of the poems of *Harmonium* the mode of the poem is dance. Its appeal is directed to the reader's power of visualizing concerted movement.

A full aesthetic response to this piece may, of course, be reached without any concern directed to the draftsman. But it is the presence of theory at the base of design which engages us in this study; and the fact of this presence is established when the arc-principle is regarded in its later projections. One of these has been cited in the earlier discussion of "Certain Phenomena of Sound" (*CP*, 286). The parasol opened to the morning sun is related to these "arching cloths" of the poet's resolve to tame the giant. It is important to note here that the longest sustained attention to the giant-presence occurs at the close of "Owl's Clover." The whole of the fifth section, "Sombre Figuration" (*OP*, 66–71), amasses like a fugue on the theme of *subman*, modulated in process to a *sprawling portent*[4] moving in the heavens. The giant-portent is to be "changed," to take on the poet's mask. He will become a shape commanded by the poet-lord, "A wandering orb upon a path grown clear" (*OP*, 70). The will of the artist has been preceded in this same poem by an image of men of the commonplace. We may call them inhabitants of the quotidian, of "a world of gutturals." They are workers "Forgetting work, not caring for angels, hunting a lift, / The triumph of the arcs of heaven's blue / For themselves, and space and time and ease for the duck" (*OP*, 60). I have presented in the Introduction as much as need be said of "A Duck for Dinner," from which these lines are taken. The irony is worth underscoring, however. In effect, it appears in the equation of the mass: the arcs of a poet's structure are no more triumphant than quotidian ease.

The metaphor of the arc is related to every mathematical projection of Stevens in the act of design. Invariably it represents the thrust into the future. Thus in "Dutch Graves in Bucks County" the marchers of a present warfare rumble "in arcs / Of a chaos composed in more than order"; they march "toward a generation's centre" (*CP*, 293). Again, in "Repetitions of a Young Captain" the soldier knows ". . . the complete / Society of the spirit when it is / Alone, the half-arc hanging in mid-air / Composed, appropriate to the incomplete, / Supported by a half-arc in mid-earth." He thinks of "Millions of instances of which I am one" (*CP*, 309). The half-arc in mid-air is the structure of the self, half achieved. The half-arc in mid-earth is the knowledge of reality, the rock of being, half achieved. We infer that war, with its tyrannical "order," arrests the free development of each individual imprisoned within it. One is conscious, with the soldier, of the fierce obstacle to completion. Lest there be any ambiguity concerning the *roundness* of the sphere which Stevens sought and the *dome* which his poetry achieves, it should be said at this point that the meditation of the young captain provides the solution that we seek. *The arc in air, the making of the singularity of self by the poet or by any other imagining individual, is the unreal above the real. The arc descending into earth and rising to meet the arc of the self is a man's mastery of the phenomena of being, the real upon which he lives in his*

---

[4] It may be noted that the ensuing line descriptive of the portent ". . . the shoulders turn, breathing immense intent . . ." seems close to Yeats's renowned image in "The Second Coming," parturition in the desert, as the lion-body moves its slow thighs (*The Collected Poems of W. B. Yeats*, p. 185).

time. Thus a completed life, regarded as a design built upon con-
joining arcs, describes a sphere. There should be no difficulty in
understanding Stevens' intention in "A Primitive Like an Orb,"
to cite one example of spherical metaphor: the orb is achieved, "As
if the central poem became the world, / And the world the central
poem, each one the mate / Of the other . . ." (*CP,* 441). We are concerned with the poetry of the half-sphere "in air" and with certain
materials from reality which are used in the process of the structure.
This is the dome of Stevens. The arcs of its structure rise and descend.
At any point on any arc the act of the poet predicts his own future
in imagination. Stevens' observation in "Description without Place"
is perfectly in accord with this principle: "The future is description
without place, / The categorical predicate, the arc" (*CP,* 344).
Place is the phenomenal fact of the rock of being. To the very end of
Stevens' poetry the requirement of *materia poetica* from reality of
place endures. Yet the dome in air, made by a free imagination, is an
aggregate description without place. Finally, when there is no
longer a future, the woman-genius of the poet takes refuge in the
enclosure of summer, as though it were a *last* summer, "Like a
shelter not in an arc . . ." ("Celle Qui Fût Héaulmiette," *CP,* 438).
She is *helmeted* there; and we shall presently see that this helmet
is the completed dome.

"The categorical predicate, the arc." It remains in this chapter
to determine the method used in establishing the arc. The following
comment will be concerned with the means employed by Stevens to
delineate the principle. He intends a visualization of movement,
the seeing of a theory in the mind's eye. The examples which I
have chosen are intended to suggest a method of reading and of
mastering the Grand Poem. I take Stevens literally when he speaks
of the arc as a *categorical predicate.* He is using *predicate* in the
sense of the logician: *in a proposition* (e.g., Stevens' A., B., etc., as
already reviewed), *that which is stated about a subject.* If this
predicate is *categorical,* then it encompasses expression turning
upon a particular subject as a class. The arc as the categorical
predicate expresses the class in its total range. Since the arc, as we
have seen, displays movement in its rise and fall, it then describes
the circumference of the sphere, or the curvature of the half-sphere,
the dome.

Prefiguration in the range of an artist's work may be initially
an unconscious act. So, too, may his acts of repetition appear to
be spontaneous and unreflective. If the artist's later work dis-

plays quotation of his earlier expression, once again he may be unconsciously motivated. But in the poetry of Stevens both prefiguration and quotation are consciously controlled. They are acts of discipline and will; and they establish a method of visualizing theory. How much Stevens may have known or cared for an evidence of prefiguration and quotation in another body of singular expression I do not know. Among his forebears in English poetry we should name Milton as the primary craftsman in a conscious architectural use of these devices. If one turns to painting and music, a cognate evidence of predictive and reflective motifs certainly exists. There is, for instance, a prefigurative movement in the early work of Henri Matisse which relates to the last drawings, just as there is a pervasive idiom in the employment of color. One senses unity in an evolving style. In the view of the critic of Matisse's art, this may amount to an architectural synthesis. From the literature of music, the uses of quotation by Wagner and by Richard Strauss provide evidence of a determined and fully conscious identification of relatedness among separate scores. In the language of the musical historian such instances of quotation may be named *signatures,* as in the dramatic synthesis of *The Ring* or in the reflective thematic summation of the last scores of Strauss.[5] These examples are intended only to propose that Stevens as a disciplinarian of thematic expression proceeding to an ordered totality is scarcely unique. Yet I wish to assume here that his evolution of a *schema* for describing continuity in the architectural line was with him original. If there are demonstrable antecedents and models for his work in this respect, a definition of these must await future criticism. My purpose is to trace certain examples of prefiguration and quotation, and to let these reveal his method as they express the principle of the arc. Self-reference is, of course, common in all important art. I regard a fully conscious and disciplined self-quotation as exceptional.

A consideration of the arc as major subject is reserved for the third section of this study, an examination of the crafting of the dome. At this point I wish only to consider a recurrence of motifs. The first appearance of each motif chosen for study prefigures its last appearance. The final quotation confirms the tenure of the line, which remains strictly within the grasp of consciousness. By this

[5] E. g., *Alpine Symphony,* "Four Last Songs."

statement I mean that retention of the motif and the re-use of it are wholly purposive as the structure proceeds. The third poem of *Harmonium,* "In the Carolinas," concludes with two italicized lines: *"The pine-tree sweetens my body / The white iris beautifies me"* (*CP,* 5). It is the symbolic pine that sweetens. The poem is a lyric affirmation of a pure sensuousness. The scent of American pine in the Carolinas is rendered as a subject of celebration. This is a physicality of American being, symbolized in the pine. A related tribute to this southern pine appears as Crispin, the American imagination, "projects" his ideal South: "The man in Georgia waking among pines / Should be pine-spokesman" ("The Comedian as the Letter C," *CP,* 38). Poets walk among pines in "Bantams in Pine Woods" (*CP,* 75). And "The Man with the Blue Guitar" closes with these lines: "The bread / Will be our bread, the stone will be / Our bed and we shall sleep by night. / We shall forget by day, except / The moments when we choose to play / The imagined pine, the imagined jay" (*CP,* 184). To "play the pine" is to defy the scantiness of the bread, the hardness of the stone of reality. The guitarist-poet makes his resolve. But these are pine-figures from the poet's early flourishing. They speak of a vitality of the imagination. When, at a late point, he continues the line of this figure, he writes in "Credences of Summer": "Postpone the anatomy of summer, as / The physical pine, the metaphysical pine. / Let's see the very thing and nothing else. / Let's see it with the hottest fire of sight. / Burn everything not part of it to ash" (*CP,* 373). The anatomy of summer is compounded of the real pine and the idea of pine which was earlier appropriated by the imagination. In this late prospect, the imagination has failed. Summer is rejected. The physical object must be seen for what it is in reality. The encounter is that of eye to object. There is no transformation. From beginning to end, the endurance of sight upon the pine is an act of the poet's will. A motif is projected in an ordered line emphasized in a continuum of metamorphosis. The springing up of the image in imaginative vigor displays a sensuousness to be celebrated. The anticipation of a failure in this vigor envisions a return to the stern reality of the object-as-it-is.

It is this retention of motifs which is apparent in the line arching between two widely separated passages intent upon the art of the poet-colorist. As he contemplates his poetic future early in *Harmonium* ("Le Monocle de Mon Oncle"), Stevens celebrates the power of the colorist's vision: "Last night, we sat beside a pool of pink, / Clippered with lilies scudding the bright chromes" (*CP*, 17). The same prospect is restored in the late poem "The Plain Sense of Things": "Yet the absence of the imagination had / Itself to be imagined. The great pond, / The plain sense of it, without reflections, leaves, / Mud, water like dirty glass, expressing silence / Of a sort, silence of a rat come out to see, / The great pond and its waste of the lilies . . ." (*CP*, 503). A comparable attention, first-to-last, is apparent in the image of the stitchings on the old black dress ("French flowers" in embroidery) of "Explanation" (*CP*, 72) and in the quotation appearing in the distant piece "The Owl in the Sarcophagus": "An immaculate personage in nothingness, / With the whole spirit sparkling in its cloth, / Generations of the imagination piled / In the manner of its stitchings, of its thread, / In the weaving round the wonder of its need, / And the first flowers upon it, an alphabet / By which to spell out holy doom and end . . ." (*CP*, 434). The first flowers of the early poem become an alphabet to this doom of the imagination.

Examples of prefiguration and quotation crowd upon the reader of the "total book." It is the early seascape of "Sea Surface Full of Clouds," "brilliant iris on the glistening blue" (*CP*, 99), that reappears in quotation in "An Ordinary Evening in New Haven." Three decades have passed since the dazzling sequence of images shifting upon the sea in the imagination's youth. Once, "The sea shivered in transcendent change, rose up / As rain and booming, gleaming, blowing, swept / The wateriness of green wet in the sky. . . . But, here, the inamorata, without distance / And thereby lost, and naked or in rags, / Shrunk in the poverty of being close, / Touches, as one hand touches another hand, / Or as a voice that, speaking without form, / Gritting the ear, whispers humane repose" (*CP*, 484). The early distance of the unreal from the real, the power of imagination to transcend the sea surface through cloud-changes, becomes the deliberate subject of this late reflection. Bright water that once shivered in metamorphosis becomes now the reality of sea. Or one turns to contemplate the rock eminence of a mountain-reality. In the early poem "How to Live. What to Do," the arc-line springs upward. A youth and his companion ascend; they pause to rest "before the heroic height." They seek "a sun of fuller fire." There is ". . . this tufted rock / Massively rising high and bare / Beyond all trees, the ridges thrown / Like giant arms among the clouds" (*CP*, 125).[6] The same mountain reappears in "Credences of Summer," as the arc turns downward. "It is a mountain half way green and then, / The other immeasurable half, such rock / As placid air becomes. . . . A mountain luminous half way in bloom / And then half way in the extremest light / Of sapphires flashing from the central sky . . ." (*CP*, 375).[7] The seeking of a sun of fuller fire is at an end. The rock rising beyond the green, beyond the "bloom," points to the flashing stars, brilliant in the downward-going of the poetry to come, in *The Auroras of Autumn* and "The Rock." But the exactitude of quotation is to be seen in the repetition of *rest* before the heroism of the height. In the earlier poem it is rest before the search for a "fuller fire." In the later, it is "the brilliant mercy of a sure repose. . . . Things certain sustaining us in certainty" (*CP*, 375).

These imagistic arcs of the colorist and of the seeker of sun and stars are matched by the line of the musician. In "Mozart, 1935," the poet resolves to "play" the present. Mozart was young; but his youth cannot be a youth of American being in 1935. His *divertimento* is a souvenir of the past. An "unclouded concerto" may be in the future. But in this present the snow is falling. It is the poet's lot, this winter of an age; it is his reality. He directs a stern command: "Be thou the voice, / Not you. Be thou, be thou / The voice of angry fear, / The voice of this besieging pain." He strikes "the piercing chord." The "wintry sound" must dominate. *Be thou* recalls the sense of *tutoyer*, discussed in an earlier chapter, as it occurs in the late poem "The Beginning" (*CP*, 427). It invokes the central self; the you of the social context is spurned. The voice is then to be of the poet in his present; his "piercing chord" will strike through the speech of everyday; it will seek the center of an age. When Stevens returns to this invocation in "Notes Toward a Supreme Fiction," *be thou* is repeated, but now with a sense of irony. Surveying the world of the commonplace again, he notes: "These are of minstrels lacking minstrelsy, / Of an earth in which the first leaf is the tale / Of leaves, in which the sparrow is a bird / Of stone, that never changes. Bethou him, you / And you, bethou him and bethou. It is / A sound like any other. It will end" (*CP*, 394). *Be-*

---

[6] Stevens probably uses here a memory of his boyhood: mountain-hiking near Reading, Pennsylvania. See Michael J. Lafferty, "Wallace Stevens: A Man of Two Worlds," *Historical Review of Berks County* (Reading, Pa.), XXIV (Fall, 1959), 111.

[7] *Ibid.*, p. 108: ". . . 'Credences of Summer' . . . seems written in reminiscence of a hike over Mount Penn. . . ."

thou is addressed not to the poet, but to men content to endure a *stone* monotony of existence. Thus, *be thou* like the bird of stone, the real sparrow repetitive in his song unaltered by the listener's imagination. Like every other sound from monotony, it will end.

The disclosure of the valedictory section of "The Rock" is indispensable. "The rock is the gray particular of man's life, / The stone from which he rises, up—and—ho, / The step to the bleaker depths of his descents. . . . The rock is the habitation of the whole, / Its strength and measure, that which is near, point A / In a perspective that begins again / At B . . . / The starting point of the human and the end . . ." (*CP*, 528). Standing as it does within the closing sequence of the *Collected Poems*, this massive memorial is a summation of theory. The motion is upward from the rock, and then downward. At *A* there is a point of beginning; again there is an initial point at *B* as perspective changes to a new line. Each is the point of origin of an arc. We understand that the line will curve downward to the same point *in projection*. The rock is both beginning and end. It is art that makes the rock endurable. As Stevens writes in "Notes Toward a Supreme Fiction": "The poem refreshes life so that we share, / For a moment, the first idea. . . . It satisfies / Belief in an immaculate beginning / And sends us, winged by an unconscious will, / To an immaculate end" (*CP*, 382). The movement to earthward is present in his earliest vision, when in "Le Monocle de Mon Oncle" he contemplates a future in poetry. "This luscious and impeccable fruit of life / Falls, it appears, of its own weight to earth." Or, again, this life is a blue pigeon that "circles the blue sky." At its end a white pigeon flutters to the ground (*CP*, 14, 17). One thinks of the "ambiguous undulations" of pigeons at the close of "Sunday Morning" ". . . as they sink, / Downward to darkness, on extended wings" (*CP*, 70). Spring itself anticipated the going down to the rock. There was a shadow, as the poet notes in "An Ordinary Evening in New Haven": "The hibernal dark that hung / In primavera, the shadow of bare rock, / Becomes the rock of autumn, glittering . . ." (*CP*, 476).

The last poem in the collected edition, "Not Ideas about the Thing but the Thing Itself," presents the most striking of all examples of the arc-line. It is as though we stood at the final point of projection suggested in the measurement of perspectives in "The Rock." In March the poet hears a scrawny cry, a bird's cry in the wind. ". . . [I]t was / A chorister whose c preceded the choir. / It was part of the colossal sun, / Surrounded by its choral rings, / Still far away. It was like / A new knowledge of reality" (*CP*, 534). It is impossible to understand this poem without grasping the significance of quotation in the *c* preceding the "choir." The poet is very probably quoting the *C* of "The Comedian as the Letter C." This is the sign of poetic beginning. Crispin, the American imagination as the letter *c*, naming the first tone of the scale. The *c* of the bird's cry is the first weak sound of the next poetic voice, beginning in spring. It precedes the choir of voices of a new age, as Stevens takes his leave. Thus at the point of the last descent of the arc a human succession in the imagination is the certainty of the future.[8]

This dominance of the arc in the announcement and repetition of motifs is related to the sequence of Stevens' separately published volumes. I add here a final note on the rise and fall of the line which this sequence represents. *Harmonium* (1923; 2d ed., 1931), as I have earlier contended, presents an inquiry into possibilities for the "amassing harmony" of the Grand Poem. Essentially, it is a volume exploring, as well, the range of sensuousness which the poet identifies as peculiar to himself. In the fourth poem of the collection, "The Paltry Nude Starts on a Spring Voyage," the beginning of Stevens' attention to the seasons of the poet-self is discovered. Even though the "hibernal dark" hangs like a shadow "in primavera," *Harmonium* is the spring quarter of Stevens. *Ideas of Order* (1935 and 1936) proposes the structure of the poetic mind as it proceeds to question the possibilities of poetic order. In *Owl's Clover* (published in 1936, suppressed in the *Collected Poems,* and republished in *Opus Posthumous*) Stevens made his own definition of the relation of the poet to society. *The Man with the Blue Guitar and Other Poems* (1937), as an interlude before return to seasonal progression, presents an image of the modern

---

[8] It appears quite certain that William Carlos Williams intended a reply to this last of Steven's poems, in *Paterson V* (completed after Stevens' death and published in 1958). The lines of Williams follow:

> *In March—*
> > *the rocks*
> > *the bare rocks*
> > *speak!*
>
> *—it is a cloudy morning.*
> > *He looks out the window*
> > > *sees the birds still there—*
> > *Not prophecy! NOT prophecy!*
> > > *but the thing itself!*
>
> [New Directions ed., p. 242]

poet as a master of variations upon dominant themes from his world. It is organized as a series of propositions concerning cognition through the imaginative life. *Parts of a World* (1942) bears in its title the sense of a world in parts, atomized. Its season is the poet's summer. Here he leaves the "prologues" of his earlier work (see "Asides on the Oboe," *CP*, 250) and in "Montrachet-le-Jardin" resolves upon the completion of the total structure. *Transport to Summer* (1947), in the sense of *rapture* or *rhapsody* addressed to summer, is a recapitulation, a "squeezing of the reddest fragrance from the stump of summer" ("God is Good. It is a Beautiful Night," *CP*, 285). The center of the volume is found in the extended reflection of "Credences of Summer." This poem serves as a prologue to the long *credo* of "Notes Toward a Supreme Fiction," ending the sequence as an apex of the whole summer span of Stevens. *The Auroras of Autumn* (1950) explores the waning season of the imagination. "The Rock," incorporated in the collected edition of 1954–55, is a valedictory. The *Collected Poems* preserves the chronology of the separate volumes; and, except for those pieces suppressed by Stevens (e.g., "Owl's Clover") and later published in *Opus Posthumous,* the "total book" is there preserved.

The arclike progression that the respective collections and their titles suggest will be obvious. This disposition of both talent and achievement must be seen as the mark of the shaper. In the chapters of this section I have wished to stress the true distinctions of Stevens as a designer and a maker of a total structure. These distinctions together make clear his approach to poetry. One area for definition yet remains before I turn to the crafting of the dome. Since it is now understood that Stevens is constantly intent upon the authority of major man and his survival, from age to age, in the arts, I wish to consider briefly his examination of central-being in the physical sense. This is the last necessity of the foreground. It may be thought of as the primacy of sight, as opposed to the singularity of mind which has been described in these initial chapters.

The Elements of Sight

II

The Sun

6

STEVENS IS NOT A MAKER OF A NEW SUN-MYTH; NOR is he an anthropological historian of an old one. As the imagination, endlessly preserved in major man, is the inner center of the individual's life, so is the sun, endlessly primary in the phenomena of earth, the outer center of the individual's sight. From these centers stream two courses of vitality, man-exerted and sun-exerted. Stevens names these *bars*. At least two passages from the poetry reveal his intent. The first occurs in "The Man with the Blue Guitar": "The world washed in his imagination, / The world was a shore, whether sound or form / Or light, the relic of farewells, / Rock, of valedictory echoings, / To which his imagination returned, / From which it sped, a bar in space, / Sand heaped in the clouds, giant that fought / Against the murderous alphabet . . ." (*CP*, 179). This bar is the attribute of the human giant of the imagination. The metaphor is refined and made comparative in the following lines from "Esthétique du Mal." "These are within what we permit, in-bar / Exquisite in poverty against the suns / Of ex-bar, in-bar retaining attributes / With which we vested, once, the golden forms . . ." (*CP*, 317). There were once myths of this *ex-bar,* the streaming of sun-fire, "Before we were wholly human and knew ourselves." Now, in our time, the *in-bar* of the individual man's imagination struggles alone against the "murderous alphabet" of the universe. Thus I must deny that any of Stevens' poetry seeks to establish a sun-myth. His humanism is entire. Through *in-bar* we understand this fact of his art. *Ex-bar* is the nourisher of sight. It is the supreme faculty of the physical universe immediately received by earth dwellers. But in the modern condition of man it will not be an object of worship.

The address to the sun opening "Notes Toward a Supreme Fiction" may seem deceptive. But the clarity of the poet's speech saves us from error. "Phoebus is dead, ephebe. But Phoebus was / A name for something that never could be named. / There was a project for the sun and is. / There is a project for the sun. The sun / Must bear no name, gold flourisher, but be / In the difficulty of what it is to be" (*CP*, 381). This radiance is the center of physical being, unnamed for modern man by any myth. In the preceding "Credences of Summer" Stevens regards the sun "in its essential barrenness . . . the centre that I seek. / Fix it in an eternal foliage / And fill the foliage with arrested peace . . ." (*CP*, 373). With this resolve the mythological sun-reference of art in the High Renaissance and the Romantic dream of reclaiming "lost" sun-symbols of antiquity are dismissed. The only celebration of the sun is in the *leaves* (foliage) of the poet's structure; the attribution to sun-power springs from the poet's rejoicing in the primacy of sight. His sovereign vision remains his own; it is singular with him. He sees as he wills.

We may think here of the long symbolic lineage of the peacock. It probably sprang, in its Western continuity, from an original Hindu sacredness; it appeared in Greece as the attendant bird of Hera; from its authority as a symbol of Hera's fidelity to Zeus, it became the symbol of the Christian faithful in the art of the Byzantine church; in medieval iconography it passed to the Romanesque and the Gothic stone-cutter as an image of the faithful drinker of Christ's blood from the Holy Chalice.[1] The radiance of life, constantly praised, endured through metamorphosis in that ancient symbol for a thousand years and beyond. It was a form made first of a creature in nature, brilliant to the sight. It was refilled again and again with a varying content before it withered and disappeared. But it is such a tenacious lineage

---

[1] On the peacock lending its feathers to wings in the hierarchy of angels, see Mary Griffin, *Studies in Chaucer and His Audience* (Hull, Quebec, 1956), pp. 49–52. Stevens uses the peacock in "Domination of Black" (*CP*, 8), but not in an iconographic inheritance. The bird appears as a symbol of acts of the imagination.

as this which Stevens, in any case, would not serve. The poet's world as he saw it must be washed clean of old images. His resolve was constant.

The parallel between Stevens' "cleansed" approach to the sun and the approach to major man in the imagination is impressive. In each it is the *center* which is sought: in the first, the "essential barrenness" of the sun, the major fact of physical being; in the second, the "nakedness" of the artist in his major fact of imaginative being. Beyond this correspondence lies the relationship existing between *ex-bar* and *in-bar*, dominant paths of energy, and the arc-in-air with its complementing arc-in-earth. We have said that it is the meeting of these arcs which makes "The roundness that pulls tight the final ring" ("A Primitive Like an Orb," *CP*, 442). The major poetry of Stevens moves constantly to the center. It may now be fully understood that his search in diction for radical forms and denotations bears an important relatedness to this movement. In principle, one does well to return to the perception of Randall Jarrell noted in the Introduction: "Setting out on Stevens for the first time would be like setting out to be an explorer of Earth."[2] It is Stevens' resolution upon freshness of sight which sets him apart from his major contemporaries in poetry. When this requirement of his mind and art has been understood, he will not be regarded as a poet of an eccentric remoteness. It is his adherence to his principle which has made him appear to some readers an artist of intentional obscurity.

The sun is the source of all life. This is the fact at the center of the physical. The symbol of Isamu Noguchi's recent sculpture for Yale University has been interpreted by the artist in the following note. "The landscape is purely that of the imagination. . . . Its size is fictive. . . . [The sun] is the source of all life, the life of everyman . . . the circle is zero, the decimal zero, or the zero of nothingness from which we come, to which we return."[3] This approach to the sun as subject matches in sculpture Stevens' approach in poetry. The paradox apparent in Noguchi's concept is to be found earlier in Stevens' expression: the sun is the source of the life of every man; it is also a zero-sign of nothingness, that nothingness from which we came and to which

[2] See above, p. xx.
[3] Noguchi's note (1965) comments on the sculpture garden that he created for the Beinecke Rare Book and Manuscript Library at Yale University. The text has been duplicated for distribution by the Beinecke Library.

we return. Stevens finds human existence a poverty of being as he regards the cosmos. The power of sight which we have rests in a physical being that came of an unyielding and absolute unknown. Yet his paradox holds, as he writes in "Esthétique du Mal": "The greatest poverty is not to live / In a physical world, to feel that one's desire / Is too difficult to tell from despair. . . . The adventurer / In humanity has not conceived of a race / Completely physical in a physical world" (*CP*, 325). Many years earlier he had asked of himself: ". . . What is there here but weather, what spirit / Have I except it comes from the sun?" ("Waving Adieu, Adieu, Adieu," *CP*, 128).

Thus it was the immediacy of physical being, the pressing necessity to see the world anew, that engaged him from his first commitment to poetry. Using one of his signs of the poet (hats, as in the *tricorn* "waved in pale adieu" at the close of "Things of August," in recollection of the eighteenth-century *décor* of *Harmonium*), he plays in amusement upon a theme of the academicians. In "Six Significant Landscapes" he turns to rationalists "wearing square hats," thinking in square rooms. "If they tried rhomboids, / Cones, waving lines, ellipses— / As, for example, the ellipse of the half-moon— / Rationalists would wear sombreros" (*CP*, 75). We note the difference between academic squareness and poetic curves and circles! These ardent rationalists are prototypes of Professor Eucalyptus in "An Ordinary Evening in New Haven." They refer, as well, to the befuddled old academician standing on the shores of the Pacific ("The Doctor of Geneva," *CP*, 24). "Lacustrine" man, the old doctor from the city on the lake, stamps the sand and tugs his shawl. He is assailed by the mighty ocean cadences. He searches for analogies: the rolling cadences of Racine or Bossuet? His "simmering mind" is set to "spinning and hissing with oracular / Notations of the wild, the ruinous waste. . . ." He uses his handkerchief and sighs.

As an early sketch for "The Comedian as the Letter C" the pathetic doctor of Geneva, incapable of a new metaphor, represents the European imagination on American shores. Abashed, he nonetheless knows what Crispin is later to tell us of the American *wild*: "Here was the veritable ding an sich, at last . . ." (*CP*, 29). At last, then, the raw reality of nature! I have digressed here upon the poet's sport with the academies, which reaches its most boisterous expression in "An Ordinary Evening in New Haven," with the intention of suggesting an ideal American freedom of meeting the *Ding an sich*. Whether or not the American imagination settled finally for the old "rationalism" of

Europe (as it does in the experience of Crispin), the fact remains
that for Stevens these American shores provided the advantageous
place for a civilized man's regard of raw nature. In "The Man with the
Blue Guitar" the doctor of Geneva is displaced by a symbol of the
nonacademic poet, "the old fantoche / Hanging his shawl upon the
wind . . ." (*CP*, 181); and in the rejected stanzas for the same poem
the sombrero belongs with the old *fantoche*, the hat cocked sunward by the poet as he strums the guitar at the gate of his reality, a
gate "not jasper," but "mud long baked in the sun" (*OP*, 72).

The coherence of sun imagery in Stevens must be studied in its
relationship to the human poverty named in this sun-baked mud. The
mud is the dirt of a contemporary reality, the failures of modern
society compounded with the facts of physical being. Certainly we do
not expect to find the poet's resolve upon a sunward gaze always
unshaken. The seasons pass with inexorable regularity, as the sun
ordains the fatal progression. In "Sunday Morning," a poem sun-
drenched to its center, the mood is one of rejoicing. "Shall she not
find in comforts of the sun, / In pungent fruit and bright green wings,
or else / In any balm or beauty of the earth, / Things to be cherished
like the thought of heaven?" (*CP*, 67). A new day of humanity is
proposed, some golden time of the future, when "Supple and turbulent, a ring of men / Shall chant in orgy on a summer morn /
Their boisterous devotion to the sun, / Not as a god, but as a god
might be, / Naked among them, like a savage source" (*CP*, 69–70).
Yet, in this same sequence enclosing this Sunday praise of physical
being, there comes the human cry from "The Man Whose Pharynx
Was Bad." The somber measure of time blocks the course of in-
spiriting power from air and light. There is the old "malady of the
quotidian." The seasons pass relentlessly over the rock. It is an appall-
ing strangulation. Summer days cannot be brought to rest "like oceans
in obsidian" (*CP*, 96). In yet another time of the poet's reflection
the endlessness of seasonal metamorphosis is borne with a shudder
as the autumn wind "spells out Sep-tem-ber," leads on "Oto-otu-bre"
and "Niz-nil-imbo," while the streets lamps dangle to and fro
("Metamorphosis," *CP*, 265–66). It is as though the strangulation of
the man of bad pharynx were merciless; the syllables break apart, pass
into nonsense, and then into the limbo of nothingness. *In-bar* sometimes fails; *ex-bar* wanes from the sun-drenched enclosure of summer
to this windy autumn suspension of life.

Yet the sun remains the source of man's existential courage. As it
rises, "Fears of my bed, / Fears of life and fears of death, / Run away"

(*CP*, 138). Once Adam woke in morning light, endowed with his first human power to make a metaphor of the world, "While all the leaves leaked gold" (*CP*, 331). His was the first human experience with the sun. But it was he who malformed the metaphor. The world malformed became paradise malformed. We may assume that with the myth of Adam's fall Judaeo-Christian man was forever to be denied the freedom of a self-wrought metaphor. The objective of human life became, in this tradition, bondage to an imagined state of existence *beyond life*. Now, far into history, we say that "the solar chariot is junk" (*CP*, 332). This saying, Stevens reminds us, is not a variation upon sun-myth, but an end of myth. (And we acknowledge, in this sense, that the myth now dead was itself foreign to the Judaeo-Christian theocentrism that began with Adam.) But the possibility of man in a world-as-metaphor remains. He has a power of shaping his world when he continues "to stick to the contents of the mind / And the desire to believe in a metaphor . . ." (*CP*, 332). The sun inspires him; the self derives from the sun a strength to believe in its metaphor of the world, a metaphor of the untrue, and yet a defiance of the reality of self-nothingness in the universe.

The island of Delos, consecrated to Apollo in his attribute as Helios, may stir the imagination of the sentimental primitivist. An aesthetic account of Jacquetta Hawkes comes very near proposing a modern primitivism of sun-worship, as this English interpreter of cosmic physics writes: "Then, as in the light of its rays, mind flowered in man, our kind looked up at the sun, were intuitively aware of its creative might and their utter dependence upon it and saw it to be bright with divinity."[4] Adoration such as this no doubt inspired the monuments of Delos. Although we will not deny that modern man retains his sense of wonder at this source of physical power, we do not find that the cult of Delos, or Zuni myth,[5] or any other archmetaphor of cultural history will serve him. I have earlier disclaimed for Stevens any form of primitivism. The only primitive states of being which engage him are those of the *center* defined in *in-bar* and *ex-bar*. It is man's science which prohibits a resurgence of a sun-myth. Stevens fully accepts this fact, even in the vision of "Sunday Morning," as he predicts some future "boisterous devotion to the sun, / Not as a god,

[4] *Man and the Sun* (New York, 1962), p. 6.
[5] See Mircea Eliade, *Myths, Dreams and Mysteries*, p. 159.

but as a god might be . . ." (*CP*, 70). The vision proposes a sun without divine attributes, but a sun as the center of wonder in a physical reality. Certainly it is this second sense which appears in his late meditation in "An Ordinary Evening in New Haven." "Of what is this house composed if not of the sun," he asks. "A recent imagining of reality," he continues, is "Much like a new resemblance of the sun. . . ." In the same poem he observes: "The sun is half the world, half everything, / The bodiless half. There is always this bodiless half, / This illumination, this elevation . . ." (*CP*, 465, 481). The tribute is directed to the power of imagining and the power of structure as these spring from the supreme power of the sun. But the tribute stops there. The identification of *in-bar* with *ex-bar* has nothing to do with ascriptions to divinity or impositions of an anthropomorphic self upon this chiefest phenomenon. Helios was once its name. But the gods imagined by men no longer flank it as keepers of its radiance.

For it is Stevens as a modern man who writes the tale of ultimate sun-disaster. In the total range of American expression in this century there is perhaps no poem approximating his "Page from a Tale" (*CP*, 421–23). If modern man has no kinship with Delos or any other sun-altar, his thought of the sun is no less awesome: he possesses modern physics. This late poem of Stevens' is compelled by twentieth-century science. It is strange that its apocalyptic vision has been so little noticed. Here is an imagery which blazes with awesome force. Mr. Riddel regards the poem as a personal disclosure, Stevens in "the winter of his discontent."[6] To a degree it is, but only in very small part. It is a masquelike projection of the end of man. The poem opens as a dream. Hans, the *persona* of the poet, huddles by his drift-fire on the shore of a frozen sea. The sea "has no accurate syllables." But the wind cries in speech. Its first syllables are fragments of a German refrain, *so blau, so lind, und so lau*; its next are phrases from "The Lake Isle of Innisfree" by Yeats. The broken poetic voices that the dreamer hears, as though in the far edges of memory, stammer through his own voice of the wintry vision. They mock him: *so blue, so soft, and so warm, Of clay and wattles made, in the deep heart's core, And a small cabin build there, And live alone in the bee-loud glade.* Nearby the great ship Balayne lies frozen in the sea. Huge stars look down at Hans "with savage faces" through the cold. It is of death that the dreamer dreams, both his own poet's death and the death of man. This turning downward is not a turning to blueness,

[6] *The Clairvoyant Eye*, p. 235.

softness, warmth. This is not the solitude of the deep heart's core, the last honey in a glade of bees. It is ice. It is a cold, "like a sleep."

Now the fitful roamings between wakefulness and sleep disappear. Hans lies awake. Visions of an apocalypse begin to rise. The transition from dream to vision appears in the dawn hour of the next day, when the men on the ship will walk the ice to shore, "afraid of the sun." The ice will gasp, "As if whatever in water strove to speak / Broke dialect in a break of memory." It is the fear of a sinister sun which obliterates the memory of a poetic promise, the turning downward of a life to the serenity of age. The poet leaves Hans and the "personal disclosure"; the broken words and phrases from poetic memory disappear.

A vision opens in wakefulness. It is peopled with men from the ice-bound ship. The sun *might rise* upon them, "ashen and red and yellow, each / Opaque, in orange circlet, nearer than it / Had ever been before, no longer known, / No more that which most of all brings back the known. . . ." This is "a motion not in the astronomies." "[A]narchic shape / Afire—it might and it might not in that / Gothic blue, speed home its portents to their ends." Or this sun *might become* "a wheel spoked red and white . . . with a second wheel below, / Just rising, accompanying, arranged to cross, / Through weltering illuminations, humps / Of billows, downward, toward the drift-fire shore." It might come in this form "bearing, out of chaos, kin / Smeared, smoked, and drunken of thin potencies, / Lashing at images in the atmosphere, / Ringed round and barred, with eyes held in their hands, / And capable of incapably evil thought." These *kin* of humankind think of "Slight gestures that could rend the palpable ice, / Or melt Arcturus to ingots dropping drops, / Or spill night out in brilliant vanishings, / Whirlpools of darkness in whirlwinds of light. . . ." The wind of change blows in these "vocables."

The dream comes in the winter of a poet. But it is overlaid with a dream of a world of ice. When the sun appears, it is a sun unknown, in "a motion not in the astronomies." It is an "anarchic shape," portentous with a "Gothic blue." *Or* it is a spoked wheel, with a second "wheel" rising and crossing in "weltering illuminations," humps of billows moving downward. Men come with it, out of chaos, "drunken of thin potencies," "holding their eyes in their hands," and "capable of incapably evil thought." They possess the power of "slight gestures" that could rend the ice or melt Arcturus.

The field of ice, the poet on the shore beside the drift-fire, and the helpless ship compose a scene of polar whiteness. Stars of the polar night and the sun of a polar dawn are unfamiliar presences in this waste. They threaten with unnamable portents. It is as though the poet looked upon the ice field of an explorer's ultimate North, as though he stood upon the very tip of the earth's axis. In this unaccustomed atmosphere, he knows a hugeness of stars and a sun luminous in colors never seen in the temperate zones of human habitation. The solitary song of the poet, fractured into "glassily-sparkling particles of the mind," ceases. The symbolic import is relentless: the ice field, the ship and its men, are figures of a total cessation of artistic power in the imaginative life of humanity. The one supreme faculty of man is locked in ice. The song of the last poet shatters upon the cold. Fear is the one emotion of the dawn, when a sun unknown appears in this polar light, nearer than it had ever been before, beyond the habit of man's sense, in a shape of anarchy. There is a break in the human memory of the sun. Stevens is using in this first vision a common fact of visual perception at the explorer's pole: the stars appear in a largeness and brilliance hitherto unknown; the sun seems to approach the earth in a spectrum of an exaggerated strangeness.

The second vision opens upon a man-induced sun action. As the imagery advances, a scene of atomic holocaust appears. The unaccustomed polar sun "might become a wheel spoked red and white."[7] A lower wheel rises and crosses the upper. Billows move downward, "toward the drift-fire shore" of the poet. Out of this chaos appear these "kin" of humankind who "lash at images in the atmosphere . . . eyes held in their hands." These are the makers of *incapably evil thought*. They are the ones of "slight gestures" capable of rending the ice, of spilling night out "in brilliant vanishings." The image of the eyes in the hands must be understood through another of Stevens' poems, "Arcades of Philadelphia the Past" (*CP*, 225). In that city there are men who hold "their eyes in their hands." As I shall show in a following chapter, they are men who refuse to see the reality of the present world. With them, the imagination is "closed." The use of this image in "Page from a Tale" extends the force of metaphor to the extreme: a world beyond the endurance of human sight. We find again the poet's obsession with the sun-center. The sun-derived power of those "capable of incapably evil thought" leads on the end of man. What is more deadly than the imagination put to an evil use? The vision of "Page from a Tale" poses the extremes of *ex-bar* and *in-bar* at their farthest limits.

[7] For a scientist's reading of the imagery of this poem I am indebted to Professor Bernice Wheeler of Connecticut College.

Because of the excessive difficulty of this poem, a brief résumé of the total vision seems desirable. It is a page *from a tale of man*. With bitter irony Stevens dreams of ice-locked man at the point of his atomic decimation. This is the last degree of human poverty. In a human time when the imagination, which makes life endurable, is immobile in a frozen waste of being, the poet, whoever he is, knows a final perdition of the cold with the men on the ship. The sun that in its familiar presence once measured human life and nourished the life of the imagination is now a sun unknown. It is unknown, threatening, sinister, because man has put his imagination to a totally evil use. He has *imagined* and invented a sun-action that is his doom. His potencies are "thin" in prospect of both his own nothingness in the universe and his inability to foresee imaginatively the death that he has decreed for himself. Survivors of the chaos are alert for a "tidal undulation" beneath the ice as the poem closes. But the tide, we infer, is not the coming on of another age of man.

The strictness of Stevens with sun-metaphor appears in two final examples. He thinks of orbital motion as he writes in "Credences of Summer" of the tower on the final mountain: "It is the natural tower of all the world, / The point of survey, green's green apogee . . ." (*CP*, 373). He names the vantage point from his poet's structure, the point of surveying the world, the point made of the green potential of reality in a green (and singular) *apogee*. The tower is imagined as the poet's point *in orbit* at the greatest distance from the earth. Gravity as physical law enters the metaphor. "Here the sun, / Sleepless, inhales his proper air, and rests." The poet's work, as a totality like the earth itself, his sphere created by his hand, is imagined to move in orbit. It remains earth-bound through gravity. Yet the apogee takes it farthest from earth, and places it in a universal motion governed by the burning star at the center of the system. In the same manner of scientific reference is his notice of a *high poetry* and a *low poetry* in the retrospective summary of "Things of August." High poetry is "Experience in perihelion"; low poetry is experience "in the penumbra of summer night—" (*CP*, 490). The orbital motion is repeated, this time with the image of the *perihelion* as the point nearest the sun. Thus high poetry aspires to the central sun-radiance. The *penumbra,* as the eclipse-shadow, qualifies the low. The radiance is there but is diffused in paleness around the dark disk obliterating the center.

A last account of the sun appears at the close of the *Collected Poems*. "The Planet on the Table" has already been noted in another context. The total book lies here before its maker.

His self and the sun were one
And his poems, although makings of his self,
Were no less makings of the sun.

It was not important that they survive.
What mattered was that they should bear
Some lineament or character,

Some affluence, if only half-perceived,
In the poverty of their words,
Of the planet of which they were part.[8]

[*CP*, 532–33]

The completed sphere is his, a roundness of makings of the self, makings of the sun. This poetry was made of the stuff of earth, seen in the light bathing earth and poet. The arc-line of the self is joined to the arc-line of knowledge penetrating physical reality. This knowledge, insofar as it was gained from the illumination and the life-giving properties of the sun, is knowledge from *ex-bar*. Two areas within the elements of the poet's sight remain for definition: light as the major attribute of the sun, and the perceiving eye. The half-sphere of the poet's *in-bar*, the dome of his own making, lies beyond.

[8] Cf. Richard Ellmann, in his "Wallace Stevens' Ice-Cream," *The Kenyon Review,* XIX, No. 1 (Winter, 1957), 103. Mr. Ellmann writes of this poem: "In the individual person, the self, as Stevens says in 'The Plant [sic] on the Table,' is the sun. This self should be dominated by the imagination, a solar light within the mind."

Light

7

"THE ACUTE INTELLIGENCE OF THE IMAGINATION, THE illimitable resources of its memory, its power to possess the moment it perceives—if we were speaking of light itself, and thinking of the relationship between objects and light, no further demonstration would be necessary. Like light, it adds nothing, except itself. What light requires a day to do, and by a day I mean a kind of Biblical revolution of time, the imagination does in the twinkling of an eye. It colors, increases, brings to a beginning and end, invents languages, crushes men and, for that matter, gods in its hands" (*NA*, 61–62). This observation of 1943 comes from Stevens' lecture-essay "The Figure of the Youth as Virile Poet." Within the definitions of the preceding discussion, light and the imagination are posed as *ex-bar* and *in-bar*. One finds in the contention of this statement Stevens' sharp divergence from a purely scientific concern with light. *Light adds nothing except itself.* The reference is clearly to physical process. When the biblical revolution in time appears, we are reminded of the process in terms of an indefinite temporality. It would be interesting to know whether Stevens thought here of the velocity of light reaching

119

the earth from distant bodies, or of photosynthesis[1] as process in the spontaneous generation of life. Sources from his thought, as yet unpublished, may define his interest in contemporary theories. But the power of the human mind in its encounter with light is clearly the subject of the reflection from the essay. With the knowledge of Stevens' scientific thought which we now have, it appears certain, however, that his poetic concern with light did not vary. He preferred to regard it exclusively as the phenomenon that illuminates. It is held in simplistic definition. The relationship between light and object amounts to direct flow, whether in the brilliance of an un-clouded summer day or in the diffusion of seasonal "darkenings." The alteration of the relationship is the work of the imagination, "its power to possess the moment it perceives." It adds nothing to reality save itself. Thus a measurement of *ex-bar* is not the objective. It is the stimulus of light to *in-bar* which engages Stevens.

By this simplistic acceptance of light as a constant of reality and by the elevation of the imagination as the faculty capable of varying the appearances of phenomena in the act of seeing, Stevens takes his position with the aesthetics of painting. I reserve a full considera-tion of this position for a later chapter. For the present it is sufficient to note that in Stevens' theory the imagination *colors* and *increases*. The physical particulars of the rock of being are seen as light identi-fies them; but thereafter perception possesses the object in the moment of seeing as the imagination directs. "A poem is a meteor . . . Poetry is a pheasant disappearing in the brush," Stevens notes in the "Adagia" (*OP*, 158, 173). Again, "The poem is the cry of its occa-sion . . ." ("An Ordinary Evening in New Haven," *CP*, 473). In the swiftness of perception light is the constant; the impression seized by the imagination is the variable. The expression proceeding from the imagination through the fixed form of the work captures momen-tariness. The streaking meteor is exact as an image for Stevens; so is the darting pheasant. A poem is light momentarily encountered, and put to the uses of the artist's will. The variable plunders the constant, and rushes off with its prize. One thinks of the bird "that pecks at the sun for food" ("Esthétique du Mal," *CP*, 318).

[1] A clear statement of modern theory with respect to photosynthesis in primitive organisms may be found in George Wald, "The Origin of Life," *Scientific Ameri-can*, Vol. 191, No. 2 (August, 1954), pp. 45–53: "Living organisms no longer needed to depend upon the accumulation of organic matter from past ages; they could make their own. With the energy of sunlight they could accomplish the fundamental organic syntheses that provide their substance, and by fermenta-tion they could produce what energy they needed" (p. 52).

The meeting of light and the imagination is described in the poem "Tattoo" (*CP*, 81). With characteristic precision the poet organizes the encounter in three stages. A process of "tattooing," image-building, is the subject.

The light is like a spider.
It crawls over the water.
It crawls over the edges of the snow.
It crawls under your eyelids
And spreads its webs there—
Its two webs.

The webs of your eyes
Are fastened
To the flesh and bones of you
As to rafters or grass.

There are filaments of your eyes
On the surface of the water
And in the edges of the snow.

In this metaphysical poem the webs are studied at three points. The two webs spun by the light are, first, the field of illumination spreading upon objects extending outward from the stance of the perceiver, and second, the stimulus of the light upon the perceiver's eyes. The webs of the eyes are unnamed in number. They are as multifarious as the imagination of the perceiver may order. But, whatever their number, they are the webs of the perceiver alone, spun in the self across flesh and bone. These webs, in the individual's act of response to light, are then the evidence of singular vision cast upon the objects over which the first web of the light is thrown. Thus the imposition of the light-web for design, a design colored in the manner of a tattoo, takes place in countermotion. First, the light "catches" the objects illuminated; second, it "catches" the eye of the perceiver. At the moment of this "captured" sight, the webs of the eyes "capture" the objects revealed by the light. Two inferences seem permissible. This light of *ex-bar* is constant in its two webs; the imagination of the perceiver is variable, *in-bar* in the design that it will choose to cast upon the scene. In the second place, the color of the tattoo in the webs of light remains constant; the color to be ordered by the eye is imposed as the observer wills. Notice of the motion implied in the opening and closing lines is important. The web of light spreads *over* water and snow; but the filaments of the eyes are *on the surface* of the water and *in* the edges of the snow. The conclusion is that the filaments of the perceiver *possess* the objects. The constant of light is exploited.

It need not be stressed that this is light reduced to its serviceableness to man. Once again the poet's humanism is underscored. We think of another encounter with light in human history. It evoked the images of the angels. "Why seraphim like lutanists arranged / Above the trees? And why the poet as / Eternal *chef d'orchestre?*" Here, in "Evening without Angels," thought travels back to a human time of less than man-centered men. "And light / That fosters seraphim and is to them / Coiffeur of haloes, fecund jeweller— / Was the sun concoct for angels or for men?" (*CP*, 136–37.) Angels divest men of their humanity. Above the trees is the imagined glitter of heaven. But we are here on earth as ourselves. "Light, too, encrusts us making visible / The motions of the mind and giving form / To moodiest nothings . . ." (*CP*, 137). This "encrusting" of us relates to the tattoo of the light webs. We are provided with the sight of objects. Yet here, in this evening "without angels," with only men, it is *as if* the sun and light existed for us alone. However much it may be of the unreal and the untrue, the assumption is a good. We live as if the bright angels of an earlier time had been transmuted. We have become them. In this vital assumption the capacity for delight rests.

"Tattoo" is Stevens' first theoretical poem of the meeting of light and imagination. A second follows in "The Glass of Water." In the center of the field of vision stands the glass. "Light / Is the lion that comes down to drink." The glass becomes a pool. "Ruddy are his eyes and ruddy are his claws / When light comes down to wet his frothy jaws. . . ." In the water, winding weeds appear to move; ". . . and in another state—the refractions, / The *metaphysica*, the plastic parts of poems / Crash in the mind. . . ." But the poet worries about the center of human life in this time, this day, this state "among the politicians playing cards" (*CP*, 197–98). The poem falls into three scenes: light strikes the glass and invades the water; the imagination seizes the object and converts it to a jungle pool with moving water weeds; the poet finds his purpose with these "plastic parts of poems" threatened as the demands of the real world, a state imperiled by a politicians' card game, intrude. Nonetheless, "One would continue to contend with one's ideas." The first thing to notice, proceeding from the last scene first, is that the wakeful imagination does not wait upon occasions. Light being the constant, the imagination, as in the second scene, may be spurred to activity at any time and by wholly unpredictable properties in a chance arrangement of objects. The symbol of light as the constant, to return to the first scene, is a lion of fierceness. Recalling the metaphor already cited from "The Man with the Blue Guitar," we confront here again ". . . the lion in the lute / Before the lion locked in stone" (*CP*, 175). The first beast is the poet's imagination, the second, the energy of physical reality. The utter commonplaceness of the glass of water is deliberately chosen. It reveals a characteristic discipline of Stevens' like that seen in the strict imagery of "Tattoo." Here is a microcosm of a prosaic world, waiting for the invasion of light and the answering jungle-spring of the imagination. Yet one finds the "drag" of the prosaic, the evil and the vitiating, in what one lives of necessity in his "village of the indigenes" (*CP*, 198.)[2] Between the village and the *metaphysica* that crash in the mind there is a tension of the artist. Yet light is with him everywhere. Its challenge is constant.

The going downward to the rock displays in the late poetry, as one might expect, a careful modulation in imagery. In "The Auroras of Autumn" the theater of life, floating through the clouds, itself made of a cloud, is transformed to cloud again, "the way / A season changes color to no end . . . / As light changes yellow into gold and gold / To its opal elements and fire's delight" (*CP*, 416). The seasons, as light governed them, are reviewed. The poet stands in prospect of the last season, as the streaks of the aurora flicker in the "peak" of night. Near the close of the last lyric sequence the plain style of "Lebensweisheitspielerei" speaks as a pianistic reverie musing on the "wisdom play" of life. "Weaker and weaker, the sunlight falls / In the afternoon." There is "an indigence of the light, / A stellar pallor that hangs on the threads" (*CP*, 504–5). It is not the light of *ex-bar* which fails. It is perception that weakens. There is no self-quotation in the late poetry of deeper quietude or farther range. The "threads" return to the "arching cloths," radiant in spring, of "The Plot Against the Giant" (*CP*, 6–7). "The threads / will abash him." Even the pianistic title seems to reflect upon the vigor of "Peter Quince at the Clavier" (*CP*, 89ff.). The last poverty is this waning of *in-bar*. The human power to exploit the webs of light stirs weakly as the final music is composed.

---

2 Cf. David H. Owen, " 'The Glass of Water,' " *Perspective*, Vol. 7. No. 3 (1954), pp. 181–82: " 'Light' [is] the imagination." "But the pool, the water itself, calms the lion, and the synthesis of imagination and fact, while including the evil aspects, can itself be a thing of beauty." Mr. Owen thinks of the lyric preceding "The Glass of Water" under the title "Poetry Is a Destructive Force" (*CP*, 192–93). The man in the poem feels "A lion, an ox in his breast." "It can kill a man."

The pallor of this late autumn was prophesied long before its reality was known. Thus the muted tercets and quatrains of "Like Decorations in a Nigger Cemetery" establish the design of the imagination's flickering. Some twenty years will intervene. I have earlier directed attention to the title. The "decorations" appear in the short bleak stanzas, succeeding in a somber file and numerically ordered as for distribution among graves. The qualification of the cemetery names the Americanness of the poet's experience as an American "dark" of central man. Now it is "a calm November" (*CP*, 156). The poem has opened with the image of the enduring sun, in its burning vitality a seeming mockery of Walt Whitman on the "ruddy shore." Save for a few lingering images of late autumn fruits and the odor of chrysanthemums, the decorations are austere: leaden pigeons, ice on the river, dry grasses. In this season of barrenness, the sun endures; but it is a sun unchallenged by the imagination of *in-bar*. "The sun is seeking something bright to shine on. / The trees are wooden, the grass is yellow and thin. / The ponds are not the surfaces it seeks. / It must create its colours out of itself" (*CP*,157–58). This faculty of "creating the colors" is the major subject of the poem. Thus the sun, unmatched by the faculty of the imagination, makes the colors "of itself." The image bends toward the poet's theory: Color as experienced by the human eye is determined through perception by the imagination working upon sun-illuminated surfaces. Color, as possessed by the individual, is made of the self in its encounter with phenomena.

It then appears that Stevens will not fully accept any scientific theory which argues for a primacy of the sun-process as the determinant of mutations in color. Such a theory may be seen in this summary statement of Jacquetta Hawkes. "Colors as we see them come from the different wave lengths of the solar radiation, which in turn come from the different elements burning in the sun's furnace. But how our eyes convey them to the brain, so that they can be used for road signals, exploited for advertisements, brilliantly employed for imaginative effects in painting, remains almost completely unknown to the brains that respond to them with such exactitude. Almost certainly it is a combination of structure (the rods and cones of the retina) and wave length—sensitive chemicals comparable to visual purple but not yet discovered in spite of most patient search."[3] This combination of eye structure and wave length as the determinant of a visual

[3] *Man and the Sun,* p. 43.

purple excludes the power of imagination as an element in sight. For Stevens there is no question of the physical reality of the spectrum. Yet it cannot follow that the qualities of each color in the spectrum will be identically perceived by several individuals examining the same object. The theory of Stevens approximates that of Guillaume Apollinaire in his manifesto for the cubist painters. He notes first the constancy of light and the power of the artist-perceiver to alter the forms illuminated: "All bodies stand equal before light, and their modifications are determined by this dazzling power, which molds them all according to its will." He proceeds with a contention for an equal power of the perceiver to *confer* color. "We do not know all the colors. Each of us invents new ones."[4] Again, in his constant concern with movement in perception, Stevens shows an unquestionable correspondence with the theory of Robert Delaunay, who advances in his essay "La Lumière" a principle for the painter. "Light in nature creates the movement of colors. Movement is conferred by relationships . . . of contracts of colors among themselves which [together] constitute *Reality*. This reality is established by *Depth* [of perception]. . . . The simultaneity in light is *harmony, the rhythm of colors* which creates the *Vision of Men*."[5] This *depth* in the exploration of the reality opened through light corresponds to the penetrating power of the singular imagination.

In the theory of Stevens both the imposition of color by the imagination and the perception of movement *within* light are sovereign. In the late poem "The Green Plant," the evidence of this primacy of human vision is wholly persuasive. Once again the waning imagination is examined: "The effete vocabulary of summer / No longer says anything. / The brown at the bottom of red / The orange far down in yellow, / Are falsifications from a sun / In a mirror, without heat / In a constant secondariness, / A turning down toward finality—" But outside this "legend" of the poet there is a green plant that "glares" with "the barbarous green / Of the harsh reality of which it is part" (*CP*, 506). The power of the imagination to invent the colors as variants of red and yellow is described in the disintegration to a "final" brown and orange. The movement of light in its nature as an inner relationship of "barbarous" or real colors and colors conferred

4 *The Cubist Painters: Aesthetic Meditations,* trans. Lionel Abel, Documents of Modern Art (New York, 1944), p. 9.
5 *Du Cubisme à l'Art Abstrait,* Documents inédits publiés par Pierre Francastel (Paris, 1957). The essay was written in 1912. In the following year it was translated into German and published by Paul Klee.

by the imagination reaches its end. There is the "turning down toward finality." The vision of one man approaches its end. Yet the reality of primary green endures in the constant light of the "harsh reality." The poem restates the interaction of *in-bar* and *ex-bar*. It is the governance of color by the singular perceiver which is both celebrated and relinquished.

It should be clearly understood that the theory of color here examined is not related to a color-symbolism. Stevens' unique signs of the poet's ritual are too well known to require more than momentary summary here. They may be designated as follows: blue signaling acts of imagination; green representing primitive potentiality or vitality in nature; yellow designating the vital light of the sun; red indicating bloodedness or emotion; gold memorializing the achievement of art; bronze invoking antiquity; purple establishing an act of ceremony and rite. The process of the poetry is frequently plotted with these symbols. The presence of one or another will be encountered as an announcement of the "key" of the work, as though the idiom of music had been transformed into a major scale for the imagination. But it is within the key-symbol that the mutations of color ordained and imposed by the imagination will be found to flourish. The difference between the key and the imaginative experience with color appears in "The Green Plant." The symbol is established in the title and reasserted in the last line: the poem returns to the artist's familiar encounter with primitive reality, the "enduring" green upon which every colorist, whether painter or poet, works.

Very probably the theory of Santayana appears again in Stevens' judgment of the genesis of color. In *The Sense of Beauty* Santayana wrote: "The values of colours differ appreciably and have analogy to the differing values of other sensations." He found these values peculiar to the individual perceiver: "There is a nervous process for each, and consequently a specific value."[6] Such an attention to the *nervous process* appears, at any rate, to govern the description of perception in "Bouquet of Roses in Sunlight." This poem, one of the most "painterly" in the entire range of Stevens, proceeds first to establish the object. "Say that it is a crude effect, black reds, / Pink yellows, orange whites, too much as they are / To be anything else in the sunlight of the room. . . ." Illuminated, sun-drenched, the roses seem to be "too much as they are to be changed by metaphor." "And yet," as we look, "this effect is a consequence of the way / We feel

6 The New York edition of 1896, p. 74.

and, therefore, is not real, except / In our sense of it, our sense of the fertilest red. . . ." We search for metaphor, realizing that the initial "effect" which we have just examined is literally made of the way we *feel*. But even metaphor is inadequate. "So sense exceeds all metaphor. / It exceeds the heavy changes of the light. / It is like a flow of meanings with no speech / And of as many meanings as of men" (*CP*, 430–31). This *sense* names the observer's experience with color, as the light changes, and the quality of a room dominated by roses remains variable. Metaphor is inadequate. The "flow of meanings" is the flow of color, as the imagination confers its singular vision upon the object. This is process, *in-bar* flourishing as the stream of sense continues. There is no reason, then, to question Stevens' relationship to impressionism. Metaphor, whether of poet or painter, seizes a moment from the flow and preserves it, in colors that the imagination knows and yet constantly alters through the metamorphosis of sense.

Recent studies of color perception at Harvard and Johns Hopkins have established that the cones of the human eye contain pigments sensitive to three prime colors. The peak sensitivities of the cones lie at three different wave lengths: in the blue-violet, the green, and the yellow parts of the spectrum. It is not my intention here to review the intricacies of scientific theory. But these recent findings extend the authority of earlier laboratory investigations: two prime colors turned upon the eye by controlled juxtaposition effect an organization of perception in which "new" colors are seen in addition to the "planted" ones. The use of three sources will produce in perception a full array of colors. Three sets of cones are thus the receivers of primary color-stimuli from light. Colors arising in individual perception from "blending" the primary sources are, then, imposed colors.[7] The scientists reporting these recent findings are primarily interested in physics. One must await definitive contributions from psychology which will establish that the mutations of color in perception are attributable in an immeasurable series to individual differences in the imaginative complement. Yet these scientific demonstrations have not been necessary to the theory and practice of recent painting. It has been known, since the experiments of European artists active during the rise of cubism, that a deliberate fitting together of two colors

---

[7] See Walter Sullivan, "How the Eye Sees," *New York Times,* April 12, 1964, Sec. E, p. 7. The Harvard research was conducted by George Wald and Paul K. Brown, that at Johns Hopkins by Edward F. MacNichol, Jr., William Marks, and William Dobelle.

of primary value will produce a perceptual illusion of other colors along the line of demarcation and extending into the primary field of each adjacent color. The current work of Josef Albers, in accordance with this principle, is a refinement of theory extended to its present limits in abstraction.

These notices of recent inquiry into the nature of color perception seem peculiarly suited to an examination of color in the theory of Stevens. One concludes that the insistence of Apollinaire upon the invention of new colors by each perceiver is of serious importance in the poetic antecedence of Stevens. On the other hand, it is fortuitous that contemporary science offers a means of factual support for Stevens' understanding of the unique sight that colors the world. His poet's theory of the imagination in its faculty of making color seems considerably authenticated in the proof of recent scientific experimentation.

The Eye

8

"SIGHT," WROTE SANTAYANA, "IS A METHOD OF presenting psychically what is practically absent; and as the essence of the *thing* is its existence in our absence, the *thing* is spontaneously conceived in terms of sight."[1] Stevens appears to be very close to this assertion when he reflects in "Poem Written at Morning," "The truth must be / That you do not see, you experience, you feel, / That the buxom eye brings merely its element / To the total thing, a shapeless giant forced / Upward" (*CP*, 219). It is this element of the eye which achieves an experience of seeing in conjunction with the elements of sun and light. The "practically absent" in Santayana's judgment is the essence of the thing-as-it-is. Its existence is not dependent upon us. But as a thing significant to us it derives its quality of being from our conception of it. The "shapeless giant forced upward" in Stevens' poem is the total thing-as-it-is. Yet it will remain shapeless if eye-*seeing* alone is the end of process. The buxom eye is merely the physical eye impressed with the shape of the object encountered. The object is not fully experienced in sight until the mind has conceived it spontaneously *as it is seen*.

[1] *The Sense of Beauty* (New York, 1896), p. 73.

Thus the eye in the theory of Stevens is not defined until one has examined the process behind the image physically received. "What We See Is What We Think," he entitles a late poem.

Cézanne conceived of painting as an art expressing itself "by means of drawing and colour . . . [giving] concrete shape to sensations and perceptions."[2] If a method of *seeing* in painting can be matched by a method of *seeing* in poetry, then Stevens is an exceptional maker of the equation. His notes on the eye in the "Adagia" support his relatedness to the painter: "The tongue is an eye. . . . The eye sees less than the tongue says. The tongue says less than the mind thinks" (*OP*, 167, 170). The spontaneous method of the mind, in Santayana's doctrine, is the act of presenting psychically what is absent. Cézanne intended to designate in the psychic content of concrete shape that full sight which possesses the object. Stevens intended the same. Language as the poet's medium expands the significance of the object. Yet the linguistic form does not use the whole psychic potential. The eye is the opening upon physical reality. The image that it presents must fall upon those inside webs strung across flesh and bone. There, in the psychic life, the inner sight becomes too copious for full use.

I propose here a brief inquiry into the process back of the eye, as Stevens conceived it. One of his most engaging comic expressions appears in "Arcades of Philadelphia the Past." The poem lies at some distance from the explicit theory of "Tattoo." Stevens has by no means forgotten the webs of the spider, light. But in old main-line Philadelphia there are no light-spiders. There are only real spiders, their dusty webs festooning a habitation of human beings blind in the midst of life. These eyes are disembodied! "Only the rich remember the past, / The strawberries once in the Apennines, / Philadelphia that the spiders ate. / There they sit, holding their eyes in their hands." These rich, who do not touch the things they see about them, even in a time of lilac bloom, "red blue, red purple," "polish their eyes in their hands." They must be very poor, the poet says, poor with a single sense, to have only a "Vallombrosa of ears," and visions of the Apennines (*CP*, 225–26). The *arcades* of the title represent imaginative structures. What are these memorials? Clearly they are useless structures fashioned of journeys abroad, as though to see and to hear, to taste and to touch Italy were the only experiences worthy of perception.

[2] Rewald edition of the *Letters*, p. 237. Cézanne here addresses Emile Bernard, Aix, May 26, 1904.

This poem is engaging in a number of ways. Clearly it relates to Stevens' insistence upon the American experience, the looking at the reality of one's land and time and place. It proposes rich old Philadelphians as makers of a nicely "classic" architecture of the imagination. It celebrates the here and now of Philadelphia which is not seen. But with memorable humor the whole poem turns upon the real spider, the symbol of dusty neglect. His kind ate Philadelphia. Because there was no seeing of Philadelphia as it is, a fullness of sight by the act and the devotion of mind, the invading light-spider, symbol of a vital seeing, was ignored. Eyes that were once capable of full sight are held in the hands of these sentimental voyagers to old Europe; and there they are polished, as one polishes the pictures of the mountains of his journey.

One pauses to think of the humor with which Stevens must have looked upon every manifestation of the American nostalgia for European scenery, of every aptitude for the sentimental journey, of every ostentatious importation of Florentine or Venetian architectural design for American "baronial" mansions along the avenues of the wealthy. These are American evidences of American sight unused. For there can be no seeing of one's reality of place without the mind back of the eye. The eyes polished in the hands of Philadelphians of the *haut monde* may be the eyes once "polished" in New York and Newport. The poet's attention to the "arcades" of Philadelphia gives us a boisterous poem; its exuberance recalls "The Comedian as the Letter C" and "Blue Buildings in the Summer Air," the latter with its antics at the expense of Cotton Mather and "wooden Boston." Yet the failure to *see* is a misuse of life. It is both strange and awesome that the only other use of this image of eyes-in-hands in Stevens' poetry occurs in "Page from a Tale." These unseeing destroyers of the world are incapable of perceiving the reality about them, but, more specifically, they are incapable of the *idea* of the destruction that they induce.

If the tongue is an eye, it is the expansion of sight to the point of possessing the object that engages the poet. We have seen that the imagination colors. So do words, in their power of establishing associations, color. "We make. . . . Variations on the words spread sail" ("Things of August," *CP*, 490). In "Variations on a Summer Day" the poet uses the images assailing the eye at Pemaquid on the Maine coast as points of articulation. As the eye shifts from object to object, the "variations" on the day extend. Midway in this musical process he pauses. "Words add to the senses. The words for the dazzle / Of mica, the dithering of grass / The Arachne integument of dead trees, / Are the eye grown larger, more intense" (*CP*, 234). But it is summer, and the imagination roams at will. In winter whiteness, when the glitter of the January sun on snow is the only object of encounter, when American ("nigger") central man has no sustenance ("No Possum, No Sop, No Taters"), the poet can choose only to join the detested winter crow. Words seem frozen. "Snow sparkles like eyesight falling to earth" (*CP*, 294).

We come into this life "like rhetoric in a narration of the eye" ("The Pure Good of Theory," *CP*, 331). It is the "rhetorician," the maker of metaphor, that Stevens thinks of again in "The Red Fern": "Infant, it is enough in life / To speak of what you see. But wait / Until sight wakens the sleepy eye / And pierces the physical fix of things" (*CP*, 365). These are affirmations of mind dominating the physical, certainly. The first plays again upon the theme of the tongue as an eye. The second advances the primacy of sight in the mind, which awakens the eye. Thus it is, as we find the poet's theory in "Crude Foyer," that mind is genetic in the power of sight: ". . . we know that we use / Only the eye as faculty, that the mind / Is the eye, and that this landscape of the mind / Is a landscape only of the eye" (*CP*, 305). If mind is the eye, then the landscape known by the mind is of its own making. The faculty admitting light and the images of the physical world is secondary. Thus it follows that Stevens will not assume any obligation to an art of representation. The mind will exert its choices and organize its landscape without obligation to exterior truth. This conclusion may seem to imply the possibility of fantasy in the poetry of Stevens. It does not, since the metaphor originating in mind is strictly governed to respond to the reality of illuminated forms. To recall the method exposed in "So-and-So Reclining on Her Couch": "She floats in the contention, the flux / Between the thing as idea and / The idea as thing. She is half who made her. / This is the final Projection, C" (*CP*, 295). The object impressed upon the eye is the thing to be made idea. Restored in the metaphor of the mind to the realm of things, the object as art displays its obligation to the initial reality that furnished the possibility of the making of an unreal. It is clear that, if there were no physical eye to supply forms, there would be no possibility of ideas from which to construct a landscape of the mind. In view of the requirements of visual perception in Stevens' theory, a poetry without sight seems for him inconceivable. It is this primacy of sight for poetry which in his regard urged a recognition of the affinities between poetry and painting.

From the biologist's point of view, Stevens' theory will not be found incompatible. The following observations from Agnes Arber are useful as a summary statement by a scientist:

> We are too apt to think of pictorial images in the mind as if they had a quality of literal "correspondent" truth to external objects; in actual fact they are based not merely upon the "raw" retinal mosaic, but upon this mosaic as played upon and made into an image or pattern by sensory organization. Such a pattern is a symbolic model, fashioned by the mind from materials supplied by the eye, rather than a photographic replica received passively by the mind. Mental images of this kind have perhaps more in common with expressions of modern "abstract" art, than with the familiar "representational" art based on the "copy" theory. The mind, moreover, has the power, not only of modifying but of rejecting the data offered it.[3]

In the fullness of a life of seeing, Stevens records in the late poem, "The Bouquet," a summary review of this power of sensory organization. A new diction is employed for his statement. "One approaches, simply, the reality / Of the other eye. One enters, entering home, / The place of meta-men and para-things, / And yet still men though meta-men, still things / Though para-things . . ." (*CP*, 448–49). The compound *meta-men* we take to denote *beyond-men; para-things* we read as *beside-things.* The "other eye" is the mind. It is the place of things related to, parallel with, objects encountered in physical sight, yet altered from reality. In "An Ordinary Evening in New Haven," very close in chronology to "The Bouquet," the poet speaks of "the eye's plain version" as "a thing apart." It is "the vulgate of experience" (*CP*, 465). The vulgate is the common perception of the certain, the fixed, eye. The other eye is the variable. All that has been reviewed in the two preceding chapters is brought to synthesis here. Home is the place of the imagination; external reality is the commonly shared physical estate of humanity. It is the power of the artist to make para-things of the world which establishes his possession. Stevens will again be found to accord with Paul Klee, who concluded that the two eyes effect a unity of the real and the unreal. "All ways meet in the eye and there, turned into form, lead to a synthesis of outward sight and inward vision.

[3] *The Mind and the Eye: A Study of the Biologist's Standpoint* (Cambridge, 1954), p. 116.

It is here that constructions are formed which, although deviating totally from the optical image of an object yet, from an overall point of view, do not contradict it."[4]

What must be seen by the physical eye spells out the difficulty of the man who would live in the weather of his time, and write of that and no other. A final image from "An Ordinary Evening in New Haven" proposes the opening upon the world of the contemporary:

> *It is the window that makes it difficult*
> *To say good-by to the past and to live and to be*
> *In the present state of things as, say, to paint*
>
> *In the present state of painting and not the*
>   *state*
> *Of thirty years ago. It is looking out*
> *Of the window and walking in the street and*
>   *seeing,*
>
> *As if the eyes were the present or part of it. . . .*
>
> [*CP*, 478]

We may take this as a projection of Stevens' long-standing resolve. The rock of being is of the present. The window of the physical eye will open upon no other than that. Furthermore, we should understand that "to paint in the present state of painting" is not, in the language of Stevens, to emulate a style. It is to determine the possibility of an art strictly related to a present reality and to develop that possibility as one's necessary expression. In the experience of seeing, this is the endlessly *present* difficulty: to be of one's time and to render the vision made of outward sight and inward idea as if this were the only sight of the world acceptable to the self.

The alternatives for the artist are clear. He may withdraw and indulge in a fantastic reconstruction of the past, thus denying the data of the present which the outward eye records. Or he may reproduce exactly what he sees, without reflection, as though he were a camera. The satiric comment of René Magritte on this meaningless reproduction, as presented in his sequence of paintings entitled *The Human Condition,* underscores the folly of the art that is not art. The easel is pushed to a window. A piece of plate glass is

---

[4] *The Thinking Eye*, p. 67.

mounted in it. The prospect from the window is framed by the edges of the glass.[5] Therefore, one has made a picture.

The eye of the body and the eye of the mind must be served. Without the poet's response to these authorities there will be nothing worth the form of language. It will have been obvious through these last chapters that the phenomenologist of the contemporary was antithetical to Stevens. The practice of art for Stevens was the structuring of a mind, a way of looking at the world and of reflecting upon it with a strict and distinctive control. In this second section I have intended to define the elements of sight which make this shaping of a mind possible. When these are related to the native aptitudes of the shaper, traced in the first section, the approach to the crafting of the dome is finally traversed. Without this way across the foreground the full structure of the Grand Poem cannot, I think, be evaluated. The ontology of Stevens is his particular *theory expressed in structure*. The process of the poetry is the demonstration of theory, as we have seen. The architecture of the building as the memorial of the process remains.

[5] For a reproduction see James Thrall Soby, *René Magritte* (New York, 1965), p. 35. This publication commemorates an exhibition of Magritte's work at the Museum of Modern Art, New York City, December, 1965–January, 1966.

The Crafting of the Dome

III

The Setting

9

If men at forty will be painting lakes
The ephemeral blues must merge for them in one,
The basic slate, the universal hue.

[*CP*, 15]

THIS IS THE PLACE OF BEGINNING, THE ROCK OF BEING. In "Le Monocle de Mon Oncle," as *Harmonium* opens, Stevens surveys the place of foundation. The "ephemeral blues" of the imagination will be described in the arcs of the dome. They will merge finally in the universal hue. Before that finality the years of the architect will be known. Time grows upon the rock ("The Man with the Blue Guitar," *CP*, 171). The poet comprehends the reality of his place: it is his knowledge of *being*, his possession of the unalterable facts of the physical and the social, *existence*, "the heroic subject of all study" (*NA*, 176). "The rock cannot be broken. It is the truth" ("Credences of Summer," *CP*, 375). This truth becomes the final subject in the valedictory poem bearing its name. In farewell the poet looks upon the rock through the *principle* of his architecture. The ephemeral blues have disappeared. At "odious evening" the rock is bright "with redness that sticks fast to evil dreams" (*CP*, 528). The "Arctic effulgence" that flares "on the frame" (*CP*, 417) of the structure glances in a red violence upon the "universal hue." But it is satisfaction in the design completed that dominates the mind. The poet concludes:

> *The rock is the habitation of the whole.*
> *Its strength and measure, that which is near,*
> > *point A.*
> *In a perspective that begins again*
> *At B . . .*
> *The starting point of the human and the end. . . .*
>
> [*CP*, 528]

From the blue lake of the early poet-painter to the final redness, the rock is the base. Without it there would have been no poem. Existence is not illusion.

I intend in this chapter a synoptic statement. The poet brings to the rock his singular talent as a draftsman; he advances in his design with constant attention to the elements of physical experience which have just been reviewed: sun, light, the perceiving eye. I turn now to the symbols related to the rock. These express the elements of the setting. They describe in the total sense the firmness of the structure. In the Grand Poem they are certain designations of the builder's intent. They present his unfailing purpose, as in the reflection on the full accomplishment in "The Rock": the poet's "fiction of the leaves" as a "copy of the sun," his leaves (poems in the total poem) that "cover the rock." "These leaves are the poem, the icon and the man" (*CP*, 526–27). Thus this symbol of the leaves and the symbols of wind, weather, clouds, frost, moon, are descriptive of process. As they recur, they signify the builder's acts of joining the parts of his work, of creating a totality.

The last poem of *Harmonium* is an address to the wind: "What syllable are you seeking, / Vocalissimus, / In the distances of sleep? / Speak it" (*CP*, 113). This most vocal force blows without ceasing. The wind upon the basic slate is the herald of change in the passing time of humanity. Crispin, arriving on American shores, ushers in "That century of wind in a single puff." Immediately it is the "mythology of self" that "counts." There will be no more "drenching of stale lives." There is only this newness of a "gaudy, gusty panoply" (*CP*, 28, 30).

The distinction to be made between these two uses of the wind-symbol is obvious. In the first "Vocalissimus" it is the wind of the poet's change which is interrogated. His perception will shift in metamorphosis. The "syllable" sought by the wind prefigures the late disclosure in "An Ordinary Evening in New Haven": "The poem is the cry of its occasion" (*CP*, 473). Yet it is the rock of being which compels adherence to the subject, no matter what the frequency in the shifts of perception. In the same meditation, the poet admits "the spirit's alchemicana"; nevertheless he concludes: "We keep coming back and coming back / To the real: to the hotel instead of the hymns / That fall upon it out of the wind" (*CP*, 471). This is *hotel* in the French sense, the dwelling, the place of habitation. It stands upon the rock. The wind ordains the hymns. In "The Auroras of Autumn" the symbol perseveres in the final question: "Of what disaster is this the imminence: / Bare limbs, bare trees and a wind as sharp as salt?" (*CP*, 419). Death is a cessation of this wind of the personal. In the early poem "The Death of a Soldier" an individual life ends "When the wind stops and, over the heavens, / The clouds go, nevertheless, / In their direction" (*CP*, 97). These images are posed in sharp contrast. An upper wind of the heavens, a wind of an age of man, continues. Below it, the wind of the fallen soldier ceases.

In the second use of the symbol, as in that initial American "century of wind in a single puff," it is the upper wind above the personal which leads on the changes of human experience. This master wind is the maker of the weather of an age. In the memorial quatrains on the death of the soldier in "Esthétique du Mal," Stevens thinks of the battle wound in the history of *man-fallen*. Each hero is surrounded by "concentric circles of shadows," the shadows of his fellows who find in him a center of being in a time of violence. The shadows are "motionless / Of their own part." Yet they move *on the wind* (*CP*, 319). "Time's red soldier [lies] deathless on his bed." The great wind of human experience takes away and restores violence. In every war the red wound of the soldier recurs as the symbol of being. This relentless wind is the master of recurrence as Stevens imagines it in "Repetitions of a Young Captain." Every young captain of every war rests in this speaker. Hence, he signifies the endless repetition of violence in the human condition which we call war. We are to understand that every war is born of a wind, "a tempest . . . on the theatre," the great building of an age. The wind beats in the roof. It levels half the walls. "The rip /

Of the wind and the glittering were real now, / In the spectacle of a new reality" (*CP*, 306).

At various points in the preceding discussion I have intended to emphasize Stevens' unyielding insistence upon the present as the only reality. The destruction of the theater by the wind is repeated throughout human history. Yet one cannot enter the reality of another time. The feeling of a past age cannot be reclaimed. From these meditations on war Stevens speaks of the cataclysmic change that the wind of war announces. It is as though war were the master attribute of wind. The reality that emerges from each time of terror is wholly new. War is a mechanism commanded by wind; every individual death represented by the fallen soldier of time is a sacrifice required by the mechanism. From this reality the red rose that is the soldier's wound (*CP*, 318) blazes with intensity. The young captain thinks of the cataclysm as "calculated chaos" (*CP*, 307). It was made in a wind of men.

To speak of Franz Hals as a maker of weather is for Stevens to think of the winds of that brush master. In the fullness of a lifetime of *weather-mindedness,* Stevens in "Notes Toward a Supreme Fiction" reflects upon the painter who visualized the idea *weather.* The creator-imaginer grasps the "giant of the weather," the central idea, "mere weather, the mere air," and gives it the shape of the particular and personal vision. The abstraction of the idea becomes "blooded, as a man by thought." The weather appropriated by Hals is "blooded"; it is "wetted by [his] blue, colder for [his] white" (*CP*, 385). But this is Stevens' reflection upon a painter's rendering of the constant idea of weather in the physical sense. The use of wind as both epochal and personal recurs in the weather of a poem of mid-career, "Wild Ducks, People and Distances" (*CP*, 328–29). The poet first observes that the life of the world depends upon the singular vision of the individual and upon the visions of other men. People make what we call the world. Yet we are not elements of the physical world, like earth and sky. As though he stood at the edge of a vast plain, Stevens thinks of a time of a coldness of his own weather. The wild ducks of autumn migrate to solitude. They are his thoughts, his imaginings. In the distances lie villages of other men. Yet the ducks cannot span these, where there is no weather, "except the weather of other lives." Nor can they migrate from other lives. They are his ducks. As though he stood in prospect of a total humanity in his age, the poet thinks of the human condition. The knowledge that other men are makers of weather in their villages, wherever they are, as solitary individuals or as communities, holds off "the final, fatal distances." If the physical rock of reality does not depend upon the human being as an element, then it is the sense of continuity in the life of the mind that is solace for human kind. We share in a human fate. As men together, we are alone in the universe. As individuals among men, we share the human condition, each in his own singular weather yet related to his fellows in the weather of the common life.

Stevens' unique way with the titles of his poems is purposive. The intention in such, for instance, as "Woman Looking at a Vase of Flowers," "Landscape with Boat," "Man and Bottle," is not to confound us. It is apparent that Stevens, continually mindful of the relatedness of poetry and painting, wishes to suggest a correspondence of these arts. But even in his uses of titles that seem to be irrelevant, the purpose is exact. The poet intends to suggest the nature of modern weather as though "Man and Bottle," apart from its sound as a cubistic title, proposed some absurd equation of the inanimate commonplace with the vitality of human kind. This poem affirms in its content the rightness of such an approach to the title. There is no bottle in the poem. There are rather furious thoughts of furious war, of the mind that has to persuade itself that war is a manner of thinking, of poetry that has the power to lash more fiercely than the wind (*CP*, 238–39). Further thought upon the theme is inviting, as though we had seen the bitter proposal: out of the clanking mechanism of the present, "the land of war," comes a machine-made bottle; yet a man is no more important than this object. It is the fury of poetry which lashes against the *reductio ad absurdum*. In this sense it is the force of poetry which defies the weather.

Wind and weather are the movements of human existence upon the rock and within the being of the poet who flourishes there. These movements are unpredictable. If the world as it is thought to be is the vision of men, one knows that these relentless shifts in the continuity of existence are happenings in a human reality without ordained design. The structure of the artist must again be urged as an act of defiance before the threat of meaninglessness in human duration. One may press upon Stevens the question of ultimate causality: What power, if any, lies beyond the play of wind or the endurance or disappearance of any weather? His only answer will be: "Fatal Ananke is the common god" ("Owl's Clover," *OP*, 59). Ananke, fatal necessity, is the unknown. One may as well inquire of a necessity in universal being which will eventually command the death of the sun, or the man-induced end of man. There is no knowing. Cosmic necessity is mute. It lies beyond human understanding; and in the thought of Stevens every philosophy that has proposed an answer is a construct proceeding from imagination. Thus every philosophy is blown upon by wind and displaced in the ceaseless progression of weather. Such is the enigma of the eternal rock. This stone cannot be broken. Neither can the enigma that is its nature. Hence, there must be an end of thought, a point beyond which no mind can proceed, save in a transcendence of the rock, into a mystique of the supernatural. It is unnecessary to assert again the resolve of Stevens upon the rock. There is a palm "at the end of the mind" where the "gold-feathered bird sings" ("Of Mere Being," *OP*, 117–18). A structure is a certainty. That is the end of being.

When one turns from wind and weather, the symbols of frost and cloud appear for definition. I have earlier cited the meditation of "Like Decorations in a Nigger Cemetery" in several contexts. I return to it again, naming it as the most searching of Stevens' earlier poems on death. The eccentric, he observes, is the base of design. By the *eccentric* he means unlike, individual, unconventional; and I suspect that he intends the word in its mathematical sense, that of *not having the same center*.[1] Hence, we take the design of Stevens to be centered as he alone willed. The setting is chosen without respect to the choices of other men. His explicitness gives no room for error: "Under the mat of frost and over the mat of clouds. / But in between lies the sphere of my fortune . . ." (*CP*, 151). Possibly there are answers for other men in the grave beneath the earth, or in the vastness beyond the clouds. For him, the design, the "fortune," must lie between the two. Frost is the certainty of human finality; cloud is the imagination above the certainty. The whole course of Stevens' thought is an alternation of engagement with the certainty of frost and the refuge of cloud. If one takes "Sea Surface" as the supreme "cloud" poem, the refuge is entire. The surface of nature is made to bloom in the artist's colors. Imaginings spread upon the sea from a light of the mind and the will. The machine of ocean is appropriated; it becomes all "cloud." But clouds alone,

[1] Marius Bewley, an expert reader and critic of Stevens, has used this image in the title of his study of the American novel, *The Eccentric Design* (London, 1959).

without a surface of the real, are evocations of "gloomy grammarians," a "drifting waste" (*CP*, 55–56).

The course between frost and cloud is difficult. Certainties of the cold, since the real must be preserved, rise to threaten the clouds. "Everything falls back to coldness," a voice heavy with premonition warns in "The Reader" (*CP*, 147). These moments in Stevens reveal the difficulty of the way. In a later poem the clouds become crystal, "an over-crystal out of ice" (*CP*, 351). Chilling prospects open from the depths of the interior monologue. Once again, the defiance of nothingness is emphasized. In the poetry of Stevens the eternal threat of this paralyzing cold is an admission to the perilous nature of the act: to build between frost and cloud is to contend against the reality of the rock, and at one and the same moment to hold to it. The making of the unreal cannot desert the obdurate substance of real being. As we have seen in an earlier examination of "The Bed of Old John Zeller," the will must be iron. Discipline must persevere. As the frost threatens the clouds, frost as "tinsel" of the ice, whether in February or in August, "There are things in a man besides his reason" (*CP*, 351).

It is unnecessary to say more of the sun in the setting of the dome. The sun is the indifferent master of exterior light. The moon is a mirror, reflecting outer reality transformed, the unreal which the private imagination conceives. Stevens' final "Note on Moonlight" presents the moon as the symbol of "an inherent life": "In spite of the mere objectiveness of things, / Like a cloud-cap in the corner of a looking-glass, / A change of color in the plain poet's mind" (*CP*, 531–32). This image of the moon-mirror has at least one companion in the poetry of this century. One finds it in Yeats's "The Crazed Moon," where the phases of man the myth-maker are reflected by the mirror in the night sky.[2] The image of Yeats presents the crazed reality of a human weariness: every myth reflected in the "wandering eye" of the moon perishes. Impermanence is the condition of every symbolism born of the imagination. Stevens' "Lunar Paraphrase" projects the same theme. In the weariness of November the moon is "the mother of pathos and pity" (*CP*, 107). This mirror of mind, the moon, as Stevens later observes, is in no sense vital. "It is the sun that shares our works. / The moon shares nothing" (*CP*, 168).

[2] See *The Collected Poems of W. B. Yeats,* p. 237.

Moonlight is the "inner" light streaming from the reflecting mirror. On the surface of the mirror the unreality of things imagined takes form. It is this moonlight which effects a synthesis of disparate objects. The process is revealed in "Les Plus Belles Pages" (*CP*, 244–45). In the life of the imagination "nothing exists by itself." St. Thomas Aquinas seemed to exist without moonlight, talking endlessly of the separateness of God. He was an "automaton, in logic self-contained." But with man substituted for God the only theology belongs to the eye, in broad daylight. Aquinas did not recognize his oneness with the moon. His theology was but another imagining of the saints. The moon-mirror was always there. Theologies dreaming beyond the limits of man are reflections of the moon. The only true theology establishes man at the center. As I have noted elsewhere, for Stevens, God and the imagination of man are one and the same.

Wind and weather, frost and cloud, sun and moon, are constant in the process of the structure. A final note on leaves is appropriate. They are momentary flourishings of the imagination, "floraisons of imagery," as Stevens calls them in "The Sail of Ulysses" (*OP*, 102). They are the "flourishings" of young lovers in the celebration of an earthly paradise; and it is among the "littering leaves" of the past that the lovers renew life (*CP*, 69). They are the leaves of Adam in the Garden (*CP*, 331). In the poet's prospect of the sea grinding on the rocks of Maine, they are the unspoken "letters of rock and water," "leaves of the sea . . . shaken and shaken" (*CP*, 232). The quick turns and forays of the imagination may often remain merely potential to language. The eye and the mind know them, as in an incipience of the unexpressed, in leaves of the sea and unfolding leaves of the day. When the potential is brought to poetic form it becomes a leaf of record. It is a written leaf. Thus the poet's leaves roof the dome, establishing the surface of the Grand Poem rounded sunward, extending the arcs of the major ideas springing from and descending to the rock.

An examination of the dome in the later poetry shows clear evidence that Stevens was acquainted with the history of domical theory in architecture. The "summer circle" of the helmeted genius of poetry in "Celle Qui Fût Héaulmiette" provides the first of this evidence. It has already been noted that in this poem the circle describes the roundness of the dome-crown. The poet has said that she marks "a circle, not . . . the arc" (*CP*, 438). This concern with curvature agrees with a major tradition of domical symbolism: the dome as a celestial helmet. E. Baldwin Smith, whose history of the symbolism of the dome is thus far definitive, provides the following summary. "The one symbolic concept of great antiquity in the Near East which can be most definitely connected with Palestine and Christian writings is the idea of a celestial helmet. Although it was also derived from the Cult of the Dioskouroi and related to the belief in a cosmic egg, it apparently had its origin in several different cultural traditions." The account names the Hittite and Syrian cultures as original among these traditions. In the classical period, "the sky was frequently visualized and described as a hat or domical helmet." Later, "the cupola of the Odeon at Athens [was compared to] the helmet which Pericles always wore in public."[3] The cult of Castor and Pollux as warriors is linked in Stevens' poem with the helmet-maker's wife of Villon's lyric.[4]

In this encompassment of the poet's symbol there is a further source: Rodin's renowned sculpture on the same subject from Villon, the aged helmet-maker's wife popularly known as "The Old Courtesan." This figure in the Metropolitan Museum of Art, New York City, by Stevens' own confession to a correspondent, had suggested "Celle Qui Fût Héaulmiette."[5] When one has considered the full dominion of the woman-genius in the total poetry, the appropriateness of Rodin's masterwork strikes us as remarkable evidence of Stevens' perception of great art. The gaunt head of the old woman bent in reflection upon the wrinkled flesh and the sagging breasts is memorable in its human submission to ravaging time.[6] In Stevens' poem the woman-genius is helmeted against the cold. She has her own beauty in age. She is the poet's tribute to the human cycle of the imagination that flourishes and fades. Thus it is that the dome as helmet is presided over by the *demoiselle* of the struc-

[3] *The Dome: A Study in the History of Ideas* (Princeton, 1950), pp. 77–78. The study probably appeared too late for Stevens' use of it as he prepared *The Auroras of Autumn* for September publication in that year. The appearance of the cosmic egg in "Things of August" in the same collection seems alike not prompted by Smith's discussion. I have not been able to fix an exact source for Stevens. But his use of this domical theory remains, in my estimation, unquestionable.

[4] See above, ch. 4, n. 11.

[5] In Stevens' letter, cited in n. 11, ch. 4 above, to Bernard Heringman, July 21, 1953, Stevens collection, Baker Library, Dartmouth College.

[6] For a readily accessible photograph of the figure see Albert E. Elsen, *Rodin* (New York, 1963), p. 64.

ture. She is the same *demoiselle* of gold seen in the early poem "Architecture." Now she is aged, and yet, in her own triumph, helmeted.

A second evidence of Stevens' knowledge of domical theory appears in his use of the cosmic egg in "Things of August." "We make, although inside an egg, / Variations on the words spread sail. . . . The egg of the sea / And the egg of the sky are in shells, in walls, in skins / And the egg of the earth lies deep within an egg. / Spread outward. Crack the round dome. . . . Breathe freedom, oh, my native" (*CP*, 490). Returning to the cult of the Dioscuri, Mr. Smith continues with this commentary on the dome as the cosmic egg. "Therefore, when their conoid bonnets [i.e., of Castor and Pollux], or helmets, surmounted by stars, became the common symbol of the cult and were identified with the cosmic egg and the similar conception of the world as a globe consisting of two halves, the upper hemisphere being the radiant heavens to which men aspired and the lower half being the earth plunged in darkness from which men desired to escape, the celestial pileus gave a deeper and more spiritual meaning to the conoid shape."[7] The image of the cosmic egg in the passage from Stevens reaches its fullness in the command, "Crack the round dome." I take this to signify the release of the poet from the process of his poetry, his total accomplishment, as though the unnamed "freedom" from life itself lay beyond. Of the poet's use of this domical theory of the globe rising to the radiant heavens, sunward, and descending to the depths of earth-darkness, there can be little doubt.

There may be further evidence that the domical theory of the cosmic house was suggestive to Stevens. Mr. Smith traces the religious significance of the house, tomb, and sanctuary in pre-Christian times as a symbol of the universe. He continues: ". . . It was the prevalence and persistence of the various beliefs in the celestial symbolism of domical coverings on ancestral types of cosmic houses which were most responsible for the growing popularity of the domical shape."[8] I have dealt sufficiently with Stevens' concept of the house of the poet. That the shape seen in the mind's eye is that of the dome appears unquestionable. That it is a cosmic house seems equally certain when one considers its relation to the sun, its representation of the stars, particularly the

[7] *The Dome*, p. 78.
[8] *Ibid.*, p. 79.

dome shape of the *aurora borealis*[9] in "The Auroras of Autumn,"
and the poet's final images of a structure in orbital motion. The
last signs that Stevens left us for a tracing of his architecture,
in the arc-perspectives beginning at points A and B in "The Rock,"
and in the symbol of the planet on the table, are mandatory. If the
accompanying evidence from the final texts of "St. Armorer's
Church from the Outside" will seem contradictory to some readers,
let it be remembered that Stevens does not picture this chapel, his
own, as a Gothic structure or a building in any traditional style.
It has arches, but they are arches of a "modern" structure, not
far from Matisse's chapel at Vence. In the inevitable coming on of
a new weather, a new age, it will disappear. But even though it must
fall to cinders, it was his structure.

On the setting and the style of the dome one comment remains.
In an earlier discussion of Stevens' devotion to four-squareness
I suggested that the portals of the structure are directly oriented
to the due compass points. One might think, then, of the dome
perfected by the Byzantine architects, the pendentive resting on the
square. I must question this as the prevailing vision of Stevens' architecture.[10] It seems better to regard it as a concept of the half-globe
resting on the rock. The arcs, in the testament of Stevens' poetry,
are anchored there. An exact orientation to the compass, portals
from South to North as the imagination endures and dies, portals

[9] Very probably Stevens' observation of the *aurora borealis* at some time comprehended the *auroral corona,* formed of bands or curtains of light streaming
upward, sometimes to a distance of 500 miles above the earth, and meeting in an
apex above the spectator. The arcs of this phenomenon, displaying at their highest
points an inclination toward magnetic north, appear at the point of convergence
as a dome. Stevens would have known that the *aurora* occurs through the entry
of particles emitted by the sun into the earth's atmosphere. The poetic value of
this sun-derived display of streaming arcs against the night sky is obvious.

[10] I use the qualification in *prevailing* with particular reference to Stevens' dome
image in the middle and the late poetry. An argument may be ventured: the
dome as half-sphere is characteristic of modern architectural design; the pendentive
is of the classic past. I suggest that the very early poem of 1918, "Architecture,"
takes the pendentive as a prototype. And certainly this design is still dominant
in the mind of the poet as he writes "Sea Surface Full of Clouds." Thus he conceives of small momentary domes of the imagination superimposed upon reality:

> . . . *And then blue heaven spread*
>
> *Its crystalline pendentives on the sea*
> *And the macabre of the water-glooms*
> *In an enormous undulation fled.*

[Sec. 2, *CP*, 100]

The blue heaven of the imagination, as it shapes the five scenes of the poem, is
understood to "spread" domical structures in the pendentive form. The major
reference is to a momentary architecture of vision.

from East to West as the vigor of life within nature rises and declines, is still apparent.

In the following chapters I shall examine the arcs of the dome. The evidence of the Grand Poem presents ten of these. The longest of Stevens' sequences under an encompassing title is "Notes Toward a Supreme Fiction." I take this as the supreme statement, the crown of the dome. In this work all the arcs will be found to cross. I think of it as the point of intersection. I add my belief that Stevens was at work on this sequence for many years, far in advance of its first publication in 1942.[11] Thus its place in the chronology of the mind may be considered as a central point.

The arcs to be examined are the major unifying themes distinguishing the poetry of Stevens. They will be treated as dominant ideas projected through and covered by the leaves of separate poems. The following designations appear in the order to be followed in the discussion.

Wing and Claw: Symbols of the Imagination

The Painter: Encounters of the Eye

The Comedian: Masques and Festivals

The Mythological Canon: Ritual Presences

American Place: Of Land-Made Men

Society: Transitions in the American Community

Existence: The Difficulty of Being

The Hero: Aspects of the Supreme Fiction

In the Northern Quarter: The Descent to the Rock

The Chapel of Wind and Weather: The Poet as Priest

[11] By the Cummington Press, Cummington, Mass.

Wing and Claw: Symbols of the Imagination

10

THE FIRST POEM IN THE COLLECTED EDITION OF Stevens, "Earthy Anecdote," presents an image of bucks running in Oklahoma. Clattering, they swerve in a "swift, circular line," to the right, to the left, "because of the firecat" that "bristled in the way" (*CP,* 3). The image symbolizes *motion* in the reality of physical being: the line of movement is "swift and circular," in an American place; the threatening firecat is the maker of the curve. Later, "the firecat closed his bright eyes / And slept." The poem of mid-career, "Montrachet-le-Jardin," discussed earlier in this study, ends in these lines: "And yet what good were yesterday's devotions? / I affirm and then at midnight the great cat / Leaps quickly from the fireside and is gone" (*CP,* 264). As the last poetic vistas close, October's "lion-roses have turned to paper" (*CP,* 506). When one reaches the final lyric of the collected edition, the "scrawny cry" of a bird rises faintly in the early March wind (*CP,* 534). This span of symbols is exemplary. The firecat of Oklahoma, the great cat leaping from the hearth, October roses of the lion, and the bird's cry are all metamorphic expressions of the same subject, symbols within "leaf-poems" expressing a constant theme. The symbols represent the imagination in action. The subject rises and descends, the certain arc, from the rock, to the rock.

Commenting on lines from the sixty-fifth sonnet of Shakespeare quoted in an English review of Epstein's paintings, Stevens surveyed the fierceness of the vital imagination. The question of the sonnet runs in the familiar lines: "How with this rage shall beauty hold a plea, / Whose action is no stronger than a flower?"[1] The colors of Epstein's flowers were found by the reviewer to explode all over the picture space. "What ferocious beauty the line from Shakespeare puts on," observed Stevens, "when used under such circumstances" (*NA*, 34). It is clear that, for Stevens, rage is the vital mode of imagination. If beauty issues from poetic speech, it is incidental; it is certainly not the end. The concluding lines of "Poems of Our Climate" urge this beauty of ferociousness: "The imperfect is our paradise. / Note that, in this bitterness, delight, / Since the imperfect is so hot in us, / Lies in flawed words and stubborn sounds" (*CP*, 194).

It was once fashionable to write of the elegance of Stevens, as though the "ultimate elegance: the imagined land" (*CP*, 250) were the major attribute of the poetry. This criticism, akin to the pursuit of *dandyisme* in Stevens, is both sentimental and worthless. Elegance was never the primary objective any more than was the creation of a limpid beauty intentional. When Stevens uses *elegance* he is again intent upon a radical diction: from the Latin *ex* (*e-*) plus *legare, to choose out,* and therefore *elegance* as *deliberate choice.* A land of elegance is a land made in the mind through a ferocious attack upon reality. The imagination of that land is a clawing and springing thing. If beauty is as delicate as Shakespeare's flower or as awesome as the *aurora borealis* in the autumn night of Stevens, it is nonetheless beauty which is captured from the heart of rage.[2]

This force of the imagination considered in its primitive strength, its power of bird wing and bird cry, its hot litheness and tension, is the subject of this chapter. In the structure of the dome it is the arching idea first chosen for description because it is an embodiment of the concept of power in all of Stevens' poetry. Like each of the other master ideas to be studied, it passes through a continuing metamorphosis as the leaves take shape and memorialize the passage of the mind, moment to moment, in its resolve upon the total structure. Stevens will not be fully read and enjoyed without comprehension of this brilliant vigor, this utter fierceness. It is blood-red, like the "red

---

[1] This review of an Epstein show at the Leicester Galleries, London (1941?), is noticed by Stevens in "The Noble Rider and the Sound of Words."

[2] "The belief in poetry is a magnificent fury, or it is nothing." So Stevens wrote to his friend Henry Church from Hartford on March 30, 1943; see *Letters*, p. 446.

weather" of his old sailor drunk and asleep, catching tigers (*CP*, 66). It must be seen as naked imaginative force, an attribute of the *naked* poet.

Among the books that Stevens ordered from his Paris dealer in the early fifties was an edition of the correspondence of Richard Strauss and Romain Rolland.[3] Addressing Strauss after the third performance of *Salomé* in Paris in 1907, Rolland wrote his tribute. "I do not believe that one can see a more manifest proof of your force. This force is, for me, the greatest to be found in musical Europe today."[4] One cannot be sure of the extent of Stevens' interest in Strauss.[5] But I submit that the *force* of Strauss had excited him long before he set out to read in the correspondence with Rolland. I suggest an excitement prompted by that fierceness of imagination again and again celebrated by Strauss in the scores for orchestra and in the operas. For, if *Salomé*, to name only one work, does not exalt the power of the imagination in the fierceness of its score, then the aesthetic of this music cannot be meaningfully discussed. Readers who feel the rage of imagination in Stevens will not, I think, find this affinity with Strauss in the least fanciful. The separate arts of these men of the century may be related in other respects, as I shall later note. For the present it must be urged that Stevens was fully aware of his poet's talent for the fierce grasp, and that he admired artistry of a like energy.

The ferocious imagination as subject becomes a dominant arc of the structure. It is a principle of the poetry as self-definition. The horde of symbols describing this force is ordered in a severely controlled lineage as the Grand Poem progresses. Taken together, the symbols confirm that Stevens possessed a native vigor scarcely equaled by any other American poet of his day. Contrary to much published opinion, urbanity is not his mode, any more than it is that of, for example, Pound. I do not argue that the force of Stevens is uniformly

[3] The letter addressed to Miss Paule Vidal is dated at Hartford, July 31, 1952; see *Letters*, p. 758.
[4] *Richard Strauss et Romain Rolland: Correspondance, fragments de Journal* [par Romain Rolland] (Paris, 1951) [Cahiers (No. 3) Romain Rolland], p. 85. Rolland's letter is dated at Paris, May 14, 1907. I use the Albin Michel edition ordered by Stevens.
[5] Stevens appears particularly to have admired among the scores of Strauss the tone poem *Till Eulenspiegel* and *Der Rosenkavalier*; see *Letters*, pp. 294, 442, 744. This last reference occurs in a letter to Barbara Church from Hartford, March 24, 1952. With respect to Stevens' persistent analogies between poetry and music his disclosure to Mrs. Church is significant. "I am very keen about Rosenkavalier, especially the music of the presentation of the silver rose. The glancing chords haunt me and sometimes I try to reproduce the effect of them in words."

maintained. But its thrusts are frequent enough to astonish us with the endurance of his energy. This attribute of Stevens' may be usefully compared with the energy of Pound at various points in the *Cantos*, particularly in the "Rock Drill" sequence. I am speaking most strictly of the essential Stevens, the poet who demands of the imagination in "Credences of Summer" a *gripping* of the object "in savage scrutiny" (*CP*, 376).

It is my intention to trace the leaves of the arc describing imaginative vigor. These poems, or parts of poems, appear as symbols. The infallible sign of the "savage scrutiny" in Stevens, the act of the imagination rather than the "blue" that is the sign of its dominant presence, is the appearance of an imagery of birds and of clawed and fanged animals. Never in Stevens are these creatures of the natural world studied as objects in themselves. They are invariably objects-made-ideas; and the import that they assume is invariably symbolic. Here, and in the ensuing chapters, I shall wish to deal with major recurrences of symbolic patterns in metamorphosis. It is not my purpose to offer a chronology inclusive of every instance of repetition. I assume that readers who wish to follow the arc of the idea will have at hand the *Collected Poems* and the poetic texts of *Opus Posthumous*.

It may as well be said at this point that I regard Stevens' longer poems as *multileaved*. I think it entirely clear that no single long poem of Stevens' is confined to a single subject. The fact is that most of the longer works are synoptic. In the sense of Stevens, they are *leafages* rather than single leaves; they are clusters of poems. The titles of these works are scrupulously demonstrative: for example, "Le Monocle de Mon Oncle" [the eye-glass trained upon multiplicity rather than singularity]; "Like *Decorations* in a Nigger Cemetery"; "*Variations* on a Summer Day"; "*Credences* of Summer"; "*Notes* Toward a Supreme Fiction"; "*Things* of August." I have italicized in order to point out the deliberate suggestiveness of these plurals. Furthermore, even the most superficial reading of "An Ordinary Evening in New Haven" will immediately indicate that New Haven is not the constant subject. Several poems are gathered under this title. I do not find it necessary to defend an approach to the *multileaved* longer work. Nor do I think that Stevens himself intended other than this multiplicity. Enough has already been asserted of his theory of the total poem of which each small piece is a part. The long poems are all inclusive of many subjects. Each is an aggregate, serving from time to time the work of the total structure as further projections of the subject-arcs are accomplished.

The firecat orders the line of movement as the bucks clatter in Oklahoma. But it is not a beginning in early youth. The poet is forty. Already, as he sets upon "painting lakes" in "Le Monocle de Mon Oncle," the red bird that flies "across the golden floor" seeks out his choir. But "These choirs of welcome choir for me farewell. / No spring can follow past meridian" (*CP*, 13). We have already noted that *Harmonium* is not exclusively a "spring" volume. The shadows of advancing age fall upon it in several scenes. This red bird is a sign of the youthful imagination. He must join his own youthful kind, his generation. The choir sings farewell to a poet who already crosses the meridian into summer. Even in this moment autumn threatens (Sec. 8, *CP*, 16). Almost immediately comes the resolve upon discipline. The poet will not take his place among the "fops of fancy." He is a "yeoman" who knows "no magic trees, no balmy boughs, / No silver-ruddy, gold-vermilion fruits" (*CP*, 16–17). But he will endure as himself. Stevens thinks of this individual mastery of being as a tree. It will grow, no matter what the process may reveal of imaginative vigor: "It stands gigantic, with a certain tip / To which all birds come sometime in their time. / But when they go that tip still tips the tree" (*CP*, 17). The tree is his individuality. It is not the domain of another man. The tip is the expression of this tree and no other. The prospect to note in this early poem is that of growth associated with the flights of birds, season to season, as age progresses.

After "Le Monocle de Mon Oncle" the imagery is very quickly refined. The first display of mastery occurs in "Sunday Morning." Certainly the "green freedom of a cockatoo" opening this renowned poem may be read as an element of the pictorial, along with the peignoir, the coffee, the oranges, and the sunlight (*CP*, 66). The composition "reads" like a Bonnard or a Matisse. But this bird is far more than pictorial in the scene. It is related to every bird of the symbol. It is *green* in *freedom* for the woman seated in her chair. She may make on Sunday morning whatever faith she likes. The bird is hers. It is the *green potential* that lies everywhere about her. For the woman, of course, is the feminine presence, the genius of poetry exalted by Stevens. She is seen here in a guise as distinctive as that of her "blue-shadowed silk" in "Peter Quince at the Clavier" (*CP*, 89). But the cockatoo is not the only winging creature of the poem. The swallow's wings of the June evening belong to the feminine presence; and so do the pigeons undulating down to darkness, prophetic images of death, as the poem closes (*CP*, 68, 70).

In the continuing sequence of *Harmonium,* the bantams of pine-woods appear soon after the cockatoo. Each bantam is a poet; the pine-woods establish an American setting. Azcan, the overweening cock of this antic piece, is the pompous "master" poet with assumptions of his grandeur and his overlordship among his supposed inferiors. In the middle couplet stands the unyielding principle: "Your world is you. I am my world" (*CP*, 75). The metamorphosis from "Sunday Morning" to this poem is impressive. Yet the subject remains unshaken. It is the freedom of the imagination which must endure: freedom from intimidation suffered at the hands of strutting poets, freedom from the words of other men, freedom from dogma, freedom to make one's world.

Stevens' fascination with the subject continues to intensify. The master poem of the symbol follows, blazing in a green and metallic iridescence. "The Bird with the Coppery Keen Claws" (*CP*, 82) has posed exceptional difficulties for criticism. Although the variety of commentary need not be reviewed, an apparent guesswork in analysis offers proof that the parts of the Grand Poem must be seen in their relationships, if they are to be fully comprehended. I wish here to comment on each of the six tercets of this lyric. In the first, above "the forest of the parakeets, / A parakeet of parakeets prevails." This quintessential bird is a "pip" (a seed) of life "amid a mort" (a death) of "tails." In the second, the master parakeet is surrounded by "rudiments of the tropics." But he does not see: "His lids are white because his eyes are blind." In the third, even though he is a master parakeet, he is not a paradise of other parakeets, as though he were an idol, in his "gold ether," this "golden alguazil" (policeman). He is a presence. He "broods there and is still." Plume upon plume ("panache upon panache") in the fourth tercet, his *tails* spread "upward and outward, in green-vented forms." His "tip" (crest) is "a drop of water full of storms" (weather). In the fifth tercet, the turbulent colors of his plumes "undulate" "As his pure intellect applies its laws." Yet he "moves not on his coppery, keen claws." In the sixth and last tercet, he "munches a dry shell" (a dry rind of a fruit) "while he exerts / His will, yet never ceases, perfect cock, / To flare, in the sun-pallor of his rock."

It need scarcely be urged that this poem is worked with an intentional brilliance of imagery. The green of the tropical forest is washed with an antique gold. But this brilliant surface conceals an exactitude of conformity with the master symbol of wing and claw. We should then review the poem through an opening of the exterior fabric. The forest is the green potential of the imagination. The parakeets, like the bantams, are bird-symbols of poets, of separate imaginers. The parakeet-of-parakeets is the presence of *central man,* here transformed as the *central imagination* in human continuity. Thus the master parakeet is the possessor of the seed of life amidst the constant deaths of individual men. The "tails" in the first tercet are related to the tails of the peacocks in "Domination of Black," the seventh poem in *Harmonium:* As the shadows of the hemlocks fall (the shadow of the winter to come after this poet's spring), the peacocks cry; "The colors of their tails / Were like the leaves themselves / Turning in the wind" (*CP,* 8). Peacock plumage, parakeet feathers—these *tails* of the imaginings of each man must perish. But the master parakeet endures *in blindness;* his white lids are closed over *unseeing* eyes. There is no obscurity in this image. Since the master bird is the presence of the imagination in central man, subman, this human force is not given the power of sight *until the individual man at his time in the great continuity opens his eyes.* The parakeet-of-parakeets is the absolute certainty of imagination, bathed in the gold of the sun, a radiant warder of all passing imaginations. Yet he is not a transcendent paradise of men. He is *of man,* and of man's earthly experience. He broods in stillness. The changes of man-made weather are in his mastery. As the central imagination, he is the law-giver: *Man shall imagine.* Seeing nothing of the color of earth's fruits for sustenance, he "munches a dry shell," an ancient rind of fruit, as he exerts his will. Yet he "flares" forever, this master bird, in the "sun-pallor of his rock." If it is argued that the coppery, keen claws belong to a symbol of the sun, the last image clearly denies the possibility. This "sun-pallor" is sun-whiteness. It relates to the whiteness of the lids covering the blindness of the master eyes. It will become sun-brilliance only to the opening eyes of the individual imaginer in his brief life upon the rock.

Parakeets die in the green forest. Peacocks spread their tails; but the winds of autumn and the shadows of the hemlocks presage their deaths. One may think of Yeats, who heard "the scream of Juno's peacock," as the clarion of an ending cycle in man's history.[6] He may reflect upon the gyre of the falcon ("The Second Coming"), or upon the

---

[6] *A Vision* (New York, 1956), p. 268: "A civilization is a struggle to keep self-control. . . . The loss of control over thought comes towards the end . . . the last surrender, the irrational cry, revelation—the scream of Juno's peacock." Yeats's observation recorded here is of 1937.

love that is like the lion's tooth ("Crazy Jane Grown Old Looks at the Dancers"), or upon the miraculous strange sea bird that shrieks at two well-matched lovers ("Her Triumph"). And one says of each of these that imagination, its power to ordain the quality of being, is represented in the symbol. If a comparative study of Stevens is yet to come, it may very well be one that contrasts his modes of being with those of Yeats. To review these casual choices from Yeats, let it be said first that it is not the aptitude for wing and claw in Stevens which is distinctive. Clearly his uniqueness lies in his use of this imagery as symbol. First, Stevens was not committed to any history save the evidence of a continuity of the imagination, the master human faculty that makes the world again and again what it is. To think of man in periods and cycles was foreign to his nature. The old myths are dead; they do not require measurement; they do not relate to us. Second, love in the sense of the self in union with another self is not a subject in the entire range of Stevens' poetry. There is, then, a history of the imagination which endures in a succession of independent selves, and there is a history unique to each self in its own time span. That is all. Hence I take it to be wholly true that Yeats intended an "open" poetry of the universal, and that Stevens sought a "closed" poetry of the particular. I have contended sufficiently in the Introduction for this poetry of a closed solitude. Of Stevens we may be sure that the certainty of the master bird is all that can be known *as human endurance*. The central creature of winging power is blind until each imaginer of every present gives him sight. Thus, in the final confessional of "The Rock," this life of the poet Stevens was made of its leaves alone: ". . . the green leaves came and covered the high rock, / . . . the lilacs came and bloomed, like a blindness cleaned, / Exclaiming bright sight, as it was satisfied, / In a birth of sight" (*CP*, 526).

"Thirteen Ways of Looking at a Blackbird" presents thirteen phases of the imagination at play upon a winter landscape (*CP*, 92–95). The frequent suggestion that the forms of the thirteen sections seem to borrow from the Japanese *haiku* is readily admissible. But as leaves on the frame, these sections are swift passages of a *jeu d'esprit*, metamorphosis proceeding at very nearly top speed. The eye turns with astonishing agility. Sight travels to the snowy mountains, to icicles along a window, to a "glass coach" traveling along the Connecticut River in the vicinity of Haddam, to the cedar limbs as snow threatens again. The blackbird darts in and out of scene after scene. The light is *green* as he becomes more than one bird or wings in images of himself in the shadows of the "coach." All this darting motion of the imagination, related to the jungle parakeet in a momentary blackbird, is of the poet's gleeful command: the unreal rising above the real. The men of Haddam are accused of being "thin." Why do they imagine golden birds, when the blackbird is here in them? It is a matter of seeing what is around one, and of projecting the imagination upon the immediate place where one lives.

These early examples of wing and claw on the arc are engaging, not only in the variety of the images related to the master symbol, but alike in their attributes of movement and tone, color and novelty. Early in the next sequence, *Ideas of Order*, Stevens returns to the cat-lion image. The comic irony of "Lions in Sweden" is perhaps well enough known to require little comment. The poem refers to "Sweden," as to any country of the poet's time. Lions may be of two kinds: those massive symbols of the architecture of savings banks, monuments to the allegories of Fides, Justitia, Patientia, Fortitudo; or the lions of one's "souvenirs" of the soul. (Here the "arpeggi of celestial souvenirs" [*OP*, 35] should be recalled.) The poet will shun the majestic images of savings banks. If the fault is with any man's lions, they must be returned to Hamburg, whence they came.[7] The "whole of the soul . . . Still hankers after lions, or, to shift, / Still hankers after sovereign images" (*CP*, 124–25). The matter depends upon the "souvenirs" one wants, cash in banks presided over by stone lions, or the lions of a poet's sovereign images. "The vegetation," Stevens concludes, "still abounds with forms." Knowing the celebration of summer in the poetry of Stevens, we then understand his image of the lions that come down in voices as the March sunlight falls at the end of winter (*CP*, 134), or his image of the tiger, "Lamed by nothingness and frost," a "failure" of the sun in another autumn (*CP*, 154).

If the soul hankers after sovereign images, if it wants its own souvenirs of claws no matter what the weather, warm or frosty, then it will require its own legend. The primitive vegetation, abounding with forms, must be made to yield a "newness" of lions. Something of the same resolve may be discovered in certain knotty passages of "Like

---

[7] See Daniel Fuchs, *The Comic Spirit of Wallace Stevens* (Durham, 1963), p. 65, n. 4. Mr. Fuchs points out that Stevens may be indebted here to Guillaume Apollinaire. The poem is suggested by "Le Lion" of *Le Bestiaire*:

> *O lion, malheureuse image*
> *Des rois chus lamentablement,*
> *Tu ne nais maintenant qu'en cage*
> *A Hambourg, chez les Allemands.*

This sequence of Apollinaire was issued in an edition illustrated by Raoul Dufy at Paris in 1919.

Decorations in a Nigger Cemetery." There is a "decline in music," Stevens notes, between oriole and crow. The crow is a "realist." But so may the oriole be the same! (*CP*, 154.) We hear the bleak caw of a detested creature in the background. His note is clearly related to the unmusical sternness of the obdurate rock. If the symbolic oriole is a realist as well, then he is songster of a *realist* originality in the unreal. In the manner of a country riddle, the following lines extend the metaphor: "The hen-cock crows at midnight and lays no egg, / The cock-hen crows all day. But cockerel shrieks, / Hen shudders: the copious egg is made and laid" (*CP*, 155). One reads: hen-cock, cock-hen = one and the same, the fabulous layer of the cockatrice-egg. This is old myth. *But* a new egg is made and laid in this moment. The hen is now the bird of the imagination; the golden sun-cockerel is the mate. The new egg is a new myth. It is the poet's own. A third tercet follows. The bird from the egg is purple, regal in the poet's ceremony. But he "must have / Notes for his comfort that he may repeat / Through the gross tedium of being rare" (*CP*, 155). The notes guarding against tedium are, of course, the poet's music. The metamorphosis in these three "decorations" from the cemetery scene of autumn spreads over the theme of the realist-poet as the maker of his own myth. The theme extends the subject: the imagination in action.

The metaphor which has just been reviewed occurs in the poetry of the mid-thirties. If one takes the opening poems of *Ideas of Order,* published in 1936, as confirming the resolve upon the total structure, then it is apparent that these explorations of imaginative power belong to a consciously deepening maturity. The imagery of wing and claw expands with the sureness of a virtuoso. It is in this period that Stevens achieves the intense power reflected in "Autumn Refrain" (*CP*, 160). This superb lyric, standing very near the close of *Ideas of Order,* is dominated by the American grackle. It is as though the purple ceremonial bird of the new egg had ordained an American myth of poetic wing. The scene is one of autumn desolation. The "skreak" and "skritter" of the grackles lead on the stillness that follows their evening flight. These grating sounds from the American rock leave behind a stillness in a desolate "key." The poet will never hear nightingales. They are not of his reality. The piece is made of iron. Relentless birds of the mind scratch at the rock, compelling it to yield its harshness to music. Not since the nightingale of Keats has there been another poem of this order in English. I am speaking here of the stillness that follows the disappearance of the bird, nightingale or grackle. In the whole of Stevens there is no poem that excels this one in a display of sheer compulsion. It is a primary example of the fierce imagination seizing beauty from the "skrittering" of these iron American throats. A lifetime of an American poetic discipline is represented in this forged image. Furthermore, it speaks of will, the discipline at the center, the decision to turn northward in "Farewell to Florida," the decision to persevere in "Montrachet-le-Jardin."

At about the same time, in "Owl's Clover," Stevens thinks of a native bird in a real jungle far from Connecticut. The metaphor leaps to Africa as he ponders the future. In the savageness of that wild vastness, the discipline of a civilized imaginer has yet to come. He displays an African fierceness as the central imagination *uncontrolled.* In Africa, "Memory moves on leopards' feet." And "desire / Appoints its florid messengers with wings / Wildly curvetted, color-scarred, so beaked, / With tongues unclipped and throats so stuffed with thorns, / So clawed, so sopped with sun, that in these things / The message is half-borne" (*OP*, 57). It is not, certainly, that in Africa the imagination of man is unrecognizable. But its fecundity is all litheness and savagery. The giver of the "message" is the worker of form, the maker of music, the disciplinarian. I have said that Stevens was not enticed by the possibility of imposing cycles upon the history of man. But he would scarcely have belonged to the twentieth century had he not repeated the question of the age: After us, what next? Is there to be a total surrender of the civilized power of controlling the imagination, a return to a primitive jungle where man, the *individual,* must discover himself again, where he must find anew what it is to possess a self? Is this African bird of unclipped tongue and throat stuffed with thorns to be the master of all wings? The question has its own importance as the twentieth century advances.

Thus, on the threshold of "The Man with the Blue Guitar" (1937) Stevens reaches the mode of wing and claw which permits an imagery of interplay between the imagination and the will. Apart from its observations turned with a searing light upon the crassness of an unimaginative society, this poem reaches a full confirmation of discipline. The clawing beast and the cutting wing are united in Sections, 17, 19 and 24, as the guitarist plucks and strums. The first variation on the theme contends: "The person has a mould. But not / Its animal." The soul is the mind. It is an animal. On the blue guitar "its claws propound, its fangs / Articulate its desert days" (*CP*, 174). Now comes the second strain:

That I may reduce the monster to
Myself, and then may be myself

In face of the monster, be more than part
Of it, more than the monstrous player of

One of its monstrous lutes, not be
Alone, but reduce the monster and be,

Two things, the two together as one,
And play of the monster and of myself,

Or better not of myself at all,
But of that as its intelligence,

Being the lion in the lute
Before the lion locked in stone.

[*CP*, 175]

This is absolute dogma in the art of Stevens. It is a *credo* expressing the fixed center of his poetics. The monster, nature, will be coerced by the passion for design, which is the energy of an "intelligence," a necessity of form. These savage lines conclude in an image that I have earlier advanced as clear refutation of Stevens' supposed agreement with Wordsworth and Coleridge. I repeat: With Stevens, imagination is not an agent patiently synthesizing; it is raw faculty, fanged and snarling, the lion in song matching the lion in nature. The sequence of the variations on the blue guitar concludes with a master image of the wing. The poet would bequeath a book, a page, at least a phrase. "A hawk of life, that latined phrase: / To know; a missal for brooding-sight. / To meet that hawk's eye and to flinch / Not at the eye but at the joy of it" (*CP*, 178). The final chord is struck in fierceness. *To know*: this is the *Latin* of the poet's *missal*. The hawk above life circles and seizes. The gross object of nature is chosen through the eye of the hawk. The prey is claimed.

Stevens' reticence to explicate his poetry has given the few disclosures that he left an excessive rareness. Thus his notes addressed to Renato Poggioli of Harvard in 1953 are among the priceless. Mr. Poggioli, laboring at the task of translating selected poems for an Italian edition,[8] sent to Stevens a set of questions with major reference to "The Man with the Blue Guitar." Scholars engaged in criticism of Stevens have known these for a decade, since they were first deposited in the

[8] *Mattino Domenicale ed altre Poesie* (Turin: Giulio Einaudi, 1954).

Harvard collection by the translator. Stevens' comment has been fully noted. But when it is taken in the context of the subject under discussion here, its importance, I think, becomes new. Stevens' note, in part, follows:

I want, as a poet, to be that in nature which constitutes nature's very self. I want to be nature in the form of a man, with all the resources of nature = I want to be the lion in the lute; and then, when I am, I want to face my parent and be his true poet. I want to face nature the way two lions face one another—the lion in the lute facing the lion locked in stone. I want, as a man of the imagination, to write poetry with all the power of a monster equal in strength to that of the monster about whom I write. I want man's imagination to be completely adequate in the face of reality.

Of his symbol of his poetry as a liturgical directive, he concluded: "I desire my poem to mean as much, and as deeply, as a missal."[9] "And then, when I am. . . ." He *was* the lion in his lute; he had been the monster taming the monster since the inception of the blue guitarist. Confronting again and again the problem of the poetic art, he found poetry in the bead of an eye, lion to lion. Thus one finds the two beasts in confrontation again as he writes "Poetry Is a Destructive Force" (*CP*, 192–93). There is a lion in his breast. "He tastes its blood, not spit." "He is like a man / In the body of a violent beast." Another lion sleeps in the sun. "Its nose is on its paws. / It can kill a man."

This is the rage from the decade of the thirties. Just how the rage of the forties is exposed in encounters of Stevens the man with the violence of war, we should expect the biographer to tell us. But from internal evidence of the poetry we may be certain that there is a transmutation, as if to create in full ferociousness on the war-smitten rock were to strain every muscle. *Parts of a World* (1942) is clearly marked with the struggle. The imaginations of men are gathered to evil. In "Dry Loaf" this bread of human kind is evil. There are birds. But they come "like dirty water in waves . . . [that were] soldiers moving, / Marching and marching in a tragic time" (*CP*, 200). It is a time of humanity when "he that suffers most desires / The red bird most and the strongest sky." The "little owl" of presumed wise men is useless (*CP*, 244). These are poems from anguish. The lion returns in the sardonic reverie of "Jumbo" (*CP*, 269), this time transformed to a fat beast with a circus name. He is the force of a war general, a "prince of secondary men." He plucks upon the iron bars of being, "clawing" his "consonants" on the ear. The consonants are the flat prose of his orders.

[9] *Letters*, p. 790. These notes of Stevens' are dated at Hartford, July 12, 1953.

This military general becomes the governor of imaginations. He pre-empts the poet's role of "cloud-clown, blue painter." He is a "bad-be-spoken lacker." Whoever he is, he is a tyrannical fat beast. What he plays on the iron of the rock is his "sing-song"; his repetition is what a generation hears, that song and no other. In the widest sense he is the maker of an age, this prince of secondary men, not of men living the life of major man as the individual imagination wills.

One finds something else in *Parts of a World*. The poet himself senses the approaching end of summer, just as he once passed the meridian of spring in "Le Monocle de Mon Oncle." Using an image of the musical scale in fusion with the bird of his lyricism, he writes in "The Hand as a Being": "Her hair [that of the feminine presence, the genius of poetry] fell on him and the mi-bird flew / To the ruddier bushes at the garden's end" (*CP*, 271). The mi-bird is the life of the imagination in the third tone of a major scale. Autumn (*mi*) approaches.

The descent of the arc of wing and claw begins at the zenith. The downward course is a continuous symbolic description of waning force. Yet every movement in the process remains strictly controlled. If there is a "gripping" of the object "in savage scrutiny" ("Credences of Sum-mer," *CP*, 376), there is a gripping of the self in the searching gaze of the man who hears the third tone. The gaze is maintained without recourse to the sentimental. If we are creatures in a human poverty, then every stage of the poverty will be confronted with a defiant scru-tiny. There is, indeed, terror in the late Stevens. But an indulgence of nostalgia is absent. As he approaches the meridian of autumn he sets his course: "picking thin music on the rustiest string, / Squeezing the reddest fragrance from the stump / Of summer" (*CP*, 285). Now, in *Transport to Summer*, the metaphor of wing and claw is divided between what was, as though in close review of a principle of fierce-ness, and what is, as the power of making the unreal from the real declines. The "bird that never settles" on the ocean—ocean that without the bird "would be a geography of the dead" (*CP*, 304)—is retrospective. It takes us back to that most wondrous of all ocean meta-morphoses in Stevens, "Sea Surface Full of Clouds." An earlier vigor is resplendent there, as the colors shift in a seemingly infinite progres-sion: the power of the lion in the breast to meet the lion in nature. This is how it was.

The lion of the blue guitarist is seen again in "Jouga" (*CP*, 337). The poem opens with the acknowledgment: "The physical world is meaningless tonight / And there is no other." "Ha-eé-me"[10] is the beast in the poet. The theme of the lion in the lute and the lion in nature is repeated. But the sound is of a diminishing echo. An imbecile seems to "knock out a noise" from the guitar. There are beasts moving about on slight footfalls which one never hears. The beast in the poet falls asleep; and the new subject in reality passes furtively, almost unheard. It may seem that the reappearance of a poetic lion-strength in "Notes Toward a Supreme Fiction" re-establishes the vigor of the first images: "These are the heroic children whom time breeds / Against the first idea—to lash the lion, / Caparison elephants, teach bears to juggle" (CP, 385). Yet this is retrospection upon "animal-tamers" approaching the universal. "Heroic children" of men have always been the furious masters. The "notes" are summations. Together they make Stevens' book of the possible for an apt, youthful inheritor.

In "Puella Parvula" (little girl) Stevens reduces the feminine presence of poetry to the infant origins of a new poet. The girl must grow to woman with him. As she grows, so will there be "The bloody lion in the yard at night or ready to spring / From the clouds in the midst of trembling trees / Making a great gnashing, over the water wallows / Of a vacant sea declaiming with wide throat" (CP, 456). This new lion is not of Stevens. The vision is projected for the next poet. Another man will bear within him a lion ready to spring, quick to descend upon a blank sea surface. This is prophecy.

Like the fluttering pigeons closing the meditation of "Sunday Morning," "downward to darkness on extended wings," the later images of wing pale steadily in color. The "seeming" of a summer's day becomes a dove alighting on a column in the desert (CP, 343). The hen-mate of the golden cockerel becomes an "old brown hen" under "an old blue sky." We live between these, the poet observes, between the bird of imagination and the radiance of the upper blue (CP, 359). The cock flies low now, alighting on a bean pole in a weedy garden, where "the gardener's cat is dead." "A complex of emotions falls apart." But the cock on the bean pole may detect "another complex of other emotions," a complex neither "soft" nor "civil." We understand that they belong to the fierceness of a new imaginer, a new poet. The sound of the cock "is not part of the listener's own sense" ("Credences of Summer," CP, 377). This state of reduction in vigor introduces the final theme of wing and claw. As one poet goes down to death, another

---

[10] I am unable to offer a certain reading of this metaphoric name. I suggest that it is a compound of the French *Ha*, of *étais* contracted to *eé*, and of the plain English *me*. Hence, the reading may be "Alas, as I was" or in the colloquial sense "It was me."

rises. The impossibility of *tradition* in poetry is thus unquestionable. There cannot be a passing on of one's own complex. The wind and the weather of the next poet and of the next age prohibit this, whether imposition or inheritance. Nothing is inherited save the power to imagine.

The poet's own reckoning of his final loss is heard in somber confession. The auroras of autumn tinge the night; "the theatre is filled with flying birds" (*CP*, 416). The discipline of poetic will is shaken; now the owl becomes the symbol of the wing. In the sarcophagus he intones of a "high sleep" and a "high peace" and of the mother, earth, "that says / Good-by in the darkness, speaking quietly there, / To those that cannot say good-by themselves" (*CP*, 431). As this mind grew from an innocence of being, so now it "is a child that sings itself to sleep."[11]

The enduring conformity of imagery to theme need not be urged. As the final sequence of leaves marks the return to the rock, there is a last look at the dove. She lies upon the roof in the morning. The sun rises. This lord, this sun of man's love of life, this master of natural process that brings man's final sorrow, "Lay on the roof / And made much within her" (*CP*, 520). She is the wing of the next poet. There is a final recollection of the blue jay from the domain of the blue guitarist (*CP*, 184) as the mother, great nature, rises a "bearded queen, wicked in her dead light." This is the time, at last, for language from "the handbook of heartbreak" ("Madame La Fleurie," *CP*, 507). A quiet normal life becomes the only mode. The poet is in his house, his room, his chair. The crickets' chords are heard. "There was no fury in transcendent forms" (*CP*, 523).

He who goes down to the rock, whose fury was a sunward thrust, hears "At the earliest ending of winter, / In March, a scrawny cry. . . . A chorister whose c preceded the choir" (*CP*, 534). C is beginning, *do* before *mi,* as the *mi-bird* flew toward the meridian of autumn. The going down is not comfortless. Central man endures. A child sleeps in its own life. It will come to know both wing and claw, as a seabird scratches on shale (*CP*, 304), as the lion in the lute meets the lion in nature.

---

[11] Cf. "A Child Asleep in Its Own Life," *OP*, 106. The poem appeared in the London *Times Literary Supplement*, September 17, 1954, less than a year before the poet's death. It should be read as a lyrical meditation upon the presence of central man over the crib as the child begins its own life of the mind.

The Painter: Encounters of the Eye

11

CRITICS WRITE OF ART IN COMPENSATION FOR THE
works they are unable to produce. In this judgment of Etienne Gilson,
the critic seeks to turn plastic works of art into literature.[1] He continues
with a quotation from Gaston Bachelard on the supposed "success" of
the effort: "One has only to *write* the painted work. . . . Through the
substitute of literary imagination, all the arts are ours."[2] These admis-
sions pertain to aesthetic criticism. If the critic *writes* the painting because he cannot paint, or, for that matter, *writes* any art which he cannot practice, it follows that his minor talent seeks to appropriate the
work examined. He writes *as if* the shaping hand were his. Hence, in
these prospects, we may conclude that there can be no absolute aesthetic
criticism. The value of aesthetic judgment would seem to be confirmed
only in the strictest explication: e.g., that Wallace Stevens refers to a
prototypic image from the art of Picasso as he writes "The Man with

[1] *Painting and Reality* (New York, 1959), p. 211. Cf. Gilson's preceding contention: "The proper ground on which the painter stands is that of the existential
possibles; the ground occupied by the critic is that of the abstract possibles"
(p. 210).
[2] *Ibid.*, p. 211 and n. 23, p. 378. The source in Bachelard cited is *La Terre et les
rêves*, p. 95.

the Blue Guitar," or that Picasso refers to a prototypic iconography of African masks as he paints "Les Demoiselles d'Avignon." For the critic such expositions of fact appear alone to establish whatever authority he has.

Stevens' lecture-essay "The Relations between Poetry and Painting," delivered at the Museum of Modern Art in New York (1951), is disappointing. The promise of the title is not realized. One soon discovers that his critical approach falls short of explicitness. There is talk of a "fundamental aesthetic" manifested by all the arts, in the sense of Baudelaire; of Poussin and Racine as "inevitable" in French classicism; of a modern reality of "decreation" common to modern poetry and modern painting (NA, 160ff.). It is not very meaningful to note simply that "poetry and painting alike create through composition," that "a constructive faculty" is common to both, or that these arts in the mid-twentieth century are "sources of our present conception of reality" (NA, 163, 164, 176). Any second-rate critic could have written as much. The burden of the argument is cliché: The temper of every age is described by its artists.

But we do not begin here with a critic who writes of art to compensate for his own lack of primary talent. We are looking at a poet of major power who for some years had written in a mode of an intense visual authority, who had celebrated the primacy of light and the seeing eye; and we regard again the frequent purposiveness of his titles, language deliberately ordered to invoke an image of the maker as a poet-painter. If the lecture on poetry and painting tells us nearly nothing of fresh value, it is nonetheless certain that painting is a true subject in the poetry of Stevens and that an explicit demonstration of relationships is fully possible in the Grand Poem.

William Carlos Williams is the only other major American poet who may be related to Stevens through a similar objective. A comparison of Stevens and Williams in this respect must be the subject of another study. I do not intend here to estimate Williams save to observe that, despite his experiments with a painterly technique from "Portrait of a Lady" to "Pictures from Brueghel," he was not chiefly engaged with a poetry of aesthetic affinities. At the same time, I must assert that he was a better *critic* of painting than was Stevens. There is, for instance, nothing in the prose of Stevens comparable to Williams' brilliant note on Matisse. He speaks of a nude displayed in a gallery on Fifth Avenue (1921). "On the french [sic] grass . . . lay that woman who had never seen my poor land. The dust and noise of Paris had fallen from her with the dress and underwear and shoes and stockings which she had just put aside to lie bathing in the sun. So too she lay in the sunlight of the man's [Matisse's] easy attention. His eye and the sun had made day over her. She gave herself to them both for there was nothing to be told. Nothing is to be told to the sun at noonday. . . . So he painted her. The sun had entered his head in the color of sprays of flaming palm leaves."[3] An ease of existence *sun-drenched* is recognized as the subject. It may be argued that Williams is *writing* the picture. If he is, it is also true that he names here the everlasting subject of Matisse: the eye and the sun as the makers of *easy attention*. It is apparent that this ease describes, as well, the heart of Williams. One must pose against it the tension of Stevens. A full reading of Stevens' poetry confirms his unease again and again. As we read, we are aware of the tension of process as the work of the architect continues.

Michel Benamou in his sensitive comment on Stevens and painting writes persuasively of affinities with Monet. Both "express the poetry of a fluent universe, a vast stage for the wind, rain, sun, and moonlight, a poem of skies and waters in which the key word is weather."[4] He finds the woman-figure in "Sunday Morning" comparable to a figure by Matisse.[5] Yet he reaches a certain exasperation before he finishes. "Poetry lies when it tries to compete with painting. Color is in painting the real thing, in poetry a reflection of words. The true nature of an image is to become a metaphor."[6] The naming of the lie may be aesthetic rectitude for most critical opinion. But for Stevens it was not falsehood. And therein lies the difficulty. He chose to make painting a poetic subject; he projected it as one of the dominant arcs of his structure. Mr. Benamou's essay is particularly revealing in its summary. Nearly all that can be said of Stevens and painting *regarded in the old way of pointing to a convergence of qualities of perception in the viewer* is either stated or implied: here and there we are reminded of Monet, Matisse, Van Gogh. The modes of artists working in different media seem to meet. Some of this *being reminded* is inevitable for criticism. But the question still perseveres. Stevens' intention in the subject is to explore an integral relationship between poetry and painting. It is explicit resolve. Can there be an explicit critical demonstration of the purpose and of the means employed by the poet to redeem it from falsehood?

The naming of colors by a poet, no matter what the virtuosity of

[3] "A Matisse," *Selected Essays of William Carlos Williams* (New York, 1954), p. 30. The note was first published in *Contact,* II (1921).
[4] "Wallace Stevens: Some Relations between Poetry and Painting," *Comparative Literature,* XI (1959), 48.
[5] *Ibid.,* p. 50.
[6] *Ibid.,* p. 56.

the range, will not approximate painting. Neither will a concentration upon painterly subjects, landscapes or nudes, arrangements of objects on a table, or striking faces for portraiture. These acts of a poet are in the end nothing more than references to another art. It has been admitted that Stevens helps us scarcely at all with his lecture on poetry and painting. Yet there is one observation in it which I intend to claim as genuinely significant. Reflecting on a passage from Leo Stein's *Appreciation: Poetry and Painting,* he writes: "By composition he [Stein] meant the compositional use of words: the use of their existential meanings." Stevens then expands upon a line from Wordsworth's "Michael," used by Stein as an illustration of a composition "in which all the parts are so related to one another that they all imply each other." The old shepherd in his sadness went, some said, day by day to the site of the fold, "And never lifted up a single stone." If the sense were merely that a workman did not do his work, "these lines would have no existential value." But this last is a line of great poetry simply because of Wordsworth's "compositional use" of the words. They become "weighted with the tragedy [Michael's] . . . and saturated with poetry" (*NA*, 162–63). Thus all the words of the line *imply each other*.

Stevens does not proceed in his lecture beyond this recognition of the compositional principle. We may infer that he means in his following contention, "poetry and painting alike create through composition," to urge this analogy: the elements of poetry which are words imposed upon a base in design and the elements of painting which are colors conferred upon line are similar elements in composition. Let these terms of design as bare structure be reduced to a single principle: the skeletal idea. But, we may add, what of composition in the other arts? The answers seem clear. Musical notation is not a cognate, since music as it stands in the written score is a direction for an ordering of time. Neither architecture nor sculpture, in principle, is chiefly realized in an interrelationship of parts that *imply each other*. Both are intent upon the control of mass and volume in relation to space. When one considers dance, composition is found to be an ideal projection of bodily movement, an interaction of exaggerated motion and pause. If any two of the arts seem to meet in a similarity of compositional ends, poetry and painting are the only ones, however much, in some desire to compel synthesis, we may talk of color in music, music in architecture, sculpture in dance. In our carelessness of description we are probably nearer to Baudelaire's "fundamental aesthetic" than we think.

For intent readers of Stevens, it is often true that his poetry leaves a residuum in the mind of visual experience. We have been reading in a master of pictorial sight, who to our knowledge never painted a picture. *Seeing in color* becomes a dominant province of our memory of Stevens. When we return to him again, the impression is intensified. Every reading of "Hibiscus on the Sleeping Shores" (*CP*, 22–23) heightens the experience in color which endures in the residual mental image. It will not be unlike the intense image that endures after we have looked at the exploding colors of Emil Nolde, his "Sultry Evening" (1930) or his "Red Poppies" (1940).[7] I shall return presently to "Hibiscus." The poem is wholly pictorial in impression. It is executed as a painting. The mind roams "as a moth roams / Among the blooms beyond the open sand." The scene explodes with blue, purple, red, yellow. But it is not enough to name the colors. These alone will not establish an interaction of this poetic art with the art of the painter. We seek to know Stevens' method. The pleasure that we experience in an encounter with the poem approximates the response we make to the brilliance of Nolde or of any other powerful colorist. What has Stevens done? The answer must be found in the compositional use of words, the use of their "existential meanings." For to use words in the existential mode is to create in composition the poetic line in which all the parts imply each other. If Wordsworth's "And never lifted up a single stone" is a line saturated with poetry, then certain lines of Stevens' and certain poems are to be perceived as saturated with the elements of the painter's craft: color, light, and shadow.[8] The major subject of the painter in Stevens becomes the arc-line distinguishing his effort to penetrate the other realm, no matter what barriers mark its dominion. At these points of crossing over, his modal use of words in their "existential meanings" is the subject for concern.

Two aspects of process in both painting and poetry must precede questions of analysis directed to Stevens. There is first the work of the hand. Etienne Gilson notes of the painter: all his work is handmade. "It is the hand of the painter that embodies in actually existing physical objects the conceptions of his mind." He is a maker who has

---

[7] For a ready source of reproductions in color see Peter Selz, *Emil Nolde* (New York, 1964), a catalog of an exhibition of the artist's work at the Museum of Modern Art, New York City. See also Bernard S. Myers, *The German Expressionists: A Generation in Revolt* (New York, n.d.), pp. 153ff.

[8] On the painter's picture as an afterimage see Charles Johnson, *The Language of Painting* (Cambridge, 1949), p. 42. As the picture takes shape, the afterimage, which I regard here as the governing idea in the mind, takes its form through the elements of the painter's medium.

struggled since the Renaissance to advance his art as one of the "liberal arts." He has urged his claim by writing of his intellect as the director of his hand. He has become a "theorist" who has determined to negate his earlier status as a journeyman.[9] But then it can be said of workers in the other arts that the achievement is just as frequently handmade. As far as we are concerned, the distinction must rest in the singular painter's hand arranging the parts of a whole, each implying all the others, in a use of "existential meanings." This is to say that colors used by the painter derive their *present* existence in the picture through the relationships they bear among themselves. This assertion would probably be inadmissible if it were applied to a Minoan painter of frescoes, or to an apprentice decorating a choir stall in the chapel of a Venetian doge. But from the masters of the early Renaissance to the masters of the twentieth century the history of painting shows an endlessly mounting concern with the relative values of colors. From our point of observation this concern appears to have intensified very quickly in the brief span from the impressionists to the present. We admit readily the disappearance of tradition in the manner of the painter's sight and in his choice of subject. But it is the disappearance of the *absolute palette* which most impresses us. The mastery of the hand as the maker of relative values is dominant. The hand shapes a composition dependent upon colors in interplay, values that are literally determined by the presence of other values relative to them. It is in no sense the hand of the journeyman. It renders a private vision of the world in a metaphor of color; and, in so doing, it describes the mind of the artist.

Stevens wrote two poems on the shaping hand. They appear together in the final sequence of *Parts of a World*. In the first, "The Hand as a Being," the woman-genius of the poet rises in "the first canto of the final canticle." "Her hand composed him and composed the tree" (*CP*, 271). Her hand in his, he composes himself as he works, and shapes the tree of his life. The second of the poems, "Oak Leaves Are Hands" (*CP*, 272), presents a historic view of the imagination in the endurance of humanity. The tree of the first poem, the singular life, now becomes in this second disclosure an oak tree of the life of man. The leaves are the shaping hands of artists in succession. The woman of this poem is the everlasting feminine presence of the artist's genius. She is the consort of central man. Lady Lowzen has been many shapes to many men. She has been Flora, of ever-recurring spring.

---

[9] *Painting and Reality*, pp. 51–52.

She has been Mac Mort, as she was once expressed in what appears to be a Hindu sculpture of Siva's dance, multilegged, multiarmed. She it is who puts her hand to her brow and broods "on centuries like shells." The centuries are husks of the fruit of the past. For this poet Stevens she has a new, a "Northern sound." Passing his way in her eternal metamorphosis, she appears in "the movement of a few words"; and in this movement she "invigorates" in "glittering seven-colored changes" her everlasting *chromatism*. Hands are creators. Every leaf on the tree of the great oak is the leaf of a shaping hand. The nature of Lady Lowzen is found in the chromatism of her changes.

If an examination of Stevens' method as a poet-painter is to yield anything, the simple delight of impression at first encounter must be surpassed. No one will deny the unique pleasure of first-reading as he turns to the lyric devoted to St. Ursula. "Cy Est Pourtraicte, Madame Ste Ursule, Et Les Unze Mille Vierges" (*CP*, 21–22). The title announces another use of the "French imagination." It is cast deliberately in Old French: this portrait of Madame St. Ursula and the eleven thousand virgins. Our first impression must refer, in this sign from Stevens, to the art of a jewel-like illumination in a medieval manuscript. The delicacy of the hand is supreme. Blue, gold, pink, and green, a woman in red and gold brocade, the marguerite and the coquelicot, roses "frail as April snow," compose this garden. The mind immediately entertains analogies. This is a leaf, we say, from a saint's life or a Book of Hours or an Easter canticle. St. Ursula makes an offering of flowers on the altars of the Lord. But in the grass she offers radishes and flowers, timorously, in fear that the Lord will not accept offerings so strange. The radishes perplex us while the analogies hold.

Yet the radishes in the grass make all the difference. We require critical exaction and we put aside the analogies. This poem can tell us much about the essential Stevens. In view of earlier discussions of the "French imagination," no explanation of the foreign title is necessary. But St. Ursula must be seen as the woman-genius of the artist in another guise. The presence of "eleven thousand" virgins with her refers to a conformity of a countless number of artists, traditional workers in an act of worship; and the tradition is that of the illuminator of a manuscript. The work of arrangement in the poem is of the hand. St. Ursula may be related to Lady Lowzen. Her hand touches the hand of this poet. He makes his "portrait," his poem. Radishes are introduced by his hand among the traditional spring flowers. The offering is placed in the grass, not upon an altar. Yet it is pleasing to the Lord who "sought / New leaf and shadowy tint / And they were all

His thought." The Lord is the lord of imagination, the only lord. He seeks new leaf and "shadowy tinct" in his garden. Radishes as symbols of a commonplace reality are arranged with frail flowers. Eleven thousand virgins may worship in the tradition of decorating a spring altar. But the hand of St. Ursula is the iconoclast. The *shadowy tinct* arranged by her bold new poet is pleasing to the Lord. It is this *tinct* which reveals Stevens' method, rather than the enamels of the illumination. The leaf (poem) is *new*; the *tinct* is *shadowy*, with its radishes and flowers in grass. The *shadowy* color is made in the poem by relative values in interplay: the crude red of the radishes and the subtle colorings of the flowers. The image residual in the mind of the perceiver is the afterimage desired by the poet. It is not a copy of any traditional reaction, any more than the poem itself is a copy in words of a traditional illumination. The radishes are assertive. The harsh tone of the word, taken singly, sets up a relation with the opposing delicacy of tone in *coquelicot*. Beyond this relation Stevens clearly intends to create a relativity of imagined colors: crude, earthy radish red challenging frail tissue, field-poppy red.

The evidence that we reach is thus a use of words *in their existential meanings*. Through both sound and visualization, radish and coquelicot become what they were not, before they entered the poem. "Ste Ursule" gives us a primary example of Stevens' painterly way of image-making. The *shadow* in the *tinct* is the comparative value *between* two colors juxtaposed. If this existential creation of color through words is residual in the mind after several encounters with the poem, then the aesthetic effect intended by Stevens is achieved. Whatever some psychologist may wish in the future to say of aesthetic perception experienced before a painting and before a painterly poem of Stevens, the theory-in-process of Stevens will remain certain. And for some of us who read him, the authority of the afterimage, whether of the painting or of the poem at hand, will remain unquestionable. It is here that the momentariness of perception before the painting and Stevens' deliberately intended elusiveness of the poem meet *in compositional use*. When Emil Nolde painted a brilliant burst of red poppies, he recorded a momentary impression of them. Stevens will not get at momentary red through reference to poppy red alone. He is a poet. He achieves it through a careful juxtaposition of values through words. The momentariness is captured as he intended: "A poem is a meteor. . . . Poetry is a pheasant disappearing in the brush"; and finally, "A new meaning is the equivalent of a new word" ("Adagia," *OP*, 158, 173, 159).

This study has already asserted Stevens' full commitment to impressionism, and his distaste for professional modernism. His well-known entry in the "Adagia," a contention that he projected in his lecture on poetry and painting, reads: "To a large extent, the problems of poets are the problems of painters, and poets must often turn to the literature of painting for a discussion of their own problems" (*OP*, 160). Yet he shunned cubism, as I have noted; and his disagreement with every school of nonobjective painting is abundantly clear, first, no doubt, because it was a school of emulation as he considered it, and, second, because it reduced the primacy of color in composition. Thus he confessed to his Paris book-dealer, whom he had commissioned to look for and purchase paintings for him, a qualified view of Braque. "While I like Braque, I like him in spite of his modern perversions. There is a siccity and an ascetic quality about his color which is very much to my liking. Some of his greens and browns are almost disciplinary. In his case his modern perversions are not particularly offensive."[10] There will be no wonder here that Stevens urges a discipline of color and omits notice of design. An exhibition in 1963 of pictures owned by Stevens, most of them acquisitions through his Paris dealer, showed not one painting in the mode of cubism or post-cubism; and the one Braque, a lithograph, had never been framed, according to the poet's daughter.[11] Whatever his taste for living with a

[10] The comment appears in a letter to Miss Paule Vidal dated at Hartford, March 6, 1947; see *Letters*, p. 548.

[11] The exhibition, arranged with the permission and the assistance of Holly Stevens, took place in the Library of Trinity College, Hartford, in May and June of 1963. It was opened on May 7 with a panel discussion of Stevens in relation to painting. Samuel French Morse, Michel Benamou, and Miss Stevens were the chief participants. The discussion established interesting affinities between Paul Klee's notebooks and Stevens' "supreme fictions," after comparative readings by Mr. Morse. A survey of references to color in the poetry was conducted by Mr. Benamou, who argued for a broad aesthetic relationship between poetry and painting. Miss Stevens disclosed that her father left to his dealer Miss Vidal all decisions for purchase, in some instances after initial correspondence concerned with descriptions of the kind of painting desired. More frequently Stevens wrote in response to suggestions for purchase from Miss Vidal.

The Trinity College exhibition comprehended five watercolors, eight etchings, three Japanese prints, one pastel, and fifteen oils. The oils collected by Stevens represent work of the following artists: Henri Lebasque, Jean Marchand, Edmond Céria, Roland Oudot, Yves Brayer, Eric Detthow, William Kienbusch, Pierre Tal Coat, Jean Cavaillès, Jean Labasque, Camille Bombois. An original lithograph by Rodin was also shown.

Two of the paintings were renamed by Stevens: a "Still Life" by Tal Coat newly designated "Angel Surrounded by Paysans," the title of Stevens' poem of the angel of the imagination, and "Port of Cannes" by Cavaillès, called by Stevens "Sea Surface Full of Clouds." The findings of the discussion were that Stevens is related to painting through his insistence upon *visual sense experience*.

Braque lithograph, it is nonetheless true that structure as the *exposed* attribute of any painting did not primarily appeal to him. The frame of design was, of course, acknowledged as the base. But, since color in painting is like the poet's leafage, it is the clothing of design. Color is the essence of painting. It is the supreme expression of the imagination; as metaphor it describes the particular quality of the mind conceiving it.

The distance of a modern structure in painting from the colorist's impression is apparent for Stevens as he sets down the rigid lines of "The Common Life" (*CP*, 221). The poem has frequently been related to the idiom of Fernand Léger. In the "down-town frieze" there are a church steeple and the stack of the electric plant. They become black line against white line, or black line drawn on "flat air." The light is "morbid." In all this severity of structure, metaphor of the implacable modern city, the "woman" appears without rose and without violet. This bony genius of a painter is not for a man. There are no *shadows* (cf. the *shadowy tinct* of "Ste Ursule"). All is glare. The paper of the draftsman is whiter "for these black lines." The scene is as "shadowless" as the severity of Euclid: glaring paper "beneath the webs of wire" (and one recalls the webs of light and the webs of the eye, so much the sight of the colorist, as Stevens has described them in "Tattoo").[12] These are geometrical webs on nothingness. This poverty of vision is *the common life*. From Stevens' condemnation we understand that there will be no existential use of color or of words in an art restricted by this poverty. Mechanical existence is abstracted here as an angularity of black on white. There is no color.

The foregoing comment has intended to describe the first aspect of Stevens' process as poet-painter. The second requires brief notice before we turn to the arc of the poems related to painting. This second aspect is the nature of the mind described by the work of the hand. J. Hillis Miller, in his recent study of Stevens, notes that many modern

---

From the Stevens-Vidal correspondence it is evident that the impressionist qualities of Cavaillès and the boldness of the Tal Coat (according to Stevens, a still life displaying a "slap-dash intensity" rather than an interest in "solids") were of first significance for the poet. (See *Letters*, pp. 655–56 and 833, opinions addressed to Miss Vidal from Hartford on October 31, 1949, and May 13, 1954, respectively.) Of further interest is Stevens' professed admiration of Paul Klee (May 4, 1948) and of Jacques Villon (May 26, 1953) and his statement on the latter date of his having known Villon's brother Marcel Duchamp, presumably during his (Stevens') early years in New York, when he was frequently in the company of Walter C. Arensberg and other *avant-garde* writers and artists. (See *Letters*, pp. 595 and 777.)

[12] See above, ch. 7.

painters "have been obsessed with the fact that even the most distorted representation of a woman or a vase of flowers is still only a picture." Since there is no representational dimension, "the paintings are just these thick drops of paint squeezed from a tube." They are merely "manifest examples of matter."[13] This may often be the case. But it is difficult to see just how Mr. Miller might have supposed that this process describes Stevens. He continues: "A poem may start coherently enough, but as it progresses the poet becomes more and more exasperated with words and things." Hence Stevens, as his language finally "dissolves into incoherence" and "nonwords," spreads "a thick linguistic paste, like the splotches of paint on an expressionist canvas." At this point Mr. Miller concludes that Stevens, by "draining all referential meanings out of words," hopes only that their "sound and appearance" will remain.[14] These judgments from a sensitive and competent critic are surprising. In the first place, Stevens strongly opposed the painter's "manifest examples of matter" in thick smears such as Mr. Miller would have him approve. In the second place, though Stevens reserved the right to exert his principle "A new meaning is the equivalent of a new word," he wrote no incoherent poetry. The structure beneath the words, even when they are used *existentially*, relates to other structures of other poems in the total poem. These structures come of a mind that would not permit incoherence. There is no example in Stevens of a thick linguistic paste or, for that matter, of exasperation with words and things.

The mind governs. Its resolve upon a coherence of expression is implacable. A second look at Mr. Miller's judgment supplies the contention that "the poems in which language degenerates toward mere sound are among Stevens' gaudiest."[15] I return to the radical use that I have earlier stressed: *gaudeamus te*. The mind rejoices in the power transmitted to the hand, its power of prefiguring the linguistic pattern. The *gaudiness* of Stevens' poetry, wherever it occurs, is both rejoicing and control *in the mind*. It follows that Stevens looked at modern painting in the modern idiom: the picture is a painting of the mind. This is his way of regard, whether one speaks of Claude or Poussin, of the impressionist mode that was most satisfying to him, of cubism or postcubism, or of some thick paste of mere "matter," disturbing to Mr. Miller. In every instance, whatever the mode, a mind was described, whether it was a mind structured or formless. One adds to this way of

13 *Poets of Reality*, p. 251.
14 *Ibid.*, p. 252.
15 *Ibid.*, 253.

looking Stevens' constant requirement: poetry must be related to present reality (e.g., the radishes in the spring garden); so must painting. Robert Rosenblum writes of cubism and its aftermath: One of its essential aspects is "to deny a single definition of reality and to replace it with a multiple interpretation."[16] But is this not true of all painting since the inception of impressionism? A multiple interpretation is inevitable as soon as the individual work is seen to exist as a description of a unique mind. Stevens accepted this condition as the supreme fact of all modern painting. He would not have argued for an apparent discipline in the greens and browns of Georges Braque had he not so believed.

Modern theories of the mind exposed in painting are, of course, abundant. I shall cite a few of these with the intention of demonstrating the contemporaneity of Stevens. Michel Benamou notes that Stevens' rage for order resembles Cézanne's, that is, when the monster in the poet meets the monster in nature. "In a sense, his aesthetics were Cézanne's subjective ('expressing onself') objectivism ('realizing the object'). It is a personal meeting, an encounter with reality on terms of equality."[17] But I have already said as much in earlier discussions of Cézanne and Stevens. Some further notice of precision in the mind of Cézanne remains. Erle Loran provides an analysis of Cézanne's principle of organization: "planes and volumes moving around an imaginary central axis . . . [in a] power of . . . circular movement that gives the painting its ultimate 'closed' effect."[18] This critic is speaking particularly of the composition entitled *Sainte Victoire, Seen from the Quarry Called Bibemus.* The importance of circular movement in the organization of Stevens has been sufficiently stressed. In both painter and poet it is apparent that this *closed* effect proceeds from the structure of the mind. It comes of a principle imposed upon reality, leading on a containment of reality transformed in the picture as a self-ordained vision. The world in this containment is created anew. In the language of Stevens from "The Rock," "the icon is the man."

Stevens professed to his Paris dealer that he admired Paul Klee because he illustrated a principle: "The physical never seems newer than when it is emerging from the metaphysical."[19] The Bauhaus notebooks of Klee, comprehending the years 1921–33, were not available in a full English translation until 1961, when they were published

---

[16] *Cubism and Twentieth Century Art* (New York, 1960), p. 62.
[17] *Comparative Literature*, XI, 55.
[18] *Cézanne's Composition* (Berkeley, 1944), p. 61.
[19] To Miss Paule Vidal from Hartford, May 4, 1948; see *Letters*, p. 595.

under the title *The Thinking Eye*.[20] Yet we should not deny the possibility of Stevens' having seen them in an earlier German edition or of his having read an early European printing of the Klee lecture on modern art at Jena in 1924.[21] There is, for instance, Klee's theory of "grey": ". . . the fateful point between coming-into-being and passing-away . . . white and black at the same time . . . neither up nor down . . . neither hot nor cold . . . grey because it is a non-dimensional point, a point between the dimensions."[22] Stevens' "Gray Stones and Gray Pigeons," included in *Ideas of Order* in 1936, suggests the *fateful point* of Klee. The archbishop is away (i.e., the poet-priest). Without his presence all is gray: the church, the clouds. The sexton's stare is "in the air." The birds are "dry." The scene will remain gray until the bishop passes again in his colored robes (*CP*, 140). Gray in this metaphor is the point between the dimensions of color. Only the "dithery" gold of the sun falls upon the scene. The stasis is a center of possibilities, as though the movement of any color, up or down, hot or cold, were contingent upon the will of the "absent" poet. From Klee again a theory of diminution in the strength of color seems reflected by Stevens. Klee writes: "There is a yellowish red (so-called warm red) and also a bluish red (so-called cool red). . . . But from the stand-point of red, bluish and yellowish mean weakening."[23] Something of this weakening must be apparent in the late Stevens as he closes "An Ordinary Evening in New Haven" with images of "the little reds / Not often realized . . . / These . . . edgings and inchings of final form . . . / Like an evening evoking the spectrum of violet" (*CP*, 488). The mind, of course, orders this use of color as a sign of weakening. When one turns to Klee on modern art, in the Jena lecture, there appears a metaphor that we can scarcely exclude from possible relation to the poet's theory. "I have already spoken of the relationship between the two elements of earth and air. . . . The creation of a work of art—the growth of the crown of the tree—must of necessity, as a result of entering into the specific dimensions of pictorial art, be accompanied by distortion of the natural form. For, therein is nature reborn."[24] The step to Stevens is a short one. In the poet's theory, the root grips the rock; the

[20] Ed. Jürg Spiller, trans. Ralph Manheim (New York, 1961).
[21] This text in English would have been available to Stevens in the translation by Paul Findlay, *On Modern Art*, with an introduction by Herbert Read (London, 1948).
[22] *The Thinking Eye*, p. 3; see pp. 425 and 428 for diagrams describing central gray in relation to the dynamics of strong color.
[23] *Ibid.*, p. 486.
[24] *On Modern Art*, pp. 19–20. The symbol of *air* in this sense is a late development in Stevens. Cf. "An Ordinary Evening in New Haven," in particular, "the glass of air" (*CP*, 488). The crown of the tree, in Stevens the "tip," appears, however, as early as "Le Monocle de Mon Oncle" (*CP*, 16–17).

crown spreads in air; hence the poet's structure is of the air as nature is reborn in a structure described in the "leafage" of his color.

An earlier reference to Kandinsky has suggested an important affinity between the painter's mental image of the moving triangle and the poet's image of the arc.[25] I add here the possibility of Stevens' having known the "prose poems" of Kandinsky, written between 1912 and 1937 and attached to the manifesto *Concerning the Spiritual in Art*. Kandinsky's pieces on the "color symphony" contain an interesting metaphoric cadence on the "Fagott" (English: *Bassoon*). The translation runs: "By virtue of distended, long drawn-out, rather inexpressive, indifferent tones of a bassoon, moving a long while in the depths of the void, everything gradually turned green. First deep and rather dirty. Then lighter and lighter. . . ."[26] The painter "sees" color in the tone of the instrument. But it is his impression of *green* in the tone, the presence of a harsh, primitive color which relates immediately to the poet.

Stevens' use of images of woodwinds is not extensive. But in two important instances they appear as symbols of the governance of the mind; and in each it is a purging of the mind of old, or inherited, images that is signified. It is as though the poet sought anew the primitive potential of his own *green*. The first instance appears in "The Man on the Dump" (*CP*, 201–3). He surveys a rubbish heap of old images. "One rejects the trash." And then, "That's the moment when the moon creeps up / To the bubbling of bassoons." The "mattresses of the dead" are rejected. The world is made new. The second instance employs a cousin of the bassoon, the oboe. In his "Asides" for this instrument, Stevens once again "washes" the mind. "The prologues are over. It is a question, now, / Of final belief" (*CP*, 250). "Asides on the Oboe" are meditations on the authority of a mind free, as though in primitive green, to make as it wills. The suggestiveness of Kandinsky's "Bassoon" is insistent. If Stevens did not know this painter's "poem," then the coincidence is remarkable. For Kandinsky the "spiritual in

25 See above, ch. 5.
26 Probably read by Stevens in the first English translation by Michael Sadleir (London, 1914). I use here the edition cited earlier (New York, 1947), pp. 81–83. Stevens' one thus far published reference to Kandinsky appears in a letter to Thomas McGreevy, dated at Hartford, October 24, 1952. "It is easy to like Klee and Kandinsky. What is difficult is to like the many minor figures who do not communicate any theory that validates what they do, and, in consequence, impress one as being without validity. And non-objective art without an aesthetic basis seems to be an especially unpleasant kettle of tripe" (*Letters*, p. 763). This observation reinforces Stevens' frequently restated principle: no aesthetic authority without a base in theory; see, for instance, the "Adagia": "The theory of poetry is the life of poetry" (*OP*, 178).

art," the painter's communication, had its own social function. One supposes that he stood in agreement with the dictum of Apollinaire: "It is
the social function of great poets and artists to continually renew the
appearance nature has for the eyes of men." Poets and artists preserve
men from wearying of "nature's monotony."[27] I return again to Stevens'
closed vision. His "playing" of the bassoon and the oboe does not refer
beyond his art. Although his renewal of nature may suggest the way
to freedom for other men, he is not dedicated to a cleansing of sight
as a "social function." As he determines in the closing line of "Asides
on the Oboe," he will be "The glass [imagining] man, without external reference."

Stevens' very limited notice of Picasso is guarded. He accepted, of
course, and admired the Blue Period of this master. He could agree
with Picasso that a modern picture is "a horde of destructions" (*CP*,
173); and he finds that the same is true of a modern poem (*NA*, 161).
Yet, in the lecture on poetry and painting, he found the uncompromising nature of modern art expressed in Picasso's "surprise" at people
who ask for meaning in a picture (*NA*, 167). Stevens was not interested
in the "social function" of his poetry, as I have said. Nonetheless, he
wrote no poetry without meaning. We may proceed beyond his statements in the lecture to say that he resisted modern art of a studious
nonmeaning for the simple reason that he believed a work of art
should clearly display the mind of its maker. How much of Picasso's
mind he may have found revealed in the more abstruse styles I am not
prepared to say. But his praise of freedom in Picasso is certainly
ungrudging. He quotes Christian Zervos on the artist-iconoclast at
work: "The expression of his spirit has destroyed the barriers which
art . . . impressed on the imagination." Stevens adds: "To take
Picasso as the modern [painter] one happens to think of, it may be
said of him that his spirit is the spirit of any artist that seeks to be
free."[28] It is clear that Stevens refers to freedom of an artist's mind
here, and nothing else. We may add that it is the freedom of the
painter which began with early impressionism.

For one must always return to Stevens' allegiance. The guideline
must hold. As he thinks of this mind in freedom, it is the "poetics" of
impressionism that endures. One should return again and again to the
note on Jean Labasque: "But if the only really great thing in modern
art: impressionism, was poetic, the poetic is not to be flipped away

[27] *The Cubist Painters: Aesthetic Meditations*, trans. Lionel Abel, Documents of
Modern Art (New York, 1944), pp. 12–13.
[28] In his address "The Irrational Element in Poetry" (*OP*, 226).

because that particular poetic expression is *vieux jeu*" (*OP*, 293). In the mid-twentieth century the *jeu* may be old. Nonetheless, for Stevens it was the only modernism that counted, this liberation of the painter's mind which began a century ago. It was freedom from bondage to the representational, freedom from reality as absolute tyranny. A tone of vexation appears in a late letter of Stevens' to his Paris bookdealer. They have corresponded about a possible purchase of a painting by Bezombes. Stevens replies that he is not interested in a picture representing a landscape on the Loire. "My only possible objection to it is that it may be a view and what I want is a pure painting. I mean by this that I care nothing about the Chateau d'Amboise but I do care for the colors of the work."[29] These remarks sufficiently establish the poet's insistence on *pure painting*, as he regarded it.

Color is the essence. Design established in reality, mind described in design, to summarize here, will preserve meaning as the colors express the work of imagination. The hand will order a relativity of values. A view unaltered is not a painting. This is the view seen through a pane of glass. If a smear of paint ungoverned by a formless mind is incoherence to the aesthetic position of Stevens, then one may say, beyond this unacceptable state, that pure representation to him expressed no mind at all. The satires of René Magritte on bourgeois complacency, cited earlier, should delight the student of Stevens' aesthetics.[30] Once again, the sequence of paintings in *The Human Condition* is appropriate emendation for the critic. The transparency on the easel frames the view beyond the window. There are no paints and brushes. The picture was finished the moment the framed transparency enclosed the prospect. One has had one's encounter with painting!

With these qualifications of Stevens' approach to the alliance of painting and poetry I turn to the arc of the painter. The method of examination to be used is that applied to the portrait-poem presenting St. Ursula. We wish to examine the continuance of Stevens' method, his compositional use of words in their existential meanings, and, therefore, his use of words analogous to a painter's use of colors in relative values. It must again be emphasized that the determined interplay of

[29] To Miss Paule Vidal, Hartford, July 22, 1953. Stevens' carbon copy of the letter is in the possession of his daughter, Holly Stevens. By permission of Miss Stevens.
[30] See above, ch. 8.

words, and not a mere naming of colors, is the poetic condition for study.

An effect of *momentariness* in sight is the objective of the impressionist painter. I have related Stevens to this aesthetic in calling attention to his view of a poem as a meteor, a pheasant. These images describe his poetic objective. The first experiments with painting-in-poetry are intent upon a metaphoric flow of water. An exposition of this preference occurs in the first stanza of "Le Monocle de Mon Oncle" (*CP*, 13). The genius of poetry is addressed. Nothing is "like the clashed edges of two words that kill." The poet wishes he might be "a thinking stone." But to be human is to know the flowing mind. Out of "the sea of spuming thought," beauty was borne in a radiant bubble. Thought alone knew this first radiance. But "a deep up-pouring from some saltier well" within the poet bursts the bubble, "its watery syllable." In this eloquent metaphor the struggle is described. A clash of words along their edges will kill the poem. The watery syllable in the mind will burst. Its momentary radiance will disappear. The prosaic sense of the passage is that the bubble from the spume must be articulated and brought to form in language that will preserve the effect of momentariness. This is a confrontation of the problem of the hand, quite as though one had named this *language* as *color* in the aspiration of impressionism or in that of the solitary Cézanne after his desertion of the impressionist school. We begin in the chronology of Stevens with a metaphor of thought that flows like water. The problem of poetry lies in the words. Radiance as set forth in the lines from "Le Monocle" is the possibility of color in the form. It must be realized in words. The painter in Stevens does not work with words *experientially,* as though the poem took form at happenstance, one word or one expressed image suggesting another. Consciousness flows. But the mind must be the tyrant of the momentary. Its design will require *the* expressive language and no other. A clash (an ineptitude) of words *kills,* we assume, both the thought and the composition.

Thus it is that Stevens' early poems are poised on water. These are true experiments with painting in poetry. The succession begins with "The Paltry Nude Starts on a Spring Voyage" (*CP*, 5). It has been long recognized that Stevens plays here with the old imagery of Botticelli's *The Birth of Venus.* A dead myth is at once recognized. Aphrodite-Venus is now merely spring. Her shell is replaced by a piece of seaweed. She will be succeeded by summer. If she is "paltry," the next season is to be a "goldener nude." The composition takes form as a painting in the interplay of words of the sea surface and sea volume with words of movement expressed by the two female figures of the seasons. The first group opens with "glitters" of the surface, continues with the "brine and bellowing / Of the high interiors of the sea," returns to "water-shine," and concludes with "spick torrent." The second opens with "scuds" as the figure moves on the surface, proceeds to the blowing of the wind on her back, to "scurry" (misprinted "scrurry" in *CP*) as her heels "foam," to "sea-green pomp, / In an intenser calm," as the second nude of summer is foretold. The action of sea surface is the base of these countermovements of scudding feet and foaming heels. The composition stands as a diptych. The second scene is qualified by sea-green pomp bearing a nude more golden than the first, by a deeper calm on the "spick torrent." The two figures are not separate, however. They are artfully joined by "scuds" and "scurry" of the first and "scullion" of the second. The sea itself has "high interiors," as though the surface, sun-illuminated, convered a bellowing space beneath. Botticelli "repainted" here falls to a hand without response to the myth. The seasons are now related to the mechanism of waves. Yet the poem as a composition has great visual expressiveness, precisely because of the interplay of the language, in "scurry," "spick," "scullion," and in such unaccustomed verbal use as that of sea "interiors." Speed of movement is determined by this diction. The effect is momentary.

"The Load of Sugar-Cane" (*CP*, 12) is a small wonder of metaphoric water movement. *Every object* in the composition is crafted to be *like every other one*. The first image of the glade boat is modified by the flowing water. It is *like* the water "flowing / Through the green saw-grass, / Under the rainbows." The rainbows are *like* birds "Turning, bedizened." The birds turn *while* the wind whistles "As kildeer do." The kildeer *rise* at the red turban of the boatman. This spot of vivid red at the close would have nothing to do with painting in Stevens' principle of composition were it not for the fluid course of words and images, all of which imply each other. The poem, weighted with no meaning save its compositional quality, is a perfect example of the common ground of poetry and painting, as Stevens saw it.

This "wideness" of the mind apparent in a likeness of images composing the picture is frequently repeated. So in "Hibiscus on the Sleeping Shores" (*CP*, 22–23) the mind is a moth "Among the blooms beyond the open sand." From its drowsing in the tropical afternoon along the "bony" shores and the "blather" of the water, it rises "besprent" to seek the flaming red of the hibiscus, "dabbled with yellow pollen." Stevens imposes a splash of red to establish the picture.

"Blather" is nonsense in this "stupid afternoon." It is challenged, shaken, by the springing up of "besprent," leading on the hibiscus red. Languor as a total verbal effect is not the objective. It is a languor intensified by the red flower, a drowsing along the shore made languorous precisely because of the red seized by the roaming mind. And by the same principle the red is intensified by the languor. One element of perception is relative to another element of perception. The poem moves from inaction to the momentary assertiveness of the flower and back to inaction. The impression left in the mind of the reader was intended to be wholly visual; and it is. The bright image at the center emerges from the lapping water and dissolves into the drowsing in which the poem opens.

Immediately following "Hibiscus" comes a scene on the beach in "Fabliau of Florida." The "French" imagination suggested in the title is appropriate for the night. A moon-lit boat on the shore organizes the picture. The black hull is the one point of stasis. Every element in perception moving about it dissolves, shape into shape, "alabasters" and "night blues," foam and cloud. The surf drones. The boat, like the red flower, establishes the moving relationships of all the colors. Both this piece and "Hibiscus" are experimental; yet they are perfect inquiries into the method of the impressionist painter and into the possibilities of transferring it to poetry. The technique of creating a composition of parts, each in itself implying all the others, is further refined.

"Floral Decorations for Bananas" (CP, 53–54) is a pause in a moment of humor as the subject proceeds. Stevens momentarily reflects upon what it may be to paint bananas without "floral" decorations. "Floral" in the title specifies the work of the individual imagination in an impressionist's composition. Let us suppose, he begins in addressing himself ("nuncle"), a composition of "blunt yellow in such a room." The "insolent" bananas glare against the décor (recalling the frequent eighteenth-century settings of Harmonium). It needs, this composition, "something serpentine." The designer observes that "the table was set by an ogre"; and here he refers to that familiar giant, central man in the imagination, who this time is expressed without the refining touch of the individual imaginer. The bananas are simply gross, oozing gum out of that insistent purple tip of bloom (as one sees it on the plant preparing for its fruit). The arrangement is one of raw yellow, raw green of leaves from the "Carib trees," raw purple. The poem expresses high-spirited satire directed to painting that is grossly representational or to color about as raw as one may encounter in, for example, any secondary cubist. The title of this piece may be altered and extended in this way: still life with bananas, leaves and stalks on a table, in need of the transforming power of a "floral" imagination. The conclusion reached is that raw reality transferred to canvas and left unaltered by the fluid mind is not masterly painting. This is composition displaying absolutely no principle of relative values. It is the exact obverse of the "compositional use" asserted in "Hibiscus."

These early poems of Stevens' often show a particular fondness for opening scenes that assume the dimensions of painting and then give place to reflection upon themes apart from the initial composition. This practice appears in the "slum of bloom" of the summer garden opening "Banal Sojourn" (*CP*, 62–63) and in the vivid range of color introducing the meditation of "Sunday Morning" (*CP*, 66–70). It is seen again in the swift passage of the first three sections of "Peter Quince at the Clavier" as the woman in blue-shadowed silk is quickly transformed into Susanna bathing in the clear green water and spied upon by the red-eyed elders. Susanna is a summer nude. After her initial garden scene she disappears; and we hear that "Beauty is momentary in the mind" (*CP*, 91). The green of summer pools in summer gardens endures forever in human imaginations. It is "a wave, interminably flowing." One summer dies; one imagination dies. But the wave is endless; and in its flowing every vision of beauty is momentary. One should expect to find in Stevens a poet's pure delight in the swiftness of the picture. Since mind is fluid, every color is fleet. On the way to his masterpiece of painting, Stevens thinks of "lightning colors . . . in me . . . flinging / Forms, flames, and the flakes of flames" (*CP*, 95).

The masterpiece is, of course, "Sea Surface Full of Clouds" (*CP*, 98–102). So much praise of this poem through all the years of Stevens' reputation seems to tell us only this: it is a supreme tribute to the imagination in its power to color the phenomenal world. Sea surface is the one reality here. All else is imagined. In the poem Stevens gives us five impressionist paintings in which color is the sole subject. Each is a morning poem. But the light changes, from the first through the last, in intensity. We regard the same scene in sunlight, in grayness of an overcast sky, in mist. The "moving blooms" (Sec. 1) are *evolved* "out of the light." Close attention shows that the five compositions are executed in variations of red, blue, and green (with an introduction of yellow in the second). The "role" of red is assumed by the "chocolate,"[31] which has, of course, no reference to the absolute value that we

---

[31] "Chocolate" appears in each of the five sections of the poem, in the following sequence of values: 1, "rosy"; 2, "chop-house"; 3, "porcelain"; 4, "musky"; 5, "Chinese" (*CP*, 99–102). On the "Chinese" value Stevens commented in a letter

name in "chocolate brown." Each of the reds, in constant metamorphosis, section to section, is furthermore associated with "umbrellas," a pervasive sign in Stevens of a brief "domical" experience of the imagination. Thus the reds signify the vigor of the imagination. The greens and the blues flow constantly on the sea surface, extending and crossing one another in a dazzling fabric of interrelated values.

The power of words in their existential meanings as related to the painter's compositional use of color was never again to be so fully exploited by Stevens. Each morning vision of these "blooms," *evolved* from the light striking the eye and from the light of the imagination, differs from the next. Yet the mechanical sea, the reality, continues the same. One may propose that this poem stands unmatched in the English language. It is not only a full demonstration of a principle, that poetry and painting may meet in the compositional use of words and colors. It is also a testament to the ultimate possibility that the afterimage produced by a poem of this aesthetic will be of exactly the same kind as that enduring beyond actual sight of a composition in pigments. A way of seeing and imagining and a technique of describing the mind may be common to the creators of both poetry and painting. A blue of Stevens' poem may be "rainy hyacinth" or "brilliant iris" or "transfigured" blue. In each instance the value is what it is because other values surround it. In the mind there is a fluid state of perception which matches the flow of the sea surface. In sheer power, mind and sea are equal.

Stevens pauses with a sense of irony in the little comment of "Tea" as *Harmonium* closes. "Sea Surface" comes from the world of the mariner of imagination. The robust voyager is the maker of his world of color. In "Tea" the umbrellas accompanying the bold chocolate-reds of "Sea Surface" are rediscovered. But how diminished they are! One thinks of Boston.[32] It is late autumn. The park is frost-bitten. Inside, in the warmth of lamplight the porcelain glows with "sea-shades and sky-

---

to John Pauker (Hartford, June 3, 1941), obviously in answer to a question of Pauker: "The words are used in a purely expressive sense and are meant to connote a big Chinese with a very small cup of chocolate: something incongruous" (*Letters*, p. 389). There is no mention of the other four values; but clearly the persistence of "chocolate" in its recurrence as a naming of color is compositional. Stevens on the big Chinese with the small cup seems oddly whimsical. It is worth noting that it is in this same letter that he contends: "The basis of criticism is the work, not the hidden intention of the author."

[32] See the comment on the poem by Harry Levin, *Harvard Advocate* (Wallace Stevens Issue), CXXVII, No. 3 (December, 1940), 30. Mr. Levin's reading agrees with the one which I offer here. He thinks of the pattern as "a piece of New England *chinoiserie*," although he does not relate the umbrellas here to the same figures in "Sea Surface Full of Clouds."

shades, / Like umbrellas in Java" (*CP*, 113). We infer the difference. A Boston parlor in autumn is warm and secure. Once there were mariners of Boston in the East India trade. The tea service is a little memento of an earlier and a bolder life. Sea-shades and sky-shades of Java are remote from this habitude. The umbrellas have become teacup size. The colors are quaint.

For a cautious tea-drinker in Boston, we suppose, not to have known the large colors is not to have a sense of loss. But a sense of his weakening in the power to color is an experience of the painter. It is an experience of the poet. Well into *Ideas of Order,* following the brilliance of color in *Harmonium*, Stevens takes the mask of his "Anglais Mort à Florence" (*CP*, 148–49). He remembers "the time when he stood alone, / When to be and delight to be seemed to be one, / Before the colors deepened and grew small." He is to remain faithful to the painter. But he knows that the height of color, its largeness, will diminish from this time to his own end in a final darkness. "Like Decorations in a Nigger Cemetery" (*CP*, 150–58) contains brief exertions of the painter's hand. But already the temper of the poetry shows strong prefigurings of the intense meditation that will mark the last sequences. The poetic tone sounds with a stark regret in "A Fish-Scale Sunrise" (*CP*, 161). Though the mind "perceives the force behind the moment, / The mind is smaller than the eye." What we look for in the succeeding intellection of "The Man with the Blue Guitar" is the mind at work in creating for itself a momentary habitation in color. We seek the theory that we learned in *Harmonium*, the freedom to experience color for itself alone. But the poem does not yield this experience. It is deep in social commentary, exposing the problem of the contemporary poet who would command reality, and the imprisonment of the imaginations of his countrymen in a quotidian existence. Two major changes in the poet are manifest: the mind no longer seeks the composition *fully* wrought by the painter, sensing its waning power to think in color; the painter's poem is itself no longer enough. Thus the pink and white carnations in the brilliant bowl, this purity that simplifies the day, are insufficient. There are torments in the self which must be answered. "The imperfect is our paradise." It is in us (*CP*, 193–94). The mind must be answered. So must the imperfect. One recognizes, of course, that it is not the technique of "Sea Surface" that has been forgotten; the later poetry provides evidence that the power to make the colors endured for many years. Yet Stevens knew that the act of the painter alone was insufficient to the total structure that he purposed. The arc of the painter advances. But we should expect a weakening of exclusive devotion. If the colors grow small, then it amounts to the poet's determination "to behold himself" as the resolve comes in "Prelude to Objects" (*CP*, 194). The mind changes, no matter what the certainties of its architecture and of the self that it is constantly completing.

When Stevens returns to the subject of the still life, he comments on academicism in painting as a barrier imposed upon both the eye and the imagination. The much-quoted "Study of Two Pears" (*CP*, 196–97) begins with a pedagogical proposition: the pears resemble nothing else; they are what they are. It follows that the colors, as they are applied, are separate and self-contained. They are not determined by an imagination ordering relationships. "The pears are not seen / As the observer wills." Thus the poem condemns pedagogy in the academies, and, in the metaphor, the imposition of any proposition upon the imaginative life. Reality of any sort must be treated as the individual observer wills. Within its limits this poem is successful. But it is not a composition in the poet's color. Nor, as a satiric piece, is it as sure in touch as the earlier "Floral Decorations for Bananas." By the time one has reached and studied the rubbish heap of "The Man on the Dump" (*CP*, 201–3), with its rejection of the trash of old images, the certainty of the future seems clear. Every painterly poem thereafter, though there may be intermittent attention to problems in composition through a relativity of words, will be directed to ideas that are outside the picture.

Such is the case with the satire of "The Common Life" (*CP*, 221) as the black lines on white are rigidly drawn, and the idiom of Léger[33] is examined in its metaphor of the modern city. Even the apparent intent to return to a full composition in color falters in a picture "Of Hartford in a Purple Light" (*CP*, 226–27). The earlier light of this day was masculine. This "irised" twilight glow is feminine, as the muscularity of the city "slops away." The images pull against one another; the metaphor is strained, as though the journey of the sun "from Havre to Hartford" or "aunts in Pasadena" had something to do with the immediacy of this composition. One does not question the eye of the impressionist. But the mind tangles here. If the picture seems to move toward a self-contained form at one or two points, in the end

---

[33] Stevens' interest in Léger is reflected twice in his letters to Mrs. Barbara Church (*Letters*, pp. 568, 713). In the second letter, dated at Hartford, April 6, 1951, he speaks of having gone to see exhibitions of Léger's pictures and books in New York.

it disintegrates. This is the last of Stevens' poems in which an attempt is made to return to the idiom of the painter's poetry in *Harmonium*.

The rest is expression in a different mode. A ship at sea is studied at the close of "Variations on a Summer Day" (*CP*, 235). At a distance the sight is blurred. "The mist was to light what red / Is to fire." This form of an equation will endure henceforth as the habitude of the late Stevens. As he returns to the painter in each instance, he will choose to employ painting as metaphor. In "Woman Looking at a Vase of Flowers" it is the bird of retrospection, the owl, that reflects upon what *was*. (This bird symbol is to figure in the last reflective poetry, in "The Owl in the Sarcophagus.") Brooding upon a state of the mind in an earlier time, the owl is to tell *how* once "High blue became particular . . . how the central, essential red / Escaped its large abstraction. . . ." It knows *how* "the inhuman colors fell" in "An affirmation free from doubt." In that time that *was*, "formlessness / Became the form and the fragrance of things / Without clairvoyance . . ." (*CP*, 246–47). The disclosure of the owl is the poet's admission. Once the imagined colors made the composition. In the poet's past there was once a form *without clairvoyance*. If painting now becomes metaphor, it is the mind unable to rest entirely in a display of color that makes it so. Clairvoyance becomes the end. The movement toward the new objective of mind is inevitable. Unlike the painter who is wholly a maker of color, the later Stevens will not be satisfied with the achievement of a pure sensuousness alone. Yet at this point, and through "Notes Toward a Supreme Fiction," retrospection upon what was continues. If clairvoyance in Stevens were directed toward a reality of the superhuman, then we should have nothing to speak of in terms of a full architecture. But the *clear seeing* in Stevens will not search beyond the human; it must be limited to a completion of design. I have already specified the nature and the limits of Stevens' ontology. These are apparent in the Canon Aspirin sequence of "Notes." The Canon at the "utmost crown of night . . . chose to include the things / That in each other are included . . . the amassing harmony" (*CP*, 403). The equation holds. Each of the subjects of the Grand Poem is equal in value to each of the others. Each stands in relation to the total harmony as mist is to light, or red to fire. This making of an "amassing harmony," and this alone, is *clairvoyance*.

And so it is that painting and the projections of a full poetic design are equated in "So-and-So Reclining on Her Couch" (*CP*, 295). "The arrangement," the poet notes, "contains the desire of / The artist." In this poem "One walks easily / The unpainted shore."

The arrangement points to clairvoyance, not to the single act of endlessly painting the shore. With age, white has become "Sharp as white paint in the January sun," and the yellow that is needed is "Less Aix than Stockholm" (CP, 312). A Northern yellow, it is "hardly a yellow at all." As the colors fade and the sharpness of white stands "in the punctual center of all circles" (CP, 366), the future becomes "description without place, / The categorical predicate, the arc" (CP, 344).

"Notes Toward a Supreme Fiction" reveals a full retrospective view of the painter that was. A one-time planter on a blue island with wild orange trees looks back before his death. He is the poet in age who thinks often "of the land from which he came" (CP, 393). "The blue woman, linked and lacquered," familiar genius of the poet, looks from her window. "It was enough / For her that she remembered." The "fierce addictions" are gone. "Feathery argentines" have become "cold silver." Through the window she names "the corals of the dogwood, cold and clear" (CP, 400). At the center of all circles stands sharp white, utter clarity of the colorless all-color, that is, the crossing of another spring meridian but now a crossing without the old festivals of spring color. "Bouquet of Roses in Sunlight" (CP, 430–31) and "The Bouquet" (CP, 448–53) extend the reverie. The first, using the plural, speaks for what is true of men: the life of feeling as a making of metaphor, a coloring of the world, until each one in age reaches white, where "the sense lies still, as a man lies . . . in a completing of his truth." The second, in summation of a total theory, speaks of colors as "questions of the looks they get." In every eye there is "a special hue of origin" (CP, 451). This for Stevens is as it *was*. The bouquet lies on the floor. Memory reflects upon the beginning. It was the inception of the poet-painter, moving as a human life must move, "toward a consciousness of red and white as one" (CP, 450).

A man begins in the green of vitality. The last poem of the painter is companion to the last poem of wing and claw. In "The Green Plant" (CP, 506) October's lion roses have turned to paper, "And the shadows of the trees / Are like wrecked umbrellas." The arc-line of the painter descends to earth. The umbrellas of "Sea Surface," now "wrecked," are in this last glance, as the green plant glares in its barbarous potentiality for another maker of color, the youth, the new poet who comes on in the endless succession.

The Comedian: Masques and Festivals

12

IN "THE AURORAS OF AUTUMN" THE REFLECTION
pauses upon the old "pageants out of air, / Scenes of the theatre."
"What company, / In masks, can choir it with the naked wind?"
Humanity stands always "in the tumult of a festival." But for this
poet, a maker of pageants, the hour is late; the wind blows, and the
night sky is streaked with sinister flames. The musicians "play at"
a tragedy. "There is no play" (*CP*, 415–16). In "An Ordinary Evening in New Haven" the maskers reappear. The *center* has been
reached. It is "a neuter shedding shapes in an absolute." There
was once a blue condition of the mind before this neuter. Of the
earlier blue, only "the transcripts" remain, "the shapes that it took
in feeling, the persons that / It became." The "neuter" has been
studied under another name in the preceding chapter: the sharp
white at the center when the colors are gone. The transcripts of the
blue are the "leaves" of the past. They memorialize the process of
an imagination in its earlier vigor. There comes a time when the
choir of maskers cannot match the wind. Then there is only a last
twilight muttering (*CP*, 479).

The subject of the comedian in Stevens, as he names it, is
"the tumult of a festival." Allowing for much that has been written

of Stevens and the comic spirit,[1] we must assert that the comedian from the moment of his first appearance was the reveler who felt the shadow. The seventh and the eighth poems of *Harmonium* are portentous. With a relentless vision they foretell the winds of autumn and a "mind of winter" when the sun will glitter on the white waste (*CP*, 8–10). The "black cataracts" (*CP*, 533) and the "white paint in the January sun" (*CP*, 312) are still distant. But the revelry of the early poetry flourishes in defiance of the poverty and the tragedy of humankind, life that moves to death in the reality of the unyielding rock. One does not expect to find Stevens and Eliot at any point in accord. Yet the close of Eliot's "East Coker" provides a language appropriate for Stevens; and so too does the last section of "Little Gidding." "In the end is my beginning." "The end is where we start from."[2] For Eliot the dove of the Holy Spirit descends, breaking the air; for Stevens nothingness is inevitable at the neutral center. Nonetheless, the end of Stevens is in his beginning. The arc rises in the knowledge of the end. His poet's reality is the dominant principle of his structure, the "amassing harmony." There is the accompanying act of foretelling, of how it will be when the actors depart, how it will be in a world of white on the threshold of black.

The expression of the comedian in Stevens reveals his delight in the multiform acts of the master of revelry. Robert Rosenblum writes of Paul Klee's fondness for his Clown: the figure "offers a reprise of a theme . . . that of duality of personality, as revealed in masks and actors."[3] The same is true in the art of Stevens, save that the actors of the poetry are not always the personae of the maker. Peter Quince, who plays the clavier in the renowned poem of his name, is Stevens (*CP*, 89); so is Liadoff at the piano (*CP*, 346–47). But these are examples of the exceptional rather than the usual in the poetry. More frequently the actors are summoned to roles expressing the poet's reflection upon conditions of art and society, as in the swiftly moving company representing the imaginations of other men in "The Ordinary Women" (*CP*, 10–12). The setting of every poet, in the sense of Stevens, is a theater of the mind. The talent of the poet displayed there is his power to create and to govern actors. But it is the distinction of Stevens that his actors

---

[1] See, for instance, the recent study by Daniel Fuchs: *The Comic Spirit of Wallace Stevens* (Durham, 1963).
[2] *Four Quartets* (New York, 1943), pp. 17, 38.
[3] *Cubism and Twentieth Century Art,* p. 257.

always relate to commonplace reality. They are not maskers of a *jeu d'esprit* alone, a pageant in the air existing as mere phantasy. Although Stevens assumes the mask of Ariel in the valedictory of "The Planet on the Table" (*CP*, 532), he was never from his beginning to his end a mere ingenuous Ariel of the clouds. In each masque of his making he was intent upon the rock. Nor was Stevens as Peter Quince solely content with the gossamer of *A Midsummer Night's Dream.* Peter in Shakespeare's play is a joiner who yearns to command revelers; Stevens referred to himself as "this carpenter" (*CP*, 478) thirty years after he had first assumed Peter's mask at the clavier. Yet every script of Stevens the comedian holds to the principle: poetry as a meeting of imagination and reality as equals.

One comes to know the roles of the poet—Peter Quince, the "father" in "The Auroras," or Ariel—and to recognize Stevens in the play; and one learns to distinguish the parts that he assigns to his actors. The troupe is a large one. Its diversity, both in the range of the poet's participation and in the variety of the performers commanded, presents another display of metamorphosis. Here is evidence again of the Grand Poem as process. The swiftness of performance accords with the impressionist vision of the painter which has just been examined. Stevens the painter gives place to Stevens the maker of masques. We shall presently consider Stevens' early interest in harlequinade. For it is to the tradition of the *commedia dell' arte* on the Continent rather than to the English masque that he was attracted. In the full range of modern American poetry Stevens is unique in this aptitude. He found very early in his career, as he put his imagination to French tutelage, a fascinating range in such prototypes as the Pierrot of Laforgue. Furthermore, the eighteenth-century *décor* of *Harmonium* reflects his taste for intimate theater. The masques of this first volume, particularly "The Comedian as the Letter C," move with the spirit of a buffoonery presented to a noble company. They may suggest Stevens as a court poet. But the impression is altered when we regard the irony: an American poet intent upon imposing, for his own amusement, an archaic dramatic form, royal in its exclusiveness, upon the homely materials of American shores. The paradox is comic. The poet intended it to be so.

Now and then, as the performance advances, Stevens enters the play with his actors. Yet the whole dramatic venture in the masques is an expression of major man, the giant of the imagination. In "Owl's Clover" the specification of the poet's office reads like a

promptbook for a director of revels. The master is major man in
the poet:

> He turns us into scholars, studying
> The masks of music. We perceive each mask
> To be the musician's own and, thence, become
> An audience to mimics glistening
> With meanings, doubled by the closest sound,
> Mimics that play on instruments discerned
> In the beat of the blood.

[OP, 67]

The affinities between actors and music[4] disclose a rich domain
of Stevens' aesthetic. We expect his mimics to "glisten with meanings." But it is this close relationship of response to the momentariness of musical "masks" and to poetic language itself which impresses us. "Beauty is momentary in the mind— / The fitful
tracing of a portal; / But in the flesh it is immortal" (CP, 91). The
familiar lines from "Peter Quince at the Clavier" present a compelling summary. The poem relates music, masque, and painting.
It is as though any one of the three arts might singularly provide
this beauty apparent to an audience attentive to "mimics glistening."

Any contention that a highly imaginative poetry will have immediate popular appeal Stevens would have regarded as spurious. One
does not justly argue that harlequinade or court masque, early opera
or twentieth-century opera,[5] have held very much genuine charm
for the majority. These arts have flourished in assumptions requiring audiences of an imaginative range sufficient to meet that of the
authors. On similar grounds we have no right to assume that
The Tempest evoked a wide imaginative response from the Eliza-

---

[4] Stevens appears to think here of music in the classic Greek sense: music as
inclusive of poetry and letters. See W. H. D. Rouse, trans., *Great Dialogues of
Plato* (New York: Mentor Books, 1956), p. 174, n. 1.

[5] The affinities of masque style in Stevens' poetry with survivals of the *commedia
dell' arte* in opera are striking. The aesthetic, for instance, of Richard Strauss's
Ariadne auf Naxos (1912), its libretto by Hugo von Hofmannsthal, seems
curiously appropriate for Stevens. This *tour de force*, with its "outrageous" mix-
ture of elements from Molière's *Le Bourgeois Gentilhomme*, *opera seria* in the
noble myth of Ariadne (recalling Monteverdi's treatment of it in *Lamento di
Arianna*) and elements from the Scaramouche tradition of the *commedia dell' arte*,
may be called an eruption of imaginative brilliance. The work obviously celebrates the agility of imagination; and the glittering chromatism of the arias,
especially the one written for Zerbinetta, derived from Columbina of the *commedia*, is something of a triumph in musical metamorphosis.

bethan populace.[6] Stevens knew and utilized Shakespeare's symbols of the "cloud-capp'd towers" of Prospero (IV, i), and of the magic of Ariel. But he did not advance this poetic idiom as comprehensible to unimaginative spectators. No more did he assume that the "Theatrical distances, bronze shadows heaped / On high horizons, mountainous atmospheres / Of sky and sea" of his own vision might appeal widely to his contemporaries. Among these images he set the little masque of his girl-persona singing beside the sea in "The Idea of Order at Key West" (*CP*, 129). The scene is solitary. The music was conceived for the singer. When it is heard by others, we recognize it as music for uncommon ears. If his countrymen have sometimes found this disdain of the poet incompatible with a "democratic" aesthetic, the objection is idle. He held to his maxim: poetry is the scholar's art. But the scholar is the thinker capable of high imagination. Stevens did not rejoice in the fact of his being rare.

The first of Stevens' masques is "The Plot Against the Giant" (*CP*, 6–7): primitive, unrefined imagination, how to tame him. Each of the girl actors prepares for his arrival. The first will check him with odors of flowers; the second, with colors; the third, with words, "Heavenly labials in a world of gutturals." We are impressed by the speed of performance. But the poem is a prophecy, as well. For thereafter every masque will answer to the poet's insistence upon metamorphosis and momentariness of impression. The fleet mind describes its brief pause. It makes a metaphor upon simple fact: Raw imagination must be compelled to yield itself to form. The three girls are three personae of the poet. In their three roles they are together the woman-genius of his craft.

But with the second masque following almost immediately, the poet is the spectator. "The Ordinary Women" (*CP*, 10–12) should be read under a nonexistent subtitle, which we may offer as "Ordinary Poets," or "Ordinary Imaginers." The women are the women-

[6] See K. M. Lea, *Italian Popular Comedy: A Study in the Commedia dell' Arte, 1560–1620, with Special Reference to the English Stage* (New York, 1962), II, 342. *The Tempest* appealed only by way of dramatic representation or spectacular qualities, not by poetry of the conception and expression. Earlier in this study Miss Lea notes the fallacy. "The assumption that a popular audience found poetry any more acceptable in the sixteenth than in the twentiety century is challenged by a study of the record of Henslowe's experience of popular taste. For every magnificent soliloquy in *Tamburlaine* or *Dr. Faustus* Marlowe threw in the sop of an episodic sensation . . ." (II, 341).

geniuses of other men. They rise from the minds of their consorts and rush about in a palace of imagination. They come "from their poverty," from "dry catarrhs" (which we relate to the commonplaceness of "a world of gutturals"); and they flit here and there to the guitar-strumming of these impoverished men. Their dresses are "cold"; they look from the window sills at the "alphabets" of heaven, "beta b and gamma g" (as though the end of poetry were some scientific reality beyond the earth and the life of man). In the signs of heaven "they read of marriage bed" (as though an unearthly consummation between "gaunt" guitarist and woman-genius were consummation at all). The women are dressed in superficial beauty: "explicit" coiffures, "civil" fans. They find no candles burning in the dark halls.[7] They quit the palace. One comes to Stevens' fact of a reality; poetry will not be commanded by "gaunt" makers of abstractions, who send their imaginations toward some script of the heavens beyond humankind. There will be no true poet's revelry in this palace of darkness, no matter what the festive dress of these ordinary women of ordinary poets. This rush of images, moving at prestissimo, needs no comment. The figures of the women rise from the dark, glitter in moonlight, crowd the halls, gaze heavenward from the windows, and disappear. The life of the poem flares in the bold tumblings of the diction. But this is not poetry without meaning, as though motion alone were its property. Reality, as Stevens saw it, is asserted: Every poet seeking his truth beyond the earth, which claims all men in its nature, is an "ordinary" poet; his halls will be "wickless"; his speech will be "dry," his music "gaunt."[8]

The coiffures of the ordinary women establish a long lineage in the poetry of Stevens. Every image of hair is the insignia of an imagining man, whether lord or pauper. One first meets the sign of the true master-artist in the "all-speaking braids" of Utamaro's beauties. The point of occurrence is the third, the "Oriental" section of "Le Monocle de Mon Oncle" (CP, 14). Stevens uses the art of a Japanese print-master to represent a triumph of imagination in a distant past. The braids are the sign of Utamaro's "festival." They do not evoke some subtle relationship between Japanese art and the American present known to Stevens. The symbol specifies the

---

[7] Cf. Stevens' symbol of the candle of the poet in his verse play "Carlos Among the Candles" (OP, 144ff.) and in the lyric "Valley Candle" (CP, p. 51).
[8] See Fuchs (n. 1 above) on a reading of this poem as "moonlight revery." The significance of *ordinary* is ignored (pp. 97–99).

achievement of another man. For in the same section the poet notes, "I shall not play the flat historic scale." In this resolve he means that he will not imitate any art of the past. In effect, he dismisses the whole range of orientalism in French poetry and painting at the turn of the century and in American imagism. Utamaro was an artist working for himself. With other masters of the past, he has become a "studious ghost."

The poet poses his question: "Have all the barbers lived in vain / That not one curl in nature has survived?" The barber is the artist; the curl, like the braid, is the sign of his work of the imagination. "Nature" here is the continuum of man. Immediately after the question, Stevens turns to his own woman-genius of poetry: she has no pity on the "studious ghosts"; she comes "dripping in . . . [her] hair from sleep." The sum of the questions is that no art of the past is to be answered to or emulated in any present. Each artist in history has flourished in his own time. His work may engage our admiration. His age may appear to us far more favorable to great art than is ours. But as an imagining man of the past he is not of us. Furthermore, one must return to Stevens' unyielding view of the singularity of all creators in any present. These men of imagination do not together make a tradition or a unanimity of art. Whoever they are—philosophers, painters, musicians, poets— they may reflect a contemporaneous reality. But they do not flock as universal spokesmen in one palace of art. Each man lives in his own structure. It is not a place of ordinary women. To each is his own woman-genius; and to her alone he directs his lyric praise.

This imagery of hair and of the work of the barber endures throughout the Grand Poem. The vaulting line from "The Comedian as the Letter C" to the late poem addressed to the waiting earth, "Madame La Fleurie," she who will receive every man, is a long one. The masque of Crispin ends with a barber image: "So may the relation of each man be clipped" (CP, 46). So may the lock, the curl of each man of imagination, each fashioning barber, be cut away by death. This is fact. In "Madame La Fleurie" the thick strings of the guitarist "stutter" the last "gutturals": "Now, he brings all that he saw into the earth, to the waiting parent. / His crisp knowledge is devoured by her, beneath a dew" (CP, 507). This *crisp* knowledge is of the imagination named in Crispin. It is the lock, the "relation" of the poet, now to be clipped, obliterated.

Curls and beards are cut away by time. Every present recedes into the past; every culture is to repeat this relentless fact of history in its own death. Thus Stevens uses a symbolism of curls in presenting the four daughters of Crispin. Each daughter seems to be a century, an age in the history of the American imagination, symbolized in Crispin himself. Each is a presiding woman-genius of an age, *curled,* marked by acts of imagining barbers. Three centuries of American history have passed, and a fourth now opens. In this fourth century at the fullness of his power, Stevens presents his own woman-genius of "glittering hair" (*CP,* 271). When the imagination wanes he names himself as "a father bearded in his fire" (*CP,* 438). Flame consumes life at its end. The boreal night intensifies; and he thinks of all true men of imagination as "bearded with chains of blue-green glitterings" (*CP,* 449). In this late use of the symbol one discovers an affirmation of every other use of the barber, the curl and the beard, hair in whatever dress it appears. These are the signs of the maker of the "festival," the comedian, the master of the masque. Invariably this hair signifies the splendor of a blue of the imagination, a green of the potential world of human sight. Every actor of Stevens displaying the symbol is related to the subject of the comedian. But in every instance of the comedy the shadow encroaches: this present pageant, too, will be finally clipped.

The major poem expressing the subject of the pageant is "The Comedian as the Letter C." Because of the intricacy of miming in this sequence, the rush of images and the rapid interplay of the diction—"waves that were mustachios, / Inscrutable hair in an inscrutable world," as Crispin makes his voyage to American shores—the poem may strike us as fantasy too brilliant for analysis. It will be well to establish at the outset certain points of anchorage. The first of these is fixed as we consider Stevens' intentional base in Crispin. No matter what the source of the character, the reference in the name is to the Latin *crispus, curled,* and hence the *curled one.* Crispin in his voyage to the unknown coast, a world of hair as it were, uncombed, is imagination-as-human-faculty brought across the Atlantic by the first explorers and settlers. Crispin arrived simply because men arrived. Stevens' own note on his intention appears in a poem of about 1920 (unpublished during his lifetime) under the title "Anecdote of the Abnormal": "Crispin-valet! Crispin-saint! / The exhausted realist beholds / His tattered manikin arise / Tuck in the straw, / And stalk the skies" (*OP,* 24). The substance of these lines is to be rendered thus: Crispin, from either the valet of French harlequinade or the third-century Roman Christian martyr, patron saint of shoemakers, Crispin, who on American shores is as poor as a scarecrow and yet vigorous enough to stalk the skies. This is major man of the imagination among us, the character whose signs are American cabins and American quilts (*CP*, 41). He may have once been a poor valet in the comedy of the French imagination; he may have been a saint of Christianity. But in America he is made what he is by dwellers in a new world. If he is poor, he is nonetheless ours. He is our American comedian, our master of the revels.

The autobiographical element in "Crispin" is certain only to the extent that Stevens regards himself as another American poet *expressing major man of the imagination* on American shores. The subject of the poem is the course of an imagination brought to this continent from Europe. Its mode is the masque. Crispin, the curled one, is the master of American revels, the American festival. His French origin may be related, of course, to the "French" quality of Stevens' imagination. But the derivation is French primarily because the poet wishes to create a masque in the style of French harlequinade. The irony of French harlequins in attitudes of comedy amidst the potential greens of the new world is obvious. Crispin, the persona of major man in comic guise, Crispin much impoverished in his comic role in the old country, sails here from Bordeaux. He has a "barber's eye." As he approaches the new world of "inscrutable hair," his eye is intent upon the land, one of "simple salad-beds" and "honest quilts." He has become a skinny sailor, shorn of his old costumes, possessing no myth save the "mythology of self." First, he walks in the South: Yucatan, Havana, Carolina (as the poet recalls imagining *conquistadores* and English mariners). In this South, as in Yucatan, where Crispin finds "a new reality in parrot-squawks," all is "green barbarism." The new world is a green potential to Crispin. He sees the green luxuriance of the tropics. Nonetheless, as he plans his "colony," America is "always north to him." Eventually, in "A Nice Shady Home," he makes a "polar planterdom." His home is a cabin; and in this North (of the early American colonies of New England, and of every settlement related to the North) this American major man, "despising honest quilts," lives "quilted to his poll." He is the American of cabins and quilts, he who once planned "loquacious columns by the ructive sea."

Crispin takes a bride, his own woman-genius of his imaginings. He has his difficulties with the enervations of the *quotidian*. But out of his union with his blonde mate are born his four "daughters with curls," the centuries of his history on American shores: the first, in a "capuchin" cloak and hood (the mien of a Puritan wife); the second, in a half-awakened state (a tentative national consciousness, as the eighteenth century advances); the third, a "creeper under jaunty leaves" ("leaves" of an emerging American poetry of the nineteenth century); the fourth, still "pent," the one not yet fully grown (the inception of the twentieth). This much has been and is true of all four daughters: "four questioners" [of this life in a new world] and "four sure answerers" [as the purveyors of doctrine]. For it is doctrine which Crispin finally concocts "from the rout." This doctrine, as the masque closes, is mere emulation of the old European way, *turnip* sacked and carried overseas. On these shores, the turnip is finally "the same insoluble lump." And Crispin, the old musician from French harlequinade, falls short of his grandiose dream of a genuinely new world. *If,* finally, "the music sticks," *if* Crispin is "a profitless philosopher" (*CP,* 45–46), "can all this matter since / The relation [Crispin's play] comes, benignly, to its end?" Such is the substance of this chief masque of Stevens' in its evocation of an American reality. The new world failed to be new. The imagination on these shores finally settled to making doctrine. There is nothing wrong with cabins and quilts, certainly. But the displaced Crispin, after all, did not reach his initial promise as "principium and lex" (*CP,* 27).

Beneath the drollery of this masque-poem lies the evidence of Stevens' delight in comic irony. Characteristic of his sense of comedy is this grotesque of a French harlequin amidst parrot squawks, Georgia pines, humble cabins, and the patchwork of American quilts. In his notes on the poem to Professor Poggioli for an Italian translation, Stevens wrote of Crispin: "The central figure is an everyday man who lives a life without the slightest adventure except that he lives it in a poetic atmosphere as we all do." Earlier in the same comment Stevens contended: ". . . It is what may be called an anti-mythological poem."[9] These disclosures support the irony of Crispin's new American setting. When one adds to them a later note to the translator on "The Man with the Blue Guitar," the poet's full purpose becomes clear. The line of the "Blue Guitar" for comment opens the third section of the poem: "Ah, but to play man number one. . . ." Stevens wrote of *man number one:* "Man with-

[9] *Letters,* p. 778, a letter to Renato Poggioli dated at Hartford, June 3, 1953.

out variation. Man in C Major. The complete realization of the idea of man. Man at his happiest normal."[10] It may seem at first glance difficult to relate these contentions for man in C Major *without variation* to the idea of Crispin as comedian. One resolves discrepancies by examining Crispin as major American man of the imagination, comprehending all Americans whose potential lies at C major, the beginning key for the boldness of *individual* imaginations. The American "poetic atmosphere" is there for the claiming. Crispin's American comedy flourishes in the shadow of a potential unrealized. The only gain is doctrine, the old turnip. Thus the poem is indeed antimythological in the sense that the unique American opportunity for a mythology of the self has not been fully grasped. In the majority we are still planters of the old European commonplace, the "insoluble lump," *turnip*.

As far as Stevens' use of the name is concerned, the common title of Crispin for the French comic character and a third-century saint is intentional. The two are related by the poet in a likeness of humble stations: Crispin's reduction to a mere valet at the end of the Scaramouche tradition, and the trade of St. Crispin's shoemakers. Crispin knew the passing of a glory of *rodomontade,* once delivered with plumes and jeweled swords; or he knew the lowly, unassuming days of cobblers. It might have been different on American shores had some fury and brilliance of the High Renaissance arrived in, let us say, the imagination of Tiberio Fiurelli, the greatest of all Scaramouches. But what the New World received was a "tattered manikin," as Stevens calls him in "Anecdote of the Abnormal" (*OP*, 24). In his derivation from harlequinade the American Crispin was essentially an impoverished Scaramouche. Once he was the imitator of the great Captain, arrogant and blustering. He ended as a lackey. The ward of St. Crispin we leave faithful to his simple craft.

Stevens' sources in French literature for Crispin have been variously traced by critics. William Van O'Connor noted some years ago that the French Crispin used as a model by Stevens was probably the character of *Le Legataire universel* (1708) by Jean-François Regnard.[11] Other possibilities have been suggested in

---

[10] *Mattino Domenicale ed altre Poesie,* trans. Renato Poggioli (Turin: Giulio Einaudi, 1954), p. 174 [translator's notes]. By permission of Giulio Einaudi Editore S.p.A., Turin. Stevens' note as quoted here was handwritten, among other responses to questions, on the face of a letter of Professor Poggioli dated July 4, 1953.
[11] *The Shaping Spirit*, p. 139.

recent years.[12] Mr. Riddell is of the opinion that Stevens' Crispin shows no distinctive qualities from the *commedia dell' arte*.[13] But this judgment would seem to remove the deliberation of Stevens' choice of his character. His reading in the history of harlequinade, in French literature particularly, was intensive and wide.[14] Crispin as adapted by Stevens may inherit from Regnard or from earlier French dramatic models of the seventeenth century.[15] From his acquaintance with Maurice Sand's study of harlequinade Stevens would have known of Raymond Poisson as the great progenitor of Crispin's role at its zenith.[16] The extensive marine imagery of "The Comedian" may have been suggested by the name of the actor and of his descendents who played Crispin to his final end as a valet. It is also probable that Stevens knew an account in P.-L. Duchartre's *The Italian Comedy*.[17] Duchartre represents Crispin as a poor, bedraggled musician in his final deterioration. He appears at last in an insipid costume. He intones well; but he has lost his command of the score.[18] Stevens appears to reflect this wretchedly inept "musi-

[12] See Warren Ramsey on the sources in "Wallace Stevens and Some French Poets," *Trinity Review*, VIII, No. 3 (May, 1954), 38. Mr. Ramsey suggests Le Sage's *Crispin rival de son maitre* (1707) in addition to the play of Regnard. The most thorough tracing of possible sources is that of Guy Davenport in his study of the poem, "Spinoza's Tulips: A Commentary on 'The Comedian as the Letter C,'" *Perspective*, VII, No. 3 (1954), 147–54. Mr. Davenport considers Crispin from his emergence in 1654 in Scarron's *Ecolier de Salamanque*. He finds several echoes of plays about Crispin, all of the seventeenth century, in the opening lines of Stevens. The evidence of Stevens' derivations in, for instance, "preceptor to the sea," "musician of pears," "nincompated pedagogue," seems unquestionable.

[13] *The Clairvoyant Eye*, p. 95.

[14] Among Stevens' books sold at auction in New York after his death were Maurice Sand's *Masques et Bouffons* (Paris, 1862), as issued in an anonymous English translation as *The History of Harlequinade* (London, 1915). Of some importance to studies of the guitar as Stevens' symbol of the poet's music is a plate facing p. 208 in the second volume of this English edition. Scaramouche, as played by Fiurelli (b. Naples, 1608), is shown in a traditional doublet and cape with sword. He strums a guitar.

[15] See above, n. 12.

[16] *History of Harlequinade*, II, 229; see above, n. 14.

[17] The English translation from the French *La Comédie italienne*, prepared by Randolph T. Weaver (London, 1929). Stevens probably read the original French edition (Paris, 1920) as he prepared the final drafts of "The Comedian as the Letter C," first published in *Harmonium* (1923).

[18] Duchartre gives a brief account of an engraving by Bonnart (date unspecified) with an accompanying verse beneath:

> Crispin, dont tu vois la figure,
> Est un pauvre musicien
> Qui n'entend rien en tablature
> Si ce n'est qu'il entonne bien.

"Crispin, whose face you see, is a poor musician who understands naught of the score save that he intones well" (the Weaver translation, pp. 249–50). A plate appearing in the account of Scaramouche is similar to that cited above (n. 14), the actor again pictured with a guitar.

cian" as he writes of the metamorphosis of Crispin approaching America: "The whole of life that still remained in him / Dwindled to one sound strumming in his ear, / Ubiquitous concussion, slap and sigh, / Polyphony beyond his baton's thrust" (*CP*, 28). The one sound is the roar of ocean in the ears of the poor voyager. Out of this the "polyphony" is to come. Crispin is the imagination at *C*; he is man in C major. A few lines later we learn that "an ancient Crispin was dissolved. / The valet in the tempest was annulled." Now Crispin is reduced to his New World beginning. The voyage has washed him clean of his Old World shame. He is free to be "intelligence of his soil . . . a man made vivid by the sea . . . Crispin made new . . ." (*CP*, 27, 30). But he became, after all, a "profitless philosopher." He who began "with green brag" concludes *fadedly*; and the opportunity of a world entirely new is betrayed.

C is the letter, the sound of the comedian. Major man in America, man in C major is bound to the key. The musical virtuosity of Stevens realizes Crispin again and again in the sound of his letter. In a comment on the poem addressed to a correspondent in 1940, Stevens notes that *C* is "a cypher for Crispin." The title of the poem, he writes, might be changed to "The Comedian as the Sounds of the Letter C." He continues with a reference to a story about St. Francis, that he wore bells around his ankles so that the crickets would hear his approach and not be trampled. "Now, as Crispin moves through the poem, the sounds of the letter C accompany him, as the sounds of the crickets . . . must have accompanied St. Francis." Furthermore, *C* for Crispin includes "all related or derivative sounds. For instance, X TS and Z." Stevens gives some illustrations from the poem, noting that "sometimes the sounds squeak all over the place." All of this is "orchestrating . . . in the background"; and, as he writes, he has in mind the "Till Eulenspiegel" of Richard Strauss.[19] Antic orchestration, then, in music and antic orchestration in poetry! C squeaks all over the place. It is Crispin's sign *as he moves through the poem.*

The buffoonery of "The Comedian as the Letter C" ends with a shrug of the poet as the scene closes—"What can all this matter?" since every "relation" has its end in a final *clipping* by death. Stevens was never again to be so debonair a master of revels. The neuter, the nothingness that sheds the "shapes" of life was there in the distance.

---

[19] These comments appear in a letter to Hi Simons dated at Hartford, January 12, 1940 (*Letters*, pp. 351–52). A shorter note on the repetition of *C* in the poem is contained in a letter to Renato Poggioli dated at Hartford, June 3, 1953 (*Letters*, p. 778).

We have noted the early domination of black. *C* is sounded through the comedy of Crispin. But Stevens the maker of masques will not return to this key. There will be other virtuoso scores, those, for instance, of "Esthétique du Mal," capacious and brooding in its various modes, or of "An Ordinary Evening in New Haven," spare as in the slender voices of a string choir. Yet the total act of Stevens the comedian is a strictly traced diminution from bravura. Somberness falls upon the pages of *Harmonium* shortly after Crispin's withdrawal. Those who went before us in the "old comedy" of existence are now the "dark comedians" of the tomb (*CP, 56*). The poet thinks of the moral law, the church nave, and "haunted heaven" as he addresses "A High-Toned Old Christian Woman," and of the "opposing law," poetry, "The supreme fiction." The architect in poetry makes a peristyle "And from the peristyle project[s] a masque / Beyond the planets" (*CP, 59*). The blithe farewell to Crispin has in it a precise element of the impersonal. The play belongs to the American comedy. It is a masque projected from the disarray and the poverty of the national imaginative experience. The short lyrics following are stern resolutions: they sound darkly, with an unyielding inwardness; they are meditative in the manner of the last poems that Stevens wrote. The voice becomes sinister: "It is with . . . malice / That I distort the world. . . . ah! that Scaramouche / Should have a black barouche." This is rage before "The sorry verities." "Yet in excess, continual, / There is cure of sorrow" (*CP, 61*). We hear astringent tonalities. On the threshold of blackness in the stern lines of "The Rock," the man of "continual excess" in the fiction wrote of the final sorrow: "These leaves are the poem, the icon and the man. / These are a cure of the ground and of ourselves" (*CP, 527*). Whoever names Stevens the comedian will remember that the maker of a script for Scaramouche works in defiance of the dark.

Stevens chose to exclude his dramatic ventures from the *Collected Poems*. "Three Travelers Watch a Sunrise" and "Carlos Among the Candles," verse plays in one act, were published in 1916 and 1917 by Harriet Monroe in *Poetry*. Both were experimentally produced. A third, "Bowl, Cat and Broomstick" (1917), was performed but remained in manuscript.[20] These pieces intended for the theater

[20] See S. F. Morse, *OP*, xxvi–xxvii. The first was a prize-winner in a contest sponsored by the Players' Producing Company; the second and the third were written for the Wisconsin Players. Morse does not print "Bowl, Cat and Broomstick."

are of little relevance to the present discussion. They provide evidence that Stevens was not a playwright. The dramatic element of the masque-poems gives us the language of Stevens. It is a speech wholly congenial to lyric poetry. But the genius of the dramatist, the power to realize a speech of other men, was not his; and nothing in the dramatic texts suggests that a continuing attention to the performing theater would have surmounted the deficiency. The masque characters are all Stevens' counterparts. They exemplify poetic theory. There is no drama. We note these experimental pieces for the theater as inappropriate in a study of the poetry. The resolve of Stevens is stated in *Harmonium*: he intends "memorials" that are "the phrases / Of idiosyncratic music . . . paper souvenirs of rapture" (*CP*, 79). When he speaks again in "Life Is Motion," two characters dance round a stump (death). They shout in abandon, celebrating motion (life) for the sake of motion. The poet stands apart in reflection: they celebrate "the marriage of flesh and air" (*CP*, 83). Thus human flesh is wedded to the certainty of nonbeing. Motion is the definition of life. The scene in the sense of Stevens is a "phrase of idiosyncratic music." We take Stevens as the literalist in this qualification of his music: *idios,* the peculiar (of the imaginer), plus *synkrasis,* the mixing together. We do not hold him to the obligation of the dramatist. With him it is always the self *as theorist* revealed through exemplifying characters summoned to the scene. This idiosyncrasy is the subject as he writes the poem of *Transport to Summer,* "The Pure Good of Theory" (*CP*, 329–33).

The way of the later Stevens with the masque is fully indicated in the method of "Peter Quince at the Clavier" (*CP*, 89–92). This renowned scene of *Harmonium* is early; yet it is prophetic of the masques to come. Peter improvises. The woman-genius of the poet-musician, Peter the carpenter-performer, appears in blue-shadowed silk. The actors arrive, Susanna and the Elders, and the attendant Byzantines. The scene closes. Stevens speaks: Susanna is the theme, again and again; whoever of the long succession of artist-imaginers may have touched her, the beauty of her in his mind was momentary; yet in the continuity of human imaginings she is immortal. This is the endurance of the human power to imagine beauty. It is deathless.

The theme continues, as *Harmonium* closes. "The Revolutionists Stop for Orangeade." In the heat of conflict, in the "real that wrenches," humankind must have more than the real. It must "wear the breeches of a mask." The single song of the revolutionary captain is insufficient. "There is no pith in music / Except in something false" (*CP*, 102–3). Stevens employs actors in metaphoric scenes that represent declaration. The mode of the future has become fully apparent as the first sequence of the poetry, distinguished by Crispin, reaches its end.

Much of the comic play marking *Harmonium* wanes in the next volume, *Ideas of Order*, published in 1935. The diminution from bravura has been noted. Scenes of masques and movements of actors continue. But they appear in fragments of setting and of gesture rather than in complete sequences. The mind with its constant questions of existence increasingly pre-empts the authority of an imagination intent upon revelry. Theory becomes more insistent. One sees the *mise en scène*; but it takes on a quality of mistiness, as though the spectator looked through a gauze screen into half-shadow. This evanescence is exactly equal to the diminution of color-as-subject in the act of Stevens the painter. Thus "an old casino in a park" is the dominant metaphor of "Academic Discourse at Havana" (*CP*, 142–45), a city of tropical luxuriance with its "canaries in the morning, orchestras in the afternoon, balloons at night." The discourse of the academicians, as though a convention of literalists sat in judgment on the conditions of existence itself, is mute. Its voices are suggested through the metaphoric pattern: the swans of the old amusement park are dead, the swans once stupid in their ease on the blank waters of the lake;[21] the casino with its boarded windows is rain-swept; earth has "come right" because of the "indolent progressions of the swans"; life is "a peanut parody / For peanut people." The myth of a common existence in the park, graced with swans and island canopies, "passed like a circus."[22] Now the poet's text intrudes: "Politic man ordained / Imagination as the

---

[21] Compare the lyric "Invective Against Swans," the second poem in *Harmonium* (*CP*, 4). It is clear that the invective through the symbol of swans, related here to the winter crow of desolation, is directed against the stupid ease of "ordinary" imaginations. It is as though swans were the topmost realizations of beauty for those of humankind unknowing of a fierceness of the imagination. Stevens may here intend an invective against the famous swan-symbols of Yeats in "The Wild Swans at Coole" (1919). The possibility seems compelling when one considers the attack on "lousy Byzantium" in the short lyric "Memorandum" (*OP*, 89), with its unmistakable reference to "Sailing to Byzantium" in the last line, and the direct quotation of Yeats's "The Lake Isle of Innisfree" in "Page from a Tale" (*CP*, 421–23).

[22] Cf. Warren Ramsey, *Trinity Review*, III, 39. He says of Stevens' line "Life is an old casino in a park": "If there is one image above all others characteristic of Laforgue's poetry, it is precisely that of existence compared to the abandoned casino."

fateful sin." It is the political demagogue who makes the "peanut parody." In the tropic luxuriance of Havana an academic discourse from the critics of modern impoverishment pontificates. We have heard the academicians lament: the earth is no longer near; in the cities of the present there is no "sustenance." The discourse is answered by the poet. It is the speeech of poets that may redeem this world without imagination. If one must begin with life as an old casino in the park, that is nonetheless the reality of the present. Poetry can address itself to it. A tense intricacy marks the closing lines: ". . . the old casino . . . may define / An infinite incantation of ourselves / In the grand decadence of the perished swans." One has to put up with the old casino. It was his inheritance. It is *now*. But the *infinite incantations* of poets can make it bearable.

A peanut parody, existence that is a circus travesty of what existence might be, is appropriate for the theater of Stevens at this point. It accords with what he saw of American life in the thirties. Before the end of the decade Stevens had published "Life on a Battleship" (*OP*, 77–81). The old casino gives place on the stage to the grim machine of war. Reality changes. The captain speaks: "Society / Is a phase. We approach a society / Without a society. . . ." This pushing vine of life grows, East to West. Human fate is our own. Every new society, whatever it is, presents the center of another circle for the man who will seize our strength, the new politician; and the full of his power is an end "without rhetoric," that is, the "rhetoric" of individual lives and imaginings, "infinite incantations." Peanut parody and battleship are related in Stevens' consistent faithfulness to reality as he measures it in the continuum, East to West. The peril of existence is the threat of tyranny over the imagination by the man who would seize "our strength." It is this peril which continues as the scene changes and the battleship gives place to a postwar reality. In "Notes Toward a Supreme Fiction" the utter repetitiveness of existence comes of adherence to the "single text, granite monotony" (*CP*, 394). The setting of "Notes" is vast; it is the scene of modern humanity. Every masque of Stevens', beginning with *Ideas of Order,* is mounted in the poet's private theater for a small audience. But the themes far transcend the intimacy of the early poetry. Increasingly the play becomes a metaphor of an age.

"The Man with the Blue Guitar" (1937) is essentially a study of the making of poetry as a means of redemption from the granite monotony. The crassness of the present is explored, "Oxidia," the gaseous, the "oxide" suburb in endless repetition, the modern

"Olympia." Nonetheless, "From this I shall evolve a man. / This is his essence: the old fantoche / Hanging his shawl upon the wind, / Like something on the stage . . ." (*CP*, 181). The man to be evolved is the poet, equally granitic in his purpose, to live in the world of Oxidia, and yet to change "things as they are" upon the blue guitar. He is a "shearsman of sorts" (*CP*, 165), related to all the barbers who went before him. The present world is examined again in the lyric reflection "Of Modern Poetry," written during the Great War. In this time, poetry "has to think about war . . . it has to find what will suffice. It has / To construct a new stage. . . . The actor is / A metaphysician in the dark, twanging / An instrument . . . a wiry string . . ." (*CP*, 240).

Stevens closed the volume of *The Man with the Blue Guitar* in 1937 with one of the most searching reflections on war in contemporary poetry. "The Men That Are Falling" was inspired by the sacrifice of the Spanish Republicans.[23] The poet is the actor. In the room arranged for sleep, yet catastrophic with the terror of the real, he is sleepless. He stares in the midnight hour at the pillow, black, prophetic of death. Life is the fulfillment of desire. But on the pillow lies the head of one of the men who are falling. The pillow is "more than sudarium," more in this *now* than the imprint on the sweat cloth of St. Veronica. It is the face of one who desired death more than life, this man who "loved earth, not heaven, enough to die" (*CP*, 187–88). This is the love of the right to be one's self. For us there is nothing beyond the earth. The poem is a masque of blackness, an enactment in the dark, a scene worked in terror and wonder amidst the "grinding ric-rac" of life.

One hears idle assumptions from some critics of our day. They propose varying degrees of terror in the expression of modern poets. If these must be, then it should be asserted that Stevens is unexcelled among his contemporaries in expressing the terror of modern war-fraught existence. There is the "Examination of the Hero in a Time of War" (*CP*, 273–81), with its parade of "young men as vegetables," its voyages "beyond the oyster beds" into "indigo shadow," the hero as the marble effigy of a national feeling, a "pinching" of an idea, the hero as his nation, an "anonymous actor." "Can we live on dry descriptions, / Feel everything starving except the belly . . . ?" There are the subsequent "Repetitions of a Young Captain" (*Transport to Summer*, *CP*, 306–10). The tempest cracks on the theater; yet

---

[23] See *Letters*, p. 798. This disclosure is addressed to Bernard Heringman in a letter dated at Hartford, September 1, 1953.

the people sit in it, "as if nothing had happened," while the "blue scene" washes white in the storm and a new reality approaches. One actor succeeds another in the fury. A soldier at a railway station departs as he is. He leaves his sense of place. He will not return in his old form. But will he find another? The young captain hears "the drivers in the wind-blows cracking whips"; and millions of his kind know this "calculated chaos." If "the people" sit in the theater as though nothing has occurred, they do not hear the winds of change. There is the white of cataclysm; there is the green potential of the new age that begins. The new reality will appear. But to sense the white of transition is anguish. Millions of repetitions of the young captain search for a few words of what is real. This is the only nourishment. The tragedy lies in the coercion of the many to the one, the idea of the hero, the departing soldier. The rage of "Esthétique du Mal" intensifies the terror. "Life is a bitter aspic. . . . A man of bitter appetite despises / A well-made scene in which paratroopers / Select adieux . . ." (CP, 322). The poet's voice storms against the well-made scene. Every image of man that coerces the many to the one is well-made. It was in this peril that the Spanish Republican died, in this that the anonymous hero became the vulgar ordinariness of an idea. The young captain was made one with millions of his kind at railway stations, and in this same peril of the well-made scene paratroopers are mere repetitions of a type. We should understand Stevens, in these bitter reflections on the terror of reality, as the master of his actors. If humanity stands always in "the tumult of a festival," the attribution of pageantry here is mercilessly ironic: a well-made scene, a calculated chaos. In the hellish festival, death is not the king, but that distant political man among us, the tyrant of endless repetitions, and the author of a granite oneness.

The arc of the comedian reaches its highest point during these war years. But the comedian has become the master ironist. The total structure memorializes process. The poetry continues as process because reality changes. Far into the sequence of Transport to Summer, the farewell to the summer of the imagination, Stevens returns to a green luxuriance of the tropics recalling the jungles of Crispin's first American vision. The scene is Brazil. The masque is a "Description of a Platonic Person," the second of the poems in "The Pure Good of Theory" (CP, 330–31). The genius of poetry, the "emaciated Romantic" came to Brazil. There the memory was purged of the past. A holiday hotel in the green glade flew "the flag of the nude"; it promised the world of the future. But an invalid came to the hotel. "He was a Jew from Europe or might have been." The sick man lay in bed "on the west wall of the sea." This platonic person had discovered a soul in the world. He was sick of the old question: What lies beyond the intelligence of man? The invalid was "what people had been and still were." "Could the future rest on a sense and be beyond / Intelligence?" This is the illness of man in the West of man. In the malady of the Jew from Europe, one returns to Stevens' frequent symbol of "rabbi" as the philosopher; and the fact of Europe is a repetition of the fact of Crispin as the maker of doctrine, the old European "turnip." This insistence upon a soul in the world, upon an intelligence beyond the intelligence of man, is malady. It is the disease of the human, the platonic curse. The end of war, we infer, is time for a nude beginning, in the green potential of the new. It is a time to feed the emaciated romantic (the imagination). But the holiday hotel is invaded by the old malady.

Again the theater of *Harmonium* is recalled in "Extraordinary References" (*CP*, 369). The scene is a spring garden. A mother ties her child's hair ribbons. These braids recall the early signs of hair, curl, barber. The ribbons are memorials of the past. The mother speaks: "*My Jacomyntje!*[24] *Your great-grandfather was an Indian fighter.*" And again, "*This first spring after the war, / In which your father died. . . .*" American wars, first to last, are imposed upon the next generation. The spring garden is "inherited," presided over by a "second-hand Vertumnus," the old Roman god of the seasons. Ordinary people make extraordinary references. This is to say, in the text of this poem, every present insists upon references apart from ordinary present reality. The questions rise from the despair of the poem: Can there be a spring washed new, a generation of new braids free of the weight of the past? The despair is stated in the central line: these references "Compose us in a kind of eulogy." We live to celebrate the dead.

Immediately following this garden scene, Stevens presents his final masque of the tropics. The setting of "Attempt to Discover Life" is a Cuban spa, San Miguel de los Baños (*CP*, 370). A waitress heaps roses (*hermosas*) on a table. A "cadaverous person" enters with a woman "pallid-skinned, / Of fiery eyes and long thin arms."

[24] According to Holly Stevens, editor of the correspondence, a name from the Stevens genealogy; see *Letters*, p. 4. On Tulpehocken see the editor's note on Tulpehocken Church, Myerstown, Pa. (*ibid.*, p. 541).

The blue-green roses drift up from the table in smoke. The blue of the petals becomes yellow, then black and white. "The cadaverous persons were dispelled." On the table lie two coins—*dos centavos.*

The roses were arranged "in the magnificence of a volcano." But of this smoldering are the volcanic fires that consume a life, as the streaks of flame in the auroras of autumn are signs of the burning at the end of the imagination. Stevens himself appears in the cadaverous person; the companion of long thin arms and mantilla who accompanies him is his woman-genius of poetry. Roses of the tropics will continue to bloom in a riot of color. But the roses on this table perish, as the visitors are "dispelled." Stevens wrote to his Cuban friend José Rodríguez Feo: "The question that is prompted by that poem is whether the experience of life is in the end worth more than tuppence: dos centavos."[25] The supreme verity approaches in the masque of San Miguel. Here, again, is the tropic luxuriance of the green potential. But the spa has no cure for the sorrow. The shadow lengthens.

"The personae of summer play the characters / Of an inhuman author . . . / He does not hear his characters talk. He sees / Them mottled . . . / Of blue and yellow, sky and sun. . . ." And yet they speak unheard (*CP*, 377–78). The poem is "Credences of Summer," by Stevens' admission a favorite of his from his later work.[26] The mute characters far outnumber Stevens' speakers. As one traces the arc of the comedian, one discovers that gesture, movement, and costume are the primary attributes of the maskers. The intimate theater of Stevens is faithful to the supreme art of the *commedia dell' arte,* miming. If the parts are voiced, the words are not recorded. The language heard, with few exceptions, is that of the poet-master rather than the characters. The *inhuman* author of "Credences" is none other than the author who excludes the speech of others. We have noted in this context Stevens' dismissal of dramatic form as an appropriate medium for his poetry. If the characters in most of the performances have been unheard to this point—the close of summer—they are entirely mute onward as autumn progresses to winter and the central white. The awesome scenes of "Page from a Tale" have been examined fully in an earlier chapter discussing the sun.[27] It should be noted that the characters, beginning with the poet Hans, speak nothing. They see and hear only, and their performances are

25 From Hartford, December 10, 1946; see *Letters*, p. 540.
26 See a letter to Renato Poggioli dated at Hartford, June 18, 1953; *Letters*, p. 782.
27 See above, ch. 6.

limited to gesture. "Page from a Tale" is a masque of terror, antecedent to the masques of war.

Parts of masques are suggested in "The Auroras of Autumn," as the father (the poet) and the mother (the woman-genius of his art) summon the maskers and the musicians who "dub at a tragedy" (*CP*, 415–17). But the last of Stevens' full projections in masque form is "The Novel" (*CP*, 457–59). The poem takes its title from the novel of the absurd, as exemplified by Albert Camus. Yet the total work of Stevens the poet, *his* novel, his total fiction, is clearly named. "Day's arches are crumbling into the autumn night. / The fire falls a little and the book is done."

Present reality was never asserted more forcefully by Stevens than here. It is a reality of 1948; and it is a reality of advancing age, the poet's "first red of red winter." Above the foyer (of the theater) of summer the crows of winter fly. The sun like a Spanish actor departs from the foyer into the past, "the rodomontadean emptiness" (as though a Scaramouche had retired to a tenantless hall of echoes). The prologue is over, and the first scene opens. A man lies in bed, in winter cold, reading a novel by Camus.

> Mother was afraid I should freeze in the Parisian hotels.
> She had heard of the fate of an Argentine writer. At night,
> He would go to bed, cover himself with blankets—
>
> Protruding from the pile of wool, a hand,
> In a black glove, holds a novel by Camus. She begged
> That I stay away. *These are the words of José. . . .*

José, Stevens' Cuban friend Feo, has provided the language. It is taken from a letter of Feo's in which he gives an account of leaving his assignment at UNESCO headquarters in Paris at his mother's request. She had heard of an Argentine writer who was forced to bed in the extreme cold of winter in a Paris without fuel. There he read, holding his book with a black-gloved hand.[28]

[28] See *Letters*, pp. 616–17, the editor's note on Stevens' letter to Feo (Hartford, October 6, 1948) in which a statement appears concerning his transcription of the account of the Argentinean writer for the poem. In the same note, the editor quotes Stevens in a letter to a Philadelphia correspondent on the Spanish quotation in the poem: *Olalla blanca en el* [*sic*, for *lo*] *blanco*. Stevens writes: "The language about the eulalia: Olalla, is from *Lorca*." Stevens was originally given the phrase by his Irish correspondent Thomas McGreevy in a letter dated May 26, 1948. The poet acknowledges his use of it in a letter to McGreevy dated August 25, 1950; see *Letters*, pp. 687–90.

The scene changes to the poet's fireside. The poet is the actor as the "red winter" begins, this last winter which will consume him. There is a metamorphosis into brief recollection—Varadero Beach, on the north coast of Cuba, where once, long ago, the sea became poetry to this poet, as though poetry were endless. But the meditation before the fire is quickly restored. The Argentine in bed reading the novel held in a black-gloved hand is oneself, "Feeling the fear that creeps beneath the wool, / Lies on the breast and pierces into the heart, / Straight from the Arcadian imagination. . . ."[29] The language of José Rodríguez Feo has become the masque of the end: the bed against the cold, the black-gloved hand, the novel that speaks of a final nothingness. Yet it is the Arcadian imagination, the faculty alone capable of making an earthly paradise, that creates the fear, the piercing into the heart. It alone can envision death.

As *The Auroras of Autumn* closes, the poet's moon becomes "a tricorn / Waved in pale adieu." The hat is flourished by the departing actor. "The rex Impolitor / Will come stamping here, the ruler of less than men, / In less than nature" ("Things of August," *CP*, 495). In the final sequence of "The Rock" the last scenes of the theater are brief. "Madame La Fleurie," the flowered woman, the mother earth, is the waiting parent. "His crisp knowledge is devoured by her, beneath a dew." "It was a page he had found in the handbook of heartbreak" (*CP*, 507). The mother is the same, she whom the poet celebrates early in *Harmonium* ("In the Carolinas," *CP*, 5). "Timeless mother, / How is it that your aspic nipples / For once vent honey?" His page is a single one in the handbook of heartbreak, the book of man. One may wonder with the poet of "Page from a Tale." Will the last page from the book be read, the final page for all men? The life of what we call the world is a mystery of imaginings. As the poet returns to the rock, and the arc of the comedian finds its terminus there, the mask of Ariel signals the end. Ariel was glad he had written his poems (*CP*, 532).

---

29 Stevens was apparently acquainted with "Arcadian" tradition in the *commedia dell' arte*. See K. M. Lea, *Italian Popular Comedy*, I, 201, on Arcadian pastorals in the *commedia* and on the use of the "lost [enchanted] island" in relation to Arcadia. Stevens thinks of two islands in "An Ordinary Evening in New Haven" (Sec. 21 *CP*, 480): the isle of the "black shepherd," where a "romanza" is made by the poet in defiance of the keeper, obviously death; and "another isle," where "the senses give and nothing take," "the object of the will," "the alternate romanza." See also the lines of the "planter's" island in "Notes Toward A Supreme Fiction" (*CP*, 393). This is a symbol of the early sensuous poetry in tropical settings.

The concluding *c* of the last poem has been discussed in an earlier chapter.[30] The scrawny cry of the bird is the note of the chorister "whose c preceded the choir" (*CP*, 534). The *C* of Crispin is sounded again, man at C major. The next poet begins in spring. His modulations will be his own.

We add that his actors will fill the stage, that his crisp knowledge will be devoured by the timeless mother beneath a dew. The continuity of the festival is the certainty. "It is a theater floating through the clouds, / Itself a cloud, although of misted rock / And mountains running like water, wave on wave, / Through waves of light" (*CP*, 416).

[30] See ch. 10.

The Mythological Canon: Ritual Presences

13

"I WISH THAT GROVES STILL *WERE* SACRED . . . THAT there was still something free from doubt. . . . I grow tired of the want of faith—the instinct of faith."[1] Stevens at twenty-six writes in his journal. As yet unmarried, he is at work with a legal firm in New York. The journal and the letters of this period are strikingly bare of observation and confession from the life of an inexperienced young attorney. But of a maturing poetic sensibility they are richly informative. Stevens was living in 1906 in East Orange, New Jersey. These records trace the shape of a careful solitude: more walking and rambling in the country and along the west banks of the Hudson, more reading than seeking friendships; more reverie and play with images and the poetic promise of objects than definitions and resolves. Later in the same year there is a note on "a half-misty, Fantin-La Tourish night."[2] Again, "The trees stand up to-night like charcoal daubs. The eastern side of the house is yellow with moonlight."[3] Responses such as these are dictated by the seeing eye. They point to the full perception of the poet-painter to come.

[1] *Letters*, p. 86, entry 107 [East Orange, N.J.], February 5 [1906].
[2] *Ibid.*, p. 92, entry 115 [East Orange, N.J.], May 2 [1906].
[3] *Ibid.*, entry 117 [East Orange, N.J.], May 29 [1906].

The stars are like "flares" in a twilight "subtly mediaeval—pre-Coperni-can";[4] and the prefiguration of the strict designer, the shaper who will impose a geometry of the spirit, extends. Five years earlier Stevens had arrived in New York from Harvard, his first objective a career as a news writer. Notices of the uncertain drift of assignments which finally led to his enrollment in the New York Law School are merely per-functory in the journal. But the stars are "geometrical," a "confoundedly new idea," he writes. He dreams of going to Paris; and the freedom of bird song becomes the dominant metaphor: "But to fly! Gli uccelli hanno le ali . . . a bird somewhere in a mass of flowers and leaves, perched on a spray in dazzling light, and pouring out arpeggios of enchanting sound."[5] The "instinct of faith" begins its assertions. The grove of the poet begins to flourish. It will become sacred.

A full tracing of these genetic obsessions of the mind is the task of the biographer. For our purposes it is enough to regard the vitality of this imagistic response. What one sees here is a rapid coalescence toward a firm habitude of looking; what one feels is the rising power of the imagination to endow the poet's world with *presences*. Not since Keats has English poetry known a comparable ardor of invocation. The wish for the sacred grove is the wish of Keats for "fellowship divine, / A fellowship with essence . . ." (*Endymion*, I, 778–79). It is well to recognize the poet's experience and the lesser feeling of the audience. We must take it on faith that Oedipus, pouring libations in the sacred wood of Colonus, felt the presences of the Erinyes, or that an ancient king of Phaestos bowed toward Mount Ida and descended into a lus-tration of sacred waters, laving himself of error in the presence of a god. We must allow the faith of Keats, however less the spectator's power to believe, as he sings the "bright roll" of mighty poets "in Apol-lo's hand" (*Endymion*, II, 725–26). We must grant to Stevens, a man of our century, the power of imagination at its farthest reach, a sum-moning of presences that in their constancy of reappearance become as real as the rock of being itself. On that April night when the stars were like flares in a pre-Copernican sky over New Jersey, he felt the rising presence of the genius who would live with him through his poet's life. "One would have liked to walk about with some Queen dis-cussing waves and caverns, like a noble warrior speaking of trifles to a noble lady. The imagination is quite satisfied with definite objects, if they be lofty and beautiful enough. It is chiefly in dingy attics that one dreams of violet cities. . . . So if I had *had* that noble lady, I should

[4] *Ibid.*, p. 91, entry 114 [East Orange, N.J.], April 27 [1906].
[5] *Ibid.*, p. 48, entry 52 [New York], November 10 [1900].

have been content. The absence of her made the stealthy shadows dingy, atticy—incomplete."[6]

The celebration of a mystery begins. The noble lady becomes the consort. Or one may take it the other way. Forty years later Stevens wrote in "An Ordinary Evening in New Haven": "He is the consort of the Queen of Fact" (CP, 485). Both are rulers of the real. She brings the world to him, she who chooses as a connoisseur the tokens of reality fit for a making of poems; and she is his shaping hand. She comes to him in nakedness, as Nanzia Nunzio to Ozymandias in "Notes Toward a Supreme Fiction" (CP, 395–96). He sees her dressed endlessly in fictive coverings. He is the lord of engendering power, the father of her children. She "invites humanity to her house / And table." The children throng the scene; the father is the master of the "pageants out of air" ("The Auroras of Autumn," CP, 415).

Stevens chose to suppress two of his finest ascriptions to the queen. The first appeared in 1924, the second in 1939. Neither was reprinted until the appearance of the posthumous collection edited by Morse. "Red Loves Kit" is scrawled as a title. It appears as though chalked on an ugly wall, on a sidewalk. Below this little sign of the commonplace she flourishes in her beauty. "So she, when in her mystic aureole / She walks, triumphing humbly, should express / Her beauty in your love" (OP, 31). The second poem, "The Woman That Had More Babies Than That," takes a long look at the sea. The wave of the swell goes on day after day, leaving its line of glitter, "like a dancer's skirt, flung round and settling down," over the sand. The repetitions are mechanical. The wheel "returns and returns, along the dry, salt shore." In this place of again-and-again-the-same, nature, the sovereign mother of all rulers, has one baby and only one. But the woman who had more babies than that breathes on her children with a maternal voice. She is the mother of those "that question the repetition on the shore." She is the giver of ideas that come to the "sense of speech." She defies the "universal machine" with her "fiery lullaby" (OP, 81–83). She is the consort of an imagination.

These are examples of a constantly accreting brilliance of tribute to the presence. One reads them feeling, as he goes, the masculine presence in central man. Generation to generation, this is the deathless dominion of the human power to imagine a world above the world, the unreal over the real. In a fulfillment as old as humanity itself, the presences in union and in consummation make together the

6 Ibid., p. 91, entry 114 [East Orange, N.J.], April 27 [1906].

219

children of the artist. The one without the other would be as nothing. To return to the young Stevens of the journal: "So if I had *had* that noble lady, I should have been content. The absence of her made the stealthy shadows dingy, atticy—incomplete."

Lionel Abel in a perceptive article of 1958 appears to be the only critic who was earlier aware of Stevens as the ritualist of the grove. He writes: "In the voice of Wallace Stevens we hear the oldest of poets, the poet of feasts and festivals, who by means of the magic of language made time stand still for the whole of his tribe."[7] This judgment is beautifully suggestive. One may add to it the celebration of the mother as the giver of the feast, the father as the master of the festival in "The Auroras of Autumn." In this analogy the tribal experience is sung again and again by Stevens in texts as disparate as "Sunday Morning," the whole of "Owl's Clover," and the "Esthétique du Mal." Yet he would have very modestly disclaimed all epic pretensions. The ritual remained consistently private. If the implications are sometimes tribal, they come of a votive service overheard. His principle was unfailing. This was the world as it seemed to him; it might have seemed so to other men who chanced upon the grove of celebration.

In his essay "The Noble Rider and the Sound of Words" Stevens takes note of the history of the human race as conceived by Giambattista Vico. The true history is "the history of its progressive mental states" (*NA*, 6).[8] How much Stevens may have read in this eminent philosopher of Naples at the turn of the seventeenth century is not determined. Vico is not mentioned in the correspondence. Nonetheless, it appears certain that Stevens was attracted by the boldness of Vico's early anthropological method in *The New Science*. Vico's discussion of poetic geography[9] in the classical world would have been of interest to Stevens as he thought of the scope of an American geography for his own poetry. It is tempting to suppose that Vico's reference to Anacharsis in this section of his study inspired Stevens' poem on the Scythian prince.[10] We take as the title of this present chapter one of the subjects of Vico: "the mythological canon."[11] Vico distinguishes between myths of the heroic and myths of the plebeian. In a later discussion Stevens' concept of the poet-as-hero will be examined.

[7] "In the Sacred Park," *Partisan Review*, XXV, No. 1 (1958), 97.
[8] Stevens refers here to a study by Henry Packwood Adams: *The Life and Writings of Giambattista Vico* (London, 1935).
[9] See the text of Vico in *The New Science of Giambattista Vico*, translated from the third edition (1744) by Thomas G. Bergin and Max H. Fisch (Ithaca, 1948), pp. 254–60.
[10] *Ibid.*, p. 255.
[11] *Ibid.*, pp. 185–86.

Of his thought in this area it may be noted here that he recognized fully the endless myth-making propensity of humankind. But his distinction between the noble canon of the poet and the least imaginative legend of plebeian origin, for example, the "peanut parody for peanut people" in "Academic Discourse at Havana," is very sharply drawn. Modern poets are not the makers of gods. Nonetheless, as Stevens thought of his art, it appears that the true poet in any age is a maker of a canon for the imagination at its highest reach. It is his aspiration that helps people to live their lives. His is the example.

Yet we grant at once that the example of Stevens was privately lived and written. If his attention to Vico was at all deep, he must have known the philosopher's vision of the human cycle as the Egyptians taught it: (1) the age of the gods; (2) the age of the heroes; (3) the age of men.[12] We take these to represent the "progressive mental states," the *true* history of the race acknowledged by Stevens in "The Noble Rider." We shall then propose that Stevens, intent upon anthropological evidence, displayed in his poetry a private re-enactment of the second and third stages. The gods are gone. The heroes remain, in the succession of artists. We live in the age of men; and the mythology of the self supplants the ancient hierachy of the gods. Of the first stage it may be simply asserted that the sacred grove is still possible. But there are no powers there other than the celebrant himself. In the mythology of the self, the presences are of his making. They are parts of him.

There are two dominant presences in the poetry of Stevens: central man of all human imaginings, deep in the being of this poet who travels East to West, from dawn to night; and the woman-genius, the queen-consort, the mother of his poems, or, as Stevens names her in a last poem on the verge of darkness, "the interior paramour" (*CP*, 524). A third endures apart. She is the universal presence: nature, the earth, the mother of men. She is the mother of the third poem of *Harmonium*, "In the Carolinas" (*CP*, 4–5). She is the "bearded" earth-queen, "Wicked in her dead light" as the "handbook of heartbreak" is closed in the final sequence of "The Rock." The open eye looks upon her constantly. She is not to be summoned; she is natural process, inevitable and omnipresent. The whole of the poetry derives its strength from her reality. She requires little interpretation, this mother, or this wicked queen of a man's age, or as Stevens once thought of her in her summer

[12] *Ibid.*, pp. 17–18.

benevolence, this "fat girl, terrestrial" ("Notes Toward a Supreme Fiction," *CP*, 406).[13]

The arc of the canon is, then, the major projection of a myth in two voices. Its leaves are celebrations of these presences, confirmations of faith, "a constant sacrament of praise" ("Peter Quince at the Clavier," *CP*, 92). Ascriptions to the power of central man, the giant, alternate with hymns to the beauty of the paramour. In the first poem of praise, the tribute celebrates both. "The Plot Against the Giant" (*CP*, 6) has been discussed in the preceding chapter as a masque. So it is. But the characters name the presences that will dominate the grove. The giant strides upon the scene. He must be governed, reshaped in this singular poet. The paramour appears in the roles of the three girls. The first will check him with flowers; the second, with "arching cloths besprinkled with colors"; the third, with "heavenly labials" (flute tones) in a "world of gutturals." In his raw state the old giant is a "yokel," an uncouth power. He is the "ogre" of "Owl's Clover" (*OP*, 67), the giant in the veins in "Gigantomachia" (*CP*, 289), the "rugged" king, a "companion presence" greater than the mountain in "Chocorua to Its Neighbor" (*CP*, 302). His sign of power in wing and claw is the old "parakeet of parakeets," blind until he is given sight by the individual seer in "The Bird with the Coppery Keen Claws" (*CP*, 82).[14] In the last dim vistas he appears as "a giant on the horizon, glistening" ("A Primitive Like an Orb," *CP*, 442); he is "the big X of the returning primitive" ("An Ordinary Evening in New Haven," *CP*, 474). He is the one immortal man, living through successive generations of men.

The first of the three girls in the "plot" is the mistress of sight in the poet-painter. The third is the mistress of the poet's music. The second is the maker of poetic form. Stevens assigned to this very early embodiment of the woman-genius a metaphor of form which was to be constantly recurrent in his invocations of the feminine presence. The "fictive covering" of the naked mistress is a precocious variable through all its appearances. "Arching cloths" sprinkled with designs in color begin the variation. Acts of the embroiderer, the stitcher, and the weaver become the signs of the genius, the woman-maker. She rises again and again in metamorphosis. She is the grandmother in the humorous play of "The Jack-Rabbit," as the poet in the guise of a black man (an essential American) bids her crochet the American buzzard on her winding sheet (*CP*, 50). Irony reappears. The early

[13] See Stevens' identification of the "fat girl" in a letter to Henry Church dated at Hartford, October 28, 1942; *Letters*, p. 426.
[14] See above, ch. 10.

domination of black in the first poems of *Harmonium* is reasserted. In this stitching, the woman will adorn a symbol of death with the image of an American scavenger. Then the mind pauses briefly to muse upon the myth of the modern. In "The Emperor of Ice Cream" the noble myth is dead. She who once embroidered fantails (doves) on her winding sheet lies cold and dumb in a poor room (*CP*, 64). By the sign of the attendant birds we know that she was Venus. The myth belonging to modern girls and boys is ice cream from an "emperor" who rules, as at the counter of a drug store. The domination of black is resumed as the womanly hand of the stitcher embroiders French flowers on an old black dress ("Explanation," *CP*, 72). The decoration comes of the "French" imagination of the master, the poet-mate. Across the final span of the symbol the threads to tame the giant are precisely treasured. The summary is exact. In "The Owl in the Sarcophagus" "the whole spirit [is] sparkling in its cloth, / Generations of the imagination piled / In the manner of its stitchings, of its thread, / . . . the first flowers upon it, an alphabet / By which to spell out holy doom and end . . ." (*CP*, 434). Somewhere a "comic infanta" rises in another marriage of another man, "among the tragic drapings" ("Long and Sluggish Lines," *CP*, 522). The two in "holy doom and end" prepare to leave, drawing about them "a single shawl" in poverty, saying that "God and the imagination are one." "That highest candle lights the dark . . . out of the central mind" ("Final Soliloquy of the Interior Paramour," *CP*, 524). The threads are used, the stitchings finished.

Stevens appears outside the poetry to have spoken only once of the candle and the mistress. In an address of 1951, delivered in acceptance of the award of the Poetry Society of America, he wrote of the "speech that comes from secrecy." "Its position is always an inner position, never certain, never fixed. It is to be found beneath the poet's word and deep within the reader's eye in those chambers in which the genius of poetry sits alone with her candle in a moving solitude" (*OP*, 243). Only the poet knows the secrecy. This is inwardness of sight in a solitude that moves. We discover the chambers where she sits beneath the words and beneath our private encounters with this language. Our knowing of this presence and our knowing of central, major man in the poet are responses of a deepening intensity.

The misted forms of the early poetry are not arresting.[15] It is only with the appearance of the *demoiselle* of gold in the poem "Architec-

---

[15] See, for instance, the "mysterious beauté" of the "Poems from 'Lettres d'un Soldat'" (published in 1918), *OP*, 12; and "Romance for a Demoiselle Lying in the Grass" (*ca.* 1919–20), *OP*, 23.

ture" of 1918 that we sense an identification of the genius who will become the mate of the designer.[16] Thus the ascriptions of *Harmonium* seem sudden in the clarity of the poet's vision. The woman-genius is fully realized in "Infanta Marina" (*CP*, 7), as she roams on the sand terraces of a tropical beach and "in the roamings of her fan" partakes of the sea and of the evening. She will age. But this embodiment will continue to the days of final submission, when the threads are gone and a "comic infanta" rises for the oncoming poet. "Long and Sluggish Lines" of that late time is a poem of return to the girl-bride of the Florida shore. She was the mate addressed in the bitter lines of "Le Monocle de Mon Oncle": "This luscious and impeccable fruit of life / Falls, it appears, of its own weight to earth. / When you were Eve, its acrid juice was sweet. . . ." The spring of bloom is past. Master and mate, the two together are the fruit in season. The autumn will come; and at its end "The laughing sky will see the two of us / Washed into rinds by rotting winter rains" (*CP*, 14, 16). But the bitter prophecy ends. The winter rains are yet distant. In the season of impeccable fruit, she roams the porches of Key West, "stooping in indigo gown / And cloudy constellations . . ."; she becomes "green Vincentine," a being "warm as flesh," a priestess redeeming "monotonous earth."[17]

The second volume of the poetry, *Ideas of Order,* opens with the farewell to Florida, where the infanta has roamed in the evening. The next poem is resolve. "The grass is in seed. The young birds are flying. / Yet the house is not built, not even begun." "Those to be born [poems, children, the "leaves"] have need / Of the bride, love being a birth. . . ." "Come now . . . / While the domes resound with chant involving chant" (*CP*, 119). The invocation is a restatement of the theory of a total structure. The beginning is late; the poet's spring has passed. The domes resounding with chant are sketches of the full dome. It will not be built without her, she who will bear his generation of the imagination. She will be the maker of a life-structure, the warder of all the threads. She will give shape to the leaves; and she will clothe the children.

The arc springs upward through the third sequence of *Parts of a World.* She washes the world of inherited vision for him who bears his "intenser love." On a December night the stars are clean of the past. "The sky is no longer a junk-shop, / Full of javelins and old fire-balls, / Triangles and the names of girls" (*CP*, 218). She is the "abstract, the archaic queen," mistress of the "green night." She walks "among the astronomers," *weaving* tissues out of their "self-same mad-

16 See above, ch. 1.
17 "O Florida, Venereal Soil" and "The Apostrophe to Vincentine," *CP*, 47–48, 52.

ness" (*CP*, 223). These hymns of praise cluster in brilliance midway in this sequence. In "the first canto of the final canticle" he beheld her naked, "seized her and wondered . . . / She held her hand before him in the air, / For him to see, wove round her glittering hair" (*CP*, 271). "Ruddy" bushes flourished at the end of the garden. There he lay beside her. It was a mating of his life with life (*CP*, 222).

The beauty of the presence receives its full tribute in *Transport to Summer*. "Certain Phenomena of Sound" (*CP*, 287) defines the shadow that she gives. Light, the principle of the sun, is Eulalia, a name meaning "fair speech." The "speech" of light is unaltered; it is without shadow. Eulalia belongs to the domain of the mother, nature. Semiramide in the poem is the woman "dark-syllabled." Stevens here takes a particular delight in the phenomena of sound. *Eulalia* has the sound of *white*. *Semiramide* sounds *in shadow*. The dark woman is the genius of speech. "There is no life except in the word of it." Then *life is words*, the poet's life mated with life. Semiramide is the mistress of shadowed speech, as opposed to the fair speech of light. The poet's desire for shadowings may be discovered in "Peter Quince at the Clavier" as the woman in "blue shadowed silk" is addressed, and, again, in "The Common Life," where the existence of men in the cities has become a life of "no shadows," "a black line beside a white line" (*CP*, 90, 221). "Shadows," in the poet's sense, are metamorphoses, gradations in coloring or, in the language of music, modulations and variations. Semiramide is the redemptive presence. The harshness of black against white in the common life is erased by her hand, weaving her hair "for him to see" in the garden, the sacred grove.

Of the same period in the building of the structure there is a constancy of tribute to major man, the imaginer in the poet. Much of "Sombre Figuration," the last section of "Owl's Clover," is devoted to him. "He was born within us as a second self. . . ." He is "Jocundus instead / Of the black-blooded scholar, the man of the cloud, to be / The medium man among other medium men, / The cloak to be clipped . . ." (*OP*, 67, 71). We recall at once the conclusion of Crispin's masque: "So may the relation of each man be clipped" (*CP*, 46). Crispin is merely the American part of him. "High up in heaven the sprawling portent moves" (*OP*, 70).[18] He looms endlessly in human history. One hears the poet's praise again in the song of "Yellow Afternoon" (*CP*,

---

[18] Stevens here comes very close to Yeats. The line seems, in fact, to echo the imagery of "The Second Coming": the slow thighs of the shape in the desert; see *The Collected Poems of W. B. Yeats* (New York, 1959), p. 185.

236–37). The "patriarch," the giant of man on the earth has spoken, in the yellow-gold of the sun. Despite this "fatal unity of war" there is the earth to love, "As one loves one's own being. . . ." It is day; there is a world of earth and of men; there is *her* presence, the woman who "caught his breath." But the giant is greater than all these. He is there in darkness. Night falls. The poet comes back "as one comes back from the sun / To lie on one's bed in the dark, close to a face / Without eyes or mouth, that looks at one and speaks." Blind and dumb until each man gives him sight and speech, he is there.

The waking from night and sleep heralds the greatest of Stevens' ascriptions to the immortality of central man. "Chocorua to Its Neighbor" (*CP*, 296–302) is a monologue of earth. The poem is exceptional in its voice. For here it is earth, the mother, who speaks, the third presence, the constant sovereign of reality. Stevens gave a song to the White Mountains of New Hampshire.[19] It should endure as long as American poetry is read. It should be heard in winter dawns, when the morning star rises and another American in solitude pauses there, seeing his northern land of birches and silent lakes in snow. Yeats memorialized Ben Bulben; and so Stevens, Chocorua. Yet there is only one reference to Chocorua in the whole of the prose record, and that is a simple note on the geographical location in answer to a correspondent.[20] Nothing could more firmly attest to the privacy of the mythological canon. This is the ceremony of a poet's hidden ritual in a faith that has become sacred. He is with the presences of titans: a mountain rooted in America; a giant of imaginings in humankind.

Chocorua, looming in the darkness, addresses her neighbor, who may be the summit of either Paugus or Whiteface, as one chooses. Eminence to eminence, she speaks, large in "large earth, large air." She has perceived men, "without reference to their form." The twenty-six sections, each set in five unrhymed lines, are a hymn of praise to the "prodigious shadow," the immortal in man, who in his poverty was but "a shell of dark blue glass, or ice, / Or air collected in a deep essay . . . / Blue's last transparence as it turned to black." The poem through the fifteenth section is set in the past tense, as though Chocorua had looked upon and heard this human presence once, and then had known again her ageless solitude. The shift to the present in the sixteenth section marks the summary of the voice, speaking of man

---

[19] To his friend Henry Church Stevens wrote from Hartford on June 1, 1939: ". . . The great point about the White Mountains is that you have to see them in order to understand New England . . ." (see *Letters*, p. 339).
[20] To Renato Poggioli, in a letter dated at Hartford, June 25, 1953; see *Letters*, p. 783.

wherever he may flourish before the face of nature. Thus the mountain once observed him. The "prodigious shadow" came "in an elemental freedom, sharp and cold" in a light congenial to him, light cast over snow by "the crystal-pointed star of morning." Chocorua felt his breath upon her top. He "breathed the pointed dark" (death). And yet "He breathed in crystal-pointed change the whole / Experience of night. . . ." She heard him say: "My solitaria / Are the meditations of a central mind. / I hear the motions of the spirit and the sound / Of what is secret becomes, for me, a voice / That is my own voice speaking in my ear." His life "is like a poverty in the space of life." He said: ". . . the flapping of wind around me here / Is something in tatters that I cannot hold." Of what, she asks, was his strength, his force? "He came from out of sleep. / He rose because men wanted him to be." She muses: Thus it is that the captain, the cardinal, the man memorialized in a statue, the mother, the scholar, were all embodiments of him, "True transfigurers fetched out of the human mountain. . . ." Chocorua speaks "of this shadow as / A human thing." "It is an eminence, / But of nothing, trash of sleep that will disappear. . . ." As an eminence he is "bare brother, megalfrere," yet a "cloud-casual, metaphysical metaphor" resting on her, thinking in her snow. His mysterious strength is summarized: ". . . Where he was, there is an enkindling, where / He is, the air changes and grows fresh to breathe." Of this insubstantial brother eminence she concludes: "How singular he was as man, how large, / If nothing more than that, for the moment, large / In my presence, the companion of presences / Greater than mine, of his demanding head / And, of human realizings, rugged roy. . . ." The rugged king of human realizings knows presences greater than hers. We know these to be the power of the giant, the power that rears this eminence of shadow, and the power of the genius in the creating hand.

The American quality of this poem in its geography and in its evocation of a solitude of the American wilderness need not be pressed. Nor is it necessary to urge the necessity of a reading within the context of the Grand Poem. Of the faith of this hymn to man it should be said only that it is the "crystal-pointed star of morning" in the canon of Wallace Stevens. As a work of art, separately considered, it takes its place among the primary devotional poems in English. Its rite is worship. We speak not of orthodoxies but of the nature of a faith, and of a language of "shapely fire: fire from an underworld," named in the brooding of Chocorua. Of the earth that once seemed "justified," complete, "an end in itself enough," Stevens finally wrote: "It is the earth itself that is humanity. . . . She is the fateful mother, whom he does not know" ("World Without Peculiarity," *CP*, 454). An eminence of mountain fastness has addressed an eminence of shadow, who rested on her, thinking in her snow. But we know that she was inhuman, unaware of the biting cold in whiteness, unfeeling of the forms of man that drift, cloudlike, to death.

He was the companion of presences greater than the mountain's. As the meditation deepens, there is a quiet alternation, a turning of reverent attention, between major man and his consort, queen and mother. The muted conclusion of "Esthétique du Mal" begins its song: "How red the rose that is the soldier's wound. . . ." The soldier of time is "deathless in great size." In his human succession the soldier is a shape of major man. Summer breathes for the fallen. And in this summer sleep, the wound is good "because life was." "No part of him was ever part of death." He is one with the immortal in us. The mother rises in pity; she gives comfort. "A woman smoothes her forehead with her hand / And the soldier of time lies calm beneath that stroke" (*CP*, 318–19). Yet it is not that he is forgotten. In major man he lives. She is merciful, smoothing her forehead. This is the gesture of the genius celebrated as the woman who weaves and weaves, becoming always "the centre of something else, / Merely by putting hand to brow, / Brooding on centuries like shells" ("Oak Leaves Are Hands," *CP*, 272). She changes the "centre" where we live, age to age. Mercifully she spares us the crushing weight of the past, as though we might have had without her to inherit the anguish of all wars since thinking men began to inherit the earth. The red rose of the soldier is the blood of life in every age. In him we suffer. But in her we know only a life of one present that was ours. Summer is her season forever, summer of the full imagination. She is the maker of metamorphosis and the mercy of release from the burden of centuries. "This green queen" is the ruler in "Description without Place": "In the seeming of the summer of her sun / By her own seeming made the summer change" (*CP*, 339).

"Notes Toward a Supreme Fiction" should be read as a "handbook" for the ephebe, the young poet on the threshold of life, as though a young Achilles sat in the presence of a master Chiron. The old poet, the master, will soon take his page from the "handbook of heartbreak." One must begin with the sun, the master sun. After him there is *one*, "in his old coat, / His slouching pantaloons, beyond the town," of whom one must "confect the final elegance" (*CP*, 389). He is the old giant. There is a second presence, passing through many shapes of woman in this virtuosity of instruction, finally a "Cinderella fulfilling herself beneath the roof" (*CP*, 405). The roof is the sign of the poet's total structure, the fullness of design wrought in the intensest poverty made endurable in the presence of the man in the old coat, beyond the town (and other men), the presence of a beautiful girl, dressed in rags, sitting by the fire of life. The teacher ends the lesson. His work is done.

Streaks of flame begin in the night sky of autumn. "The house will crumble and the books will burn." She whom he has loved has grown old. "The necklace is a carving not a kiss" (*CP*, 413). Yet the father summons the actors; the mother sets her table, and the children run to her. She is the eternal genius, the queen, the weaver, but only as she was *one*, alone his, in the brief interval of his life. As he embodied the old giant along the span of human duration, so she embodied for him all the passion that he gave her. In her life through time, she has been many women to many men. In her essence she is endless summer. Now she withdraws from him. The irony of "The Beginning," following upon "The Auroras of Autumn," is at once obvious. It is a beginning for another man who will love her and make her his. "So summer comes in the end to these few stains / And the rust and rot of the door through which she went. / The house is empty. But here is where she sat / To comb her dewy hair, a touchless light . . ." (*CP*, 427). She says good-by "in the darkness, speaking quietly there, / To those that cannot say good-by themselves" (*CP*, 431). It is as though he denies the farewell. In his last "World Without Peculiarity" he approaches her again. "But she that he loved turns cold at his light touch" (*CP*, 453). The heart and the mind rage. *He* speaks to the poet in his last desperation for her. It is the voice of the old man in us. She is "Puella Parvula" for another, the youth rising, but not for him. He must "write *pax* across the window pane. / And then / Be still . . ." (*CP*, 456).

These are the final invocations. The last presence of major man comes with another dawn. For the youth, the ephebe of "Notes Toward a Supreme Fiction," there is "A giant, on the horizon, glistening . . .," he who is the "patron of origins . . . ever changing, living in change" (*CP*, 442–43). A new Ulysses comes from the East. "A form of fire approaches the cretonnes of Penelope, / Whose mere savage presence awakens the world in which she dwells" (*CP*, 520). In the last "Long and Sluggish Lines" of the old poet, the "comic infanta" of the youth rises, the presence among the "tragic drapings" of this earth of men. Spring yellow is her sign, "babyishness of forsythia, a snatch of belief. . . ." The yellow patch beside the house "makes one think the house is laughing . . ." (*CP*, 522). His infanta began as a marine genius, roaming on tropical beaches (*CP*, 7–8). Where will this new infanta of the comedy roam, *puella parvula* of this youth of dawn? Stevens wrote in his notebook of the newcomer from the East. "The poet is a god, or, the young poet is a god. The old poet is a tramp" ("Adagia," *OP*, 173).

The withdrawal of the aging poet and the aging mistress precedes this last depth of release, the letting-go of the love. "Celle Qui Fût Héaulmiette" has been discussed earlier in other contexts. The once radiant presence, as he has loved and celebrated her, takes refuge against the cold, his winter, paradoxically in "the first warmth of spring." Yet the spring is not his; there is a last season within him. "Into that native shield she slid, / Mistress of an idea, child / Of a mother with vague severed arms / And of a father bearded in his fire" (*CP*, 438). It has been noted that the poem bears a title from Villon, and that, by evidence of the poet's disclosure, it was suggested by the Rodin sculpture of an old woman bearing the same title and popularly known as "The Old Courtesan."[21] When one has finished his tribute to the lyric power of Stevens in these five quatrains, the documentation of the poem remains. It is as firm as a lexicon. She is the mistress, loved and honored since the poet's beginning. As his realization of the eternal feminine presence, she has been his consort, the mother of his art. She has grown old with him. She takes her shelter from the cold of his winter in his *native shield, She who was the helmet-maker's wife*. Her form in the eye is, no doubt, Rodin's. But in the mind of the "father bearded in his fire," the conflagration of the end, she will expire with him *beneath his shield*. The shield against the cold is the total structure of the *helmet-maker*. The architect, the maker of the helmet, is the designer of the helmet-dome. We have discussed in an earlier chapter the symbol of the dome in the Middle East as a *celestial helmet*.[22] Thus the helmet-maker's wife was the genius of the domical structure, she who began, long ago, as the *demoiselle* of gold in the poem "Architecture." With the father she has been both associate and artisan. A dome of life in art, rising sunward, is the final refuge: it is fulfillment. One adds that it is a memorial, however great its peril in the flames of time, to the faith that the architect desired, a human sacredness of belief. This was the privacy of Stevens, the central act that the poetry alone reveals.

[21] See above, ch. 4 and 9.
[22] See above, ch. 9.

American Place: Of Land-Made Men

14

"MAN IS THE INTELLIGENCE OF HIS SOIL, / THE SOVER-eign ghost. . . . principium and lex." This proposition opens the first section of "The Comedian as the Letter C." *Or,* there is a companionable opposite as the poet introduces the fourth section: ". . . His soil is man's intelligence. / That's better. That's worth crossing seas to find" (*CP,* 27, 36). Crispin in his old French home was an intelligence of his soil. That is to say: the imagination was the beginning and the law, the ruling spirit, an intelligence as a power of choosing qualities to be imposed upon the land. But Crispin on American shores finds a new soil, which will shape his intelligence. The land compels him. Ideally, it will determine his Americanness. It will dominate him with its newness. In this fresh world there is no need of *lex, rex, principium.* "Here was prose / More exquisite than any tumbling verse: / A still new continent in which to dwell. . . . [a] shape . . . in Crispin's mind, / . . . to drive away / The shadow of his fellows from the skies, / And, from their stale intelligence released, / To make a new intelligence prevail . . ." (*CP,* 36–37). For *intelligence* we read the imagination as the sovereign of perception. For *prose* we read American soil, American place. The masque of Crispin is a revel of Stevens'. But the text at the center of the comedy is serious: The American earth beneath a man's feet and before his eye is (or ought to be) his intelligence, the prose of reality which urges new vision. We submit that this text is law for its author. It requires of him a faithfulness to American soil. We who read him sit in judgment. We interpret the law: This land, a face of nature, is to be known in its prose; it is to shape men of singular minds, of unique ways of sight and speech. We judge the text of Stevens, the letter of his law, to have been fully honored and celebrated. He desired a land of men with eyes washed clean. Certainly he knew the tutelage of old cultures. Every great originator, whatever his land and time, is an artist of perception and imagination in full freedom, a master of the ordinary raised to the extraordinary. But an American must be a man in his present place.

Stevens' foreign travel has been noted: twice to Cuba; once in Mexican waters, through the Canal to Tijuana. Early in his years in New York there was a brief vacation journey to British Columbia. It is fully apparent that the youth who dreamed of Paris became the poet of an American resolve. He declined Europe, we contend, in his strength of purpose. An American artist must see his land in clarity. For the man who wanders, there is a risk of clouding the vision. This ardor of discipline in Stevens came to a fullness of rejection; there could be no yielding to a fugitive impulse. The whole of an American aspiration for a poetry of the native, from Emerson onward, bears upon him. Physical reality must be the substratum of American poetic geography, the land at the core; and in the "ultimate elegance, the imagined land" (*CP*, 250) that he builds upon it, Stevens becomes an Emersonian poet-as-namer of American perception. It should be fully understood that this emphasis upon perception radically separates Stevens from epic intent. Whitman's way of transforming native setting, however abundant, into metaphor serviceable to the democratic ideal is foreign to him. The poetic geography of Stevens is first and last a celebration of earth in its American aspect. The land is the only epic, "prose more exquisite than any tumbling verse." The poetry of American place in the structure of Stevens is an arc of praise.

This insistence upon the prose of the land is a constant passion. What is sought is the essence of American soil, region to region, the feel of reality with men of the place to express it. Thus, "The man in Georgia waking among pines / Should be pine-spokesman. The responsive man, / Planting his pristine cores in Florida, / Should prick thereof, not on the psaltery, / But on the banjo's categorical gut, / Tuck, tuck, while the flamingoes flapped his bays" (*CP*, 38). The

American earth in Crispin's adventure is richly sensuous. The melon demands a ritual; the peach "should have a sacrament and celebration" (*CP*, 39). Georgia smells of pine. Florida is a rhythm of banjo strings and flamingos. And the American house is a cabin. For Stevens, there must be invocations and awakenings, as in the "Hymn from a Watermelon Pavilion" (*CP*, 88). The man in his cabin knows the watermelon in an endless purple (in Stevens the invariable color-sign of ceremony and rite). There is plantain by his door. A cock of red feather crows for him; and the blackbird spreads his tail under the sun. In this South the essence of land is the essence of the black man and the cabin. "Cotton" and "black Sly" are summoned as "Some Friends from Pascagoula" (*CP*, 126). The black visitors are bidden to speak of the eagle in the morning sky: "Say how his heavy wings, / Spread on the sun-bronzed air, / Turned tip and tip away, / Down to the sand, the glare / Of the pine trees. . . ." The eagle is the American bird of the imagination, the native wing and claw. He descends, to the sight of black men made what they are by the pine trees and the sand.

Among Stevens' first published pieces following his Harvard days is the sequence "Poems from 'Primordia'" (*OP*, 7–9).[1] They express precociously the resolve upon the essence of place, the *primordial* in a native American feeling for the land. Minnesota and the name of a Swedish immigrant are the sounds of a region. Somewhere in the American hinterland "The child's hair is of the color of the hay in the haystack, around which the four black horses stand. / There is the same color in the bellies of frogs, in clays, withered reeds, skins, wood, sunlight." In the South "The black mother of eleven children / Hangs her quilt under the pine-trees. / There is a connection between the colors, / The shapes of the patches, / And the eleven children. . . ." *Connection* is the phenomenon. If the soil is man's intelligence, man embodies his region. He is drenched in its colors. Leaving aside our poet as the maker of a deliberate structure in American art, we take the average man of imagination as one whose life is a patchwork quilt of American colors. It may be a quilt under pine trees in the South. Or by analogy it may be the patchwork of clay colors in the flat farmlands stretching westward. These are American lives of *primordia*, of the native. We add that these primordial colors are those never seen in

[1] Holly Stevens in a biographical note places the date of Stevens' first publication after his association with the *Harvard Advocate* as September, 1914; see *Letters*, p. 165.

233

another country. The American poet writes of them. They are the source of American expression.

A late poem of 1947, excluded from the collected edition, is a final corroboration. "Memorandum" (*OP*, 89) was written thirty years after these reflections on the primordial. The reference is multiple: to communist scorn of capitalistic "decadence" in American art; to the vigor of the American native element; and most clearly to the Byzantine refuge of Yeats.

> *Say this to Pravda, tell the damned rag*
> *That the peaches are slowly ripening.*
> *Say that the American moon comes up*
> *Cleansed of lousy Byzantium.*
>
> *Say that in the clear Atlantic night*
> *The plums are blue on the trees. The katy-dids*
> *Bang cymbals as they used to do.*
> *Millions hold millions in their arms.*
>
> [*OP*, 89][2]

This is praise of an ideal freshness of American sight. The land is the wealth of American being. The strength is here, immediate, artless. It is ours. Among these contemporaries Stevens bears his distinction, that of the *eye* that perceives the Atlantic night for what it is on American shores. The intelligence that it stirs has no concern with Byzantine gold. The palace of art will be built here, or nowhere. There is an "Anecdote of Men by the Thousand," he says: "The soul . . . is composed / Of the external world. . . ." Men of the East are the East. Men of a valley are that valley. "There are men whose words / Are as natural sounds / Of their places. . . ." "The dress of a woman of Lhassa, / In its place, / Is an invisible element of that place / Made visible" (*CP*, 51–52). In truth there is no soul without the reality of place, sensuously known. This soul is the essence of being. For Stevens it is clearly won by looking where one is. Nothing save his land will nourish it.

One must speak of embodiment rather than incarnation. Emerson's theism is immeasurably distant from the aesthetic of Stevens. The namer in Emerson's ideal poet is the master of a language defining the

---

[2] Cf. Yeats's "Sailing to Byzantium," in particular the opening images of old and young men; see *The Collected Poems of W. B. Yeats*, p. 191. Yeats's poem is of 1927. Stevens published "Memorandum" in 1947. See *Opus Posthumous*, p. 299.

spiritual fact symbolized in the natural fact. Man is spirit incarnate. Stevens may speak of the young poet as a god (*OP*, 173). But the youth is a god only of the imagination. His flesh is none other than his containment of natural process. No word lives in him save his own. He embodies nothing other than the facts of his place. But it is his imagination that makes essence from the facts. These conditions of Stevens' thought are appropriate thresholds as one studies his poetry of place. It has been noted that the total process moves from South to North. Florida and tropical luxuriance, Georgia pines and the vividness of quilts in the sun, compose the metaphor of youth. The American North, as Florida is finally rejected at the opening of *Ideas of Order*, must be sought. Its fact of place will be appropriate for age and the approach of winter. As for Crispin, the inevitable American place for him is the North. There the spring comes in "half-dissolving frost" and the winter overtakes the summer, "green palmettoes in crepuscular ice" (*CP*, 34). But, if one lived all his days in the South, we know from Stevens that he would reach the North, even in this ease of sun. It would be foolish to argue that Stevens deliberately chose New England. As a man of business, he probably settled where his best fortunes lay. But the place was singularly appropriate for him. His attention to the American land turns inexorably to the North as the poetry advances. It is as though by the casual circumstance of business he was permitted the master analogy. Travel through the South at an end, and Florida vacations no longer desired, he found the northern places in agreement with the later state of the soul, "composed of the external world." The achievement of his poetic geography of America is a record of embodiment, as his American life reflects the land and its power to shape the sentience that moves from youth to age. The land conforms to a deep interior knowledge of duration.

Thus Stevens celebrates American place in a conformity to the life of the mind. He is remarkable and unique in this, one of his most arresting acts as a poet. From the voice of night in Florida, voluptuous music requiring of his woman-genius "dusky words and dusky images" (*CP*, 86), to the flashing of the Connecticut River in the sun and the glistening steeple of Farmington (*CP*, 533) he goes. Throughout his endurance, the land he walks and sees, region to region, is his changing intelligence.

In the span from far South to deep North he is now and then engaged with the qualities of American cities. A blaze of canna flowering on the terrace of the politician's capitol becomes the "mighty thought" of the great man himself. The spires of color in this "Anecdote of Canna" (*CP*, 55) describe a political flamboyance. It matters little whether we propose that the canna, a familiar summer sight at the state capitol in Hartford, speak of Connecticut, or whether, as Stevens asserted, of Washington.[3] They signify the quality of an American city of politics in a summer season. Or there is the humor of "Arcades of Philadelphia the Past," its picture of old families of social eminence with dim memories of strawberries in the Apennines and with no perception at all of American lilacs. The town and the fragrance of lilacs "were never one, / Though the blue bushes bloomed . . ." (*CP*, 225). This is gentle reflection on an American blindness to the land. There is the sharp portrait of the American traveler at the Waldorf, home again in a "wild country of the soul," where the hotel in its comforts of an American city is to him as much as moonlight or sunlight (*CP*, 240–41). Or there is the amusing reflection upon the vagaries of city imaginings as Stevens recalls the "influence" of the Picts (Scottish romanticism, as he thinks of an American nostalgia), "the taste for iron dogs and iron deer," set about on Hartford lawns (*CP*, 155).[4]

These are intervals of humor. Yet Stevens, a city dweller through most of his life, distrusted the city. The evidence of "The Man with the Blue Guitar," with its reflections on suburbia (*CP*, 182), the stern lines of "The Common Life" (*CP*, 221), or those of "Loneliness in Jersey City" (*CP*, 210) press his conviction upon us. Cities breed conformity; the imagination is exchanged for stereotypic images; men become one social man. The life of the extraordinary American, the man who senses the geography of his place, flourishes only in solitude. The preservation of the self was the promise of the land. This country began in "a health of weather" and came to be the "repeated drone / Of other lives becoming a total drone . . ." (*OP*, 93–94). The bleakness of "Americana" (1950) describes the loss. The "first soothsayers" on this soil were "remote from the deadly general of men, / The overpopulace of the idea. . . ." Now, "A man . . . looks at himself in a glass and finds / It is the man in the glass that lives, not he." This is the unreal, the abstraction. "He inhabits another man, / Other men, and not this grass, this valid air. / He is not himself." He thinks of the

---

[3] See *Letters*, p. 465. Stevens in a letter to Hi Simons dated at Hartford, April 20, 1944, says that the canna were in the beds of terraces around the Capitol in Washington. X in the poem is the President. We might have thought him the Governor of Connecticut.

[4] See *Letters*, p. 349. Stevens writes to Hi Simons in a letter dated at Hartford, January 9, 1940: "When I first came to Hartford, I was much 'taken' by the castiron animals on the lawns."

flaunting of that "first fortune," "the buckskin hoop-la." The poem mirrors the distant address to this primordial American in "Owl's Clover": "O buckskin. O crosser of snowy divides, / For whom men were to be ends in themselves, / Are the cities to breed as mountains bred, the streets / To trundle children like the sea?" (*OP*, 61.)

The full scope of Stevens' thoughts on American society is reserved for the following chapter. One turns from the cities to know him as the celebrant of the land. The American who wished to be an end in himself is the poet of an American solitude. One touches its element of the native in the recurring moments of stillness. The northern places are known. The *skreak* and *skritter* of the grackle fade with the autumn evening in the North, leaving a stillness "in the key of that desolate sound" (*CP*, 160). This is not a land of nightingales. The poet endures his reality and no other. He celebrates the desolation. It is of his American being.

This display of resolve impresses us as a sign of the will, a deliberate seeking out of the severities of the North. Stevens on the Maine coast is Stevens of an intelligence far removed from the intelligence of Florida. The bays of flapping flamingos and the drowsing afternoons once evoked a speech of the South. At Pemaquid Point the granite spills into the surf. "Variations on a Summer Day" is cast in a speech made of "letters of rock and water." Here, for this northern sea, "It is cold to be forever young, / To come to tragic shores and flow, / In sapphire, round the sun-bleached stones, / Being, for old men, time of their time" (*CP*, 232–33). This is a tragic shore of North, this shelving rock where the clinging spruce trees "bury soldiers": Hugh March, a British redcoat, and his men, killed beyond the barbican.[5] And here spruce trees bury spruce trees in the endless cycle of nature. The poem closes with two prophetic tercets. A ship is sighted off the coast. "You could almost see the brass on her gleaming, / Not quite.

---

[5] Stevens and his family spent a summer vacation at Christmas Cove, Maine, adjacent to Pemaquid Point, in 1939; see *Letters*, p. 341 (n. 7). The letter is addressed to Pitts Sanborn from Hartford on June 26 of that year. The history of this area was no doubt of interest to Stevens. Captain John Smith landed at Christmas Cove on Christmas Day, 1614. New Harbor on the Pemaquid Peninsula was the home of the Indian chief Samoset, who deeded land to John Brown in 1625. Fort Frederick, built at Pemaquid in 1729 under royal commission, was destroyed during the Revolution by local residents to prevent its occupation by the British. Hugh March, the British redcoat, no doubt fell in a skirmish during the Revolution. But a search for a gravestone that might have proposed the name in Stevens' poem has been unsuccessful.

The mist was to light what red / Is to fire. . . . It was not yet the hour to be dauntlessly leaping" (*CP*, 235–36). On these rocks of Maine, old stones for old men, the imagery of "The Auroras of Autumn" is prefigured. "The mist was to light what red is to fire" is the somber equation. The eye has passed its full strength of sight. The red of winter fire that will consume the poet's house is already known. Maine rock is a place of prophecy. An American poet stands here, the one who will write in "The Auroras": "He observes how the north is always enlarging the change, / With its frigid brilliances, its blue-red sweeps / And gusts of great enkindlings, its polar green, / The color of ice and fire and solitude" (*CP*, 413).

The North enlarges the change. The arc of ascription to the land bends toward the rock. Much of the later poetry recalls an earlier strength of perception. The black man of the South returns in the striking title of "No Possum, No Sop, No Taters" (*CP*, 293). This poem of waning light is a song of desolation: "The field is frozen. The leaves are dry. / Bad is final in this light." Yet in this bad, there is the "last purity of the knowledge of the good." In the South the black man, major man on American soil, satisfies his hunger with his American country fare. In the spare North the poet hungers for the good of southern abundance. The title betrays the loss. The vigor of full perception in the sun, the nourishment of the imagination, fails.

Our recognition of "Chocorua to Its Neighbor" is perhaps complete. In this starry dawn over winter silence in New Hampshire the voice speaks for all men. But its incantation comes from an American mountain crest, an American rock towering above a procession of American imaginings. It is an intelligence of Stevens'. Yet in the "enlarging North" it is an intelligence of his country as well. Chocorua is history;[6] but she is also northern solitude. Her fastness is the threshold of the late poetry of Stevens; and one senses in the poet's approach to his own night of flame an enlarging compassion. To this mountain and to these sinister skies we are as nothing, as Chocorua has spoken, a "shadow as / A human thing . . . of nothing, trash of

[6] The following legend appears on the wooden plaque marking the Piper Trail of the White Mountain National Forest at Conway, New Hampshire, where an ascent of Mt. Chocorua begins.

Mt. Chocorua is named for an Indian chief and prophet who revenged his son's death from poisoning by killing the wife and children of Cornelius Cromwell who lived in the settlement of Tamworth. Chocorua was pursued to the mountain where he was shot. Before his death the chief called to his gods to forever curse nearby settlements of the white man.

The elevation of Chocorua is 3,475 ft.

sleep that will disappear . . ." (*CP*, 300). It is our power to speak, to find the words for our desolation, that makes the onsweep of nothingness endurable. The deeps of "Description without Place," which appeared in the same volume with "Chocorua," speak to us of human words. It is *place* that compels language. It is the present alone, as we stand in the place, that we describe. The quality of a place is present quality. The poet chooses Spain as an example: ". . . men make themselves their speech: the hard hidalgo / Lives in the mountainous character of his speech; / And in that mountainous mirror Spain acquires / The knowledge of Spain and of the hidalgo's hat— / A seeming of the Spaniard, a style of life, / The invention of a nation in a phrase . . ." (*CP*, 345). We suppose the hidalgo, a persona used at other points in the poetry, to represent in analogy Stevens himself. The land we walk is a mirror. To know a country is to know its speech, a "seeming," "a style of life." Of past and future there is no place. We are not there: ". . . everything we say / Of the past is description without place, a cast / Of the imagination, made in sound . . ."; and "what we say of the future must portend, / Be alive with its own seemings . . ." (*CP*, 346). We return to "Chocorua" with the question. What language was spoken of this summit before the white man came? What language will be spoken of it by future Americans? Chocorua in relation to human time is ageless. It is a place to be described in every present. The speech of the *now* is the only speech we have.

It is this swift passage of human vision over the endurance of American place that engages Stevens in the poems recalling the Pennsylvania geography of his boyhood. He thinks of festivals on the Schuylkill near Reading, flotillas of lighted canoes in night processions. They were signs of imaginings on the surface of an American river in a present that he once knew. But the Schuylkill flows into the future. His friends are shadows. The poem bears the title "A Completely New Set of Objects" (*CP*, 352–53). The reality of the river continues. The objects arranged there in a human future will be another present. He remembers the Perkiomen, where the wood doves are singing, and "the bass lie deep, still afraid of the Indians" (*CP*, 356). They shrink from Indian spears. A man of the present fishes there. He is all "one eye." He does not guess the variations of intelligence, past of Indian or present of his own day, that have distinguished the surface of the Perkiomen, or its wood doves, or its fish always looking ahead, upstream. He does not know, this American, that this place has been seen, from its first appearance to men, with different eyes. A poet thinks of the stream; and his eye is his alone in a present of an endless sequence of presents. These late reflections on Pennsylvania reach their deepest intensity in the beautiful vision of Oley Valley, a place of American haymows and summer ripeness. "There the distant fails the clairvoyant eye / And the secondary senses of the ear / Swarm, not with secondary sounds, but choirs, / Not evocations but last choirs, last sounds. . . ." There was a present, which he once knew, in Oley Valley. It has become a past. The evocations that its beauty demanded were once *first sounds,* beginnings, we may say, of an immediate speech. Now the sounds are *last sounds.* Nothing is left save the "Pure rhetoric of a language without words" (*CP,* 374). The difficulty of these meditations from "Credences of Summer" is unsurpassed in Stevens. He tells us in this finality that the *pure rhetoric* in man is his native power to form a language, to describe the reality of a present. Words express the rhetoric. But the poignance of a beauty known in a seeing and a hearing of the physical earth is its passage from an immediate speech. One ponders this. It is totally opposed, we see, to Wordsworth and Proust. For Stevens the reality of beauty is of a moment captured in the words of *a present.* It is not a reality discovered in recollection. Time gives us nothing. In "This Solitude of Cataracts" (*CP,* 424–25) the rush of waters is the reality of human time. "He never felt twice the same about the flecked river." The poet thinks of another American mountain. He wishes for "thought-like Monadnocks" in the turbulence. "He wanted to feel the same way over and over." But the river in its seeming never flows the same way twice; and it flows through many places.

A union of everlasting place, of major man of human imaginings and his constant mistress, appears in the third section of "Notes Toward a Supreme Fiction." "There was a mystic marriage in Catawba, / Between a great captain and the maiden Bawda." "The great captain loved the ever-hill Catawba / And therefore married Bawda, whom he found there, / And Bawda loved the captain as she loved the sun. / They married well because the marriage-place / Was what they loved. It was neither heaven nor hell" (*CP,* 401). The captain is major man of the American land. The mate is his genius of artifice, expressing his intelligence given by the earth he knows, "the ever-hill Catawba." Stevens names the ever-hill from the geography of his land. This was a southern marriage. The hill bears the name of a South Carolina river.

The last praise is of Connecticut, the place of final rest. We think, with Stevens, "when the houses of New England catch the first sun. . ."

in the "sprawling of winter . . ." (*OP*, 95–96).[7] In these last years he wrote his affecting tribute to the Connecticut River. Like the Schuyl-kill and the Perkiomen, it is a stream of his land. Like them, it is "Space-filled, reflecting the seasons, the folk-lore / Of each of the senses. . . ." It is "the river that flows nowhere, like a sea. . . ." We know that it is an intelligence of men of Connecticut, and that, like a mirror, it receives again and again the seasons ordained by the master sun and a lore of imaginings that spring from its constan presence. "The mere flowing of the water is a gayety, / Flashing and flashing in the sun" (*CP*, 533). "[T]his side of Stygia," it is known by the sight of succeeding generations. In 1955 Stevens wrote for the Voice of America his prose statement "Connecticut."[8] The piece matches the address to the river. It is an exaltation of the reality of his American place.

The man who loves New England, and particularly the spare region of Connecticut, loves it precisely because of the spare colors, the thin light, the delicacy and slightness and beauty of the place. The dry grass on the thin surfaces would soon change to a lime-like green and later to an emerald brilliance in a sunlight never too full. When the spring was at its height we should have a water-color, not an oil, and we should all feel that we had had a hand in the painting of it, if only in choosing to live there where it existed. Now, when all the primitive difficulties of getting started have been overcome, we live in the tradition which is the true mythology of the region and we breathe in with every breath the joy of having ourselves been created by what has been endured and mastered in the past.

[*OP*, 295]

The final sentence is compelling. Men of Connecticut are made what they are by this spare region of American land, "endured and mastered in the past." They live in the present joy of a place shaped for human dwelling, and yet a place everlastingly of spare colors and thin sur-faces, delicacy and pale sunlight. This is an external world that shapes the soul.

Stevens calls this tradition of Connecticut joy the true mythology of the region. In one of his last poems, presumably of 1955, the year of the prose statement and of his death, he returned to the theme.

A mythology reflects its region. Here
In Connecticut, we never lived in a time
When mythology was possible—But if we had—

---

[7] "A Discovery of Thought," published in *Imagi*, Summer, 1950; see *Opus Posthumous*, p. 300.
[8] See *Opus Posthumous*, p. xxiii.

That raises the question of the image's truth.
The image must be the nature of its creator.
It is the nature of its creator increased,
Heightened. It is he, anew, in a freshened youth
And it is he in the substance of his region,
Wood of his forests and stone out of his fields
Or from under his mountains.

[*OP*, 118]

The image of a mythology must be the image of its creator. If men of Connecticut had created a race of gods, these would have been images of Americans of the region. Yet the men are in the substance of the land. We return to the text of Crispin and the law of Stevens: His soil is man's intelligence. His imagination is what it is from his sense of place, his seeing of his part of earth. The man in Georgia should be pine-spokesman. The man in Connecticut, we continue, should be the spokesman of spring like a water color, or of houses catching the first sun in winter.

Society: Transitions in the American Community

15

THE ROCK IS PLACE, THE PHYSICAL SETTING OF THE individual life; for the artist, it is the abundance of natural phenomena to be plundered by the transforming imagination. The rock is also society, the condition of men in the aggregate. For the present study a distinction must pertain: in the view of Stevens the quality of any phenomenon of place is susceptible to appropriation by the poet; the quality of society is unyielding. In his time Stevens found the obduracy of the rock in society itself. We have understood that the structure of the dome is a design apart, conceived and wrought in the sovereignty of the self. It may very well be that Stevens in society was a man impressive in both social theory and political ardor. This disclosure, if it is to be made, is the task of the biographer. The evidence of the poetry is another matter and, for our concerns, the whole matter. The art of Stevens is neither social nor political in purpose. Throughout his years of poetry, society was a human condition that had to be acknowledged and studied. In his conviction, it was a contemporary reality that no artist would change, even as a demagogue bristling with arms and rhetoric might change it overnight. It was a state of existence not subject to the metamorphoses of the artist's imagination.

One goes back to think again of Stevens in the mask of Ariel, as he surveyed his structure in "The Planet on the Table" (*CP*, 532). He was another wonder-worker under the sun. The voice of Caliban had been heard and known; but its guttural, muddy mouthings were granted no authority. Stevens consistently chose the perfection of the unreal. Caliban, voicing the imperfection of the real, was the actual of everyday. But, since Caliban is by his nature gross beyond redemption, he is merely obdurate in his presence. Stevens has no part in the debate dramatized by W. H. Auden in *The Sea and the Mirror*.[1] Art for Stevens is not ultimately frivolous, nor does it fail to satisfy, as Auden affirms its failure through his Stage Manager: "Between Shall-I and I-Will, / the lion's mouth whose hunger / No metaphors can fill."[2] The hunger of the lion in Stevens *will* be filled with metaphor; and the lion will lie in the sun, for this day satisfied. But the agility and the plenitude of metaphor must derive from the poet's mastery of the object. Cloud and sea surface, bird song and pine tree, Maine rock and New Hampshire mountains—these can be possessed by the imagination and transmuted. The sun-fire of a dominant Ariel makes them what they never before were to another man. In the other substance of the rock, America *en masse* resists the virtuosity of metaphor.

The attention of Stevens to society diminishes after the mid-thirties, in that decade when the crowd was made the sum total in American expression. Those were the days of Rooseveltian mastery, an American feeling of one man where many men had stood. Stevens reacted strongly to the national feeling, which, as we shall notice, he regarded as a mode of imagination impressed upon the public. Yet his reflections upon society both before and after this neo-American era are constant. Together they form an arc of the total structure. We do not approach them as minor metaphor. They are, rather, the least typical of Stevens' acts as a poet. The subject itself does not undergo change as the poet turns from South to North, from the tropics of *Harmonium* to the boreal night of *The Auroras of Autumn* and "The Rock." It remains constant. Toward the close of *Ideas of Order* (1936) Stevens observes: "It is curious that the density of life / On a given plane is ascertainable / By dividing the number of legs one sees by two. / At least the number of people may thus be fixed" (*CP*, 157). This quatrain appears within the

---

[1] See the discussion by Monroe K. Spears, *The Poetry of W. H. Auden: The Disenchanted Island* (New York, 1963), pp. 218–30.
[2] See *The Collected Poetry of W. H. Auden* (New York, 1945), p. 351.

bleak engagements of "Like Decorations in a Nigger Cemetery," the searing irony of the title revealing a poet in contemplation of November in his countrymen, when only the poetic eccentric is a possible base of design. People are to be counted by their legs. As a text these lines are superior. The grimness of this mass agglomeration underlies the heroics of *The Man with the Blue Guitar*, published in the year following. In the far distance it remains unchanged in "Notes Toward a Supreme Fiction": "One voice repeating, one tireless chorister, / The phrases of a single phrase . . . / A single text, granite monotony" (*CP*, 394). The text of society in the structure of Stevens is single. Very probably he ordered it so, to match the single phrase of society. The view and the theme remain unaltered. In less than a master poet the granite monotony of society would have been equaled in the verse. Our interest is in tracing the skill of the poet in ordering a succession of new images to project the repeated text.

By two legs one counts the man in the mass. An early poem of *Harmonium* prefigures the theme, man in a society expressed in commodity, man who measures his existence by his legs. "Last Look at the Lilacs" is the poet's directive to the "caliper." The man of the mass walks in the alleys of the lilacs. His companion is the "divine ingénue," spring, the feminine presence. Scratching his buttocks, he tells her that "this bloom is the bloom of soap / And this fragrance the fragrance of vegetal" (*CP*, 48). To this vulgarian of soap and lotion, spring lilac is a commercial scent and nothing more. But spring is process, a seasonal reality; and in her naked beauty she is indifferent to the chance of her paramour. The caliper is commanded to a last look at the lilacs, since he sees nothing there save trash. He will be dismissed by the poet, a man like the "fantastic star" of night, "Prime paramour and belted paragon . . . / Patron and imager of the gold Don John [the sun]." He will embrace her before summer comes. The poem is a paradigm. The arc of society is to be marked again and again by this immutable separateness: "Calipers" distinguish the crowd, whose only rite is determined by synthetic commodity; the poet is a master of perception, an arrogant ravisher of spring, the imager of the sun; he is a godlike man apart. Stevens in this bravura of irony describes his self-appointed eminence. In this he assumed a distance that he was never to relinquish. Compassionate as the later poetry shows him to have become, in, for example, the "Esthétique du Mal," a charismatic assumption for his poetry was impossible for him. "Calipers" were to become men of a universal human poverty. The sharpness of rejection in the lilac garden was to be exchanged for the quiet speech of a man bearing his humanity in the autumn night. But the distance remained.

"Life on a Battleship" (*OP*, 77–81) has been noted earlier in another context. This poem of 1939, omitted by Stevens from the collected edition, is a primary explication of his poetic attention to society, from the scene in the lilac garden to the late meditations on an evening in New Haven. At this point in time, heavy armaments dominate the mind. The world comes to live on armaments, actually and imaginatively. Two figures pre-empt the poem: a captain of a battleship and a poet. The speakers are alike in two respects. Each knows that the life of the crowd is made what it is by rulers of the imagination. Each knows that the character of an age, whether debased by tyrants of arms or ennobled by poet-gods of the mythical, is destined to pass to another character. The strongest hand will always grasp the scepter, the magic wand; and thus the mass is always governed by the high imagination of the man who seizes its strength.

The poem opens with "the rape of the bourgeoisie accomplished." The men have returned to the ship. The captain speaks of the final simplification: How would it be if the whole world were moved to one huge battleship, "a divinity of steel," and he, the captain? Yet the simplification for him seems inexplicable. Why should it be a battleship, this ultimate, rather than a cockleshell? A man of supreme intelligence, he answers his question: The part, however small, is equal to the whole. If the symbol of the whole of life is a battleship to a "raped bourgeoisie," then it is the ultimate. Young men on the threshold of life speak of the race, the nation, the state, as the whole. But the captain of experience contends: ". . . Society / Is a phase. We approach a society / Without a society, the politicians / Gone, as in Calypso's isle. . . ." Nothing endures, save the vine of life, which pushes East to West. We follow the captain's thought: If society is merely a phase of humanity, how can there be the *regulae mundi* that he seeks? He concludes that the whole of an age cannot exist without the parts. Thus the master of the ultimate battleship is nothing without subjects aboard to command. There are no rules of the world in the phases of society; and hence there is no absolute race, nation, state.

The reply of the poet follows: "Your guns are not rhapsodic strophes, red / And true. The good, the strength, the sceptre moves / From constable to god . . . moving toward / A hand that fails to seize it." This is the voice of Stevens, through the mask of the poet-challenger. There is an ultimate. It is the endurance of the power of succeeding prophets, the power, whatever the phases of society, to ennoble the estate of man. The scepter to govern public imagination has not been seized by a prophet in this modern time. Yet the dominance of steel war machines is a dominance in transition; it does not signify that the captain of the master battleship, the rapist-ruler of the bourgeoisie, is the final ruler. The constable will be succeeded in time by a god of strophes, the celebrant of life, not death, the master of "an end without rhetoric," he who affirms the enduring power of master men to imagine nobly. The rhetoric will change, age to age, with the phases of society. The power to seize the scepter endures in the power to make a poetry of life itself. And in this rich texture of a poet's response lies the unchanging principle of Stevens: "Our fate is our own."

Thus the poet's dismissal of the "caliper" in the lilac garden is a rejection of the vulgar crowd. The poet-speaker in "Life on a Battleship" agrees with the captain that society is a phase, and yet condemns the ugly poverty of a modern public destiny, life literally known as obsession with armaments. One regards the facts as Stevens saw them: The modern phase is a society dominated by commodity and gross sensuality, and in its sterner portion by the steel of war. It is a phase to be endured. The time of a new poet-prophet has not yet come. The present is a present unable to realize a poetry of life. Stevens does not, of course, attribute the phase to a divine causality recognized by theology. In "Owl's Clover" the only source is Ananke, fatal Necessity (*OP*, 60). Ananke is inscrutable, beyond the knowledge of man. How Stevens regarded this mysterious force, apart from his acknowledgment in the third section of this long poem, is unclear. One hazards the guess that the chance of Ananke in causing a new phase of society to be barren of high imagination, crass in its satisfactions, or meekly subservient to demagogues is chance even less measurable than that of a volcanic island rising from the ocean floor. Historians may demonstrate the provenance of war in generations antedating the time of holocaust. But they fail in accounting for the precise qualities of life in the mass, the feeling of existence itself, at any given time.

Before a tracing of the arc of society is undertaken, it should be firmly noted that Stevens expected nothing better of his society than it displayed, and yet, that his assumptions concerning its impoverishment were thoroughly romantic. We will agree with him that we cannot recapture the feeling of existence in any phase of society in any part of the past. Nonetheless, it seems certain that there has never been a society fully dignified by the scepter-bearer, the poet-ruler. Caliban may be deplored; but he is not purged. If Ananke is chance beyond human knowledge, Caliban is the certain dross of each chance phase. He was present, as far as we can know, in every society of Western history, even in that of the Hellenes. He will be present in every society of the future. But most of us will grant that he was the dominant part in the age of Stevens in America and that his largeness perseveres as the century advances.

Irving Howe observed of Stevens a decade ago: "[He]. . . does not examine society closely or even notice it directly for any length of time; he simply absorbs 'the idea' of it."[3] This judgment disregards, in part, the fullness of poetic evidence. We are prepared to agree that it is the idea of society rather than the scrutiny of any group or any one of the members of the crowd that appealed to Stevens. This idea comes of "the density of life / On a given plane." One divides the number of legs by two. But there are admissible examinations of society apart from those of the sociologist, the philanthropist, the proletarian writer. Stevens' examination is both close and direct, and it continues for a very considerable length of time. His intent is steadily trained upon aggregate consciousness— the feeling of mass existence in the age—rather than upon economic and political conditions. His question is directed to what people see and imagine of the world rather than to what they do in the acts of community.

The intricacies of "The Emperor of Ice Cream" (CP, 64) have been more frequently examined than those of any other of Stevens' poems. Its significance as an early reflection on American society will not be apparent without cognate evidence from other parts of the total expression. Ice cream, contrary to the opinions of some readers, is not death.[4] Ice cream is an American commodity; its

[3] "Another Way of Looking at the Blackbird," *The New Republic*, Vol. 137, No. 20 (November 4, 1957), p. 17.
[4] See, for example, Alfred Kreymborg, "An Early Impression of Wallace Stevens," *The Trinity Review*, VIII, No. 3 (May, 1954), 15.

maker is the emperor of boys and girls in the milk-shake paradise of the corner drugstore. The "roller of big cigars" is the tycoon of American business who controls the commodity. The remarkable third line, "In kitchen cups concupiscent curds," describes the rite of the milk shake. It also repeats the sounds of *C* that "squeak all over the place," American *C* of the imagination deliberately repeated in the diction of "The Comedian as the Letter C."[5] The wenches "dawdle in such dress / As they are used to wear." The boys "Bring flowers in last month's newspapers." "Let be be finale of seem." Let what *is* in this concupiscent rite be the end of noble *seeming*. In almost immediate sequence in the collected edition the important explicative text appears. It is found in the fifth stanza of "Sunday Morning" (*CP*, 68–69), with its ritual of youthful beauty, the longing of boys for girls in a setting of the willow shivering in the sun, of fruit presented with decorous homage, as though a procession of libation bearers passed over a spot of green earth. In twentieth-century America of the time of Stevens, the longing is concupiscence, and the rite is a feast of ice cream. The flowers offered in last month's newspapers are flowers surpassed by the image of the daily news-tyrant of the imagination, the supreme determinant of public rite. We extend the reading by the discovery that flowers at the milk-shake counter are to newspapers what spring lilac is to a soap manufacturer, and by tracing the image deep into the poetry of the early forties, in "The Man on the Dump," as "Days pass like papers from a press. / The bouquets come here in the papers" (*CP*, 201).

The second stanza presents the famous image of death in an adjacent room. The winding sheet is to be taken from the dresser of deal, lacking the three glass knobs. A woman has died in poverty. "If her horny feet protrude, they come / To show how cold she is, and dumb." Horn is the color-sign of death. The poet himself confirms his intention in a later poem of *Harmonium*, "Cortège for Rosenblum" (*CP*, 80), "the wizened one / Of the color of horn. . . ." It is Venus who lies in death, in a room of slovenly ugliness. Her sign is clear. It was she who embroidered her symbolic birds, her fantails, on the sheet. Her death is a symbol of a greater death in a society of the youthful. The rite of longing and the rite of courtship are at an end. Venus, once an empress of youthful ceremony, gives place to the emperor of ice cream. As for the fantails, we observe

5 See again Stevens' comment to Hi Simons in his letter dated at Hartford, January 12, 1940; *Letters*, p. 352.

that Stevens earlier introduces in *Harmonium* another image of stitching on a winding sheet. It appears in "The Jack-Rabbit" in an ironic phantasy of a possible American myth in a wholly American setting. The jack rabbit sings to the Arkansaw. The black man, major man in the American imaginative life, exhorts the grandmother: "Crochet me this buzzard / On your winding sheet. . . ." And to the caroling rabbit he addresses a warning: "The entrails of the buzzard / Are rattling" (*CP*, 50). The rabbit is the American poet. The old American scavenger is hungry. On the winding sheet of a mythless American, he is a symbol of death. The American buzzard has no iconography, and no rite. The fantails of Venus had a long and illustrious history. In such an incongruous succession as buzzard to fantail Stevens expresses the comic spirit that was expressly his. We expect it to reach us in irony as he looks intently at the poverty of modern social ceremony in the final couplet of "The Emperor of Ice Cream": "Let the lamp affix its beam." Let the light of the mind be trained on this reality and no other. This *let* is his true imperative. As he was to write in the high surveillance of "Notes Toward a Supreme Fiction," we must accept: "The death of one god is the death of all. / Let purple Phoebus lie in umber harvest, / Let Phoebus slumber and die in autumn umber . . ." (*CP*, 381).

The recurrence of the subject through the remaining poems of *Harmonium* presents a broadening metaphoric range. In "Disillusionment at Ten O'Clock," white nightgowns are the colorless signs of colorless lives, of people going to bed again with no dreams; only the drunken old sailor "Catches tigers / In red weather" (*CP*, 66). The import is clear: there is no fury of the imagination save in a derelict and drunken solitude. The scene gives place to the American cabin and the American field in an imperious address bearing the most ingenious of all Stevens' titles, "Frogs Eat Butterflies. Snakes Eat Frogs. Hogs Eat Snakes. Men Eat Hogs" (*CP*, 78). This is voraciousness, the satisfaction of the stomach at several levels of organic being. The cabin and the field return to the symbols of American existence established in "The Comedian as the Letter C." The address to the "average" American appears in the third triplet: ". . . the man who erected this cabin, planted / This field, and tended it awhile, / Knew not the quirks of imagery." His days were arid. He did not know what some men (and certainly the poet among them) know, that the rivers went "nosing like swine," while the air was "heavy with the breath of these swine," and with "thunder's rattapallax." And the rivers went swinelike to the sea mouths. What the arid man thinks is the strictest prose: living things eat to live; the higher orders feed on the lower; life is, then, eating to live. What the man of imagination knows is that life is made of imagery if it is life at all: river and summer and thunder, swine and sea, and, beyond the poem, all that he encounters will become metaphor; this metaphor is his food; and this will sustain him until his life flows to the sea, in death.[6]

In the final sequence of *Harmonium* the subject changes in tone. Stevens left no comment on "Two at Norfolk." The poem is cryptic in reference. Two skeletons are addressed in a southern cemetery dark with myrtles and magnolias. One man had a daughter, the other, a son. Is each grave a memorial to a mere perfunctoriness of propagation? The daughter was "foreign thing" to one father; the son's "music" was unheard by the other, who praised instead Johann Sebastian Bach. And now the son and the daughter meet in the summer air, touching closely, yet feeling an escape from ardor "in the lapses of their kisses" (*CP*, 111–12). The injunction to the Negro caretakers of the cemetery is simple: "Make a bed and leave the iris in it." Premonitions of death, clearly his own death, crowd the mind of the poet. Stevens' first volume closes here in a compassionate regard. Father to daughter, father to son, we are strangers. Even in the ardor of union between daughter and son, there are lapses. What shall be said of the common prose other than that it becomes the whole of life for some men, that it threatens each of us, even as we begin in the need that is love? Society appears to be the enemy of life as poetry. But to stand in danger of its common prose was, for Stevens, as much of reality as to know the truth of society as a phase.

Ideas of Order and *Owl's Clover* of 1936 and *The Man with the Blue Guitar* of 1937 together present the major span of Stevens' attention to society.[7] Whatever the disposition of earlier criticism to read these volumes as documents of theory in a decade of American crisis, we maintain here a sole concern with metaphor. Images of mass without motion or without ordered vision dominate the opening sequence of *Ideas of Order*. The title is itself mocking

[6] Cf. the river image in "The River of Rivers in Connecticut," at the close of the *Collected Poems*, p. 533.
[7] The most thorough discussion of this period in Stevens' career yet written for publication is that of Joseph N. Riddel, *The Clairvoyant Eye*, in a chapter entitled "Poet's Politics," pp. 104–48.

and despairing. In "Sad Strains of a Gay Waltz," the fourth poem of
the volume, the dance of a dying phase of society has become
"motionless sound." The poet himself, in the persona of Hoon,
confesses the loss of all form and order in his solitude. The scene
in the theater of life changes. "There are these sudden mobs of
men, / These sudden clouds of faces and arms, / An immense
suppression, freed, / These voices crying without knowing for
what, / Except to be happy, without knowing how. . . ." They
require an order "beyond their speech" (*CP*, 121–22). "Too many
waltzes have ended." This is a new hiatus between order and order,
music and music. The poem ends very much in the manner of "Life
on a Battleship." "The epic of disbelief" will become belief in some
unpredictable future, when a new master of the imagination seizes
the scepter. But the interim is chaos. Our recognition of Stevens in
full response to this chaos is central to our understanding of the
Grand Poem, the total structure. It was his fate to live between
phase and phase in the continuity of belief. Society at the end of a
phase always moves toward a new center. But there is an inevitable
phase of disorder between these successive states of order. Stevens
did not discover before his death in 1955 that the pain of transition
was about to end. Nor did he at any time suppose that he was to
be the new master who would wield the scepter. Insofar as Ananke
determines the duration of disorder, we may say only that the poet
who is caught between has no choice save the necessity of self. This
is the larger view, beyond a poet's politics. We speak here of a
politics involving a society. The politics of Stevens the poet (and
I disclaim again for this study the individual living in a society) is
a private endeavor. The sentence recorded by his hand in the
"Adagia" is granitic: "Politics is the struggle for existence" (*OP*, 161).
We take this to be the struggle of the poet, the artist who would
place his whole belief in the self.

Thus the surveillance of Stevens in the thirties is maintained
at a distance; and one looks in vain for signs in the poetry that the
distance was diminishing in the forties and the early fifties. The
statue of Andrew Jackson by Clark Mills[8] stands today, as it stood
in the time of Stevens, in Lafayette Park, facing the White House.
"Dance of the Macabre Mice" follows the strains of the gay waltz.
"In the land of turkeys in turkey weather" we go round and round
the base of the statue. The horse is covered with mice; and we are

---

[8] See Stevens' comment on this sculpture in "The Noble Rider and the Sound of
Words," *The Necessary Angel*, p. 10.

the mice in a "hungry dance" with no name (*CP*, 123). Here stands a symbol of a past glory, bearing no relation to a present of disorder. The nation hungers for a statue of a new belief. In a gray November of another turkey-eating, we are mice. We are the "mickey mockers" of the ensuing poem, "The American Sublime" (*CP*, 130–31). The reference is quite clear. The best we can do with our hunger for a poetry of life is to reduce ourselves to the stature of the famous mouse created by Walt Disney! There is a terrible desperation in the poet's concluding lines: "One grows used to the weather. . . . What wine does one drink? / What bread does one eat?" The statue is the center for Stevens, exactly as it is to be in "Owl's Clover." Each new society requires a new statue. But as the poet contends in "The Greenest Continent" ("Owl's Clover"), Ananke alone "caused the statue to be made / And he shall fix the place where it will stand" (*OP*, 60). A man of power, one fit in his strength of imagination to seize the common lot, to rescue men from the destiny of hungry mice, will design the statue of the future. We add that if Ananke shall fix the place where it will stand, the new scepter-bearer will be the sculptor appointed by him.

The leaves of the arc of society through this period are shaped in many of Stevens' characteristic images. The performing artist at the keyboard, like Peter Quince, returns in "Mozart, 1935," to play the present on a jazz piano as the dead master of music is carried down the stairs. The body of Mozart assumes the place of the dead Venus in "The Emperor of Ice Cream." The work of the master architect of the imagination is contemplated anew in "Botanist on Alp (No. 1)" (*CP*, 134–35) as the poet contends that "Marx has ruined Nature / For the moment." He muses upon the art of Claude Lorrain. How near one is in that master, "(In a world that was resting on pillars, / That was seen through arches) / To the central composition, / The essential theme." "The panorama of despair" succeeds the prostrate pillars and the haggard arches. Joy lies only within the self. In "A Fading of the Sun" (*CP*, 139) the only redemption from this modern desolation of society is for each man "Within as pillars of the sun, / Supports of night." Men hunger. If the sun fades in this time, there is strength to be had from the sun-pillars of the self. In this strength one can eat of his portion and live.

"Owl's Clover," issued initially as a separate volume in 1936, was revised by Stevens within a year for inclusion with *The Man with the Blue Guitar* (1937). Thereafter it remained suppressed.

The original text appears in the reprinting of *Opus Posthumous*. The following comment on the poem is based on the version of 1936 in which Stevens' answer to the criticism of Stanley Burnshaw appears. The Burnshaw-Stevens encounter is of no consequence in our present considerations, even as the original text is chosen. It is sufficient to note that Stevens had perhaps very small reason to answer an adverse review of *Ideas of Order*. Within recent years, since the poet's death, Mr. Burnshaw has made clear the strange disproportion in Stevens' attention.[9] But it was Marxist egalitarianism that occupied Stevens as he wrote the first version of "Owl's Clover"; and, contrary to what the reviewer in the mid-thirties may have thought of *Ideas of Order,* it was not a poet in search of "philosophical adjustment" who wrote a reply in "Mr. Burnshaw and the Statue." Stevens was not occupied with the business of his own poetic salvation, but rather with a measurement of the distance between the poet and the contemporary mass. To specify, he was engaged in examining the poverty of the American consciousness under the aegis of the New Deal, the poverty, then, of a society moving from a last phase to a phase to come. Nor had politics anything to demand in the poet's view. Stevens' denial of a usual politics for poets may be found in the reply to Mr. Burnshaw: *If* there were to be a time "in which the poets' politics / Will rule in a poets' world. Yet that will be / A world impossible for poets, who / Complain and prophesy, in their complaints, / And are never of the world in which they live" (*OP*, 48). The reply is clear. To the Left, to the Right, politics is not poetic business. If the poet's politics is the struggle for his existence, then his art is exemplary to the mass. It may show to his contemporaries the possibility of life ennobled by the unreal of the imagination, ceremony and rite in an elevation of being, above the politics of the usual.

[9] See "Wallace Stevens and the Statue," *The Sewanee Review,* LXIX, No. 3 (Summer, 1961), 355–66. Mr. Burnshaw had reviewed *Ideas of Order* in *The New Masses* of October 1, 1935. He reprints the review in this retrospective comment. At that time, to quote Mr. Burnshaw on himself, he was among "those writers within the Left who were wrestling with their private angels" (p. 359). "But within a year after writing the Stevens review, his private angel had pinned his shoulders to the ground" (p. 360). So much for Mr. Burnshaw's aspirations of an earlier decade. He had admired, he freely confesses, the Stevens of *Harmonium.* Of *Ideas of Order* he wrote: ". . . It is verse that Stevens can no longer write. His harmonious cosmos is suddenly screeching with confusion." As of that time Mr. Burnshaw's charge was that Stevens had failed as an artist precisely because he felt his membership in a class "menaced by the clashes between capital and labor." Hence he was "in the throes of struggle for philosophical adjustment" (pp. 365–66).

The major subject of the five sections of "Owl's Clover" is the statue. In the revised text, prepared for publication in *The Man with the Blue Guitar,* Stevens, having excised references to Mr. Burnshaw, renamed the second section "The Statue at the World's End." Of the central symbol, he wrote in reply to one of his critics: "[T]he statue is regarded not as a symbol of art, but as a manifestation of the civilization of which it is a part. . . . It will be replaced, as part of incessant change. *What this poem is concerned with is adaptation to change.* One assumes that change is the evolution of what ought to be." He continued with the reflection that "life is chaos." "[T]he progression from one thing to another is archaic, as archaic as being born and dying."[10] The statue as a manifestation of a civilization will not, then, pass through a new progression to a new significance. Every statue fails eventually, in the process of human time.

The first section of the poem, "The Old Woman and the Statue," describes "the bitter mind in a flapping cloak." The old woman is the symbol of a destitute society asking of an archaic statue an answer to its need. Among the rotting leaves of autumn, the statue is a civilization in decay. It is the "manner of a mind" that has fallen in ruin. The statue is no longer "the sovereign shape in a world of shapes" (*OP,* 45). "Mr. Burnshaw and the Statue" moves about the central text: *"The Mass Appoints These Marbles Of Itself To Be Itself."* But in these memorials of an age, there is only "a trash can . . . immense detritus of a world / That is completely waste" (*OP,* 48–49). The third section turns to Africa, "The Greenest Continent." "The heaven of Europe is empty, like a Schloss / Abandoned because of taxes . . ." (*OP,* 53). Could the statue stand in Africa? Meanwhile, habitués of café intellection expound the end of all the gods. "The black will still / Be free to sing, if only a sorrowful song." Ananke alone is the final god. He will cause the statue to be made and will fix its place (*OP,* 56–60). In "A Duck for Dinner," Stevens is intent on the provision of the age. Physical hunger is assuaged by the ministrations of a new politics. Through his persona of the Bulgar[11] the poet speaks; and he answers in his own voice. These people, with "a duck to a million," rise a little, "inch by inch, Sunday by Sunday." In the Sunday park, "they keep to the paths of the skeleton architect." But "pay-roll

---

[10] In a letter to Hi Simons dated at Hartford, August 27, 1940; *Letters,* pp. 366–67.
[11] Cf. Riddel, *The Clairvoyant Eye,* p. 131, on the Bulgar as "a composite mask of the immigrant."

water-falls" and "the clank of the carrousel" are not enough. The statue will one day be known. Now the distances converge upon its place, "white and high." Stevens advances here an American faith, in his evocation of "the buckskin. . . crosser of snowy divides." He speaks of a native American hunger for a vision which is poetry (*OP*, 60–62). The statue to come will be the image that will satisfy the mass, in this present time fed only with ducks, payrolls, and Sundays in the parks. "Sombre Figuration," the fifth section of the poem, turns to the presence of major man of the imagination. He is the "sprawling portent" above us. Stevens observes that this contemporary mass is "the form / Of a generation that does not know itself. . . ." But the portent moves; the future comes on. The poem arrives at full circle. The statue of the present stands in "hum-drum space." "Even imagination has an end, / When the statue is not a thing imagined, a stone / That changed in sleep. It is, it is, let be / The way it came, let be what it may become." The new statue will be known, a new thing imagined among the people. But in this time of transition the poet's passion is "merely to be / For the gaudium of being . . ." (*OP*, 68–71).

As a programmatic composition, "Owl's Clover" assumes a monumental character that is ill-suited to the major idiom of the Grand Poem. The metaphor, with few exceptions, is demonstrative and ponderous. Stevens' later rejection of the poem for the collected edition appears amply justified. Yet this ambitious sequence remains one of the most unique of American poetic excursions into the unnamable, the quality of mass consciousness at a singular time in social history. What Stevens here sought to define was the feeling of a nation destitute of faith during an unprecedented economic collapse. What he sought to render was the quality of the national mind stripped of its commanding structures of the imagination. Material bankruptcy is not at issue. The need for metaphor is relative, as Stevens regarded it. The poet lives by metaphor. But in the mass apart from the poet, there is also a need for images without material form, images given by master men. One metaphor strongly entertained by the crowd may become a symbol of existence itself. In the end the question asked by Stevens in "Owl's Clover" is perhaps unanswerable: What is the inner, the hidden life of society without symbols that represent some degree of belief?

When he turns from the American condition in "The Greenest Continent," it is at least interesting to find him intent upon Africa.

In the light of political events since his death, his speculation in these metaphors is prescient. This is a savage green of the possible. Will the next commanding civilization rise in the luxuriance of these jungles under the "antiquest sun"?[12] Stevens is thinking of the place of the next statue. But the statue, as it has been known in Western history, is of the "northern sky" (*OP*, 54–55). It has never appeared in the tropics. The historical fact of imagination is its northern continuity. The statue in Africa seems unthinkable. The poem returns to the American scene, as though, with the bankruptcy of Europe in the distance, the final hope of our civilization must rest there. In this contention the poet completes his examination of this vast range of the possible. The only certainty is the transition of the present. Stevens takes leave of the theme for a private rejoicing in the "gaudium of being," as much as to say that, without the statue, the self is all. His disengagement bears the mark of finality. He was not again to undertake so large a metaphor of mass existence. With all its faults "Owl's Clover" remains indispensable in a full tracing of the arc of society. It seeks to specify the nature of mass consciousness, of mass aspiration, mass hunger for a nourishment that the crowd itself cannot name. There has been no purpose larger than this in American poetry. With it Stevens had arrived at the threshold of epic intention. He withdrew.

"The Man with the Blue Guitar" should be read as a sequence of thirty-three variations on the theme of a poet's resolution and independence. The rock of society is accepted for what it is; the threshold of "Owl's Clover" is abandoned; the celebration of a "gaudium of being" will endure. This is not a nostalgic plucking of the strings. At times the blows of the musician's hand are savage. Not a single one of the sections, all of varying length, fails to return to the reality of social decay. The brilliance of the poem derives from its constantly shifting metaphoric luster. The blue guitar is, of course, the imagination. Its music displays a hard and polished surface, as though to reflect the gaunt images of mass existence. This is virtuoso writing, masterful in a constancy of restatement again and again preserved from monotony. The poem closes with the following six couplets:

12 *Ibid.*, p. 128. Mr. Riddel advances the following opinion: "Above all, the poem ["The Greenest Continent"] is Stevens' initial excursion into the jungle of the Jungian unconscious, there to discover man's constant rage for order as 'Fatal Ananke,' the 'final god' and author of that 'aesthetic order' which lies behind all other orders."

That generation's dream, aviled
In the mud, in Monday's dirty light,

That's it, the only dream they knew,
Time in its final block, not time

To come, a wrangling of two dreams.
Here is the bread of time to come,

Here is its actual stone. The bread
Will be our bread, the stone will be

Our bed and we shall sleep by night.
We shall forget by day, except

The moments when we choose to play
The imagined pine, the imagined jay.

[*CP*, 183–84]

In *aviled* Stevens adapts the French *avilir,* to debase. He intends a fresh qualification beyond English diction: the debased dream of a generation in the light of the inevitable Monday. Its time is measured, then, by Sundays. Its bread is stone. Nor does the oncoming future promise bread for stone. So be it. The poet will sleep upon this rock. Some part of the day will be transformed by his music, a music played in solitude.

This terminal section serves as well as any other to illustrate the mode of variation. The range of metaphor preceding is the change made by the hand on the guitar. In the fifth section, the people, "a million on one string," cry: "Do not speak to us of the greatness of poetry / . . . Of the structure of vaults upon a point of light. / . . . Day is desire and night is sleep / There are no shadows anywhere" (*CP*, 167). The dominant image here has been examined earlier. It is the poet's structure of vaults, erected upon his point of *light,* his briefly held place in time. The rest is dark. "The fields entrap the children, brick / Is a weed and all the flies are caught, / Wingless and withered, but living alive. / The discord merely magnifies. / Deeper within the belly's dark / Of time, time grows upon the rock" (Sec. 11, *CP*, 171). The subject becomes the musician himself: "Do I sit, deformed, a naked egg, / Catching at Good-bye, harvest moon, / Without seeing the harvest or the moon?" (*CP*, 173.) Does he catch at a popular song, the man who earlier leans from the steeple, rolling a drum upon the blue guitar, with which to confront his adversary "hoo-ing the slick trombones" (Sec. 10, *CP*, 170)?[13] The resolution attains its greatest intensity in the nineteenth section. "That I may reduce the monster to / Myself, and then may be myself . . . / Being the lion in the lute / Before the lion locked in stone" (*CP*, 175). The lion is locked in the stone of society. Only the master of wing and claw will match its latent power within himself.

"Oxidia, banal suburb, / One-half of all its installments paid" (*CP*, 182). If Stevens had created no other metaphor for his society than this, the poem would be memorable. "Ecce, Oxidia is the seed / Dropped out of this amber-ember pod, / Oxidia is the soot of fire, / Oxidia is Olympia." In his comment on the poem for Renato Poggioli, he wrote of his oxide-gaseous suburb: ". . . If I am to 'evolve a man' in Oxidia and if Oxidia is the only possible Olympia, in any real sense, then Oxidia is that from which Olympia must come."[14] This is to say that the artist-hero has never had any birth other than from the condition of his society. If the American industrial suburb is the ultimate of this civilization, then the Olympian poet will be born of this reality and no other. As for major man, the progenitor of all imagination, he yet lives in modern American man of Oxidia. But we find him, "suddenly and at last, actually and presently, to be an employe of the Oxidia Electric Light & Power Company."[15]

The metaphor of society from these clustering poems of the mid-thirties is scarcely repeated in the remaining two decades. In Stevens' full achievement it is the metaphor of a sternly willed artistic endurance. But with respect to a continuing attention to structure it should be noted that the first poem of *Parts of a World,* published in 1942, returns to the major subject of "Owl's Clover." In "Parochial Theme" the poet is the man of health: "This health is holy, / This halloo, halloo, halloo heard over the cries / Of those for whom a square room is a fire, / Of those whom the statues torture and keep down" (*CP*, 191).

Parts of a World is primarily a sequence of lyrics related by the subject proposed in the title. Order was the major theme in the

---

[13] See Stevens in his notes on the poem, addressed in a letter to Renato Poggioli dated at Hartford, June 25, 1953; *Letters*, p. 783. He had in mind a song entitled "Good-bye, Good-bye Harvest Moon." The title was actually "Shine On, Harvest Moon." Of the image of the trombones, he wrote: "Hoo-ing the slick trombone means making Bing Crosby: performing in an accomplished way."
[14] From Hartford, July 12, 1953; *Letters*, pp. 788–89.
[15] To Professor Poggioli in the same commentary; *Letters*, p. 791.

years of the Depression. It is succeeded by imaginative studies of a society at war. Whatever the affirmations of the poet's private mastery of phenomena, the dominant impression of the volume is one of fragmentation. In "Dry Loaf," "dry men" are blown "Brown as the bread, thinking of birds . . . that came like dirty water in waves . . ." while the drums batter. The birds of the imagination are clearly air-borne machines of destruction. In this time "the waves were soldiers marching." The hunger of men in the thirties for a nourishment of the mind is now a different hunger. But it is still the pain of desire. The present is a new present. It is made of days that "pass like papers from a press." "United Dames of America," with its bitter title, anticipates the compassionate address that will distinguish the later poetry. The mode is confessional; and as we approach Stevens in his last decade it shows a change in regard. "There are not leaves [poems] enough to cover the face . . . of the man of the mass." This was never the face seen by the hermit-poet on his reef by the sea, nor that seen by the naked politician (*CP*, 206). In this *now*, it is the face of humanity. One thinks of Stevens in the valedictory of "The Rock." "It is not enough to cover the rock with leaves. / We must be cured of it by a cure of the ground / Or a cure of ourselves . . ." (*CP*, 526).

Yet it is true that this is compassion at a distance. The poet returns to look upon the dull poverty of the street as he muses at a hotel window. In "Loneliness in Jersey City" the steeples and the people are empty. "They think that things are all right, / Since the deer and the dachshund are one" (*CP*, 210). Life is graceless in this wry equation. But since it is that "The people grow out of the weather; / The gods grow out of the people . . . ," there will be no gods. One must expect in Stevens this juxtaposition of the imperious mood and the urgency of a common emotion. This is less paradox in the poet than recognition of divergences among the modes of public being. The vulgarity of Jersey City may be of the usual; yet it is a mode among modes. Stevens did not assume the poverty of his society to be of a single kind. It was variously known. His geometric measurement of the modern American city in "The Common Life" emerges as more descriptive of a cage than of a common lethargy of the citizens. The power that builds Oxidia is here. The light is "morbid" (*CP*, 221), but not of the citizens' making. In *Parts of a World*, society is barred against its humanity. Wherever people enter these poems, they move mechanically, in a succession of days and nights. The pitiable prospect is that of a human mechanism limited in the power of response to existence. The weather is in the city; and the weather is as well in the mind of the poet, who is not exempt from its blight. The imagination fails, even in the time of the dogwood blossoms. Spring is merely a confection; there is no rite (*CP*, 228–29).

"These days of disinheritance, we feast / On human heads." The poem is "Cuisine Bourgeoise" (*CP*, 227–28). Humanity is disinherited of its power to see the physical world. The seasons pass without human perception. The only food is the bitter meat of heads, politicians' heads, the copious provision of ideas. Thus it is that Stevens speaks of the people who avoid "central things," who are insensible to the "blood-red redness of the sun." "On the Adequacy of Landscape" (*CP*, 243–44) summons again the image of the man of solitude and open eye: ". . . he that suffers most desires / The red bird most and the strongest sky—" (*CP*, 244). The ideas of the world are not the food of physical men. The transition of ideas, we may assume, is the passage of politicians. It would be foolish to argue that Stevens in society did not attend to the demanding conflict of current ideas. Every man of intelligence so attends. But the question is one of a satisfaction in the midst of suffering. Without the eye open to light and to the forms of the physical world, the essential nature of the human being is denied.

It is this conviction which becomes the impressive strength of the following volume, *Transport to Summer,* notably in the "Esthétique du Mal." The evil of our time is less the evil of ungoverned passion in men, of bestial instinct, than the evil of slavery to ideas made by politicians, themselves masters of imagination. Konstantinov in the fourteenth section of the poem is the example (*CP*, 324–25). "Revolution / Is the affair of logical lunatics." One might meet Konstantinov at Geneva, in that famous gathering place of political logicians. "He would not be aware of the lake. / He would be the lunatic of one idea / In a world of ideas, who would have all the people / Live, work, suffer and die in that idea / In a world of ideas." For Stevens this logical lunacy was the mark of the totalitarian state. There is an evil beyond war itself. It is the evil of indenturing the mass in servitude to the single idea of the state. It is a further imposition of that greatest poverty: the loss of freedom to perceive as one wills, to imagine upon the world as one chooses. "The greatest poverty is not to live / In a physical world,

to feel that one's desire / Is too difficult to tell from despair"
(*CP,* 325). The following "Sketch of the Ultimate Politician" suggests the final dehumanization of the race, very much as though
the captain of "Life on a Battleship" had at last built the final
monster to contain the world. "He is the final builder of the total
building, / The final dreamer of the total dream, / Or will be.
Building and dream are one" (*CP,* 335). Lenin, like Konstantinov,
is a paradigm of the ultimate. For him ". . . tomorrow's regions
became / One thinking of apocalyptic legions" ("Description without
Place," *CP,* 343).

The statue is restored to the theme as Stevens takes his final
leave of society. These reflections on a communist Russia of *one*
idea lead to the prospect of "railway-stops . . . at which the same
statue of Stalin greets / The same railway passenger . . ." The poem
is entitled "Mountains Covered with Cats," which is to be rendered:
mountain eminences, above the plain, covered with cats of the
imagination, potential claws. Then why was the same statue indefi-
nitely tolerated by the same railway passenger? The personality
was "invalid"; the imagination sought peace. The ghost of Freud,
Stevens concludes, may meditate the impotent dead, "And quickly
understand, without their flesh, / How truly they had not been
what they were" (*CP,* 367–68). This is the last compassion of
Stevens. As he reflects finally in "Notes Toward a Supreme Fiction,"
the great statue of General Du Puy becomes rubbish in the end
(*CP,* 391–92). There is an end of all statues. But there is also a
sadness of exhaustion and impotence in men too long tyrannized
by ideas, a graying of energy, a loss of individual force. The battle
for existence as a single self is too arduous. There is a death of the
corporate mind of men. This is total death. Beside it the petty
deaths of individuals are the deaths of "small townsmen" (*CP,* 362).
In the vast city of humanity the death of all imagination is the great
death-in-life negating the whole of existence.

As Stevens turns to the deep introspection of *The Auroras of
Autumn* and "The Rock," society is put aside. But the final statement
is certain and compelling as the meditations of "An Ordinary Evening in New Haven" proceed in quiet succession. It is an American
city of Connecticut, a city with an American past. The fourth section of
the poem suggests that these men have sought the plainness "of a

man who has fought / Against illusion. . . ." If New Haven is a city in the "plain" style, nonetheless, "Plain men in plain towns / Are not precise about the appeasement they need." This is to say that plainness is not the end, as if a universal truth of many men together in a city were a plain truth. A harmony of men is a harmony of individualities, each bound to the others by the major talent of imagination. This is the ideal community of the poet. New Haven is not here the subject. The vision is of a city, a society unknown in America in the years of Stevens.

Existence: The Difficulty of Being

16

THE ART OF STEVENS, AS WE HAVE NOTED IN EARLIER chapters of this study, is a continuous process of encounter. Perception is momentary; and so is the act of the mind, before the hand establishes its description. A poem is a meteor; it is a pheasant disappearing in the brush (*OP*, 158, 173). These notes from the "Adagia" qualify the essential character of the total poetry. It follows that the swift passage of *the now* is constantly reflected in the major work of Stevens and that existence can be only what is known in immediacy. In his lecture-essay on poetry and painting Stevens regards existence in the sense of the immediate as "the heroic subject of all study" (*NA*, 176). When we speak of existence as thematic in the Grand Poem, we name the Grand Subject that dominates the total structure. When we purpose an examination of the arc of existence with its own leaves, we turn to those poems which are intended definitions of mind as transient consciousness. No matter what the demands made upon this mind by realities that surround it, the known of its experience at a given moment is of its individual governance and no other.

All being is difficult, as Stevens asserts in the opening lines of "Notes Toward a Supreme Fiction" (*CP*, 381). When existence is a full awareness, the difficulty is then supreme. For the realities that the mind confronts must be fully admitted and known; and at the same time it must possess the strength to maintain its own singularity. It must fend off the threat of the "pressure." This is precarious poise in the difficulty. Men of lesser strength know a lesser difficulty of assertion. The limitations of consciousness, as we have seen in examining Stevens on society, derive from the inability of the mind to grasp reality, to know what it is that threatens one's autonomy or to experience what may be, in a full perception of the physical, a satisfaction in being. There are, of course, no absolute states of limitation subsuming untold numbers of men in the same degree, as if man in the abstract were the simple total. Each individual requires of existence what his capacities may permit. Each directs questions toward what he perceives, in strict accord with the nature of his own intelligence. If his will to know pierces toward the enigmatic center of being, as the poet's imagination of transmuting power seizes the object in "savage scrutiny," he is a man of supreme intelligence. If his will has no force save that of contributing to the monotony of everyday in the most somber plebeian sense, he is a man of the rankest poverty. The variables of major questions are made one in that all of them, whether of poet or any other artist, of master politician, or of scientist, are founded in the difficulty of what it is to be.

The eleventh section of the "Esthétique du Mal" is remarkable in what it tells us of Stevens as the poet of existence. The terse assertion "Life is a bitter aspic" opens the passage. This poetic choice of *aspic* for the stinging serpent need not be pondered. The bitter sting is felt in every line. The people are called "dishonest." A meticulous reading is demanded. This is a "dishonesty" of failing to grasp reality, in this case the surging violence of war. "At dawn, / The paratroopers fall and as they fall / They mow the lawn." The supposition that the second pronoun bears the same antecedence as the first would be absurd. In a distant battlefield the paratroopers fall, and as they fall . . . The shift comes with a searing effect: *"They* mow the lawn," they, American householders in mid-summer. What are the limits of a present awareness for them? Shall we say that dawn over the battlefield breaks with a reality so huge that it cannot be comprehended? We are all "natives of poverty, children of malheur." Language is our only lord. For by this alone can the abysses of existence in cataclysm be described; and in its "gaiety" is the only health we have. The sting increases after this interpolation. "A man of bitter appetite despises / A well-made scene in which paratroopers / Select adieux . . . / A ship

that rolls on a confected ocean. . . ." "The tongue caresses these exacer-
bations." *But* "They press it as epicure, distinguishing / Themselves
from its essential savor, / Like hunger that feeds on its own hungriness" (*CP*, 322–23). *It* is this chaos of war. *They* are the same who
mow the lawn, who entertain the "well-made scene" of paratroopers
falling, the "put-together" setting of an imperiled ship. Their hunger
feeds on hungriness, a longing for life which they scarcely identify.
The man of bitter appetite will taste the full, whatever the venom of
the serpent. The man of lesser mind will perform the clanking mechanics of the day and the season; whatever he sees of war, in the mind's
eye, will be framed in the limits of his own habitude. To exist is to
taste the full, to admit the fullness of terror. It is to stand in *the now,*
in the difficulty of being, to know.

One may pose against the bitter sting of these lines the gentle
reflection of a late poem from *The Auroras of Autumn*. The poet
observes in his title, "Questions Are Remarks" (*CP*, 462–63). The
questions that the individual asks of existence are actually his statements of what he comprehends of existence. The scene is an amusing
one. A mother is asked by her two-year-old son, "What is that?" In her
"rhetoric" she tells him an old story. Peter's question is for him "the
extreme." It is "complete because it contains / His utmost statement."
He has seen the sun. In asking his mother what it is, he says *the all*
that he has perceived. It is certain that his mother's response with the
myth of the sun-chariot describes a red horse "he will never ride." As
he grows, he will follow his own sun-myth. His imaginings under the
sun will be his own.[1] The poem closes in a masterly compression. The
little boy "does not say, 'Mother, my mother, who are you,' / The way
the drowsy, infant, old men do." The final mystery of existence is the
individual himself, bearing his own vision of life, his own personality.
These cannot be defined. Peter will grow, we hope, as Peter, like no
other. His questions as remarks will grow with him. But his end, like
that of every other man, will be poignant as it meets the final question
of "drowsy, infant, old men." A passage in "An Ordinary Evening in
New Haven" extends the scene. The stages of the individual life are
thought of as the succeeding letters of the alphabet. We begin with
reality, "Naked Alpha, not the hierophant [the priestly] Omega." "It
is the Infant A standing on infant legs, / Not twisted, stooping, poly-

[1] The probability of the "red horse" of the poem as a figure representing the myth
of the sun-chariot is a matter of conjecture. For a reading of the poem at vari-
ance with the one that I offer here, see Marie Borroff, "Wallace Stevens: The
World and the Poet," in *Wallace Stevens*, ed. Marie Borroff, *Twentieth Century
Views* Series (Englewood Cliffs, N.J., 1963), pp. 6–7.

mathic [all-learned] Z, / He that kneels always on the edge of space /
In the pallid perceptions of its distances" (*CP*, 469). To begin with Z
would be to begin at the ends of other lives. Each life, if it is to know
existence to the full, must move from *A* to *Z*. The eye opens; the child
perceives and states "his utmost." As he goes he learns to appropriate
reality, both the beautiful and the bitter. He will transform his perceived world through his imagination as he can. He will end at *Z*,
unable, as he kneels on the edge of space, to know the answer to the
final question: *Who* are you? In that we begin by stating what we
see, separated from our elders because their seeing has been transmuted to idea, in that we end by knowing fully no one save the self
in its own span, each one of us lives alone. It is understood here that
we speak of the man of questions and remarks, not of the man who
mows his lawn and reads the news of paratroopers and sinking ships
through the stereotypes of mass vision.

Thus existence as a subject in the poetry of Stevens comprehends
his thought of the difficulty of being in *the now*, as oneself and no
other. I exclude here any possible use of the terms *existential* and
existentialism as designations of a categorical mode. I wish to avoid
false claims of alliance in justice to this mind. Stevens' dismissal of the
professionalism of philosophy for himself has been sufficiently discussed in the opening section of this study. Once again, a close
adherence to poetic evidence is necessary. Whatever he wrote of existence was of his own thought. One grants, of course, that French existentialism was strenuous in the intellectual fabric of his time. He could
scarcely have been indifferent to it. But if we wish to speak of his
affinities with any school, it is better, even so, to regard modern philosophical proposals as comprehended in *the philosophy of existence*.
I follow here the reasonable insistence of Jean Wahl, French philosopher and teacher, with whom Stevens was occasionally associated
during some ten years, from 1942 to 1951. Professor Wahl objects to
the term *existentialism* on the ground that certain important "philosophers of existence" have objected to inclusion among the French. He
has in mind particularly Heidegger and Jaspers in the opening discussion of his *Les Philosophes de l'Existence.*[2] This study (1954) came

[2] (Paris, 1954), p. 7. It is worth noting that Stevens in 1952 requested of his
Paris book-dealer, Miss Paule Vidal, a study of Hölderlin by Heidegger; see
Letters, p. 758. The letter is dated at Hartford, July 29. He also requested of his
young Korean friend Peter H. Lee a description of Heidegger as a lecturer at
Fribourg. At the time [1954] Lee was traveling and studying in Europe; see
Letters, pp. 839, 846.

too late to have had very much importance in Stevens' last months of reading in French sources. Nonetheless, its arguments are appropriate for Stevens, particularly its contention for philosophies posed upon immediate human circumstance rather than upon abstract essentiality. "Philosophies of existence," he writes, "must not be regarded as a succession of philosophical dogmas; man is the being who places in question his own existence, who stakes it play by play, who subjects it [willfully] to danger. Existence is the stake in the question itself. Man is the being who is philosopher for the sake of his own being."[3]

Professor Wahl,[4] who came to the United States as a refugee from Paris early in the Second World War, taught for a time at Mt. Holyoke College. It was for a conference under his direction at South Hadley that Stevens prepared his lecture-essay "The Figure of the Youth as Virile Poet" (1943). In 1951 Stevens wrote to Wahl in Paris as he prepared an essay under the title "A Collect of Philosophy." Apparently certain questions were directed to his friend for comment. The essay itself, unpublished until the appearance of *Opus Posthumous*, is one of Stevens' less successful prose pieces. Yet occasional references to his French correspondent are interesting, particularly the first: ". . . When I wrote to Jean Wahl, who is both a poet and a philosopher, about ideas that are inherently poetic, he said immediately that no ideas are inherently poetic, that the poetic nature of any idea depends on the mind through which it passes" (*OP*, 183). We conclude that Wahl's particular authority on the philosophies of existence was much respected by Stevens. A brief review of other responses by Wahl follows: citations of historic "exchanges" between poetry and philosophy, as Hölderlin's influence on Hegel, Hegel's influence on Mallarmé, Shelley's indebtedness to Plato. Yet Stevens clearly disclaims "philosophical influences" for himself as he writes of his interest in the poetry of philosophers rather than the philosophy of poets. He concludes: "I am not a philosopher" (*OP*, 195).

---

[3] *Les Philosophes de l'Existence*, p. 136; translation mine.
[4] Jean Wahl appears initially to have been known to Stevens' friend Henry Church; and probably it was through Church that Wahl first became interested in the poetry of Stevens. Among certain miscellaneous papers of Stevens' in the microfilm collection of the Baker Library, Dartmouth College, is a duplicated sequence of poems in typescript by Wahl, the first collection of which, under the title "Connaître sans connaître," is inscribed to Stevens. The date is 1938. A second group, dated at Paris in 1940, follows. The third and final group is dated 1941 at the Prison de la Santé, Camp Drancy. The date of the first sequence and the inscription suggest that Wahl had been an enthusiastic admirer of Stevens' poetry for some years in advance of his arrival in the United States. Stevens' knowledge of Wahl may be traced through the *Letters*, pp. 429–30, 438, 446–47, 452, 721, 725, 729.

Stevens has been developing the argument of the "Collect" on a principle fixed early in the discussion. "Nor are we interested in philosophic poetry, as, for example, the poetry of Lucretius, some of the poetry of Milton and some of the poetry of Pope, and those pages of Wordsworth, which have done so much to strengthen the critics of poetry in their attacks on the poetry of thought. Theoretically, the poetry of thought should be the supreme poetry" (*OP*, 187). In the introduction and the first chapter of this study we have defended an initial premise, that Stevens was interested in the lyric aptitude of philosophy rather than in its doctrinaire elements. Philosophy that reveals a metaphoric design is an art adjacent to poetry. This is to say that a philosophy that is a poetry of thought is to be regarded as a poetic structure. But Stevens nowhere assumes that pure poetry is a restatement of philosophy. Each has its own domain. We maintain the principle set down earlier: In the life of the human mind philosophy and poetry may stand in adjacency; they are not interchangeable. Thus, in "A Collect of Philosophy," Stevens somewhat elliptically seeks to outline an approach to the poetic element in philosophy. Despite his acknowledgment of Professor Wahl, we contend that his relationship to philosophies of existence was none other than a poet's interest in a mode of inquiry belonging to another province of expression. The philosopher of existence studies the immediacy of being; Stevens the poet studies the same phenomenon in a mode that is entirely his own, singular perception, which constantly revitalizes the process of mind and requires a description in the language of the poetry itself. To restate the subject of Stevens, existence is that primacy of being which is *knowing* in the greatest difficulty, the point of mastery between the strongest pressure of reality and the will to be as oneself. Perhaps the summary statement of recent philosophy most apt for Stevens as a poet is that of Ramon Fernandez. "Allowing that the visions of art are by definition imaginative, we can say that *aesthetics must be an imaginative ontology, that is to say that the fundamental problem of aesthetics is no other than the metaphysical problem of being, but transposed to the plane of imagination.*"[5]

Stevens does not borrow from the philosophers. Yet his early reflection on the essential whiteness of the universe of being provides a strong American analogy for the familiar *l'être et le néant* of the

5 *Messages*, p. 7.

existentialistes. "The Snow Man" (*CP*, 9–10) stands in the early poetry as the prefiguration of the sharp white at the center, or, as Stevens puts it in "An Ordinary Evening in New Haven," "the dominant blank" at the end of existence (*CP*, 477). "For the listener, who listens in the snow, / And, nothing himself, beholds / Nothing that is not there and the nothing that is" (*CP*, 9). Stevens begins in the difficult comprehension of the ultimate reality, the central white. This difficulty is assessed again in the image of the "ancient star," the sun, in "Nuances of a Theme by Williams" (*CP*, 18). The italicized initial couplets state the theme, the distance between man and the source of light. The second "nuance" opens: "Lend no part to any humanity that suffuses / you in its own light." This ironic address to the sun turns in the manner of Stevens: the sun, in its own gorgeous indifferency, is made what it is to men by the "suffusing" imagination. It is a supreme reality brought to personal vision. And yet it shines "like fire, that mirrors nothing." The "nothing that is" in "The Snow Man" is the nothing of humanity before the enormity of a universe of being. Space is at the edge of human life, "the dominant blank" of the late poetry. Thus it is that Stevens as a fully committed poet begins in *Harmonium* with a long regard of the final human reality, this nothing, and returns to its certainty "on the edge of space." The vision of the end was the vision of the beginning. The realities studied between the two appear in the major themes derived from the physical world and from society. These themes establish the structure of an individual life between the point of rising up from the rock and the point of return.

The first of Stevens' poems describing the pressure of reality against singular perception is "Metaphors of a Magnifico" (*CP*, 19). The poet stands in the *persona* of the title. "Twenty men crossing a bridge, / Into a village, / Are twenty men crossing twenty bridges / Into twenty villages, / Or one man / Crossing a single bridge into a village." The "old song that will not declare itself" is the first of the two statements. It is "certain as meaning." Each man achieves meaning exactly as he perceives. Twenty men as one man on one bridge entering one village are engaged in motion without meaning. The bridge resounds with the steps of twenty men marching as one. Suddenly "the first white wall of the village / Rises through fruit-trees." The individual perceiver, momentarily engaged in a fresh encounter with these objects, senses the heavy thud on the bridge. The meaning escapes. Of what was he thinking? The poem explores the significance of the two initial statements. It was always thus in the "old song," many men with many meanings, or many men as one, with no meanings. This is the difficulty of being: the point between recognition of the many as one, the threat of the thud on the bridge, and recognition by the exquisite eye, sight exerting its own individuality. This is existence, *the now* of the poet who seeks to master the old song. In succeeding poems he will return to the supreme reality of the nothing that finally *is*. But the footfalls on the bridge signify the pressure of a man-made reality in his time; the brief composition of wall and fruit trees predicts the constant evolution of meaning through singular perception.

As a poet of existence Stevens prefers a strict simplicity of declaration. The difficulty of being appears at times in aphoristic statement. This is the choice of a poet "writing and reading the rigid inscription" (*CP*, 495), the poet at the pivot of endurance. Such is the explicitness of "Anatomy of Monotony" in its commanding position near the close of *Harmonium*. We came of earth; we "parallel the mother's death"; above the bare sky of autumn, she sees "a barer sky that does not bend." We walk forth naked in the sun as we come to this life. "Yet the spaciousness and light / In which the body walks and is deceived, / Falls from that fatal and that barer sky, / And this the spirit sees and is aggrieved" (*CP*, 107–8). It is fatal deception that spaciousness and light should conceal the infinite "sky" of spatial distances. The passion for structure intensifies as the poet moves through the sequence of *Ideas of Order*. Yet the resolve upon acceptance is equally passionate: ". . . to sip / One's cup, and never to say a word . . ." (*CP*, 128). To taste the cup, to accept, is to dare the contemplation of the sky above the sky. It is to will a knowledge of the darkness. No one need pre-empt a special distinction for the desert places of Robert Frost; they are matched by those of Stevens. "All night I sat reading a book, / Sat reading as if in a book / Of sombre pages." They "bore no print / Except the trace of burning stars / In the frosty heaven" (*CP*, 146–47). This is the book of humanity, and the solitary reader is the confessor of a coldness without words. Ideas of order must be, the ideas of his book in defiance of the cold, when the garden is bare of the summer muscadines, the melons and the pears. This way of Stevens in prospect of the final reality has opened in the first pages of *Harmonium*; and the burning stars are those of the high night in "The Auroras of Autumn," stars "putting on their glittering belts" and "cloaks that flash / Like a great shadow's last embellishment" (*CP*, 419).

This is the somberness that becomes majesty in the late Stevens, "one's shadow magnified," as he speaks in "The Man with the Blue Guitar," the self beneath the greater shadow of Chocorua, "One's self and the mountains of one's land . . . / The flesh, the bone, the dirt, the stone" (*CP*, 176). It marks the upsurge of the arc and predicts its final anchorage. To exist fully in any time of man is to know in every act of the flesh the enduring stone of one's human place. But the sternest man-made reality of the rock changes. In the time of Stevens this sternness was the chaos of war. It is upon a contemporary chaos, rather than upon the mechanisms of a society without imagination, that his poetry of existence turns in the middle sequences. *Parts of a World* and *Transport to Summer* reveal a constant scrutiny of the "haggardie" (*CP*, 321) of suffering. The war poetry of Stevens has scarcely been assessed in the years succeeding its appearance. One expects a dominant attention to the phenomena of catastrophe through the poet's view of imagination and human destiny. War is a phase of existence, just as society is a phase. The phase is the theme of Stevens, rather than emotion, real or imagined, in the experience of the individual. Thus the subject is none other than the condition of the human mind in a time of war. The field of existence must be described in the question: How is the mind of an age to meet the enormity of cataclysm induced by men? It will be remembered that the longest of all Stevens' war poems, the "Esthétique du Mal," opens with the groan of Vesuvius. Briefly we contemplate the old fact of physical upheaval. Of this there is no human control. Yet almost immediately the volcano becomes a symbol of human continuity, a mountain commanding terror, "because the sound / Was ancient" (*CP*, 314). Nothing that *is* has the capacity to feel destruction, the pain of violent ends, save the human mind. The eternal paradox rises in the poet's verdict, that in the human power to experience pain we know a part of the human sublime, and yet it is a sublime from which we shrink. The pain he surveys is of human origin. It is genetic in all destructive uses of the mind. Herein lies the import of his title, the *aesthetic* of evil, in his literal sense the *perception* of evil, straight from the Greek root *aisthanomai*. How is the mind to *perceive* pain? We are not in the presence of a poet toying with aesthetics as a "philosophy of art." "The genius of misfortune / Is not a sentimentalist." This is our world, "Spent in the false engagements of the mind" (*CP*, 316–17).

Thus, in *Parts of a World*, Stevens begins with the modern mind as "the great poem of winter." In "the land of war," the mind "has to persuade that war is part of itself, / A manner of thinking, a mode / Of destroying, as the mind destroys. . . ." This world of the modern is "averted / From an old delusion, an old affair with the sun. . . ." Yet in this winter snow the poem of the mind "lashes more fiercely than the

wind. . . ." The mind is its own fury. It destroys "Romantic tenements
of rose and ice" (*CP*, 238–39). This is to say that the buildings of
another time are wrecked. The mind must discover "what will suffice."
For a poet, this imperative is answered in his acceptance of *the now*.
"Of Modern Poetry" follows immediately as a *credo*. The mind "has to
think about war / And it has to find what will suffice. It has / To
construct a new stage." The modern actor, the poet, "is / A metaphysician in the dark . . ." (*CP*, 240). The inexorable pressure of the
present difficulty and the irrelevance of the past need not be demonstrated. For in these poems Stevens formulates his primary question:
What will suffice in the act of *knowing* the tragedy of human truth,
that no age learns from the evil of the past? Mind has within it an endless incipience of chaos. It makes a winter of the earth again and again
in the records of humanity, averting successive generations from the
"old delusions," in the sense of Stevens, salvations from chaos through
the singular imagination. The depths of the adjacent "Landscape with
Boat" open perilously. What is the truth of this desolation? Is there
some causality "at the neutral centre . . . / The single-colored, colorless primitive"? For it was in this "primitive," this "ominous element,"
that human time began. The center is arcane. The poet says only that
it may be supposed. On the instant Stevens seems to approach the
major inquiry of all theologies. But the darker deep suddenly closes as
he turns to himself. Because he is a man, it is "his nature to suppose /
To receive what others had supposed, without / Accepting." "He
never supposed / That he might be truth . . ." (*CP*, 242). The mind
questions. Being the finite mind of man, it supposes a power in the
"ominous element," and yet, being of man, it will not accept the
supposition as truth. Man is the cause; he is his own truth. Or,
as the poet concludes, if he is a part of a central truth, then
"divine things" do not "look divine." This sequence in the scrutiny of *Parts of a World* establishes the major mode. From this point
on, the terror of existence in chaos is to be regarded as the truth of
the mind of man. The problem of the inscrutable center, of "divine
things that do not look divine," is dismissed. Man is his truth; and the
way is prepared for the stark assertion of the "Esthétique du Mal":
"The death of Satan was a tragedy / For the imagination" (*CP*, 319).
Satan came of the human mind in its desperate struggle to make a
truth beyond itself, truth of all supposed mysteries beyond the power
of human ascription, the contradivine imperious with the divine. Thus
all causality is imagined; and, when belief in the agent of evil is at an
end, men are left with the truth of the satanic within themselves.

There can be no ascription save to the destructive force of man-made ideas. The authors of the tragedy are few. Chaos, in "Extracts from Addresses to the Academy of Fine Ideas," is a human law, "Of improvisations and seasons of belief." "Chaos is not / The mass of meaning. It is three or four / Ideas or . . . six. / In the end, these philosophic assassins pull / Revolvers and shoot each other . . ." (*CP*, 255–56). The assassins make their seasons of belief. And not one, we know, is magisterial in this making of chaos without his dogma of freedom addressed to his armies. It is this clash of freedoms among the demagogues of imagination, the progenitors of chaos, that dominates the range of "Dutch Graves in Bucks County." This poem is a rock eminence in the landscape of *Transport to Summer*. Its incisiveness is its own; it is like no other scrutiny of reality in the achievement of Stevens; and it is probably unexcelled in English as a war inscription upon the rock of all human flourishings. The subject, meditation over the graves of early settlers in a placid corner of Pennsylvania, is deceptively simple. These lines are forged from the center of the Second World War. "What is this crackling of voices in the mind, / This pitter-patter of archaic freedom, / Of the thousands of freedoms except our own?" "Freedom is like a man who kills himself / Each night, an incessant butcher, whose knife / Grows sharp in blood. The armies kill themselves, / And in their blood an ancient evil dies— / The action of incorrigible tragedy." The dead lie in Pennsylvania earth. Their chaos was their own; they taught us nothing. In this present, evil is assuaged anew. Freedom in the dogmas of the world's demagogues is the incessant butcher. The knife is whetted in each new chaos. What is it in us which makes in a *now* that was and in another *now* this violence without certain end? "This is the pit of torment that placid end / Should be illusion, that the mobs of birth / Avoid our stale perfections, seeking out / Their own, waiting until we go / To picnic in the ruins that we leave." The stars shine only "on the very living of those alive." Another generation in this *now* is marching to its center, "in arcs / Of a chaos composed in more than order . . ." (*CP*, 292–93).

The companion eminence in *Transport to Summer* has been variously regarded here. The "Esthétique du Mal" is Stevens' last statement in this lyricism from chaos. Crickets "chant" in the dry desert of the West. But the need for another incantation to drown the crickets' sound is the need of song in the old pit of torment, ". . . music / That buffets the shapes of its possible halcyon / Against the haggardie . . ." (*CP*, 321). The tragedy of the rock, the "incorrigible tragedy," has been known. Ananke, Fatal Necessity, whose genesis is in the unknown neutral center, returns to the theme: ". . . the unalterable necessity / Of being this unalterable animal." By this acceptance of the creature Stevens returns to the necessity of nature in us. We mirror nature; for in us "The force of nature in action is the major / Tragedy." (*CP*, 324). Humanity refers in truth to itself alone. Whatever there be of the beauty of order in the universe, of the constancy of stars, of sun and moon, it is "the human that is the alien . . . the human that demands his speech / From beasts . . ." (*CP*, 328). Stevens speaks here in a poem very closely following the "Esthétique." If we are alien, there is nonetheless the saving power of sight which is ours. It is to this that he returns as his reflection on evil reaches its close. The green corn is gleaming; there are "rotund emotions" in the August heat. "The adventurer / In humanity has not conceived of a race / Completely physical in a physical world" (*CP*, 325). Life without this physical redemption is what it is in the torment of existence, "propositions about life." "The human / Revery is a solitude in which / We compose these propositions, torn by dreams, / By the terrible incantations of defeats / And by the fear that defeats and dreams are one" (*CP*, 355–56). In "Men Made Out of Words" these incantations are accepted as laws of human endurance. They are the laws *ex tenebris* of a place of man whose life is governed by the ideas of the few assassins, the makers of his chaos.

"Day is the children's friend." Children make images "of themselves, / Not of perpetual time" (*CP*, 368–69). In "The Prejudice Against the Past" and "Credences of Summer," as Stevens moves to "Notes Toward a Supreme Fiction," the theme of existence reaches the prospect of the final solitude. We return to the sufficiency of objects, of existence experienced with the singularity of sight and in the last examination of the self. Nearly everything that Stevens wrote from this point on is quietly intent upon review. The rage for order in the difficulty of being oneself diminishes. The mind turns in longing toward the fresh perception of early youth. Children who make of themselves images, unknowing of perpetual time, recall the first world evoked in "Questions Are Remarks." We begin in an innocence of perception. We end in innocence, ". . . a child that sings itself to sleep, / The mind, among the creatures that it makes, / The people, those by which it lives and dies" ("The Owl in the Sarcophagus," *CP*, 436). Between the first innocence and the last is the torment of the chaos. As Stevens reflects in "Notes Toward a Supreme Fiction,"

"There is a month, a year, there is a time / In which majesty is a mirror of the self: / I have not but I am and as I am, I am" (*CP*, 405).

The majesty of this art was a mirror of the self. The distinction of "An Ordinary Evening in New Haven" is its admission of both a final poverty and a final innocence. Whatever was for Stevens majestic here is immeasurable for us with respect to what he wished to summarize of the long difficulty. We share incompletely a man's existence in retrospect; and a commonplace evening in a city in Connecticut has very little to do with the tranquil review itself. This is a non-occasional poem written, with wry humor, for a great occasion of the Connecticut Academy convening with the pomp of the academic. And yet the only certain majesty for those who read the Grand Poem of Stevens is recognized in this unflawed music, scene giving place to scene, as though the seasons of an artist's life passed in silent array. This majesty, the final satisfaction, is the sense of the completed structure, even in the sense of fear, as the autumn evening closes into darkness. "The point of vision and desire are the same. / It is to the hero of midnight that we pray / On a hill of stones to make beau mont thereof" (*CP*, 466). In the vision of a young poet was his desire for the end. This, too, is human, this desire, and the prayer to the unknown at midnight. A poet, kneeling on the edge of space (*CP*, 469), distinguishes between the unknown and the known. Human life is all that we know; the end of desire is the "neutral center." "Life fixed him, wandering on the stair of glass, / With its attentive eyes" (*CP*, 483). "*C'est toujours la vie qui me regarde....*"

The Hero: Aspects of the Supreme Fiction

17

THE HERO IS THE YOUTH CAPABLE OF THE SUPREME fiction; he becomes the maker of it—his alone—in his time. The near-heroes are men who dare to comprehend reality and to live imaginatively in a knowledge of the rock, but they are nonetheless men whose achievement of a fictive supremacy is less than complete. The title "Notes Toward a Supreme Fiction" is absolutely precise for the poet's intention. Stevens does not inscribe these "notes" as though they were total records of *his* supreme fiction. Despite the reflective mode of this long summary, its frequent pauses upon the youthful imagination that was, the poem is not alone confession. The toward-ness of the title and the didactic opening, "Begin, ephebe, by perceiving the idea / Of this invention, this invented world . . ." (*CP*, 380)—these makes all the difference. Age speaks to youth, urging the beginning of "invention" in the beginning of a life. The notes point toward the possibility of a supreme fiction, in the condition that the beginning is made when the youth inherits the estate of early manhood. The urgency of the title and the directive should be compared with Stevens' personal disclosure as he writes in *Harmonium*: "If men at forty will be painting lakes / The ephemeral blues must merge for them in one . . ." (*CP*, 15). This is lament in the late beginning, when "a red bird flies across the golden floor" (*CP*, 13), the creature of passion and song seeking out his choir, the choir that speaks a farewell for the poet who reaches the end of spring. The best of all human life is fiction; but there will be no supreme fiction without a beginning in beginnings. In his reflection upon his own fiction, not that of the possible supreme for another life, Stevens is perfectly clear. Very modestly he observes that a late beginning promises only a partial mastery of the essential rock. "Begin, ephebe," by perceiving the idea of the sun, see the sun "with an ignorant eye," admit the death of the gods, assume the difficulty, avoid "the celestial ennui of apartments" (the structures of other men) (*CP*, 380–81), . . . but begin. The passage of time to come will be swift. Life is a fluttering thing, as we read in the earlier poetry of Stevens. The hero is the youth who dares.

There is a threshold for every youth. In anticipation of the "Notes," Stevens thinks of a portal in "The Pediment of Appearance" (*CP*, 361–62). "Young men go walking in the woods, / Hunting for the great ornament, / The pediment of appearance." The face of an architecture is there, in this high stone marking the place of footstep, entrance. In "full-blown May," with its promise of "the months of understanding," these young men are "full of their ugly lord." The pediment is "appearance," and the ugly lord is a dictator of conformity to him. Potential heroes, these youths search for "the great ornament." They choose appearance; they will not be lords of themselves. The pediment under which they pass is an ornament without a building. We have been examining the conditions of human life beyond it. Reading in the ellipsis of the poet, we know the existence that these youths search for and accept. There is a time for stepping to the work of the builder of the total building or to the anonymity of a life of appearances. It is as though "the necessary angel" stood at the threshold, just as we see him in a later poem. In "Angel Surrounded by Paysans" one of the "countrymen" speaks to his companions: "There is / A welcome at the door to which no one comes?" The angel of the sovereign imagination of the supreme self, the angel who offers to redeem life for all men, replies: ". . . I am the necessary angel of earth, / Since, in my sight, you see the earth again, / Cleared of its stiff and stubborn, man-locked set, / And, in my hearing, you hear its tragic drone / Rise liquidly in liquid lingerings, / Like watery words awash. . . ." But one must choose the welcome quickly. The angel concludes in warning: ". . . A turn / Of my shoulder and quickly, too quickly, I am gone" (*CP*, 496–97). There is a time. One chooses "the great ornament," the pediment of appearance; or one chooses to see the earth again, cleared of the stubborn, man-locked set. We add that he will be a man half-living like millions of his kind; or he will be the heroic maker of his own design.

In his study of Stevens Robert Pack writes of the solitary master as unrealized. "Stevens' hero is not a man among us, but a man beyond us. He does not exist in our world except as abstraction."[1] The hero, when he becomes man, will be the author of the central poem, and he will be its subject.[2] To regard the hero as abstraction is to see him as an enduring possibility. We agree. But Mr. Pack's reading is restrictive and confining. Stevens associates the endless possibility of the hero with the endless presence of major man in all men. The possibility of the hero knows its phases just as society knows its continuing mutations. Mr. Pack believes that the hero of Stevens "is not a human individual"; he is "the essence of human qualities."[3] We must answer no. An "essence of human qualities" does not make a hero; and a hero is always the human individual. In a rejected stanza for "Examination of the Hero in a Time of War" Stevens wrote: "The hero is the man who is himself, who / As a man among other men, divested / Of attributes, naked of myth, true, / Not true to this or that, but true, knows / The frame of the hero. Yet, willingly, he / Becomes the hero without heroics" (OP, 84). The date of these lines is 1941. This text in mid-career is a full statement of concept. The hero is, now. He is any man, not necessarily the poet, who exists among his fellows in a mythless age, true to himself, and most certainly without heroics in that far-gone, once-traditional understanding of a race conceiving of heroic deeds.[4] The modern hero is the man who dares to be himself,

[1] *Wallace Stevens: An Approach to His Poetry and Thought*, p. 147.
[2] *Ibid.*, p. 148.
[3] *Ibid.*, p. 162.
[4] Cf. Riddel, *The Clairvoyant Eye*, in a discussion of Stevens' sequential concerns with the hero, pp. 149–85. Mr. Riddel begins with the following contention: ". . . His [Stevens'] poet has become the intermediary between man and reality (there being no god), and in his words the poet-hero rescues himself from absorption in things of this indifferent world. The poet as warrior, the poet as hero—there is in Stevens' figure just enough hyperbole to indicate man's possibilities of self-transcendence, and yet maintain his root being in the physical world. Clearly enough, Stevens' hero owes his image to Nietzsche (the philosopher of moment for Stevens in the later thirties)" (p. 152). The publication of the *Letters* followed Mr. Riddel's study by a year. Stevens himself seems to deny the possibility of this claim. Writing to Henry Church from Hartford on June 12, 1942, he obviously addressed himself to a question from his friend. "About Nietzsche. I haven't read him since I was a young man. My interest in the hero, major man, the giant, has nothing to do with the Biermensch" (*Letters*, p. 409). In another letter from Hartford in the same year (dated December 8), he wrote to Church: "Nietzsche is as perfect a means of getting out of focus as a little bit too much to drink" (*Letters*, p. 432).

to build his own life-structure, to shun the great ornament, to take the welcome of the necessary angel. He will stand, to recall the strict image of "The Man with the Blue Guitar," the maker of his own structure of vaults upon his brief point of light (*CP*, 167).

Society, we conclude, may make its own heroes, by its own election. But whether they evolve from the chaos of war or from, the longing for the new statue, a longing for heroics, let us say, expended upon animated cartoons, athletic or movie stardom, or the daring of space-travel, they are fashioned by the mass. Stevens, confronting existence, would drink of his cup and never say a word. The modern hero of Stevens does not know a setting of heroics. He might be an unknown man of singular power who created a world of his own artistry and yet was never recognized in his time. And even as a lesser man, he might have been the unrecognized hero of quiet strength, perceiving the world through his own freshness of vision. The "frame of the hero" is always with us and in us. The hero does not require a tradition of heroics to be as himself, in defiance of the pediment of appearance.

One of the first of Stevens' reflections upon the potential of childhood and early youth, and upon the welcome of the angel at the door, appears in a poem of 1919. It bears the significant title "Piano Practice at the Academy of the Holy Angels" (*OP*, 21). "The time will come for these children, seated before their long / black instruments, to strike the themes of love— / All of them, darkened by time, moved by they know not what, / amending the airs they play to fulfill themselves. . . ." The striking anticipation of the keyboard image that will describe the mastery of Peter Quince is not the first mark of this passage. The instruments in this academy of the angels are black, in the certainty of the domination of black. The young performers will strike themes of love in the darkness of human time, *amending the airs they play to fulfill themselves*. Far along the arc of the hero it is this great necessity of angelic *amending* which recurs in the picture of the ephebe addressed in "Notes Toward a Supreme Fiction," the youth who is warned of the danger of a world of appearances. "But you, ephebe, look from your attic window, / Your mansard with a rented piano." The rooftops of other men stretch away in prospect from his window. He clutches the corner of his pillow (the inevitable sign in Stevens of the place of final communion with the self at the moment of death) (*CP*, 384). What will he play of his own *amending*, the airs *to fulfill himself*? Or will he be tyrannized by the adjacency of other men under other roofs? Here again is the tenacity of both theme and image in the mounting design of Stevens. The hero is the man who fulfills himself. His themes of love are those necessary for him in his answer to the angel.

"Where shall I find / Bravura adequate to this great hymn?" For, "I am a yeoman, as such fellows go." These questions are of the early poem, "Le Monocle de Mon Oncle," of *Harmonium*. The great air, the hymn, has been conceived. Where and how shall he find a bravura of speech to express it? And how shall he dare, a yeoman among the master poet-technicians of his time? The pediment of appearance has been fully rejected. But, as we have noted with him in this same poem, he begins late. The scene of the youth with the rented piano, intimidated at his window as he looks out upon the roofs of other men, seems to dominate this hesitant moment of Stevens'. The strength of a wholly independent resolve succeeds before the poem closes. It intensifies later in the sequence of *Harmonium* in "A High-Toned Old Christian Woman" (*CP*, 59). The first determination upon the total and unique structure appears. "Poetry is the supreme fiction, madame. / Take the moral law and make a nave of it / And from the nave build haunted heaven. . . . But take / The opposing law and make a peristyle, / And from the peristyle project a masque / Beyond the planets." The "nave" of the moral tradition is rejected, along with the old pediment of appearance. The peristyle, his own enclosure, is to be his "masque beyond the planets." This is heroic vision. Yet Stevens shunned to the end of his life a fully heroic image of himself. *To fulfill the self* was always heroic aspiration. Stevens' own measurement of his success is nowhere set down. He was willing only to say in "The Planet on the Table," "Ariel was glad he had written his poems" (*CP*, 532). To study the structure that he left, prefigured in the early dream of the peristyle and fully realized in the dome, is to contemplate the speech and form of the "great hymn" and the emergence of the later master from the yeoman-beginner. Stevens was a man of his time, content to affirm the possibility of the hero without heroics.

No doubt certain critical views of the hero as pure abstraction have taken form in a misreading of important lines in "The Man with the Blue Guitar."

> *I sing a hero's head, large eye*
> *And bearded bronze, but not a man . . .*
>
> *Ah, but to play man number one,*
> *To drive the dagger in his heart,*

> *To lay his brain upon the board*
> *And pick the acrid colors out.*
>
> *To nail his thought across the door,*
> *Its wings spread wide to rain and snow . . .*
>
> [*CP*, 165–66]

One begins, in these initial lines of a major statement on society, in the strength of the poet's will. He determines his airs as *he* must. He "cannot bring a world quite round." He "patches" it together as he can. The song of the hero's head of large eye and bearded bronze is an invocation to major man of the imagination. In this age the old genius cannot be wholly realized, complete as hero in a new form. He is corrupt, truncated, But then, so be it. The poet will nonetheless play him, this major man "number one," pierce him to his heart, open his brain, pick out the acrid, ugly colors, without question the colors of Oxidia. He will nail his thought across the door, its wings open to rain and snow. The sun, we note, is absent. The heroic singer, banging out his music from "a savage blue," is not an abstraction. Neither is the old man, major man of humanity. But major man is only the immortal potentiality. He will be perfect in form, or ugly, as each inheriting age gives him substance. He will be known by this poet aspiring to the only possible heroism of his time, no matter what his ugliness. The hero-poet exerts his own courage in the face of existence. He is not an abstraction. He is a man of the century. As Stevens notes later in *Parts of a World*, "This chaos will not be ended, / The red and the blue house blended . . ."; he, the poet, "the poorest of all," cannot be "mended," as though in another time he might have known major man whole and complete within himself ("Idiom of the Hero," *CP*, 200–1). Abstraction has no place among these savage principles. The mind of Stevens discloses here a pure and superior logic, operating upon the facts of existence thrust upon it by an ugly reality: major man is realized in this age in monstrous form; in the dominion of his presence the hero-singer will nonetheless answer with an unrelenting scrutiny of the real. He knows nothing of heroics for the hero. He has nothing of stature save his own honesty.

Stevens begins his address to the youth, as in the role of teacher to novice, in *Parts of a World*. One hesitates to adorn this role with a traditional heroism, such, for instance, as the mythic grandeur of instruction celebrated in Chiron or Socrates. Stevens did not lay claim to a mythic wisdom; nor did he think of any certainty of a wisdom to be passed on through his poetry. Yet he thinks intently of the example of a life, even as he thought of the full structure of Santayana, "an inquisitor of structures" (*CP*, 510). The passage of Stevens to the office of poet-teacher is scarcely announced. We sense its occurrence as the theme of the hero advances; but the lesson is always understated in strict avoidance of an insistent morality. As Stevens begins, he addresses a boy: "Some things, niño, some things are like this, / That instantly and in themselves they are gay . . ." ("Of Bright & Blue Birds & the Gala Sun," *CP*, 248). It is a commonplace of human perception, that we are sometimes moved to joy by sunlight on objects and by the blue workings of the imagination. It is a simple good of life. Yet one is not the hero in this. If there is a grim necessity of solitude, the solitude deliberately willed in "Montrachet-le-Jardin," a man becomes heroic in making "the cell / A hero's world in which he is the hero" (*CP*, 261). The boy must grow to manhood, to know what his rock of being will permit, to know whether there be exactions of the heroic from a man in solitude, or possibilities of heroic virtuosity among his fellows.

The lesson of Stevens in his "Examination of the Hero in a Time of War" extends the possibility of heroic action, certainly. But, as it rejects the vulgar insistence upon public heroes made of men who suffer "the voyage beyond the oyster-beds," it celebrates the heroes self-contained, unknown: "There are more heroes than marbles of them" (*CP*, 274, 276). "Familiar man," man thought of in the vulgar sense, as though to make of every soldier a hero, is not "veritable man" (*CP*, 280). The counterform, the falsity of the true heroic, is the stereotype of the hero in the mass mind of society. Who can know what private cells of private heroes existed in a time of war, or what eyes of heroic vision saw the world anew? The hero is a public idea, or he is the man of the rejected stanza for the "Examination of the Hero," "the man who is himself," "true," in the potentiality of major man within him, knowing in this truth "the frame of the hero," and yet "willingly . . . the hero without heroics" (*OP*, 84).

Youth, whether the *niño* of the simplest joy in things touched by sunlight, or the constantly repeated captain of a solitude self-willed, may come to know heroism in his own shaping of the self. Then he is the good man. But the crowd will endlessly oppose him. "The Good Man Has No Shape" (*CP*, 364) looms throughout the late work of Stevens in bitter summary and prophecy. *They* crucified the good man, the man who grew as the solitary hero. They mocked his flesh with the feathers of the imagination. They gave him sour wine and an empty book in the tomb. They denied, and they deny him. Who shall do him honor? He is entombed again and again. Yet his honor is to be his own, the sufficient prize of the good man who became of his own truth "willingly . . . the hero without heroics."

"A young man seated at his table / Holds in his hand a book you have never written / Staring at the secretions of the words as / They reveal themselves" (*CP*, 303). The poem bears the title "The Lack of Repose." There is no final repose for a poet-teacher. He has no knowledge that his truth will serve as the truth of the novice. Each generation succeeds the last. Every new youth will write his own book. What he reads is not what a man before him wrote. The poem is preparatory to the instruction offered in "Notes Toward a Supreme Fiction." "Begin, ephebe, by perceiving the idea / Of this invention, this invented world, / The inconceivable idea of the sun" (*CP*, 380). Book succeeds to book, or individual man of shape to the one of shape who departs, or hero to hero. The sun, light upon human life and upon this earth, is the only constant. It is the center of life, just as the "neutral centre" is the final center of the unknown beyond the sun, and beyond every phenomenon measurable by man. What is the supreme fiction to be, if this ephebe wills to make this his supreme life on the rock? *It Must Be Abstract; It Must Change; It Must Give Pleasure.* The three sections of this directive are, of course, frequently comprehensive of Stevens' reflection on his own making of his structure as a fiction, not *supreme* in his judgment, as I have contended, but certain in its demonstration of the possible. The lesson for this day is not easy, as one follows the intricacies of the metaphor. And yet, read in answer to the three principles, it is to be mastered. *The fiction must be an abstraction* of the *personal*, the singular experience lived amidst the phenomena of existence in the time of a man's life. Hence the advice against the danger: Do not be intimidated by the structures of other men; play the airs *amended* which are alone yours; even as you clutch the corner of the pillow in your knowing of the end (*CP*, 384), act "in the difficulty of what it is to be" (*CP*, 381). *The fiction must change.* It is the nature of both the power of perception and the mind that works upon perception to change. A life in its vision is continually metaphoric. The nature of sentient being is movement. *The fiction must give pleasure.* It must be a celebration of existence, the *gaudium* of being. It must be "the more than rational distortion, / The fiction

286

that results from feeling" (*CP*, 406). "Notes Toward a Supreme Fiction" is an intended lesson, asking nothing of youth in adherence to any tradition and urging nothing save insistence upon newness of perception and absolute freedom of mind. In its epilogue it is also a statement of the final problem of existence as Stevens saw it: "Soldier," he closes, once again addressing the youth, "there is a war between the mind / And sky, between thought and day and night. It is / For that the poet is always in the sun, / Patches the moon together in his room / To his Virgilian cadences, up down, / Up down. It is a war that never ends" (*CP*, 407). Every hero is a soldier, in the thick of the war. His mind holds its certain knowledge of the rock, its recognition of human poverty, its thought of the truth. Standing in the sun, he struggles against the bitterness of the reality. He patches the moon of the imagination together as he can in his "Virgilian" cadences; for the cadences in his chaotic world are to become his own epic, in recollection of an ancient poet and a time when the hero of heroics was not only possible but actual.

Aeneas is of the past. And so is the heroic Ulysses. But Stevens chooses Ulysses, as the first of all great heroes celebrated in heroics, for his last symbolic vision. A potential Ulysses always comes with the dawn. Yet, if he is hero, he will be the modern hero alone, "the center of the self," a man "as an absolute, himself" ("The Sail of Ulysses," *OP*, 101). He will be free of "the rumors of the speech-full domes" of other men (*OP*, 102). He will know his consort, his woman-genius of imagination. She waits for him as the light breaks in the East and "winter is washed away." When he comes, her "barbarous strength" will never fail ("The World As Meditation," *CP*, 520–21). The last encounter with the ephebe, the long instruction past, anticipates the poet's hope in the symbol of Ulysses. In "An Ordinary Evening in New Haven" the youth is seen at a distance. "The ephebe is solitary in his walk / . . . [he] enjoys / A strong mind in a weak neighborhood . . ." (*CP*, 474). He begins. He may become the maker of a supreme fiction. The voice of Stevens in the going down to the rock is a voice of hope, and the affirmation of the possible is strong. There is hope for the child "asleep in its own life" as the ancient of all ancients, major man of endless possibility, broods above the bed. He it is who can wake the "chords" of a new song (*OP*, 106). The song and the supreme fiction, if they are to come of this child, will be the hymn of a hero, "willingly . . . the hero without heroics."

In the Northern Quarter: The Descent to the Rock

18

"BUT NOTE THE UNCONSCIONABLE TREACHERY OF FATE, / That makes us weep, laugh, grunt and groan, and shout / Doleful heroics, pinching gestures forth / From madness or delight, without regard / To that first, foremost law" (*CP*, 17). Stevens advances the modern hero without heroics. Here in "Le Monocle de Mon Oncle" he speaks of a commonplace heroics of paradox, vital expression seemingly indifferent to the "foremost law" and yet "doleful." The paradox is itself the treachery of human fate. We live as if we knew nothing of the law, and yet we affirm it in every act. What ones comes to, as he approaches his end, is *regard*, his necessary regard heroically meeting the gaze of life which fixes a man "wandering on the stair of glass" (*CP*, 483). Every supreme lyric poetry, whatever its time, owes its greatest moments of authority and compulsion to the poet's sense of his own finitude. This we know. Yet the poetry of Stevens is unique among all evidences of this truth. The vision of the seeing eye is constantly intent upon the object scrutinized in brief encounter. At the same time, the vision of the mind, springing from the deepest strength of the imagination, is constantly trained upon the final knowing of existence. The knowledge of the law is commonplace; but the urgent projection of the

mind into *how it will finally be,* this "doleful" insistence in the midst
of momentary "madness or delight," is a distinctive act of Stevens'. In
this act he responds constantly to the "pressure" of the ultimate. One
does not speak of the "willed" act of the poet. It is rather a response
to the necessity of consciousness. If death is the mother of beauty, in
the poetry of Stevens there is a constant present simply because
every moment known to consciousness is of a life motion defined by
the inevitable. The poet's sense of his world flourishes upon the
supreme fact. It is identifiable motion because of the terminus. With
Stevens the universal law becomes the supreme law of the self. The
architect designs and builds in faithfulness to the law. He builds in
gratitude for the "unconscionable," and yet accepted, treachery. One
cannot read "Sunday Morning" without sensing this gratitude. The
metaphor of the final stanza (*CP,* 70) is the most gently wrought in
the entire range of Stevens' poetry.

The cycles of nature and the cycles of humanity involved in
natural process move from East to West. The life of a man moves
from South to North; and, in his going, he encompasses his own knowledge of the East-West movement because he is bound to nature and to
the span of one common present as it recedes to join the memorials of
the past. In his life there is a whole that may satisfy him,
however minute it is against the hugeness of repetition in the South-
North course of all men and in the East-West response to a supreme
necessity. It is a knowledge of the four provinces of being, the great
unalterable quarters, marking the limits of human comprehension.
Thus, in the South, as we have many times observed in this study, Stevens imagines the North. He searches, through his imagination, the
possibilities of what it will be to stand there. He wishes its certainty
to enliven and to expand his perception of the South. He knows that
without the ultimate North a completed design is impossible. There
is no way to account for the remarkable passion and the mastery of
this poet in his sixties without assent to these principles. The act of
completion in the North is triumph. And as the northern quarter is
summation and resolution, so is the steady gaze toward it a private
necessity among the colors of a southern "madness or delight." Thus
South and North are interdependent. One cannot be fully read in the
total structure without the other.

A strict attention to recurrences of the "Northern" prospect in
Harmonium will show that Stevens was intent upon a comprehensive
sequence of "leaves." Immediately after the shrugging and diffident
close of "The Comedian as the Letter C" and before another tribute to

his woman-genius of the Florida shore, Stevens speaks "From the Misery of Don Joost." This is how it must be with a man in age, his "combat with the sun" finished, his final knowledge of "the powerful seasons" that "bred and killed, / And were themselves the genii / Of their own ends" (*CP*, 46). The Don is the old poet; the great struggle of his life was his brash rivalry of the master sun and his deepening knowledge of the seasons of his duration. Against the brilliance of all *Harmonium* a lyric very near its close seems deliberately placed. "In the Clear Season of Grapes" envisions the reality beneath the fruit, the frost, and the fox-cries. Color and the crispness of a seasonal well-being are brushed, almost carelessly, against the rigor of the final lines: "Autumnal passages / Are overhung by the shadows of the rocks / And his nostrils blow out salt around each man" (*CP*, 111). The salt of our mortality is the salt of life. The hues of the clear season are matched by the shadows of the rocks. It is the mind of deep recess dreaming upon the final rock as the eye and the ear satisfy the senses. The shadows *overhang*.

As Stevens opens his next volume, *Ideas of Order,* he assigns to the first place in the sequence the most significant of all his poems of passage. "Farewell to Florida" is more than rejection of the tropic imagination and resolve upon a northern sternness of reality. It is as though the poet has traversed the mid-point between opposite quarters. A text from the late expression may serve here as a metaphor of metaphor: "What We See Is What We Think," the mind observes, as in summary (*CP*, 459–60). The description turns upon one day of sight, as though that day, any day, were the emblem of a lifetime of sight. At twelve the trees "stood . . . green as ever they would be." This is the exact hour, this noon, of "the imprescriptible zenith." The "first gray second" comes immediately after the "free" moment, "the end of normal time," that is, "normal" in the power of full perception and the power of the imagination to color as it wills. The zenith is the fixed point midway between the "fore-part" of intensifying green and a sky "blue . . . beyond the vaultiest phrase," and the "after-part" of gradually impinging gray. The "imprescriptible" between South and North must be crossed; and the graying will be known with an ardor matching that lavished upon the green. This is the intelligence of "Farewell to Florida." This, and the impressive symbol of the serpent of the self,[1] first introduced here at this point of passage across the "imprescriptible." The waves "make a refrain / Of this: that the snake has shed

[1] See the preceding discussion of the serpent of the self in ch. 2 above.

its skin upon / The floor" (*CP*, 117). Poetry is process, and so is the seasonal mutation of the serpent. The self in its metamorphosis is embodied in that shape. It sheds its skin by constant necessity, until the final season announced at the opening of "The Auroras of Autumn": "This is where the serpent lives, the bodiless. . . . This is his nest." He has become "form gulping after formlessness, / Skin flashing to wished-for disappearances / And the serpent body flashing without the skin" (*CP*, 411). We add that since the time of passage from Florida, across the "imprescriptible zenith," the serpent has watched the graying prospect northward.

So much of the process of diminution to the "neutral centre" has been considered in earlier chapters that it is unnecessary to describe the full course of the arc. The "deepening" and the "growing small" of the colors in "Anglais Mort à Florence" (*CP*, 148) are of the graying, as the poet assumes in irony the guise of an Englishman dead in a place of grandeur not his own. The poem is clearly related to Stevens' resolve upon an "American grandeur" of his design, and no other; and one senses again the pressure of brevity, the late beginning, as this is confessed in the poem following "Farewell to Florida" (*CP*, 119). "The grass is in seed. The young birds are flying. / Yet the house is not built, not even begun. . . ." The "bride" must come now, while "the domes resound with chant involving chant." The resounding domes are acts of the imagination in its fleet moments of structure. The great house remains to be built with the necessary presence of the consort-shaper. It is "the sense of the serpent" in Ananke, Fatal Necessity, the sense of the self moving to the bodiless, that is prescriptive (*CP*, 152). In "The Man with the Blue Guitar" it is the presence still to be named in the far distance, "the rex Impolitor" (*CP*, 495), that looms: "The approach of him whom none believes, / Whom all believe that all believe, / A pagan in a varnished car" (*CP*, 170). If none believes the law for himself, and yet believes that all save himself know the "unconscionable treachery," this is to argue that the self carries within it a paradox of knowing. It knows the limitation of its time and yet denies it. Again, it endures its changes as its duration proceeds; yet it desires the final nest, the bodiless, the "wished-for disappearances."

The endurance of Stevens in paradox is the whole of his anticipation toward the northern quarter and the final surveillance. His steady regard of paradox may sometimes appear playful, as it does in "A Rabbit as King of The Ghosts" (*CP*, 209). What if this animal awareness were the all of creatureliness! Let him be king of all ideas and senses, and there is nothing to think of. He saw a cat in the day; and now the moonlight is only "rabbit-light" to him. It makes no matter that "east rushes west and west rushes down." The night is for him alone. He becomes a self "that fills the four corners of night." But a man knows that there are "four corners" under the moonlight. "Pain is human. . . . This is a part of the sublime / From which we shrink" (*CP*, 314). We are the ones who feel "Panic in the face of the moon" (*CP*, 320), the moon that in the late time of a man is no longer the mirror of his imaginings. In the vortex we know the certain loss, even as we know the sublime. With the "Esthétique du Mal" Stevens moves toward the certain sublimity, which is none other than an innocence of acceptance and an end of desire.

Transport to Summer, despite its fullness of power and its commanding eminence in "Notes Toward a Supreme Fiction," is the least unified of all Stevens' separate volumes. Faith is its great subject. Yet in the sequence approaching the "Notes" it is a description of passage through crisis. The early acceptance of "the nothing that is" in "The Snow Man" (*CP*, 10) seems marked by an almost simple ease when one looks back from the stress of "Flyer's Fall." "Darkness, nothingness of human after-death, / Receive and keep him in the deepnesses of space— / Profundum, physical thunder, dimension in which / We believe without belief" (*CP*, 336). What, we ask, is this nothingness, this *profundum* as *dimension*? In this we believe without belief. And what is to be received and kept in the deepnesses of space? We expect to find in related poems of this span that color has become meditation (*CP*, 338); that "Tomorrow will look like today" (*CP*, 349); that the form of the poet was always a figure "meant to bear / Its poisoned laurels in this poisoned wood" (*CP*, 379). These are sequential metaphors full of prophetic voices that were heard in earlier years, images of speculation brought now to fulfillment. But the questions are new and of this late crisis alone. "The human ocean beats against this rock / Of earth, rises against it, tide by tide, / Continually." In "Two Versions of the Same Poem" Stevens thinks of his grandfather, old John Zeller. The final questions press upon him. Since there is no "golden solvent here" for these creatures, no reconciliation of elements, no "undivided whole," it must be that this is "an ocean of watery images," made by men. Perhaps these forms, these human creatures, "are seeking to escape / Cadaverous undulations" of this human sea. These are the questions of old John. But the poet enjoins: "Rest, old mould . . ." (*CP*, 354–55). The cadaverous sea is the containment of all human time. It is the *profundum*, the deepnesses of space by another name. The poet has begun a late dialogue within the paradox of self. The questions of old John have become his questions. There is crisis in the conflict, between the desire for escape into a wholeness beyond human knowing and the rational injunction: Rest, in the certainty of the impossible. A flyer falls to the earth; a poet goes downward to the rock. What is the "dimension in which / We believe without belief"? How can a man *believe in a nothingness*, even though there be a "nothingness of human after-death"? All that he knew was human, reception of light, flourishing of imagination, acquaintance with the rock of reality. The house of the self was built of these. Without the self, what may *be* at the neutral center?

Mircea Eliade writes of "the anxiety of modern man" as being "obscurely linked to the awareness of his historicity. . . ." "Anguish before Nothingness and Death seems to be a specifically modern phenomenon. In all other, non-European cultures, that is, in the other religions, Death is never felt as an absolute end or as a Nothingness: it is regarded rather as a rite of passage to another mode of being; and for that reason always referred to in relation to the symbolisms and rituals of initiation, rebirth or resurrection."[2] Stevens' "modern" experience will not be qualified. He is intensely modern, acutely aware of his historicity in the everlasting "unconscionable" fate. But I cannot regard him as the anxious man in anguish before nothingness. The act of completing the structure fends off the anguish. This is the essential fact of the late poetry. Beyond it there is a possibility of transcendence which must be recognized if we are fully to know Stevens "at the edge of space." It is the paradox of the self that is inimical, paradox of denial of the possibility and admission to it bound together in one and the same moment of consciousness. The opening tercets of "The Auroras of Autumn" are explicit. "This is where the serpent lives, the bodiless." This is his nest. This, then, is his final place. "Or is this another wriggling out of the egg, / Another image at the end of the cave, / Another bodiless for the body's slough?" The northern lights streak the midnight sky. They "may finally attain a pole / In the midmost midnight and find the serpent there, / In another nest, the master of the maze / Of body and air and forms and images, / Relentlessly in possession of happiness. / This is his poison: that we should disbelieve / Even that" (*CP*, 411). One hears the awesome questions. The last skin is shed; the self becomes "bodiless." This

[2] *Myths, Dreams and Mysteries*, p. 235.

is acceptance of the end, denial in prospect of the edge and the nothingness beyond. *Or* does another "bodiless" come of this end, destined to assume the "slough" of an unknown state of being? Do these red-pale streaks at midnight, fatal fires threatening the poet's structure, the whole of his process, reach a pole in "midmost midnight," where the serpent lives in another nest? There are no answers. The possible in this heroic vision is both denied and, in the very act of admitting the questions, affirmed. This is the poison of the serpent-self, that we should disbelieve even that, a transcendent possession of happiness, a happiness, if it could be, in the *whole* that no man knows as a man of earth. The self is the agent of faith in the humanly possible; it is the agent of disbelief in the suprahumanly possible. It bears within it, in the paradox of human existence, its own poison.

It is obvious that Stevens "finally satisfied himself that 'God and the imagination are one.' "[3] Mr. Riddel accepts with other critics the evidence of the lyric preceding "The Rock," the "Final Soliloquy of the Interior Paramour." "We say God and the imagination are one . . ." (*CP*, 524). Stevens' sign of ellipsis here is perhaps the most eloquent use of punctuation in his total poetic achievement. The principle is not punctuated as a declaration of final fact. The sign of ellipsis represents the unknowable beyond the principle. Ralph J. Mills, examining this final soliloquy of the woman-genius of the poet, believes it "evident that the existence of Stevens's 'God' depends completely on the existence of man and is, further, a creative force within him. . . ."[4] His reading, then, would argue for Stevens an absolute: without man, the creature possessing the power of imagination, no God. I must contend that the ellipsis in its own eloquence of silence represents the limits of human knowing: Insofar as we know the reality of God, we *know* only in the fact of imagination. Northrop Frye finds in the late poetry, "The Auroras" in particular, the *"Morgenrot"* of a "new recognition."[5] This approach was itself new a decade ago; yet its rightness has scarcely been extended in subsequent studies. The "new" recognition of Stevens in the *Morgenrot* of the mind, as it contemplates the auroras, is *admission* of the possible in this crucial scrutiny of the self's knowing a simultaneous *denial*, the taste of the serpent's poison. Stevens in "The Owl in the Sarcophagus" examines the "mythology of modern death." We stand at last on "the edges of oblivion,"

---

[3] *The Clairvoyant Eye*, p. 230.
[4] "Wallace Stevens: The Image of the Rock," *Accent*, XVIII, No. 2 (Spring, 1958), 79.
[5] "The Realistic Oriole: A Study of Wallace Stevens," *The Hudson Review*, Vol. 10 (1957), p. 362.

where, flinging out a last word, we are "beyond artifice." We know that the mind, as humanity knows it, has only a "light-bound space." We lie down in innocence. The mind "is a child that sings itself to sleep" (*CP*, 435–36). This is a gentle piety; and in the quiet music of the lines the overwhelming thought of this innocence is unobtrusive. Stevens is using this final innocence in the sense of unknowingness. A modern death, then, has no mythology. For Stevens the imaginings of all theologies became the myths of an envisioned immortality. The rites of death and burial became the great *introit* of such mythical projection as the imagining theologian fashioned. A modern death is of a mythless time. The artificer of a life is the possessor of a mind intent only upon an earthly reality. He goes in satisfaction; and in the innocence of that going, the unknown, which was given all its various forms in the succession of priestly hierarchies, is the possible. One reaches in one's contemplation of Stevens the irresolute paradox that makes man what he is while he breathes in human life: paradox of longing to exist as he is and of the "wished-for disappearances," paradox of denial and admission, of disbelief and "dimension in which / We believe without belief" (*CP*, 336). How shall a man live? For Stevens, in the making of an architecture of his life. How shall a man die? For Stevens, in acceptance of the paradox that must ultimately describe his humanity. The coarseness of much flagrant contemporary discourse on "the death of God" might be offset by an examination of Stevens in the northern quarter. What we need is the lesson of the poet; what we get is the vulgarity of sensational announcement. The idea of God changes. Stevens knew this to be a major phenomenon of human history. He also took the constant paradox, as he regarded it, to be the matrix of change. The triumph of the late poetry is discovered in the metaphor of description. There is a rising incidence, in this late expression, of "we" in place of the personae from solitude. The strict avoidance of universal statement characteristic of Stevens, the rejection of man in the abstract, is in part displaced by the persuasion toward paradox in the North as a human truth.

The Auroras of Autumn as the name of both the major poem and the volume is the most significant of all Stevens' titles. A man of autumn stands under the night sky deepening toward midnight. The light of the sun has been succeeded by these sinister paling streaks of red as they rise toward the zenith. A man who designed a gold dome for the perfected spirit, his radiant structure under the sun, sees above him the design of a dome of night. These are the lights of the northern quarter. The presence of the dawn, Aurora, in the old name of these boreal streams signifies, of course, a promise of immediate morning which is false. We take Stevens' sense of the name as related to the paradox: false dawn, which in his symbolistic intent is denial, or portent of a new light to come, which is admission. The *aurora borealis,* transmuted from its phenomenal reality to poet's symbol, is appropriated to the paradox. It is a name from the experience of simple human sight; and it is a designation of deep counterforces in the mind.

Upon this northern theme of a multiform significance Stevens wrote a poem exceptional in its imagery of space and time. In the prospect of illimitable distance it has few equals in English. The scope is Miltonic; and, among the boldest thrusts of imagination in twentieth-century poetry, perhaps certain passages of Eliot's *Four Quartets* stand nearest to it. The precise shape of the symbol was very clear in Stevens' mind. At the close of the year of publication of *The Auroras* Stevens was in correspondence with his Paris book-dealer, Miss Vidal, with respect to a French binding for his personal copy. "The piece of leather which was your [Miss Vidal's] personal preference, and which I am enclosing, that is, the one marked par une encoche, will do very well, particularly if there could be included among the lignes platinées a few red lines. In this part of the world the northern lights are not only misty and white but they have a definite redness."[6] It is as though the mind were branded with the structure of this night vision. Red is its sign, but red unlike that red of vigor and bloodedness in the high summer of the imagination. This is red apart from the poet's red, the color of a conflagration inevitable in natural process. On it Stevens expended a lavishness of design which in certain of its sections achieves a baroque majesty. These are extraplanetary engagements of the mind. If this modern diction lacks the diapason of Milton, the dynamic sweep of the imagination appears in strong likeness. If human time and infinity do not intersect at Eliot's point of man's salvation, the mortal is nonetheless dared against the illimitable. "He observes how the north is always enlarging the change, / With its frigid brilliances, its blue-red sweeps / And gusts of great enkindlings, its polar green, / The color of ice and fire and solitude" (*CP*, 412–13). The theater of masques, theater floating through the clouds, is filled with flying birds. "This is nothing until in a single man

---

[6] The letter, dated at Hartford December 15, 1950, speaks of a Paris binder desired for the work. Apparently he was known to Stevens by other examples of his skill: ". . . I have always liked Mr. Aussourd's work . . ." (*Letters*, p. 702).

contained, / Nothing until this named thing nameless is / And is destroyed. He opens the door of his house / On flames. The scholar of one candle sees / An Arctic effulgence flaring on the frame / Of everything he is. And he feels afraid" (*CP*, 416–17). By these lights the fulfillments of all mediations, his and those of all his kind, become "a blaze of summer straw, in winter's nick" (*CP*, 420–21).

The center of the poem, the seventh section, is a series of questions from the paradox. Certainly it lacks the assertions of a pure baroque style as the seventeenth century knew these. What one notices is steady contemplation of space and the imperious line of relationships through the metaphor. The passage requires no interpretation; in thought its reappraisal of the paradox is entirely clear.

> *Is there an imagination that sits enthroned*
> *As grim as it is benevolent, the just*
> *And the unjust, which in the midst of summer stops*
>
> *To imagine winter? When the leaves are dead,*
> *Does it take its place in the north and enfold itself,*
> *Goat-leaper, crystalled and luminous, sitting*
>
> *In highest night? And do these heavens adorn*
> *And proclaim it, the white creator of black, jetted*
> *By extinguishings, even of planets as may be,*
>
> *Even of earth, even of sight, in snow,*
> *Except as needed by way of majesty,*
> *In the sky, as crown and diamond cabala?*
>
> *It leaps through us, through all our heavens leaps,*
> *Extinguishing our planets, one by one,*
> *Leaving, of where we were and looked, of where*
>
> *We knew each other and of each other thought,*
> *A shivering residue, chilled and foregone,*
> *Except for that crown and mystical cabala.*
>
> .   .   .   .
>
> *The stars are putting on their glittering belts.*
> *They throw around their shoulders cloaks that flash*
> *Like a great shadow's last embellishment.*
>
> [*CP*, 417, 419]

With the title poem of *The Auroras* Stevens completed his exploration of the North, long anticipated and at last undertaken in the preceding *Transport to Summer*. The final poems add little to the knowledge of *how it now is*, this final reality. "In a Bad Time" speaks of an order of the northern sky and of the poverty of the man who reaches this "glacial beauty" (*CP*, 426). Images of the Swatara and the Schuylkill, Pennsylvania streams of the poet's boyhood, enter "The Countryman " (*CP*, 428) and "Our Stars Come from Ireland" (*CP*, 455). Stevens once spoke of the Swatara in a letter as a country stream of innocence.[7] Now it becomes the black river. The innocent eye of the boy no longer sees it in its country freshness. The waters darken in the vision as the dweller in the North makes his way toward his final innocence. In "The Novel" the firelit room darkens; "Day's arches are crumbling into the autumn night" (*CP*, 458). One reaches the last sorrow of "Madame La Fleurie" (*CP*, 507), "His crisp knowledge is devoured" by his mother earth, "beneath a dew. . . ." The last page of the poet is of "the handbook of heartbreak," a language that he did not know, but nonetheless must speak now, in this northern place. And one discovers the last triumph, the certainty of the "Final Soliloquy." An order, a whole, exists in the mind: "Within its vital boundary . . . / We say God and the imagination are one . . ." (*CP*, 524). What is beyond this saying? Stevens leaves us with the unknowable in the final punctuation.

"Among time's images, there is not one / Of this present, the venerable mask above / The dilapidation of dilapidations" (*CP*, 476). In "An Ordinary Evening in New Haven" the present is every man's inevitable present in the northern quarter, and the venerable mask is the poet's. There is not one *image*, we learn, of what it is to be in that late autumn place. When one ponders the assertion, he remembers the hero without heroics. It is a distinction of Stevens that he left an image of this northern present which was finally his. Few artists have so vigorously purposed a celebration of age as the fulfillment of design.

[7] To his Irish correspondent Thomas McGreevy, in a letter dated at Hartford, August 25, 1948; see *Letters*, p. 611.

The Chapel of Wind and Weather: The Poet as Priest

19

"LET US FIX PORTALS, EAST AND WEST, / ABHORRING green-blue north and blue-green south. / Our chiefest dome a demoiselle of gold" (*OP*, 17–18). The poem is "Architecture"; the date is 1918. "And then blue heaven spread / Its crystalline pendentives on the sea / And the macabre of the water-glooms / In an enormous undulation fled" (*CP*, 100). The crystalline parts of a dome rise over "Sea Surface Full of Clouds," superior among the structures of *Harmonium* in 1923. In "Ghosts as Cocoons," second in the sequence of *Ideas of Order* (1936), the mistress of the gold dome is invoked: "Come now . . . / While the domes resound with chant involving chant" (*CP*, 119). In the next year the vision of "Owl's Clover" is turned upon "The spirit's episcopate," "a heaven once" when among the domes of human making there was of each noble self ". . . the middle dome, / The temple of the altar where each man / Beheld the truth and knew it to be true" (*OP*, 53–54). The man with the blue guitar plays in a poor time to the unknowing ones ". . . of the greatness of poetry . . . / Of the structure of vaults upon a point of light" (*CP*, 167). One goes with the poet to "Variations on A Summer Day" in *Parts of a World* (1942), to stand with him on the rock of Maine, in prospect of the northern quarter: "Round and round goes the bell of the water . . . / The bell of its dome, the patron of sound" (*CP*, 235). In 1950 the midnight dome is streaked with its arcs of northern light (*CP*, 411–21); and, in the cold, "Celle Qui Fût Héaulmiette," she who was the helmet-maker's wife (she who once was the "demoiselle of gold"), takes refuge "not in an arc / But in a circle, not in the arc / Of winter, in the unbroken circle / Of summer. . . ." Her place of shelter is "Like a meaning in nothingness . . ." (*CP*, 438). There is "The Plain Sense of Things" of "The Rock," when "The great structure has become a minor house" (*CP*, 502). There is the prophetic vision of Santayana's Roman death: "Its domes are the architecture of your bed" (*CP*, 510). In a final inspection, Stevens the architect surveys his structure in "St. Armorer's Church from the Outside" (*CP*, 529–30). "Its chapel rises from Terre Ensevelie, / An ember yes among its cindery noes, / His own. . . ."

It is not my intention to summarize the vast range of Stevens' architectural metaphor. The reappearances of columns, arches, arcs, roofs and canopies, and total buildings have been fully apparent in the preceding chapters. I have intended to isolate in these references certain dominant assertions of the principle. In brief review, the assignment of the "demoiselle of gold" as the mistress of the "chiefest dome" is the announcement of the principle, and the solitary architect who takes a last look at St. Armorer's Church is the fulfillment. The "pendentives" of "Sea Surface," the concave triangles vaulting from the corners of the basic square, are prefigurations of the master design. In the architectural vision of Stevens the single poem of perception is frequently a paradigm of the total design. The swift encounter of the eye, the imagination, and the shaping hand render the great dome in miniature. It is an enclosure, a "roundness," in which the object has been fully claimed by the imagination and transformed from the commonplace to the wondrous, just as the smallest part of any good architect's design is a detail of transformation toward the full image of the mind. Thus the domes of brief encounter in "Ghosts as Cocoons" and in "Variations on a Summer Day" are small likenesses of the great structure. But a full achievement pre-empts the vision in "the middle dome, / The temple of the altar" of each great imaginer, exemplified finally in Santayana; in "the structure of vaults upon a point of light"; in the "summer-built" circle of refuge for the woman-genius of the poet; in the awesome analogy of a dome flaming in the autumn night; in a great structure as a minor house; and, at last, in a chapel glowing as an ember among the cindery annihilations of time.

The dome was the master pattern. In this examination of the structure of Stevens we have reached an account of the tenth and the last arc: the enduring intention of the dome as a house of priestly acts, the chapel of a poet. The "pendentives" of "Sea Surface" suggests that the master design was evolved upon the pendentive principle in domical theory. Four concave triangles rise from a square. The sides of this square, as we know Stevens, would represent the East-West course of nature and the South-North course of the self. But the pendentive principle suggested in "Sea Surface" gives place to modern design, the half-sphere on the rock, with its dominant rounding of arcs. The basic square, then, is not the foundation of the dome. The rock of reality is the base. Yet the supreme quarters of East, West, South, and North are the provinces of experience from which it was built; and the dome exists in constant reference to the four. The ritual of its making is the process of the poetry; its distinction is a response to the necessities of rise and fall in nature and of youth and age in the self. Stevens does not disclose that St. Armorer's Church is completed in the form of a dome. But it must be certain that this fulfillment is accomplished in the freedom of the modern draftsman. The reference to Matisse at Vence is not idle. The modern boldness of his famous chapel in southern France is no greater than the daring of the poet's structure. The chapel of Stevens is "like a new account of everything old, / Matisse at Vence and a great deal more than that . . ." (*CP*, 529). It is of the modern, on the rock. It is the icon of a poet's life in poetry. "The gold dome of things is the perfected spirit" (*OP*, 168).

The evidence of Stevens' deliberation upon this domical structure is complete in St. Armorer. He was the "saintly" priest-builder. He was the armorer. To understand the poet as the armorer one turns to "Celle Qui Fût Héaulmiette," she who was the helmet-maker's wife. The poet was the husband, the armorer, the maker of the helmet. She was his mistress, woman-genius, shaping hand, the feminine presence of his days and nights. When she takes shelter from the cold, "not in an arc / But in a circle" (*CP*, 438), the auroras have been seen in the midnight sky. "Into that native shield she slid. . . ." The armor is the structure, the house of the poet and of his consort, the chapel of St. Armorer. It has been noted earlier in this study that the symbol of the helmet-maker's wife derives from Villon and from the sculpture of Rodin based on the same poem.[1] The realization of a once beautiful

[1] See above, ch. 4, n. 10, and ch. 9, n. 5. Stevens' letter to Bernard Heringman dated at Hartford, July 21, 1953, in which he names Rodin's "The Old Courtesan" (in "Celle Qui Fût Héaulmiette") as a prototype of the "wife" in the poem. I use here, as noticed above, the full text of the letter, Stevens Collection, Baker Library, Dartmouth College. By permission of Holly Stevens.

woman in age must have appealed to Stevens as he thought of the attendant geniuses of other creators, distant poet and recent sculptor. We take the armorer in the lineage that Stevens followed. He was a maker of helmets. It is but a step to that domical theory already discussed, the ancient symbolic concept of the Near East, the dome as a celestial helmet.[2] St. Armorer's Church is the chapel of the poet, completed, a helmet against the cold, and yet a structure that is destined to join the cinders of the past.

In ancient Peking the emperor performed rites of burnt offerings at the summer and winter solstices. He ascended to the central altar of the Temple of Heaven, the great shrine rounding upward in canopies of blue tile under the dome of the sky, celestial dome that was thought to cover the structure and the celebrant like a hollow turquoise. Its tiers of stone ascending toward the sanctified chamber support steps and portals oriented directly to the points of the compass.[3] Whether Stevens knew of this majestic design, one of the supreme achievements in the history of all temple architecture, and of these rites performed under the symbol of everlasting blue is a matter for pleasant speculation. An imagining of these should have given him joy.[4] Such a geometric formalism set in a brilliant symbolic range of color, such a total act of imperial blue marking the seasonal passages of earth in tribute to the golden sun, seem the right metaphors of majesty for Stevens. The passion for design in Stevens the architect and his strenuous compulsion toward a rite that would order and celebrate his poet's life stand in accord. The structure of an American mind in the twentieth century daringly commands its own fitting analogies. For it was subman, major man in the architects of old Peking, who gathered to himself his fortunes of another time in the Temple of Heaven; and

[2] See above, ch. 9.
[3] See Juliet Bredon, *Peking* (Shanghai, 1922), pp. 132–35.
[4] Stevens' correspondence with Harriet Monroe should be of interest to any reader who wishes to argue for an active orientalism in his work. Miss Monroe's sister, Lucy Monroe Calhoun, was living in Peking in 1922. Stevens' letters addressed to Miss Monroe in this year express an interest in exotic teas to be had from Mrs. Calhoun. The reverie on China is exotic. Stevens' image of Peking is clearly of the ideal; and one finds his imagination playing upon the ideal in his correspondence with Leonard C. van Geyzel in Ceylon, friend of a friend of a friend, with whom he exchanged observations and from whom he now and then ordered a "few things." (See the *Letters*, pp. 228–29 on Peking, and pp. 323 *et passim* for the correspondence with van Geyzel.) Stevens mentions Peking once in the poetry, in "The Comedian as the Letter C" (*CP*, 34).

it was the old giant in us who authorized the solitary triumph of Stevens.

One supposes that, had Stevens been able to accept an orthodoxy of the Christian tradition, he would have embraced Roman Catholicism with its ritual and order, its feasts, its colors of the seasonal year, and its disciplines of meditation. The splendor of Christian Rome which surrounds the dying Santayana, "inquisitor of structures," will seem to many of us a metaphor for Stevens himself. The domes of the great city, wrote Stevens, "are the architecture of your bed" (*CP* 510). They stand in adjacency to the central dome of Santayana, whose "design of all his words takes form / And frame from thinking and is realized" (*CP*, 511). So it may have been for Stevens, thinking of domes adjacent to his own, as he paused for a last look at St. Armorer's Church and, in American poetry, memorialized the greatness of Henri Matisse, the faithful Christian designer of his chapel tribute to a Roman reality.

Some of the most affecting of Stevens' letters are those addressed to Sister M. Bernetta Quinn late in his life. Sister Bernetta, at work on her study *The Metamorphic Tradition in Modern Poetry*,[5] sought the advice of Stevens as she prepared her commentary on his work. At the beginning of their exchange Stevens chose to note an affinity: "Your mind is too much like my own for it to seem to be an evasion on my part to say merely that I do seek a centre and expect to go on seeking it."[6] The correspondence gained steadily in confidence, as Stevens attested some six years later: "Your Easter message made me happy, as all your notes do, because they seem to come from something fundamental, something isolated from this ruthless present. . . ."[7] In April of the year of his death, Stevens, doomed by an inoperable cancer that would be disclosed by surgery in the following month, wrote finally: "I can think of no one to whom Easter can mean more than it means to you."[8] These confessions in friendship are beyond mere tolerance. They are tributes to the faith of another, in their own way as affecting and honest as the tribute to the faith of Matisse.

The firmness of Stevens' resolve against the structures of other men, demonstrated particularly in the foregoing discussion of "Montra-

---

[5] (New Brunswick, N.J., 1955). Sister Bernetta is a member of the faculty of the College of St. Teresa, Winona, Minnesota.
[6] In a letter dated at Hartford, April 7, 1948; *Letters*, p. 584.
[7] Dated at Hartford, April 21, 1954; *Letters*, p. 828.
[8] Holograph letter in the Stevens Collection, Baker Library, Dartmouth College. By permission of Holly Stevens. On Stevens' fatal illness see *Letters*, p. 882, n. 5.

chet-le-Jardin,"[9] does not signify a lack of discrimination among adjacent structures. The dome is the symbol of a structure of the imagination. Yet one can be very certain that Stevens had no interest in domes and rituals native to primitive societies building of mud and blood. No one need attempt to relate him to a red-rawness of consciousness, to the dome of the ceremonial *kiva* of the Amerindians of the Southwest, or to the earthern domes of *kubbas* in tomb-structures on the way to Mecca. The old giant of the everlasting imagination in man authorized these as well. But he was the giant unrefined. Mud in the sun is not the equivalent of the Temple of Heaven or of Periclean Athens seen by Anacharsis. When Stevens thinks of sun-baked mud, as he does in the "Stanzas for 'The Man with the Blue Guitar'" (*OP*, 72), he thinks of himself in supreme irony: The materials of a man in "this ruthless present," named in his letter to Sister Bernetta, are mud to the wealth of some past builders. Stevens left no evidence of enthusiasm for the memorials of primitive societies in this hemisphere. What he had to say on the Mayans is perhaps eloquent enough. To his Cuban friend José Rodríguez Feo he wrote in a clear disdain. "One sees pictures of the Mayas, and this, that and the other. These things never take one below the surface and I have yet to feel about any Maya that he was made of clay. Publications like Cuadernos Americanos convince one that he was made of putty."[10] Later he observed in a letter to his correspondent in Ceylon, Leonard C. van Geyzel, that American pride in Mayan antiquities is mere pretense. "I don't know whether you know about Maya art. This consists very largely of glyphs and sacrificial and calendar stones, all of them completely hideous. . . . Many people believe that these early Indians came from the South Pacific. We feel a special interest in things of this sort because they give us the antiquity which the English like to deny us."[11]

One comes back to the structures of Catholicism, to the poet of respect without faith. We have regarded him in other adjacencies, as he contemplates the sun, as he invokes presences in the manner of a priest of the pagan, as he perceives with the savage scrutiny of a first earth-dweller the radiance of natural forms. And yet one cannot discard the paradox. Stevens was a *first* man seeing with eyes washed clean, but nonetheless a man who knew keenly of the ultimate refinements of the giant imagination in the Western heritage. *How to tame*

[9] See above, ch. 2.
[10] From Hartford, December 19, 1946; *Letters*, p. 543.
[11] From Hartford, September 14, 1948; *Letters*, p. 614.

him, as in that first ascription in *Harmonium,* "The Plot Against the Giant" (*CP*, 6–7), is *how to know that he can be tamed* by evidence from other men. The race did not struggle from the mud for naught. The proof of civilized man is no more than the proof of the power to refine. It is for this reason, more than for any other, that one can propose the significant adjacency of the domes of Catholicism in the final hours of Santayana. And, if this great elegy be regarded as metaphor for the final bed of Stevens himself, perhaps we say with justice that the structures of Rome were nearest in his final regard—that and nothing more. This is the sympathetic vision in the final analogy of the chapel at Vence: a structure adjacent to St. Armorer's Church.

It is the rite of Rome which lingers in the images along the arc of this chapel of Stevens'. The building is a structure made in the winds of the poet's change and in the weather of his time. Wind is the process of passage from South to North; weather is the climate on the rock. We have noted in the preceding chapter Stevens' reflection on "the mythology of modern death" (*CP*, 435–36). One has one's time, one's present reality. Stevens' chapel is the structure of the only faith possible for him. Yet the language of the priestly ritual, the intoning of the poet-celebrant, is the speech of the traditional. "The poet is the priest of the invisible," Stevens wrote in the "Adagia" (*OP*, 169). The full structure of the dome-chapel of this poet, then, is invisible save in his language and in the design of the mind. We are chiefly interested, in this final inspection of the arcs of design, to show the coherence of priestly language.

Harmonium is marked with images of ritual. In "The Comedian as the Letter C" the peach of the American South "should have a sacrament / And celebration" (*CP*, 39). In "Peter Quince" the immortal longing for beauty plays "on the clear viol" of Susanna's memory "And makes a constant sacrament of praise" (*CP*, 92). An equivalence between a religious procession and a poet's masque has been proposed in "A High-Toned Old Christian Woman" (*CP*, 59); and Susanna and all her successors in the poet's theater seem to follow in a procession to the high and central place of sacrament. It is clear from these initial images that Stevens intends consecrating acts of the imagination, acts which signify the poet's power to transform the grayness of the real to the beauty and color of the unreal. The "leaves" of his structure-in-process appear to invite sacramental participation of his fellows *as if* this priestly solitude were, instead, a congregation of the faithful.

Such is the implicit significance of "Gray Stones and Gray Pigeons" (*CP*, 140) in the following sequence of *Ideas of Order*. "The archbishop is away. The church is gray." In the church are "Birds that never fly / Except when the bishop passes by, / Globed in today and tomorrow, / Dressed in his colored robes." This *globed* in the diction refers directly to the curvilinear structure in the mind of Stevens; it is the sign of the archbishop, the poet, as he transforms the gray of reality. One adds that the colored robes are of the high imaginings of Christian ritual. "Winter Bells" follows closely upon these colors of the archbishop. Why did the Jew desert his synagogue? Like every other man, he wanted a church with bright bells and "The *mille fiori* of vestments" (*CP*, 141). As Stevens notes in "Lions in Sweden," "the whole of the soul . . . hankers after sovereign images" (*CP*, 125). In the widest sense the soul of humanity longs for the order of ceremony. As one studies the earlier poetry of Stevens, it is procession in the rising chapel which most engages the mind: a procession of American makers of celebration for the native peach, of succeeding players upon the viol of Susanna's memory, of a poet's masque in passing array, of vested priests in seasonal colors. The correspondence with the high coloring of the painter's poetry is exact, perception at the full when the world at its best is seen as color and motion.

At about the time of his naming of the "spirit's episcopate" in "Owl's Clover," "the middle dome, / The temple of the altar" of each man (*OP*, 53–54), Stevens turned to a language of instruction, the relationship of teacher to ephebe cast in a liturgical directive of priest to novice. In "The Man with the Blue Guitar" the poet aspires to be the giver of a manual of praise. "A poem like a missal found / In the mud, a missal for that young man, / That scholar hungriest for that book, / The very book, or, less, a page / Or, at the least, a phrase, that phrase, / A hawk of life, that latined phrase . . ." (*CP*, 177–78). This missal for the youth is none other than the poet's handbook of life. The diminution from *book* to *phrase* in this resolve is the mark of reflection upon the possible: not that the youth should copy the example, but that the Latin text at the center of all great imaginative acts should be universal at the altar of every man, *I will to be a hawk of life*. This role of the priest-celebrant in solitary readings of the missal is thereafter persistent. In "The Hand as a Being" (*Parts of a World, CP*, 271) one turns to "the first canto of the final canticle. . . ." Stevens thinks of the beginning of the last office of the canonical hours. The *final canticle* is the final hymn. In "Examination of the Hero in a Time of War" the will of the soldier-hero "opposed to cold, fate / In its cavern, wings subtler than any mercy" makes a *psalter* of existence in this chaos (*CP*, 273). The Latin phrase of the hawk is reasserted in these wings of courage, unflinching in seizure of the grim reality. As the major directive of "Notes Toward a Supreme Fiction" approaches in *Transport to Summer,* the book of the poet becomes scripture set against scripture. Description of this known human life is revelation. The vision of the Book of Revelation describes nothing relevant to man. The text of a man's description is "the book of reconciliation . . . canon central in itself, / The thesis of the plentifullest John ("Description without Place," *CP*, 344–45). The creator of the full description of a life is of the world; St. John was not of the world.

It is the poet's scripture of the world which one finally hears in "Notes Toward a Supreme Fiction." In the strictness of the text, *It Must Change,* is the ringing denunciation of the "bloodless episcopus, / Eye without lid, mind without any dream—" (*CP*, 394). The episcopus repeats the "single text, granite monotony." One understands that in the rite of Stevens constant metamorphosis in the language of the ceremony is the necessity in every act of celebration. There is a *vulgate* of reality, Stevens observes; and this we know to be endless repetition in the experience of the human. What the poet seeks is "a peculiar speech to speak / The peculiar potency of the general, / To compound the imagination's Latin with / The lingua franca et jocundissima . . ." (*CP*, 396–97). This is to say that he seeks to compound the central Latin, *a hawk of life,* the direct opposite of *bloodless episcopus,* with his free and, for him, most appropriate language. These Latin emphases in the diction are faithful to the rite conceived in "The Man with the Blue Guitar." The missal offered to the young man is to be of his own making in "the imagination's Latin," bird of wing and claw which seizes the objects of its vision with a savage force. For this is the way to the parable of the Canon Aspirin. *It Must Give Pleasure,* the supreme fiction. The Canon's legend is the legend of Stevens in the chapel of his making. The pleasure was in "the whole, / The complicate, the amassing harmony" (*CP*, 401–3). The "Notes" become a missal for the youth, the potential hero.

The rest of the celebration is private. In *The Auroras of Autumn* the *"summarium in excelsis* begins" ("Puella Parvula," *CP*, 456). Not the *Gloria* of the mass, but *summary* in the highest: "Flame, sound, fury composed. . . ." The structure nears its completion; and the poet-priest turns briefly in reflection upon his distant past. "The Old Lutheran Bells at Home" sound out faintly from his boyhood, "the voices of the pastors calling / In the names of St. Paul and of the halo-John . . . / the voices of the pastors calling . . . / Generations of shepherds to generations of sheep." "Deep in their sound the stentor Martin sings" (*CP*, 461). What shall be said? That Martin Luther propounded in the deep past the rite of faith which was commanded of a young man in Pennsylvania? That he knew no priest of the essential phrase, the imagination's Latin, *a hawk of life*? The poem ends in a *summary in the highest* of the freedom in that phrase. "Each truth is a sect though no bells ring for it. / And the bells belong to the sextons, after all, / As they jangle and dangle and kick their feet" (*CP*, 462). Stevens approaches the last inspection of St. Armorer's Church. His chapel is his truth, his sect, though no bells ring its praise. The sextons of the world ring the bells of all "stentor Martins" who advance their separate truths as the final truths of the sheep. In "The Man with the Blue Guitar" Stevens inscribed his first defiance of the stentorian voices: "The bells are the bellowing of bulls" (*CP*, 181). Immediately he likened himself to a Franciscan of a "fertile glass," the "fertile" unreal above the real, and so the place of his truth.

In a note on the passage written for Renato Poggioli he confessed: ". . . I imagine that I chose a Franciscan because of the quality of liberality and of being part of the world that goes with the Franciscan as distinguished, say, from a Jesuit."[12] Martin Luther was a bull of the bells; and so, we assume, was any Jesuit of eminence. However faithful to the persuasion of the Franciscans Stevens may be, his election of this affinity for his role as priest is of clear significance. The lingering of Roman rite in his ascriptions to the chapel in process, in his resolve upon the missal, or, at the least, the central text, "A hawk of life, that latined phrase," is a mark upon the dome. It speaks of adjacencies upon which he never looked with indifferent eyes. If Rome had been all Franciscan . . . But Wallace Stevens was a man of the North in the completing of his truth. The air of Mediterranean lands was not of his place. "America was always North to him," he wrote of the displaced Crispin (*CP*, 34). And there, in the way which he thought of as American, he took the life of Crispin to himself, and assumed an inevitable solitude.

The reference to Matisse at Vence in "St. Armorer's Church from the Outside" is of final significance. In this one fleet moment Stevens related his achievement in poetry to the triumph of the painter and the

12 From Hartford, June 25, 1953; *Letters*, p. 784.

architect. Matisse had designed the Chapel of the Rosary of the Dominican Nuns of Vence in its entirety: in its exterior and interior architecture, its *vitraux*, its frescoes, and its vestments. As a summation of
a life of devotion to beauty and as a testament of praise to the glory
of God, the structure was consecrated in the early summer of 1951.[13]
Stevens' recognition seems utterly casual in his poem. His own structure, he notes, "is like a new account of everything old, / Matisse at
Vence and a great deal more than that . . ." (*CP*, 529). But he honors
a man of Mediterranean air in a completing of his truth. The little
chapel at Vence is the *summarium in excelsis* of his life. He thinks of
his own poet's chapel, house of wind and weather, for a little time "An
ember yes" among the "cindery noes" of "Terre Ensevelie. . . ." In
every sense the act of Stevens the architect was an act of dedication
comparable to, even though unlike, that of Matisse. In 1950 Stevens
wrote to his Irish correspondent, Thomas McGreevy, "On my death
there will be found carved on my heart, along with the initials of lots
of attractive girls, that I have known, the name of Aix-en-Provence."[14]
Country that he had never seen, this southern clime of France, of Paul
Cézanne and of Matisse! Did he think of some blessing of this place,
that the love of beauty in a youth of women was like the love of life
itself in this land of sun and Mediterranean grace? Each master creator fulfills himself as he must. One concludes that Matisse and Stevens
were fellows in the rarest of satisfactions known to man: the sense of
the ultimate, the design realized. The "great deal more than that"
which Stevens claims for his structure as he thinks of Matisse should
be quite simply read. The painter turned in his last five years to an
architecture as a final triumph; the poet lived an architect's full life
in a crafting of one structure, the chapel of wind and weather. In his
own, his "native," as he often named it, he was "the priest of the invisible" ("Adagia," *OP*, 169).

13 Of his labors at Vence, Matisse wrote the following notes. ". . . This chapel is
for me the conclusive achievement of a whole life of labour and the flowering of a
huge, sincere, and difficult striving. It is not a labour I chose but rather one for
which I was chosen by destiny as I near my journey's end. . . . I regard it, despite
all its imperfections, as my masterpiece . . . as an effort which is the culmination of
a whole life dedicated to the search for truth." (In a Chapel pamphlet guide
published by the Congregation of the Dominican Nuns of Monteils Aveyron.)
14 From Hartford, March 20, 1950; *Letters*, p. 671.

Afterword

IV

The Poet in His Time

20

IN A FLORIDA MIDNIGHT THERE WERE "LINES STRAIGHT
and swift between the stars." A poet's celebration of the perceiving
eye was to be his delight, "Wading the sea-lines . . . / Mounting the
earth-lines" (*CP*, 72). His arrows of the mind would fly and fall,
"straightway for their pleasure." They would make "recoveries of young
nakedness / And the lost vehemence the midnights hold." From
this full southern sight to the prospect of glittering winter stars
in the North, the courses of the arrows would be delight (*CP*, 71–72).
Such was a poet's resolve upon a strict geometry of the perfected
spirit. As he looked seaward from Maine rock on a day of high
summer, the mind behind the eye contemplated a seeming "to grasp
at transparence." A premonition of the death of sight was delicate
and yet certain, this misty paling after an unclouded radiance known
to youth. "It was not yet the hour to be dauntlessly leaping" (*CP*,
235–36). The time of leaping came as the auroras smoldered in an
inevitable midnight of "lost vehemence." Was there, then, "an
imagination that sits enthroned / As grim as it is benevolent. . . .
Goat-leaper, crystalled and luminous, sitting / In highest night?"
(*CP*, 417). The arrows had traveled from South to North. A poet

would then leap dauntlessly from the "edge of space" (*CP*, 469). Beyond his leaping would there be a leaping of an imagination greater than his imagination of the human, Capricornus dauntless among the stars of his constellation? Yet even this power, goat-leaper, would "dare not leap by chance in its own dark." Even he would leap by some design, tracing a structure, and finding at last a means of an unmaking of the shape (*CP*, 417–18). We reach a final acquiescence of Stevens. The law is universal entropy, irreversible tendency of all systems toward increasing disorder and inertness. The final admission to entropy is matched by the constant celebration along the arrowy courses of a man's imagination. We recognize the arc-principle of the poet's mind. By its authority he shaped a house of life.

The design realized is the memorial of one man's process, a structure destined for an early oblivion, and yet in its time an evidence of supreme human capacities. "Poetry is a health," wrote Stevens in his notebook (*OP*, 176). He had earlier reflected in the same sequence upon poetry in the universality of the human. "Poetry is a purging of the world's poverty and change and evil and death. It is a present perfecting, a satisfaction in the irremediable poverty of life" (*OP*, 167). As readers of Stevens we ponder the ultimate barrier, irremediable and enduring poverty of human existence, and the ultimate hope, a purging of the poverty, a health through poetry. When we return to his analogy of a poet's scores and of his readers as performers,[1] we do not expect to find a coda, his truth as universal truth. The only truth is the enduring power of the imagination. In this sense the achievement of every artist in human history is an *aria da capo,* whatever its harmony among all the "'amassing harmonies" (to use Stevens' term, *CP*, 403), aria in praise of the one redeeming faculty. Poetry is not *the* health, as Stevens named it, but *a* health among healths. The choice of any maker of the satisfaction, any man who treasures imagination, is his own. The poverty of the rock has never relented; it will endure. We may suppose a kinship of artists in their sharing of the change-less condition, a little gain before the threat of loss. There is a bond between Anacreon and Wallace Stevens, between Praxiteles and Giacometti. To have in some degree purged the poverty of life is to have found a brief health in the midst of danger.

[1] See the Introduction to this study.

An earlier chapter has reviewed Stevens as an interpreter of transitions in the American community. Society is a *phase*. We should have expected him to study the phases of his time in terms of the imagination. The poverty of America was to him apparent in the starvation of men who hunger for a metaphor of life and who await the coming of the prophet, the man "that seizes our strength" (*OP*, 81). In the reflections of "Life on a Battle-ship" Stevens admitted the equation between the politician and the prophet-god as the leader. Each is a master of imagination. But the one perpetuates the hunger; the other, when he comes, will assuage it. We should remember that Stevens lived in a politics-ridden era. Two cataclysmic wars and the struggles of the Depression ordered the character of the nation as he knew it. His last years ended in the portentous mid-fifties, shadowed by global American destinies of such ambiguity and paradox as to resist definition. His world, and that of every other American, was a theater of political strategists. Yet this is not to say that he regarded the poverty of his time as unprecedented. His total poetry attests to his acceptance: every age relives the insufficient; the matter for recognition and study is the nature of the present poverty. If poetry is a means to a health, if it is a "present perfecting" in the irremediable, we should then conclude a reading of Stevens with an objective view of the American poetic estate in this century. The degree of public receptivity to poetry is as elusive of definition as are the hazardous ventures of global politics. American conditions in the twentieth century are in no wise unique among those to be found in other politics-ridden modern nations. There may or there may not be more unacknowledged desire for the health of poetry among humankind than ever before in history. It is impossible to know. In his years as an artist Stevens held to his principle: "Poetry is the scholar's art" (*OP*, 167). But he hoped for a future of poetry as redemption from the ordinary, a poetry for "non-scholars" satisfying the hunger for metaphor. I am speaking here of Stevens apart from the context of his particular art, of a man who made no assumptions about the viableness of his work and who yet looked toward a time when Americans would not be nourished on politics alone.

When one regards the poetry of Stevens, with its geometry of sea-lines and earth-lines and its final star-lines, one thinks of the aesthetic remoteness of Stevens' American countrymen. The nonscholar in the audience does not easily grant the possibility of this difficult art in the life of a business executive, an investment-banking specialist. That this man was intent upon defying a poverty of life in the midst of success is an idea strange to American judgments. But we should emphasize that a like strangeness to popular judgment might be found in any other contemporary nation, its citizens regarding in dismay a poet serving the mechanics of economy. There is no American distinction here. The attitude expresses scarcely more than a universal curiosity about the exceptional. We are concerned only with peculiarly American conditions in the American inheritance, the "sweating changes" of the American imagination as Stevens personified its history in Crispin (*CP*, 33). For though it is certain that the inheritors of old cultures across the Atlantic have lived in proximity to art longer than have Americans—the cathedral with its frescoes beyond the fields, the doorways of painters and poets near the market—yet the American has his own heritage. For him it is an endurance of "sweating changes" as he learns to accommodate art to life and to respect his imagination as a faculty of redemption from the ordinary. He has had much to live down.

The bifurcation of art and what we please to call life is, as the course of American social history demonstrates, the legacy of a demonic Puritanism. A long American public distrust of supreme works of the imagination should by this time have been judged by all scholars as a mark of an earlier national poverty. Of our illustrious Puritan forebears William Carlos Williams wrote from the dead center of a modern intolerance of their prized legacy. "Having in themselves nothing of curiosity, no wonder, for the New World . . . they knew only to keep their eyes blinded, their tongues in orderly manner between their teeth, their ears stopped by the monotony of their hymns and their flesh covered in straight habits. . . . It is an immorality that IS America. Here it began. You see the cause. There was no ground to build on, with a ground all blossoming about them—under their noses."[2] This irrefutable observation of Dr. Williams' may have come of Stevens as well. Our social history tells us enough of the awesome facts of Puritan conformity, every man like every other man: in his elevation of scriptural authority as the sanction of existence, in his distrust of the unreal of art, his feigned abhorrence of the flesh, and his meek submission to the dogma of an oligarchy. His realities were of a human nonentity under the subsuming will of the Lord and of the

---

[2] *In the American Grain* (1956 ed.), pp. 112, 114.

will of devils in every vision of self-rightness. The inevitable consequence in the depths of national consciousness was suspicion
of that serpent of the self held in full view, for instance, in the
poetic grasp of Stevens. In the widest sense it was suspicion of any
man who advances the act of imagination as the end of being. For
this freedom in the making of art, the first American expatriates
went to Italy to paint, and the first ambassadors, in the intensely
modern sense of Henry James, sought a dominion of imaginations
called Paris.

The historian's account of expatriation among American artists
and writers in the twentieth century has yet to be written. But one
knows the urgencies without the account. It may be seen that Ezra
Pound was impelled by these to live abroad an epic life of the
rebellious American defector. Where Stevens, Williams, and Frost
maintained a strict faithfulness to the native, certain of their
contemporaries in American literature, for peculiarly American
reasons, chose residences abroad. The choice must be read in
these afteryears of the sixties in terms of personal requirement
rather than of cultism. There was a foreign air that seemed to
these Americans a greater freedom toward a self-elected and honest
art. Mr. MacLeish's complaint against the expatriate "Irresponsibles"
in the mid-thirties has for us scant justification. It makes no difference where Americans choose to live and work. We judge them without respect to their various "desertions." If we examine the history
of their years abroad, we know that they were in search of freedom
from that American "immorality" named by Dr. Williams, too long
a heritage of Puritan blindness, lack of curiosity and wonder "for the
New World." In the sense of this condemnation, every world of
every new generation is new.

The transitions of American culture from 1920 to 1950, roughly
the span of years in which Stevens wrote his major poetry, will be
read by future historians as remarkable "sweating changes." For
our purposes here, upheavals in the moral code and in political
and economic institutions are not at issue. We are concerned only
with the crisis in American letters, particularly with the living down
of the long American immorality. The major achievements of American literature were not discovered until a totally new and vigorous
American criticism began in the twenties to define them. The collapse
of the American idea of polite fiction and fireside poetry widened
into crisis. Whitman's poetic "nakedness," as in Stevens' concept
of a "central" poetry, was first understood in Whitman's land. The
significance of the Concord rebellion against the American past was

first defined. The paradoxes of Hawthorne, Melville, and Henry James were found to be unique American contributions to the metaphysics of the novel in its world stature. The discoveries, as one may wish to name them, are all examples of a new American energy at work in the complex task of defining American culture, often too easily named "the American experience."

In the rush of this scholarly energy toward the American center, one finds also a counterforce, a spreading of expression beyond American reference and into nonnational modern experience. The passage of American literature toward universal conditions of twentieth-century man is a phenomenon of the crisis. In the decades of upheaval, when so much of our present understanding of literature was being constructed, this phenomenon among the literary arts was particularly evident in poetry. The vast distances separating the major American poets from 1920 to the present need not be stressed. There is no tradition among them to be named; there is only the simple fact that each wrote, and yet writes, a poetry of crisis. Clearly this poetic art is critical in the sense that it reflects American iconoclasm with respect to poetry and "life." Its idiom is diverse and difficult; and in these recent decades of its emergence it has often seemed wholly private and granitic, impervious to wide public inspection. A paradox of the present comprehends a poetry of America established in questions of human existence unlike any known in the American heritage, and yet a poetry removed, because of its unaccustomed speech, from the wide audience that it should have. In his thought of poetry as a redemption, a health, Stevens is in no way exceptional. One infers a like conviction in a reading of Whitman; and certainly in this century evidence of the same in the thought of Frost, of Eliot and Pound, of Roethke and Lowell, is fully apparent. Poetry as a means of purging existence of its poverty, of raising the life of the American individual above the ordinary, is offered again and again. We need to study the distance between the offering of poetry and the audience desired. A broad estimate by Irving Howe in 1957 presents one of the challenges from the American crisis in poetry: Stevens needs to be read "as if poetry were that which can help liberate us from the tyranny of mechanical life and slow dying."[3]

---

[3] "Another Way of Looking at the Blackbird," *The New Republic*, Vol. 137, No. 20 (November 4, 1957), p. 19. Yet this same critic has also objected to Stevens' "withdrawal" from "the life of men living together" (*A World More Attractive* [New York, 1963], p. 165).

The impossibility of measuring a public ardor for this liberation from tyranny is granted. But it is very certain that public awareness of poetry in the national expression increases. Modern American poetry is publicly known to be distinguished, however dismaying its variety and its innovation. In the media of popular journalism and advertising, attempts have been made to establish criteria for American public judgment of the "usefulness" of poetry. Two examples from these sources provide somewhat bizarre instances of an executive effort to justify contemporary poetry as commodity. The first of these comes from a popular informant of public taste, *Time* magazine. Some five years ago a reviewer, unnamed, wrote of "Poetry in English: 1945–62" that no one is stopping recent poets in the English language. If these poets will, they may "rejoin the human race." Of Stevens and William Empson this historian of recent poetry wrote as follows: "But as the '30s stumbled toward catastrophe, poetry blundered deeper into obscurity and ambiguity, into the talented but precious minutiae of Wallace Stevens and William Empson, whose poems often suggest esthetic scrimshaw, a cathedral carved in a cherry pit. Poetry became a world unto itself, a self-sealing vacuum in which poets engaged in a conspiracy of mutual self-approval, safe from the embarrassing questions of the bewildered public, safe from what Stefan George called 'the indignity of being understood.' "[4] The emphasis, of course, falls on the "blundering" into obscurity and ambiguity. The unlikely linking of Stevens and Empson is itself bizarre. Stevens, at any rate, is not of the race: as the thirties stumbled, so he blundered deeper. Poetry must be an instrument of immediate communication in the national life. The inference is that the poet of the ambiguous has denied his humanity. How could it be otherwise, for human existence in the twentieth century is, of course, quite free of ambiguity! It follows that poetry ought to be a medium among media, a simple affirmation of the simple mechanics of living. In this form it might become a currency among commodities, passing easily from hand to hand and insulting no man's intelligence.

A second example from advertising displays an act of industry in "honoring" poetry. Since modern poets are known to be difficult to read, perhaps their work can be made immediately accessible in a "suggested" design. The recent effort of the Steuben Glass Company is the case here: a selection of thirty-one contemporary

[4] The issue of March 9, 1962, p. 95 and p. 92.

American poets by the Poetry Society of America, each to supply a new lyric to be "expressed" in crystal form. The completed "sculptures" interpreting the lyrics submitted were exhibited in the Company's showrooms in New York, presumed illustrations of how poetry can be visualized in a commercial art that in the context of trade is commodity.[5] One does not hold the participating poets in the slightest disrespect. But a distinctly modern question is reasserted: What does the nation do with its poets, to relate them to "life"?

Yet the relationship grows, however slowly. The years of the century advance. In each year more Americans feel the presence of the arts. The future may know a dependency upon the work of great imaginations; and this will be an accommodation of art unknown in the formulas of journalism and merchandising. It will come of a need at the center of existence. Stevens' reflections upon the society of his time are not uniformly dark. In "Owl's Clover," midway in the transitions of his American years, he wrote: "We have grown weary of the man that thinks. / He thinks and it is not true. The man below / Imagines and it is true . . ." (OP, 66). There is a sprawling portent in the heavens. "It is the form / Of a generation that does not know itself . . ." (OP, 68). Yet, there will come a knowing of the self of another generation, a time when politics is not the sustenance of life. We feel this hope in Stevens; for, as long as there is a continuity of the human, there will be a cyclical return to a new strength of purging the old poverty. If one thinks of the nation as Stevens did, what one wants is poetry in the mind's encounter of each day. He wished it to be the "vulgate" of experience, each man's work brightened and made individual by his poems flourishing above reality through his imagination, poems, if unwritten, yet beautiful acts of the mind. In the widest sense this is simply poetic experience mixed with the bread of daily life. One has only to contemplate the poet's meaning in the lyric from the depths of the Depression, "A Fading of the Sun" (CP, 139). Poetry *could* be for every man. If poetry is a purging of poverty, then we may say that the furious decades of contemporary America have marked a purging of the past. And the "sweating changes" continue.

[5] See a review of the exhibition by Brian O'Doherty in the *New York Times*, April 26, 1963, Sec. 1, p. 10. Among the poets whose work was represented were Marianne Moore, Kenneth Rexroth, and Mark Van Doren. Mr. O'Doherty noted: "For the semi-educated in expensive surburban homes, these crystals are just the thing—good conversation pieces over cocktails."

Stevens knew, and we know, terrors made by imaginations put to evil use. Yet these may be inevitable terrors in a chaos preceding a new form of man in America.

The weather of humanity always changes, in Stevens' view, in a generation of the very young. He believed that public education must find a way to remove poetry from its place as "a thing apart" and to bring it to the individual's life. His concern is fully reflected in his correspondence with his friend Henry Church. Stevens wrote of the possibility of a first Chair of Poetry in an American university. The *Letters* variously preserve the record of his devotion to the idea of his friend, the man who wished to endow the venture. Stevens' proposals need not be reviewed here. It is enough to note that he thought of a professor of poetry as a man who would work to bring poetry to the vitality of men and women, poetry that would enrich for them the aspects of the world.[6] His hope was that this effort would generate its own liberating force as it passed into the objectives of all American education. This was aspiration, that poetry might one day be taken from its isolation and known as evidence of the possible: for every American a singular life as a health of self-fulfillment. The public *credo* of Stevens is expressed in his statement read at Princeton in 1941, in a symposium on The Language of Poetry, made possible by a gift from Mr. and Mrs. Church. "I think that his [the poet's] function is to make his imagination theirs and that he fulfills himself only as he sees his imagination become the light in the minds of others. His role, in short, is to help people to live their lives" (*NA*, 29).

Stevens accepted the degrees and honors that came to him with a modest gratitude. He was in no sense indifferent to those institutions and committees which wished to recognize him. But one must see him finally in his ardent conviction: "Poetry is (and should be) for the poet a source of pleasure and satisfaction, not a source of honors" ("Adagia," *OP*, 178). The candor of his acceptance of the National Book Award in 1955 for the *Collected Poems* agrees with the principle. "Now, at seventy-five, as I look back on the little that I have done and as I turn the pages of my own poems gathered together in a single volume, I have no choice except to paraphrase the old verse that says that it is not what I am, but what I aspired

---

[6] See a letter to Henry Church dated at Hartford, October 15, 1940; *Letters*, p. 377.

to be that comforts me" (*OP*, 246). Of his avoidance of identification with any poetic Establishment there should be no wonder. His truth is inscribed in the "Adagia": "One has a sensibility range beyond which nothing really exists for one. And in each this is different" (*OP*, 161). This means, in effect, that each poet has his own sensibility; and, consequently, each works in solitude. Yet he knew the supremacies of his American contemporaries in poetry. If he wished not to read them widely, he was faithful to his resolve upon keeping his own mature vision clear of the hazards of influence. There was to be one architect alone of his structure; and the full design and its realization, even to the smallest detail, were to be his.

The predictive faculty of the critic is itself plain assumption. Stevens did not expect his chapel of wind and weather to endure among the "cindery noes" of time. Nor would he have had his sensibility and perception become the paradigm of a "great style" in a poetry of the future. The art historian is just in speaking of the moments of great innovation when a new style in painting becomes so important that it seems to dictate the careers of artists contemporaneous with it, and following. Around 1510 the monumental style of the High Renaissance was shaped by Michelangelo, Raphael, Bramante; in 1870 impressionism was realized by Monet, Renoir, Pissarro; in 1910, cubism by Picasso and Braque.[7] We shall not venture such an authority for Stevens in the history of American poetry and in the wider history of poetry in English. He would not have us do so. We should say simply that he refreshes life and that we learn of him how poetry is a health. Stevens with all his contemporaries in American art spoke from a metamorphosis of a nation. The process of the Grand Poem was as restless and inexorable as the reality encountered. It was originally suggested in this study that the memorial structure of Stevens towers like nothing else in its time. But it was not my purpose to evaluate its uniqueness or its strength in comparison with other eminences of the century. I adhere finally to Stevens' intention: that his poetry should be an evidence of the shaping power within us, the supreme talent endlessly forming the lyric history of humanity.

[7] See Rosenblum, *Cubism and Twentieth Century Art,* p. 9.

Indexes

Title Index

Not all the titles of Stevens' poems listed below appear in the text; however, lines quoted from a particular poem can be found on the page or pages indicated.

Subject Index

Stevens' major subjects are comprehended in the chapter headings above and are accordingly omitted in this index. Only minor subjects of Stevens' treated in the discussion have been listed. Artists and writers mentioned in relation to Stevens, but not included below, may be found listed in the Title Index.

THE JOHNS HOPKINS PRESS

THE DOME AND THE ROCK
Structure in the Poetry of Wallace Stevens
by James Baird

Designed by Gerard A. Valerio
Composed in Baskerville by Monotype Composition Company, Inc.
Printed offset by Universal Lithographers, Inc., on 60 lb. P&S R
Bound by L. H. Jenkins in Columbia Fictionette